Non-Fungible Tokens (NFTs) in Smart Cities:

Advancements and Security Challenges

Usman Khalil
Universiti Brunei Darusalam, Brunei

Mueen Uddin
College of Computing and IT, University of Doha for Science and Technology, Qatar

Owais Ahmed Malik
Universiti Brunei Darussalam, Brunei

Abdulhalim Dandoush
College of Computing and IT, University of Doha for Science and Technology, Qatar

IGI Global
Scientific Publishing
Publishing Tomorrow's Research Today

Vice President of Editorial Melissa Wagner
Director of Acquisitions Mikaela Felty
Director of Book Development Jocelynn Hessler
Production Manager Mike Brehm
Cover Design Jose Rosado

Published in the United States of America by
IGI Global Scientific Publishing
701 East Chocolate Avenue
Hershey, PA, 17033, USA
Tel: 717-533-8845
Fax: 717-533-7115
Website: https://www.igi-global.com E-mail: cust@igi-global.com

Library of Congress Cataloging-in-Publication Data

LCCN: 2024058266 (CIP Data Pending)
ISBN13: 9798369388761
Isbn13Softcover: 9798369388778
EISBN13: 9798369388785

British Cataloguing in Publication Data
A Cataloguing in Publication record for this book is available from the British Library.

This book is humbly dedicated to Allah, The One and The Almighty, whose boundless grace and unwavering support made the realization of this project possible. Without Divine guidance, this endeavor would not have materialized.

With deepest gratitude, we extend our heartfelt thanks to our beloved families, whose patience, understanding, and constant encouragement provided the steadfast foundation for the countless hours of research, writing, and collaboration that brought this book to life. Their unwavering trust in our vision fueled this collective journey.

To the dedicated researchers, esteemed collaborators, and insightful peers who contributed their expertise, time, and intellectual rigor to this volume, your collective efforts have truly enriched this work. Your support and belief in the importance of this subject matter have been invaluable.

Editorial Advisory Board

Table of Contents

Detailed Table of Contents

This chapter provides a comprehensive overview of the evolution of smart cities, tracing their roots from the Web2.0 era to the emerging Web3.0 ecosystem. It delves into the historical development of IoT-enabled smart devices and the enabling communication technologies that underpin their functionality. The chapter explores the layered architecture of smart cities, comprising application, transmission, and sensing layers, and identifies the associated security challenges at each level. A particular focus is placed on IoT-enabled smart device authentication, examining the state-of-the-art authentication models, including single-factor, two-factor, and multi-factor authentication. The chapter delves into the specifics of multi-factor authentication, discussing biometrics, token-based, certificate-based, hardware security module, and trusted platform module approaches. By understanding these concepts, readers will gain insights into the intricate workings of smart cities and the critical role of security in ensuring their resilience and reliability.

This chapter delves into the fundamental concepts of distributed and non-distributed systems, laying the groundwork for understanding the intricacies of blockchain technology. A comprehensive overview of public, private, and hybrid blockchain networks is provided, highlighting their unique characteristics and applications. The chapter explores the concept of blockchain tokenization, with a particular

The fusion of blockchain technologies and non-fungible tokens (NFTs) into smart city ecosystems presents new security challenges, impeding the widespread adoption of NFT in urban settings. Accordingly, this study comprehensively reviews the cybersecurity aspects surrounding NFTs within smart city environments. Firstly, a discussion of the various applications of NFTs in smart cities is provided. This is followed by an exploration of the unique cybersecurity vulnerabilities emanating from implementing NFTs in smart city ecosystems, including data privacy issues, smart contract vulnerabilities, token theft, and the potential for market manipulation, etc. Moreover, various countermeasures and best practices to negate NFTs' cybersecurity concerns and vulnerabilities have been detailed. Finally, emerging trends in NFT security are equally also analyzed. This review study provide urban planners, policymakers, technologists, students, and researchers with a refined understanding of the cybersecurity concerns of NFT in smart cities.

Foreword

28th Mar, 2025, Bandar Seri Begawan, Brunei Darussalam.

In an era where urbanization and digital transformation converge, the concept of smart cities has emerged as a beacon of innovation. Yet, as cities grow smarter, the challenges of security, governance, and equitable resource management intensify. Enter blockchain technology and its groundbreaking derivative, non-fungible tokens (NFTs), which promise to redefine how we conceptualize ownership, trust, and participation in urban ecosystems. This book, *Non-Fungible Tokens (NFTs) in Smart Cities: Advancements and Security Challenges*, stands at the forefront of this revolution, offering a critical lens through which to examine the fusion of decentralized systems and urban infrastructure.

The transition from Web2.0 to Web3.0 marks a paradigm shift in how data and assets are managed, moving from centralized control to distributed, user-centric frameworks. Within this evolution, NFTs emerge not merely as digital collectibles but as tools for securing cyber-physical systems (CPS), enabling transparent governance, and fostering community engagement. This book masterfully navigates these intersections, addressing both the transformative potential and the inherent vulnerabilities of integrating blockchain and NFTs into smart cities.

From exploring blockchain's role in therapeutic treatments to dissecting the ethical quandaries of deepfakes, the chapters reveal a multidisciplinary approach rarely seen in technical literature. The authors meticulously analyze NFT-enabled solutions for urban resource management, tokenized voting mechanisms, and decentralized authentication systems while candidly addressing scalability, regulatory compliance, and cybersecurity risks.

What sets this work apart is its balance of visionary optimism and pragmatic caution. It does not shy away from the complexities of hybrid blockchain architectures or the limitations of current authentication mechanisms. Instead, it proposes actionable strategies, such as permissioned networks and IBFT 2.0 consensus protocols, to fortify smart city infrastructures.

For policymakers, technologists, and academics alike, this book is an indispensable resource. It challenges readers to envision cities where blockchain fosters inclusivity, NFTs empower civic participation, and security frameworks evolve alongside technological advancements. As smart cities transition from theory to reality, this compilation serves as both a roadmap and a cautionary tale—a testament to the power of innovation tempered by vigilance.

Moayad Aloqaily
Carleton University Ottawa, Canada

Preface

28th Mar, 2025, Bandar Seri Begawan, Brunei Darussalam.

Welcome to *Non-Fungible Tokens (NFTs) in Smart Cities: Advancements and Security Challenges*, a comprehensive exploration of how blockchain and NFTs are reshaping urban landscapes. This book bridges the gap between theoretical research and practical implementation, offering insights into the opportunities and challenges of decentralized technologies in smart cities.

MOTIVATION AND SCOPE

Smart cities represent the pinnacle of human ingenuity, integrating IoT, AI, and blockchain to create sustainable, efficient urban environments. However, the rapid adoption of these technologies has outpaced the development of robust security and governance frameworks. NFTs, with their unique ability to authenticate and tokenize assets, present novel solutions to these challenges. This book aims to:

- Illuminate the role of NFTs in enhancing transparency, ownership, and civic engagement.
- Analyze security risks inherent to blockchain-integrated CPS.
- Provide comparative studies of emerging technologies, including deepfakes, in therapeutic and urban contexts.

ORGANIZATION OF THE BOOK

Chapter 1: Introduction to Smart City Infrastructure Overview and its Evolution from Web2.0 to Web3.0

This chapter traces the evolution of smart cities from Web2.0 to Web3.0, emphasizing Blockchain's potential to secure IoT-embedded assets. It discovers the emerging concept of decentralized smart cities within the framework of Web3, examining how distributed ledger technologies can redefine urban landscapes. It delves into the potential of Blockchain, smart contracts, and decentralized applications (dApps) to revolutionize city operations and enhance resident quality of life. We will investigate how these technologies can foster transparent, secure, and efficient management of essential urban resources. Furthermore, the chapter will analyze the crucial role of the Internet of Things (IoT) in this context, focusing on the interconnected network of low-powered devices that facilitate real-time data collection and communication. We will discuss how decentralized smart cities can promote democratic governance through decentralized voting systems, empower residents with greater control over their data privacy, and foster innovation and collaboration among diverse stakeholders. By examining the integration of IoT with Web3 principles, this chapter aims to provide insight into the development of citizen-centric, secure, and efficient urban environments.

Chapter 2: Decentralized Principles of Blockchain and BC Tokenization in the Era of Smart Cities

This chapter dissects decentralized systems, contrasting public, private, and hybrid Blockchains while critiquing NFT-based authentication gaps. It probes into the fundamental concepts of distributed and non-distributed systems, laying the groundwork for understanding the intricacies of Blockchain technology. A comprehensive overview of public, private, and hybrid Blockchain networks is provided, highlighting their unique characteristics and applications. The chapter explores the concept of Blockchain tokenization, with a particular focus on non-fungible tokens (NFTs) and their potential to revolutionize security, authentication, and asset digitization. A critical analysis of the challenges and future directions of Blockchain technology is presented, followed by an examination of existing NFT-based CPS authentication mechanisms and gaps within the Web2 & Web3 architectures. The chapter concludes with a comparative literature review of NFT-enabled solutions for the cyber-physical environment, highlighting their strengths and weaknesses.

Chapter 3: Cyber-Physical Systems and Security in Smart Cities

This chapter evaluates CPS security vulnerabilities, advocating for Blockchain-driven countermeasures. It further discovers the integration of Blockchain technology within cyber-physical systems (CPS), focusing on its application in smart houses, smart districts, and federated mechanisms. The chapter delves into the potential of Blockchain to enhance security and privacy in IoT-enabled environments, particularly through Blockchain-enabled IoT-embedded assets. A thorough examination of the challenges associated with current Blockchain-based authentication systems is presented, highlighting issues such as security concerns, communication vulnerabilities, and inadequate authentication mechanisms. To address these limitations, the chapter proposes NFT-enabled solutions for the cyber-physical environment, leveraging permissioned networks and IBFT 2.0 consensus mechanisms to prioritize security services.

Chapter 4: Understanding Non-Fungible Tokens (NFTs) in Smart Cities

This chapter positions NFTs as catalysts for participatory governance, illustrating their use in tokenizing public assets and enabling decentralized decision-making. It depicts the role of Non-Fungible Tokens (NFTs) in the development of smart cities in this digital era, focusing on their perspective on boosting urban governance, community engagement, and resource management. A unique digital asset fosters transparent ownership and provenance tracking of urban resources, such as public art, land, and community spaces. The integration of NFTs enhances service delivery and planning as demonstrated in the chapter advance participatory governance, granting citizens to engage in decision-making processes through tokenized voting mechanisms. Moreover, NFTs promote community engagement and tokenized identity expressions, thereby boosting local economies. Finally, the study highlighted the transformative potential of NFTs in creating sustainable, inclusive, and innovative urban environments.

Chapter 5: The Era of Blockchains, Deepfakes, and NFTs in Therapeutic Treatments: A Comparative Study

This chapter explores the transformative potential of blockchain and deepfake technologies in therapeutic treatment, offering a comparative analysis of their roles in enhancing patient care and medical data management. It highlights how blockchain—particularly through the use of NFTs—can bolster healthcare data security, transparency, and traceability, while also enabling more personalized treatment approaches. Simultaneously, deepfake technology is examined for its promising applications in creating immersive and realistic simulations that support rehabilitation and psychological therapies. However, the chapter also addresses the ethical challenges these innovations introduce, such as concerns over data privacy, informed consent, and the potential misuse of manipulated media. Grounded in a comprehensive literature review, the study outlines both the benefits and risks associated with these tools and concludes with key recommendations for their secure and ethically responsible integration into healthcare practices.

Chapter 6: NFT Innovation: Past the Fad

This chapter delves into the structure and significance of NFT marketplaces as central hubs in the digital asset economy. It examines how these platforms enable the buying, selling, and trading of unique digital assets—non-fungible tokens (NFTs)—which are securely recorded on the blockchain. By allowing artists to tokenize their work, NFT marketplaces validate authenticity and open new revenue streams through secondary sales and royalties. The chapter emphasizes the essential role of blockchain technology in ensuring transparency, security, and traceability, while also highlighting the importance of community engagement and artist visibility. It further outlines key considerations for building and maintaining effective NFT marketplaces, including the integration of social features, robust security protocols, scalability, regulatory compliance, and ongoing platform optimization. Through this analysis, the chapter provides insight into how NFT marketplaces are shaping the future of digital creativity and commerce.

Chapter 7: Blockchain Integration for Smart City Infrastructure: Advancing Urban Connectivity and Security

This chapter tackle Blockchain integration challenges in energy, transportation, and data governance, culminating in a roadmap for NFT security best practices. It discusses the transformative potential of Blockchain technology in the evolution of metropolitan areas into smart cities, a necessity driven by urbanization, population growth, and the pursuit of sustainable development. It delves into how Blockchain's decentralized, secure, and transparent nature can address the compatibility, security, and data management challenges inherent in smart city systems that rely on IoT, AI, and big data analytics. We will investigate Blockchain's applications across critical urban domains, including energy management, transportation, public services, and data governance, examining both existing case studies and potential future implementations. The chapter aims to illuminate how Blockchain can foster peer-to-peer energy trading, enhance data interchange between infrastructure and vehicles, and bolster the security and reliability of public services. Furthermore, we will analyze the challenges associated with Blockchain integration, such as scalability and regulatory compliance, and propose solutions to facilitate its effective deployment. By providing a structured approach to business model development and showcasing successful implementations, this chapter seeks to guide entrepreneurs, policymakers, and urban planners in creating sustainable, efficient, and secure urban ecosystems.

Chapter 8: NFT Security in Smart Cities: An Exploration of Challenges, Countermeasures and Emerging Trends

This chapter examines the burgeoning intersection of Non-Fungible Tokens (NFTs) and smart city frameworks, a convergence that offers significant opportunities for digital asset management, property ownership, and enhanced public participation. While NFTs, unique digital assets leveraging Blockchain technology for ownership and authenticity verification, have gained traction in various sectors, their integration into smart cities presents both potential and complex security challenges. As smart cities increasingly adopt digital transformation, NFTs emerge as tools for digital identity management, property tokenization, and service provision. However, this integration introduces cybersecurity vulnerabilities that extend beyond traditional frameworks, necessitating a deep analysis and innovative solutions. This chapter delves into the unique security considerations arising from NFT implementation in smart city ecosystems, exploring the potential impact on critical infrastructure and citizen privacy. It analyzes the cybersecurity threats, including phishing attacks and smart contract vulnerabilities, and investigates countermeasures and best practices to mitigate these risks. Furthermore, the chapter examines ethical frameworks and emerging trends in NFT security within smart city contexts, providing valuable insights for smart city planners, security professionals, and decision-makers. By offering a comprehensive overview of NFT applications and their associated security challenges, this chapter aims to contribute to the development of secure and resilient NFT implementations in smart city environments.

AUDIENCE AND ACKNOWLEDGMENTS

This book caters to researchers exploring decentralized systems, urban planners designing next-gen infrastructures, and policymakers navigating regulatory landscapes. We extend gratitude to contributors whose diverse expertise enriched this work.

As cities evolve into interconnected digital-physical ecosystems, this book underscores the imperative of balancing innovation with ethical and technical rigor. We invite readers to engage critically, envisioning a future where technology serves not just efficiency, but equity and resilience.

Usman Khalil
School of Digital Science, Universiti Brunei Darusalam, Brunei

Mueen Uddin
College of Computing and IT, University of Doha for Science and Technology, Qatar

Owais Ahmed Malik
School of Digital Science, Universiti Brunei Darusalam, Brunei

Abdulhalim Dandoush
College of Computing and IT, University of Doha for Science and Technology, Qatar

Acknowledgements

28th Mar, 2025, Bandar Seri Begawan, Brunei Darussalam.

In the Name of the Almighty Allah, the Most Gracious, the Most Merciful. All praises and prayers are for the Creator of the universe. May blessings and peace be upon Mohammed, His devoted servant and messenger.

First and foremost, we must acknowledge our limitless gratitude to Allah, the Ever-Magnificent; the Ever-Thankful, for His help and blessing. We are absolutely sure that Without His guidance, this endeavor would not have materialized.

The creation of *Non-Fungible Tokens (NFTs) in Smart Cities: Advancements and Security Challenges* has been a collaborative endeavor, blending expertise from diverse domains to address the intricate relationship between blockchain innovations and urban ecosystems. We extend our deepest gratitude to everyone who contributed to this intellectual journey. We express our sincere appreciation to the **Editorial Team** for their unwavering commitment to maintaining the academic rigor and coherence of this work. Their meticulous attention to detail, constructive feedback, and relentless pursuit of excellence ensured that each chapter met the highest scholarly standards.

We are profoundly indebted to **Dr. Mueen Uddin** (Associate Professor), **Dr. Owais Ahmed Malik** (Senior Assistant Professor), and **Dr. Abdulhalim Dandoush** (Associate Professor & Head of Department) for their visionary insights into Blockchain-based solution, BC tokenization and decentralized systems. Their critical analysis and discussions were instrumental in balancing technical depth with accessibility.

This book would not have been possible without the collective efforts of researchers, practitioners, and institutions pioneering blockchain-NFT integration in smart cities. We acknowledge the anonymous peer reviewers whose critiques strengthened the manuscript, as well as the academic institutions that fostered interdisciplinary collaborations between technologists, urban planners, and policymakers.

Finally, we thank our families and colleagues for their patience and encouragement during countless hours of research, drafting, and revisions. Their unwavering support reminded us of the human element behind every technological advancement, a principle central to designing inclusive, secure, and sustainable smart cities.

This book is a testament to collaborative innovation, and we hope it inspires future explorations at the nexus of Blockchain, NFTs, and urban evolution.

Chapter 1
Introduction to Smart City Infrastructure Overview and Its Evolution From Web 2.0 to Web 3.0

Usman Khalil
https://orcid.org/0000-0001-8550-1557
Universiti Brunei Darussalam, Brunei

Mueen Uddin
University of Doha for Science and Technology, Qatar

Owais Ahmed Malik
https://orcid.org/0000-0002-4888-5448
Universiti Brunei Darussalam, Brunei

ABSTRACT

This chapter provides a comprehensive overview of the evolution of smart cities, tracing their roots from the Web2.0 era to the emerging Web3.0 ecosystem. It delves into the historical development of IoT-enabled smart devices and the enabling communication technologies that underpin their functionality. The chapter explores the layered architecture of smart cities, comprising application, transmission, and sensing layers, and identifies the associated security challenges at each level. A particular focus is placed on IoT-enabled smart device authentication, examining the state-of-the-art authentication models, including single-factor, two-factor, and multi-factor authentication. The chapter delves into the specifics of multi-factor

DOI: 10.4018/979-8-3693-8876-1.ch001

authentication, discussing biometrics, token-based, certificate-based, hardware security module, and trusted platform module approaches. By understanding these concepts, readers will gain insights into the intricate workings of smart cities and the critical role of security in ensuring their resilience and reliability.

INTRODUCTION

In the context of Web3, a decentralized smart city is an innovative urban concept that utilizes blockchain technology to enhance city operations and improve the quality of life for its residents. By leveraging decentralized technologies such as blockchain, smart contracts, and decentralized applications (dApps), a decentralized smart city can offer greater transparency, security, and efficiency in managing urban resources such as energy, water, and waste. An exponential number of smart devices connecting to the internet with every passing day results in a network of low-powered devices that communicate with each other. For the smart city, it is inevitable to refer to a ubiquitous computing system, as it develops a system where all the connecting devices can communicate with each other through the miner, making it possible to create a device-to-device (D2D) or a machine-to-machine (M2M) network (Cisco, 2020). One of the key benefits of a decentralized smart city in the context of Web3 is the ability to create a more decentralized and democratized system of governance. By utilizing decentralized voting systems, residents can have a greater say in how their city is run, ensuring a more equitable and democratic approach to urban development. Another important aspect of a decentralized smart city in the context of Web3 is the increased security and privacy of citizen data. By utilizing decentralized data storage and management systems, residents can have greater control over their data, ensuring that it is not exploited or misused by government or private entities. Here Internet-of-Things (IoT referred to as a network of low-powered smart devices that communicate with each other through mining machines or servers, etc.) has an important role in realizing the smart city concept as these devices play an important role in every domain. They make the edge of the network where real-time data collection is carried out in cyber and physical space. It can also be defined as a system in which things, people, processes, and data connect to the internet and each other (Cisco, 2020). It requires merging other technologies to make a ubiquitous computing system. Due to the ease of carrying out day-to-day activities, IoT-enabled smart devices have become an integral part of cyber-physical systems (CPS/s) in which they operate such as energy management, medical, retail, transport, manufacturing, etc. (Hussain et al., 2020). These CPSs may eventually be operating in a smart city realizing the concept of a smart plant. Furthermore, a decentralized smart city in the context of Web3 can enable greater innovation and collaboration among stakeholders. With the ability to easily share data and collaborate on decentralized platforms, developers, entrepreneurs, and other stakeholders can work together to create new applications and services that benefit the entire city. Overall, a decentralized smart city in the context of Web3 holds significant promise for the future of urban development. By leveraging decentralized technologies, cities can create more efficient, transparent, and citizen-focused urban environments that are more democratic and secure.

WEB 2.0 TRANSITION TO WEB 3.0 ECOSYSTEM

Web2 is the infrastructure that operates on the traditional TCP/IP internet which in actuality was not designed for such a huge number of devices connected all together. The increasing number of IoT-enabled smart devices due to the underlying network models such as the client-server-based, centralized Web2 ecosystem, inherits the issues concerning the privacy and security of the connected devices and associated CPSs (Chaabouni et al., 2019). Issues exploited by the attack vectors on different communication layers have been categorized concerning layers such as physical attacks, physical and link-layer attacks, network layer attacks, transport layer attacks, application-layer attacks, and multilayered attacks (Hussain et al., 2020). Web2 provides backend support for the applications that are hosted on a server owned by businesses like Microsoft Azure, Google Cloud, etc., enabling these tech giants to position the restriction on consumers' private data for financial gains. Cloud computing from Web2 on the other hand is one major contributor as it provides a framework for IoT infrastructure in three basic levels referred to as tiers for the choice of customers such as IaaS (Infrastructure as a Service), PaaS (Platform as a Service), and SaaS (Software as a Service) (Lee & Lee, 2015). Since these deployments still raise concerns for the security concerning assets and the communication data generated by these devices. Architectures based on Web3 provoke the motivation that refers to the next phase of the internet based on decentralized networks. The lack of permission and trust for Web3 applications provides unbroken inter or intra-platform communication in a Permissionless manner while there is no users/nodes trust for the network and resources by any central regulatory or controlling body which strengthens the trustless features. Both of these features are indispensable for Web2 apps to operate. The mechanisms based on the distributed environment have become an obvious choice for solutions, while they have not been limited only to a specific domain (i.e., crypto-currency). Hence architectures that would provide the authentication mechanism of all the assets operating in the smart city model are a sheer need. Since blockchain technology provides distributed ledgers of transactions that are distributed in nature and operate on the Web3 platform, the identification and authentication can be dealt with the same way so the choice was obvious for its integration into CPSs for smart cities.

HISTORY OF IOT-ENABLED SMART DEVICES

The concept of IoT was conceptualized in 1982 when the connection of a Coke machine was made to the internet and was capable of reporting whether the drinks were cold or not (Teicher, 2018). Later on, Mark Weiser was the first person who gave vision to IoT (Weiser, 1991) however a British entrepreneur named Kevin Ashton in the year 1999 came up with the term IoT for a system of all the interconnected devices while he was associated with Auto-ID Labs as presented in (Matta & Pant, 2019; U.Farooq et al., 2015). A meaningful statement was given by him in the year 2009: "The IoT has the potential to change the world, just as the Internet did. Maybe even more so". (Matta & Pant, 2019).

International Telecommunication Union-Global Standard Initiative ITU-GSI projected IoT as one of the major fields in the research arena that includes mobile computing, wireless sensor networks, pervasive computing, and cyber-physical systems (CPS). According to Kevin Ashton, IoT is a disruptive phase of Internet technology, as IoT can enable the end-user to access sensitive information, which he/she could use inappropriately or cleverly. The development of IoT-enabled smart devices kick-started and LG electronics advanced it further by incorporating it in a smart fridge in 2000. The advancement did not stop here rather the utilization progressed to different domains in the production line such as a smartwatch, Google's self-driving cars, smart TVs, Google Lens, Echo, and Autopilot in Tesla self-driven cars as shown in Figure 1.

Figure 1. Evaluation history timeline of IoT-enabled smart devices

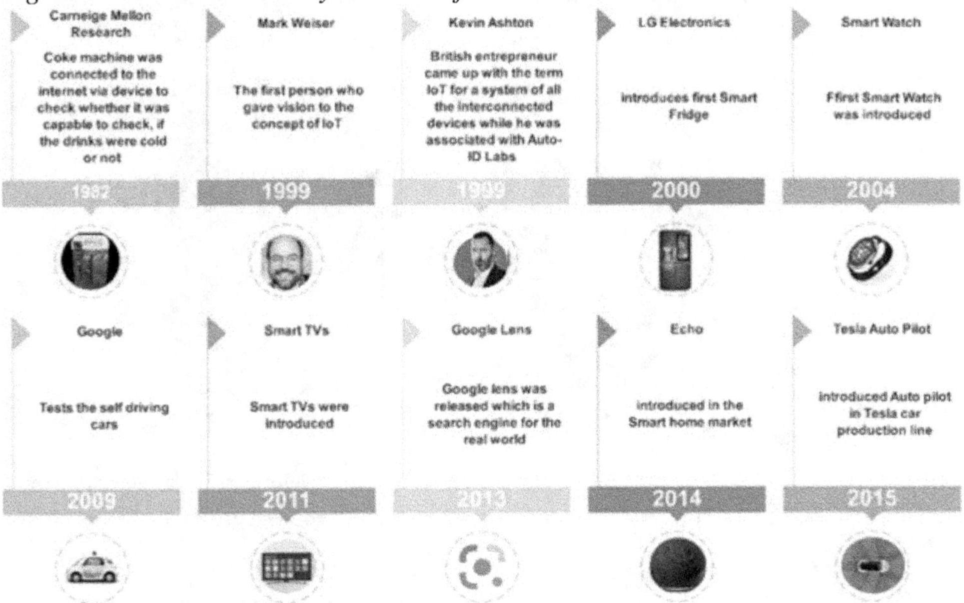

According to the Cisco Internet Business Solutions Group (IBSG), “IoT is simply the point in time when more things or objects are connected to the internet than people.” According to the survey, as shown in Figure 2. the world’s population in 2003 was 6.3 billion, while connected devices were only 0.5 billion. The figure was 6.8 billion in 2010, while 12.5 billion devices were connected. In 2015, the population grew to 7.2 billion, while the connected device count was 25 billion. The survey projected the world’s population and connected devices to be approximately 7.6 billion and 50 billion in 2020, respectively. Figure 2. also depicts the ratio of connected devices per person on a year-wise count that shows the immense use of connected smart devices (Burhan et al., 2018; Vinet & Zhedanov, 2011).

Figure 2. Roadmap of world's population vs. connected devices by 2020

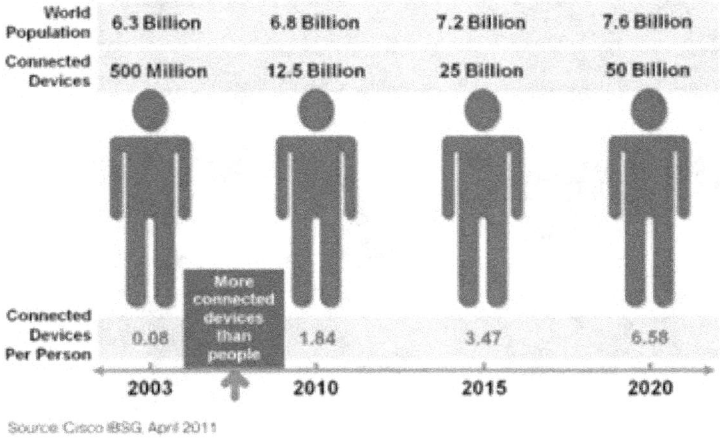

(Vinet & Zhedanov, 2011)

The survey also depicts the projected year-wise count of connected IoT devices, which shows 15 billion connected devices by 2023, as shown in Figure 3. (Burhan et al., 2018). Since IoT uses low-powered devices with limited resources in terms of efficiency for data collection, storage, and processing, the architectures have been an open playing ground for attackers. These IoT-related objects and processes have been developed based on the traditional transmission control protocol/Internet protocol (TCP/IP) stack-based internet. They are not designed for such a huge number of connected devices. It requires robust solutions that may provide the foundation for its implementation and integration. Due to the underlying network models, the increasing number of smart devices inherit the issues concerning privacy and security of the connected smart devices and the network itself (Chaabouni et al., 2019). These devices play an important role in every domain as they make the edge of the network where real-time data collection is carried out in cyber and physical space.

Figure 3. Connected IoT-enabled smart devices by 2023

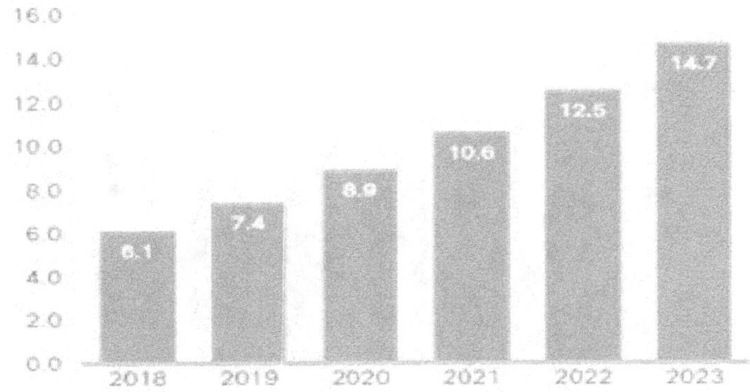

(Cisco, 2020)

The wide adoption of these smart devices has led to the concept of smart cities, where many smart devices operate in different CPSs. It supported the realization of other cyber-physical systems such as smart houses, smart parking, smart buildings, smart healthcare, etc., as depicted in Figure 5 (Hussain et al., 2020). Since these devices operate at the edge layer, they are referred to as edge nodes and are typically low-powered and responsible for sending a specific piece of information. The edge nodes work under smart city architecture hence known as IoT-enabled smart devices (U.Farooq et al., 2015). Leading to the spike in the number of devices there is exponential growth for the connections to the internet daily. On the other hand, the internet has become a global arena for connecting these IoT-enabled smart devices. Yet, exponential growth has been observed in the number of connected smart devices. According to the recent Cisco Annual Internet Report (2018–2023), nearly two-thirds of the global population will have internet access by 2023 which means more devices may be connected to the internet in the future.

Figure 4. Growth projection in internet users from 2018 to 2023

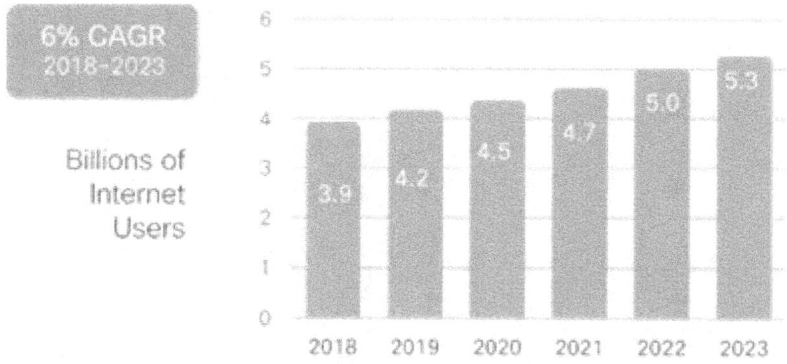

(Cisco, 2020)

The report projects approximately 5.3 billion total internet users, i.e., 66 percent of the global population, by 2023. It estimates a rise of 51 percent for the worldwide population noted in 2018 (Cisco, 2020), as depicted in Figure 4. These devices hold a pivotal position across various sectors, serving as the network's edge where real-time data collection takes place within the realms of cyberspace and the physical environment. The widespread integration of these smart devices has paved the way for the emergence of the cyber-physical environment, where diverse IoT networks accommodate numerous smart devices. This expansion has, in turn, facilitated the establishment of various cyber-physical systems, including but not limited to smart residences, automated parking systems, intelligent buildings, advanced healthcare services, efficient retail operations, streamlined transportation networks, optimized waste management, sustainable energy grids, and modernized agricultural practices, as depicted in Figure 5 (Hussain et al., 2020).

Figure 5. Generalized cyber-physical environment

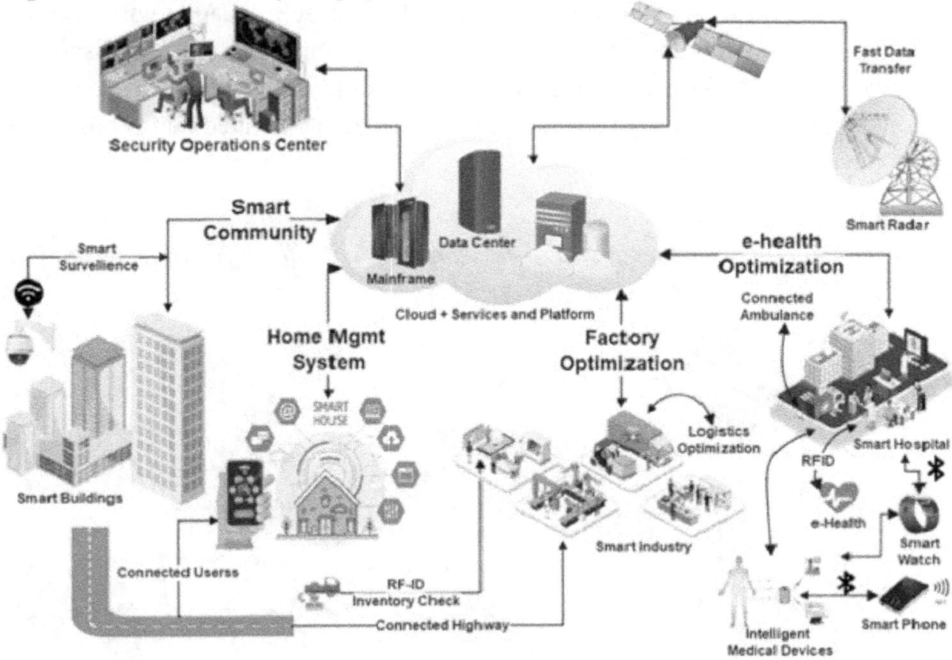

(Khalil, Malik, et al., 2022)

These IoT-enabled smart devices operating in their respective domains would eventually lead to the concept of a smart planet where all systems will be interoperable and interconnected. The periphery of the network links these intelligent devices, encompassing sensors, aggregators, and actuators capable of functioning within the tangible environment and gathering data, which is subsequently harnessed to facilitate well-informed decisions via subsequent actuation. Since these devices operate at the edge layer, they are referred to as edge nodes and are typically low-powered and responsible for sending a specific piece of information. The edge nodes that work under an IoT infrastructure are IoT devices (U.Farooq et al., 2015). The edge nodes or IoT devices depend comprehensively on enabling technologies that play a vital role in data collection and analysis such as WSN, cloud computing, fog/edge computing, and software-defined networks. The background information has been given in Appendix A for clarity. Since these IoT-related objects and processes have been developed based on the traditional transmission control protocol/Internet protocol (TCP/IP) stack-based Internet. They are not designed for such a huge number of connected devices. It requires robust solutions that may provide the foundation for its implementation and integration. Due to the underlying network models, the escalating proliferation of intelligent devices has introduced concerns surrounding the confidentiality and safeguarding of both the interconnected smart devices and the underlying network (Chaabouni et al., 2019). Figure 6 recaps Figure 5, illustrating the various components in a cyber-physical environment and associated potential security risks (represented with the red dotted lines) for clarity. Among the several potential security risks, a few have been demonstrated that persist in the cyber-physical environment.

Figure 6. Generalized cyber-physical environment with attack vector demarcations

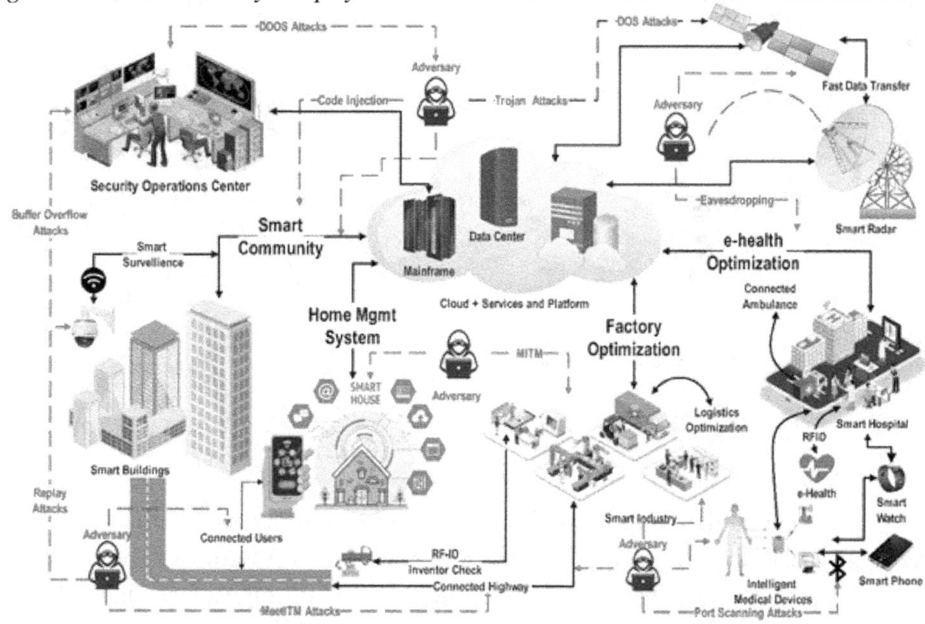

As depicted in Figure 1.6, it may include Denial-of-Service (DoS) and Distributed Denial-of-Service (DDoS) Attacks, these attacks aim to overwhelm a system with traffic, rendering it inaccessible to legitimate users. Man-in-the-middle (MITM) attacks involve an intruder intercepting communication between two parties and possibly altering the messages. Buffer Overflow attacks exploit software vulnerabilities to inject malicious code. SQL Injection attacks involve inserting malicious code into SQL queries to manipulate data. Eavesdropping for unauthorized interception of communication. Data theft for unauthorized acquisition of data etc. A snapshot of detailed security risks is shown in Figure 6 based on the layer-wise distribution and an elaborate explanation has been provided in our prior research study for reference (Khalil, Malik, et al., 2022).

Enabling Communication Technologies

These smart devices utilize enabling technologies based on the type of network, as depicted in Table 1 (U.Farooq et al., 2015). The connectivity provided through these traditional network technologies supports data collection and transfers, as depicted in Figure 5. Since the smart city architecture also relies on the conventional internet supported by communication and transmission technologies for data collection and transmission, respectively, it is evident it may inherit security and privacy challenges. The core of each network is the communication technology through which it communicates. If the medium is not secure or reliable (protocols) enough to provide less resistance for digital signals in the form of the data packet flow, the communication between the devices and data transmission would result in high latency affecting the quality of service (QoS) and security of the network. As discussed in the section above, communication technologies play an important role in connecting devices (i.e., M2M) in an IoT infrastructure; some have been discussed. As shown in Table 1, communication technologies have different purposes depending on the range, baud rate, and power consumption (BehrTech, 2020).

Table 1. Enabling Communication Technologies (Khalil, Mueen, et al., 2022)

Technology	Range	Baud Rate	Power Consumption
RFID	1m - 2m	1 Kbps	Low
ZigBee	10m - 15m	10 Kbps - 100 Kbps	
Z-Wave			
BLE			
Bluetooth	10m - 15m	1 Mbps	
Wifi	10m - 15m	10 Mbps - 100 Mbps	Medium
Wifi HaLow	10m - 15m	1 Mbps - 10 Mbps	
LPWAN - Licensed			
MYTHINGS	1KM - 2KM	10 Kbps - 100 Kbps	High
LoRa			
SigFox			
LPWAN - Unlicensed			
LTE-M	1KM - 2KM	1 Kbps	High
EC-GSM			
NB-IoT			
Cellular			

continued on following page

Table 1. Continued

Technology	Range	Baud Rate	Power Consumption
5G	1KM - 10KM	1 Mbps - 100 Mbps	High
4G/LTE			
3G			

The range differs concerning technologies from less than 1m to more than 10Kms (i.e., < 1m to >10Kms). As depicted in Table 1, Radio Frequency Identification (RFID), ZigBee, Z-Wave, Bluetooth (BT/LE), Wireless Fidelity (Wi-Fi/HaLow), and Near Field Communication (NFC) transmit the data with low power consumption and hence have been in use by many industries especially the retail and logistics for their business needs. Low-Range Wide Area Networks (LPWANs) and Cellular are cloud-based protocols. It operates on the medium access control (MAC) layer and is generally responsible for high data rates over long ranges with medium to high battery power consumption.

With the increase in range, the power consumption increases, which provides a better data rate. It increases as the data rate also differs from 1kbps to 100Mbps depending on the type of service and the power source it uses (BehrTech, 2020; U.Farooq et al., 2015). Most of these essential technologies have been developed keeping in mind the resource-constrained nature of the IoT-enabled smart devices that eventually supported deploying these smart devices in cyber-physical systems to realize smart city infrastructure. The use of communication technologies supported data acquisition and transfer using IoT-enabled smart device technologies. Wireless Sensor Networks (WSNs) and Cloud Computing (CC) have enabled data storage, processing, and analysis in real-time, making industries save time and expenditure for maintenance in case of machine breakdown due to unforeseen events.

WIRELESS SENSOR NETWORKS

Wireless Sensor Networks utilize the physical and MAC (Medium Access Control) based on IEEE 802.15.4 standard. It enables using LR-WPAN protocols such as 6LoWPAN, CoAP, etc., for WSNs (U.Farooq et al., 2015). It is a network of bi-directional sensors wirelessly connected. They are connected so that each sensor senses the environment and sends object-specific data, e.g., location, temperature, humidity, and speed of an IoT device or its surroundings (Khan & Salah, 2018). The collected information is passed to the *customer-premises equipment* (CPE) for processing. Sensors in WSNs are connected in a multi-hop fashion, allowing multi-hop communication in different network designs for transmitting data from one sensor node to another and then to CPE, as shown in Figure 7 (Lee & Lee, 2015). WSNs operate in different topologies such as Bus Topology, Tree Topology, Star Topology, Ring Topology, Mesh Topology, Circular Topology, and Grid Topology.

Figure 7. WSNs scenario with sensor node structure

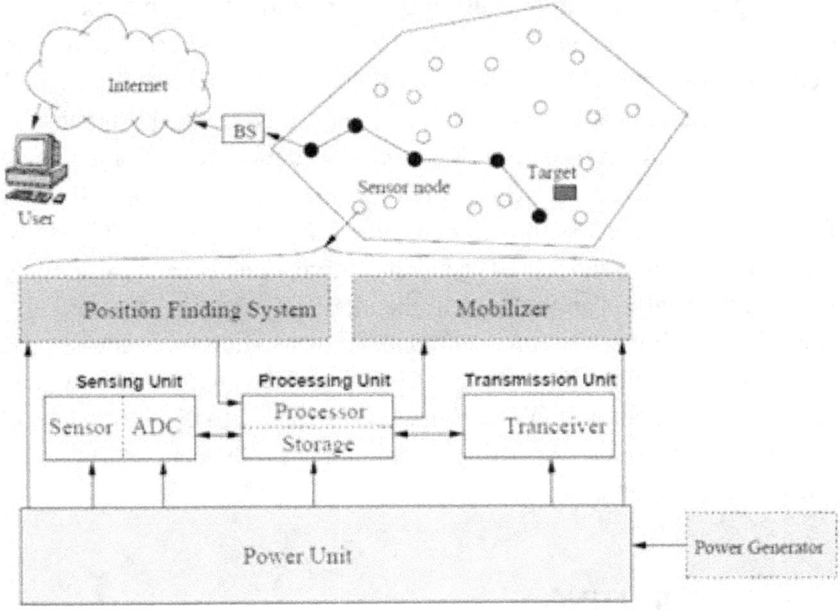

(PKtronics: Structure of a Wireless Sensor Node, 2017)

The figure further depicts that a sensor node has four main components: the sensing unit, processing unit, transmission unit, and power unit. Every sensor node has a Power Unit powered by the power generator to keep the node alive for collecting data. The node must be powered and active at the time of data collection; otherwise, the data shall be lost (i.e., not in a sleeping state). The collected data is stored and processed by the Processing Unit. The Sensing Unit has a sensor that records the data as specified. The transmission unit transmits and receives the data from the node to the others or CPE via a base station (BS) (Sandeep Verma, 2013; U.Farooq et al., 2015). As aforementioned, the sensor node collects the object-specified data, and it needs to be alive, which consumes power. That is why the applications and protocols must be developed to prolong the sensor life since the node has an inadequate supply of energy resources (battery power) (Sandeep Verma, 2013). WSN is used in different industries such as tracking, navigation, security, maintenance systems, etc. For instance, General Electric has used WSN in jet engines, turbines, etc., which analyses the data in real-time, making GE save time and expenditure for maintenance in case engines break down due to overheating (Lee & Lee, 2015).

CLOUD COMPUTING CONCEPTS

Cloud computing is one major contributor as it provides the framework for smart city infrastructure. It has been defined in three basic levels referred to as tiers for the choice of customers such as IaaS (Infrastructure as a Service), PaaS (Platform as a Service), and SaaS (Software as a Service) (Lee & Lee, 2015). Cloud computing provides a platform-based service model for data access, storage, analysis, and network to centralized data centers and backbone IP networks. Since smart city infrastructure connects with different cyber-physical systems (CPSs) where devices of different make and models generate heterogeneous data, this data is further processed for analysis and storage in the cloud. By the time the data uploads to the cloud, it loses important information as far as its analysis is concerned, and that's where fog computing takes its place for acting on IoT data and analyzing it to get useful information out of it (Wikström & Emilsson, 2014). The trend for cloud computing has shifted to fog computing, keeping in view the demands of emerging IoT-based smart city infrastructure.

FOG/EDGE COMPUTING

Fog computing is one of the latest research trends in computing, storage, control, and networking in which the services are provided to the end-user alongside the cloud (Chiang & Zhang, 2016). IoT-enabled smart devices within a CPS that generate data are called fog nodes deployed anywhere in the smart city network. For instance, the sensors alongside roads, on the poles, in a vehicle, or on an oil rig are called fog nodes. These nodes also include switches, routers, and servers, so any device with computing, storage, and network connectivity can be a fog node (Wikström & Emilsson, 2014). Thus, the sensing layer in smart city architecture comprises an edge and fog layer. It deploys edge and fog devices such as sensors, aggregators, actuators, and Raspberry Pi/servers to get real-time data processing. Later, the collected data can be used to make informed decisions based on CPS requirements in a smart city, as depicted in Figure 8.

SOFTWARE-DEFINED NETWORKING (SDN)

Software-defined networking (SDN) technology is another communication approach that enables network management dynamically and efficiently to improve network performance. The software-defined networking is different from conventional network management techniques as it programmatically improves network performance and monitoring. The core concept of SDN is to take out all the control functions from the network devices and merge them in a centralized location. It is one of the drawbacks of SDN from a security and privacy perspective, but it varies with the characteristics of different SDN implementations (Cisco Academy, 2014). It provides an interface more like cloud computing, enhancing network management features more easily. On the other hand, it is meant to provide the elasticity for easy troubleshooting as far as the current networks are concerned. This property is important for the smart city infrastructure as scalability and monitoring can be done proficiently. However, the centralization of the intelligence has its drawbacks to scalability and security, compared to distributed architecture (Cisco Academy, 2014; Hussain et al., 2020).

Here, the security of IoT-enabled smart devices in smart cities becomes immensely important, specifically from an authentication standpoint. In the case of unauthenticated/malicious assets, the whole infrastructure would be at stake. Many researchers in academia and industries have proposed different methods to secure these smart devices and the data generated by them. Considering these issues, we will be reviewing the literature focusing on authentication mechanisms and the representation of IoT-enabled smart devices in smart cities.

SMART CITY LAYERED ARCHITECTURE

The smart city architecture can be classified into layers based on the assets operating in a physical cyberspace environment that provides connectivity with the network for data flow, such as the Internet. The data captured by the physical assets, i.e., sensors, aggregators, and actuators, are processed in the physical layer referred to as the sensing layer. The command-and-control work on the application layer defines the applications for the asset's behavior at the physical layer. The network provides connectivity using communication and transmission technologies at the transmission layer. Though different researchers have different opinions (Perera et al., 2014), smart city architecture can mainly be divided into three-layered architecture, as depicted in Figure 8. The layers' functions, issues, and weaknesses are further explored and discussed below in this section.

APPLICATION LAYER

The application layer plays an important role in the applications defined with different functions for respective CPSs, such as application deployment for smart homes, smart hospitals, or smart cars. As depicted in Figure 8, this layer provides a path for the interaction using received information from the transmission layer. The commands are executed based on data received from the devices at the sensing layer. The deployment is carried out in a smart city's security operations center (SOC). It is the center point for service providers in a smart city architecture for utility companies connected to several applications located at different locations. The automated services provided at this layer may be centralized or distributed depending upon the nature and requirement of the CPS for its application and scalability.

TRANSMISSION LAYER

As shown in Figure 8, the data from the application layer is transmitted through this layer. It is responsible for the communication among the devices between the upper and lower layers. These devices connect through the traditional network technologies already in use for transferring the collected data, i.e., Wireless Fidelity (Wi-Fi), Radio Frequency Identification (RFID), Bluetooth (BT), Near Field Communication (NFC), etc. In contrast, transmission technologies such as 3G, 4G, LTE, 5G, internet, or satellite play an important role in data transfer and act as the backbone for communication (U.Farooq et al., 2015). Routing devices such as routers and switches use communication and transmission technologies to route the data. In contrast, cloud computing platforms, internet gateways, firewalls, intrusion detection systems (IDS), and intrusion prevention systems (IPS) platforms facilitate smooth and secure data transmission. The data centers by web servers such as Facebook, Google, etc., also function at this layer which may be centralized or distributed in nature, as in the case of Interplanetary File System (IPFS), Swarm, S3, etc.

Figure 8. Generalized smart city layered architecture

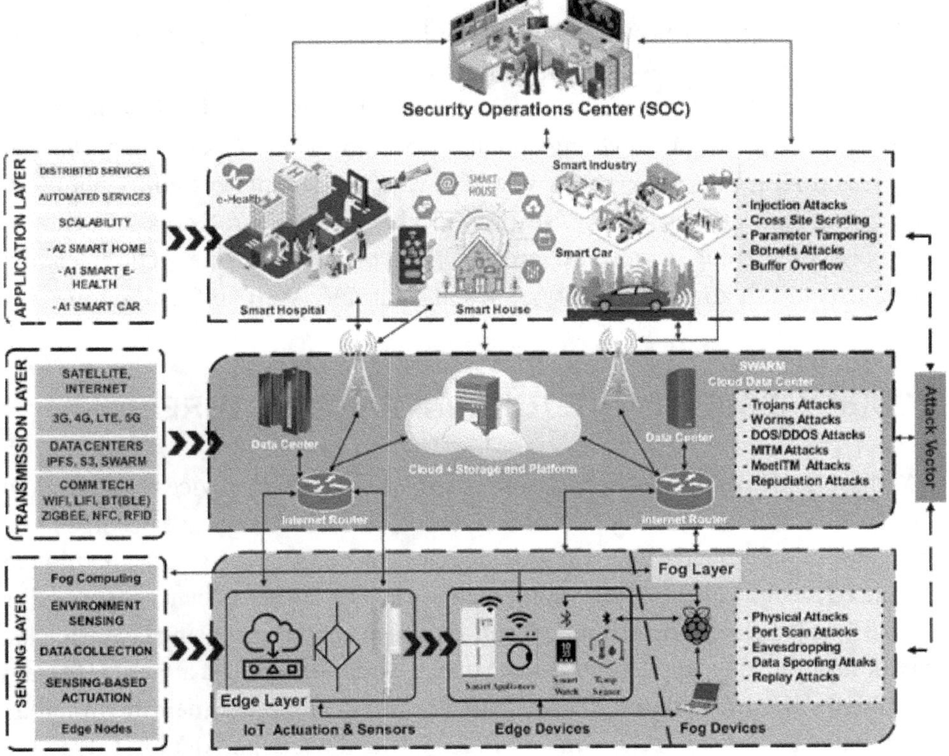

(Khalil, Malik, et al., 2022)

SENSING LAYER

Next to the transmission layer is the sensing layer. It comprises an edge and fog layer and deploys the edge and fog devices such as sensors, aggregators, actuators, and Raspberry Pi/servers to achieve real-time data processing. Later, the collected data can be used to make informed decisions based on CPS requirements in a smart city, as depicted in Figure 1.8. For instance, actuating the lights to switch on/off, recording a video whenever any moving object is detected, or turning on/off any smart device whenever sensing the heat signatures triggers environment sensing that can be used to intimate the SOC for further action, etc.

SMART CITY LAYERED SECURITY ISSUES

Though the Internet provides a platform for connectivity and creates a Web2 ecosystem where all the assets will communicate (D2D, M2M, etc.), it is fundamentally unsafe. Many specialists and researchers believe that "IoT is going to hit us hard if we're not doing anything about it." (Sandoval, 2017). For every service, process, and API, the attack vector would always be looking to find loopholes to break through the various layers of security mechanisms and protocols. A review of security issues keeping in view the same has been discussed in this section, leading to the current evaluation of security issues in smart city Web2 infrastructure.

SECURITY ISSUES IN INTERNET INFRASTRUCTURES

As discussed in earlier section, the use of IoT-enabled smart devices is not limited to any specific field or industry. The objects associated with them have become more intelligent and smarter. It causes these devices to be prone to security issues exploited by the attack vectors on different communication layers that have been categorized as physical attacks, physical and link-layer attacks, also known as sensing layer attacks, network layer attacks, application-layer attacks, and multilayered attacks (Hussain et al., 2020). If compromised, these smart devices become the mainstream arena for cyberattacks to exploit the vulnerabilities of the devices and deploy IoT botnet attacks that cause major issues in the internet core for data transmission.

An example, in this case, is MIRAI BOTNET. The group utilized "Mirai" to scan the internet and found the IoT-enabled smart devices vulnerable to a cyberattack with their default login details. The assets were hacked and were used to attack a huge botnet that choked half of the internet in the United States and was named "the most serious distributed denial-of-service (DDoS) attack in the history of the country (X-Force, 2017). Attacks like DoS and DDoS jammed the network flow (Doshi et al., 2018), while the increasing number of IoT networks have faced challenges based on the security and privacy of the smart devices and data generated (Dorri et al., 2017).

SECURITY ISSUES IN CYBER-PHYSICAL SYSTEMS

Security is critical for building IoT-enabled smart devices in a smart city, including secure communication and strong authentication for users and devices. In context to CPSs such as fields of smart grid, health monitoring, smart vehicles (UAVs, UGVs), process control, oil, and gas distribution, transportation systems, etc., more complex large-scale systems have been developed and deployed at the industry level, such as Supervisory Control and Data Acquisition system (SCADA). These CPSs provide command, control, communications, computer, intelligence, surveillance, and reconnaissance (C4ISR) facilities, considered the backbone of any industrial architecture (Department of the Army, 2006).

Security Issues in Industrial Cyber-Physical Systems

As detailed earlier, the customer premises equipment (CPE) in cyber-physical systems (CPSs) generates data (sensors) that is crucial to making informed decisions (actuators) or decisions for corrective measures to resolve operational issues. In contrast, implementing these devices in a corporate system such as supervisory control and data acquisition (SCADA) is critical. Here, authentication becomes of immense importance from an adversarial point of view that may cause serious damage to the CPS, as in the case of industrial programmable logic controllers (PLCs). The automated engagement of electromechanical processes for controlling the machines and industrial processes such as separating nuclear material from the centrifuges is performed. In case of a data breach, wrong data fueling may cause serious damage to the overall system or, in worst-case scenarios, be destroyed, causing a system halt (Department of the Army, 2006). A similar kind of security breach was reported in 2007. The Iranian Nuclear Program was hit by the Stuxnet virus, which works by propagating information across the network and the USB sticks (Kelley, 2013). The virus compromised Iranian PLCs, collecting data on industrial systems, and caused the fast-spinning centrifuges to tear apart (Department of the Army, 2006). According to Reuters, an asset protection US-based company, "Target," was breached via the network to access the embedded devices with impunity. It caused a serious security risk to the data breach that hit 40 million payment cards data breach in the year 2013 (Finkle & Skariachan, 2013). The cyber-attack on the German steel plant in 2014 caused significant damage. The attack vector accessed the corporate network and moved unilaterally throughout the control network or operation network without any operational defenses (*German Steel Plant Suffers Significant Damage from Targeted Attack - Nouvelles de Sécurité - Trend Micro FR*, 2015).

Security Issues in Health Care

In the case of the healthcare CPS, the issues related to the weak security in the wireless embedded medical devices such as pacemakers and insulin pumps (which record the patient details and treat the respective patients accordingly) may leak the patient's critical health information. In case of false data injection, the results may be fatal. There had been major adversaries in the past where the vulnerabilities in the smart assets were exploited. A report was released on 29 December 2016, by the U.S. Food and Drug Administration (FDA) about the smart devices currently available in the market. It mentioned the issues related to the network security in wireless embedded medical devices such as pacemakers and insulin pumps, which could leak the patient's critical health information. Here, the authentication of connected devices has to be ensured while sending data to the corresponding storage devices, which is critical as far as the patient is concerned.

Security Issues in IoT-Enabled Smart Devices

Another factor is the manufacturers' low concentration of security features in the CPE, such as easy-to-guess default login credentials, open ports, unencrypted and weak versions of SSL (v2, v3, and CBC mode) services, self-signed or expired security certificates, etc. Thus, it becomes an easy target for the attack vector who exploits these features to attack the system as a botnet that happened a couple of times in the past. The manufacturers of these devices left unattended authentication and access control schemes which increases the chance of the attack vectors' exploitation.

In (Doshi et al., 2018), an analysis of the ten most popular consumer IoT devices showed 250 susceptibilities concerning outdated operating systems, open telnet ports for making a remote connection to the device for exploitation, and weak encryption protocols configuration for data transmission. Authors in (Alrawi et al., 2019) evaluated 45 IoT devices from well-known vendors such as Amazon (Echo, Fire TV), Apple (HomePod, TV), D-Link (Cloud Camera), Google (Home, Home Mini, OnHub), Philips (HUE), TP-Link (Wi-Fi Bulb, Wi-Fi Plug), Samsung (Smart Things, Smart TV) and Logitech (Harmony), etc. They found almost the same kind of issues together with 84 running services. Secure Shell (SSH), Universal Plug n Play (UPnP), HyperText Transfer Protocol (HTTP webserver), Domain Name System (DNS), Network Virtual Terminal Protocol (Telnet: A service for remote connection to devices), Real-Time Streaming Protocol (RTSP) and custom services to name a few, while 39 issues related to those services were found. Though many state-of-the-art authentication and authorization mechanisms have been proposed for devices in smart cities, most are centralized and offer high communication overhead, which results in higher energy consumption.

Security Issues in Heterogeneous IoT-Enabled Smart Devices

Different manufacturers and vendors produce IoT-enabled smart devices that use various security and communication protocols to connect to the same IoT infrastructure. Since these heterogeneous devices connect in the same CPSs, creating a heterogeneous infrastructure for data transfer and communication mechanisms at respective layers. It also causes the infrastructure to generate a huge amount of heterogeneous data. The authors in (Hussain et al., 2020) also discuss the IoT infrastructure regarding the heterogeneous data generated by the heterogeneous things (IoT devices). The collection of this data poses an open challenge because of its volume and nature. It is important to take care of this data as hackers can easily hack it from IoT assets and later use it to manipulate the devices, such as in the case of Botnet attacks.

IOT-ENABLED SMART DEVICE AUTHENTICATION ARCHITECTURES IN SMART CITIES

As discussed earlier, the issues in the Web2 smart city infrastructure can also be put into fundamental security traits categories, i.e., Authentication, Authorization, and Audit (AAA). It further classifies the security services into Confidentiality, Integrity, and Availability (CIA), whereas user confidentiality and authentication aspects have been explored. For any CPS in Web2 smart city infrastructure, the authenticity of users and customer premises equipment (CPE), i.e., sensors and actuators, are major concerns. With the rapid increase in usage and low concentration on the security and privacy details of the devices, challenges have been evident, pushing the need for solutions that could address these security issues.

Since the work in this thesis focuses on IoT-enabled smart device authentication schemes in a smart city, the upcoming section discusses the review of traditional state-of-the-art authentication mechanisms already deployed, followed by the newly proposed authentication mechanisms in upcoming chapters.

STATE OF THE ART AUTHENTICATION MODELS

The authentication of CPE is as crucial as other CIA traits. The schemes would force legitimate users to access the resources; otherwise, the whole system would be at stake. As shown in Figure 1.9, the state-of-the-art authentication model is based on authentication architecture with two main categories, i.e., centralized/non-distributed and non-centralized/distributed authentication models.

Figure 9. Authentication model

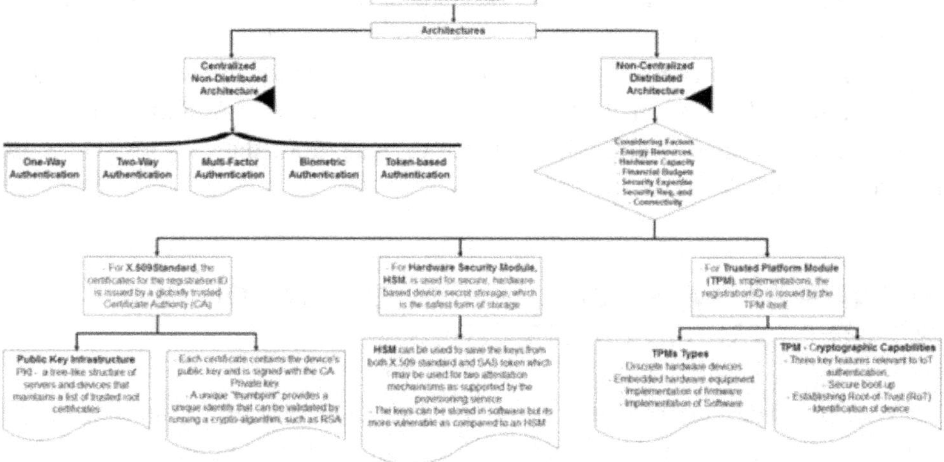

(Khalil, Malik, et al., 2022)

The traditional authentication mechanisms have been developed on mostly centralized architecture based on Web2 architecture where resourceful machines play an important role in providing authentication services. The attack vector always finds ways to intervene in the security protocols. That is where the additional authentication protocols come in handy such as OpenID (Esposito et al., 2021), Security Assertion Markups Language (SAML 1.1/2), Fast Identity Online (FIDO), or Open Authorization (OAuth). At the same time, the implementation relies on trusted third-party (TTP) solutions. OAuth is the most adopted Web2 solution because it is one of the most powerful open authorization solutions available to API developers today. Its powerful functions can be utilized to protect the vast Internet of Things. Though it provides a strong and single sign-on (SSO) authentication mechanism, it also poses threats to its centralized architecture (Tahir et al., 2020). The centralized/non-distributed mechanisms, as depicted in Figure 1.9, involve the following authentication mechanisms that have been used traditionally and are discussed as under.

Single-Factor Authentication (SFA)

SFA, referred to as One-Way Authentication, provides primary authentication such as password, secure PIN, PIV card, etc.

Two-factor authentication (2FA)

2FA referred to as Two-Way Authentication, provides one-time authentication such as a one-time password, secure PIN, registered device, etc.

Multi-Factor Authentication (MFA)

MFA depends on two to three factors that provide authentication, such as password, secure PIN, texting OTPs to users' phone numbers and magic links sent via SMSs or emails, locational info, etc. In all the password-protected environments, protocols such as PAP and CHAP are used, which provides sufficient usability for the authentication mechanism.

Biometrics

Biometrics includes biological traits, such as fingerprint ID and face shapes for user authentication. In 2011, a fingerprint scanner was introduced to the Motorola ATRIX Android smartphone, and since then, it has been commonly used for user authentication for device logging or completing digital purchases.

Token-Based Authentication

It is a protocol used to authenticate the users to verify their identity based on the unique token received after verification of the credentials. These tokens are then used to access websites, applications, or any protected resource by mitigating the hassle of repeatedly re-entering the credentials. The token-based authentication mitigates the risk of stolen authentication factors as tokens are protected against misuse. It does not utilize system processing power like a password-based mechanism. In smart city infrastructure, the authentication of the IoT-enabled smart devices in a cyber-physical system is immense. Though it is an important yet hard-hitting decision to choose the relevant model for authentication, the factors affecting the overall network's performance would be at stake. The performance affects energy resources, hardware limitations, budgets, security expertise, security needs, and connectivity. As depicted in Figure 1.9, the distributed security model works on certificate-based authentication, hardware-based authentication with secret storage, and trusted platform-based authentication solutions (WorkOS, 2020).

Certificate-Based Authentication

This authentication mechanism utilizes X.509 Standard, one of the most implemented and preferred choices that rely on certificates for authentication and authorization. These certificates are used for ID registration and issued by a globally trusted Certificate Authority (CA). It is referred to as Public Key Infrastructure (PKI), which consists of a tree-like structure of servers and devices that maintain a list of trusted root certificates. The certificates contain the device's public key and are signed with the CA's private key. A unique "thumbprint" provides a unique identity that can be validated by running a crypto algorithm, such as RSA (Mumtaz et al., 2019).

Hardware Security Module

Further shown in the figure, the other type of authentication is provided by hardware-based devices. It offers the Hardware Security Module (HSM), which secures the hardware-based device's secret storage and is considered one of the safest forms of secret storage. HSM can save the keys from X.509 standard and SAS token, which may be used for two attestation mechanisms supported by the provisioning service. The keys can be stored in software, but it is more vulnerable than an HSM (Arcenegui et al., 2021).

Trusted Platform Module

The Trusted Platform Module (TPM) implementations include the registration ID issued by its hardware. TPMs come in several forms, such as discreet hardware devices, embedded hardware equipment, firmware, implementation of software, etc. TPM has several cryptographic capabilities, while a few key features may be quite relevant to IoT authentication, i.e., secure boot-up, establishing the root of trust (RoT), and identification of the device (Siddiqui et al., 2018). The aforementioned authentication schemes have traditionally been used; however, new authentication mechanisms have been proposed.

Up to this point, the smart city literature and associated issues with its Web2 architecture have been presented which offer a motivation to propose a novel architecture based on Web3 services. Due to the benefits of Web3, solutions may be developed from previously unimaginable possibilities. The permissioned cyberspace and decentralization were pure science fiction concepts however progress in the Web3 architecture resolves the problems of Web2. The next section discusses the chattels of possible solutions based on Web3 architecture which will eventually help address the ambiguities for improvement and escorting in a decentralized digital future.

CONCLUSION

The developments in Web 3.0 have steered, a new era of decentralized and interconnected smart cities. With significant upgrades in the capability of the IoT-enabled smart devices and advanced communication technologies, the aim is evident to enhance urban living, optimize resource utilization, and improve overall quality of life. However, there are implications of these technologies that also introduce new security challenges, demanding robust authentication mechanisms to safeguard sensitive data and prevent unauthorized access. This chapter explored the foundational aspects of smart city infrastructure, including its historical evolution, enabling technologies, and layered architecture. It has delved into the specific security challenges associated with IoT-enabled smart devices and presented various authentication models to address these concerns. As smart cities continue to evolve, it is imperative to prioritize security and privacy to ensure the trust and confidence of citizens. By adopting strong authentication measures, such as multi-factor authentication, and staying abreast of emerging technologies, we can build secure, resilient, and sustainable smart cities for the future.

REFERENCES

Abideen, S. (2019). *Blockchain Expert* (Sainul Abideen CEO (ed.)). CYBROSYS Technologies. www.cybrosys.com, www.blockchainexpert.uk

Almadhoun, R., Kadadha, M., Alhemeiri, M., Alshehhi, M., & Salah, K. (2019). A User Authentication Scheme of IoT Devices using Blockchain-Enabled Fog Nodes. *Proceedings of IEEE/ACS International Conference on Computer Systems and Applications, AICCSA, 2018-Novem*. DOI: 10.1109/AICCSA.2018.8612856

Alrawi, O., Lever, C., Antonakakis, M., & Monrose, F. (2019). SoK: Security Evaluation of Home-Based IoT Deployments. *Proceedings - IEEE Symposium on Security and Privacy, 2019-May*, 1362–1380. DOI: 10.1109/SP.2019.00013

Aman, M. N., Chua, K. C., & Sikdar, B. (2017). Mutual Authentication in IoT Systems Using Physical Unclonable Functions. *IEEE Internet of Things Journal, 4*(5), 1327–1340. DOI: 10.1109/JIOT.2017.2703088

Ammi, M., Alarabi, S., & Benkhelifa, E. (2021). Customized blockchain-based architecture for secure smart home for lightweight IoT. *Information Processing & Management, 58*(3), 102482. DOI: 10.1016/j.ipm.2020.102482

Arcenegui, J., Arjona, R., Román, R., & Baturone, I. (2021). Secure combination of IoT and blockchain by physically binding IoT devices to smart non-fungible tokens using PUFs. *Sensors (Basel), 21*(9), 3119. Advance online publication. DOI: 10.3390/s21093119 PMID: 33946227

Armando, A., Carbone, R., Compagna, L., Cuellar, J., & Tobarra, L. (2008). Formal analysis of SAML 2.0 web browser single sign-on: Breaking the SAML-based single sign-on for google apps. *Proceedings of the ACM Conference on Computer and Communications Security*, 1–9. DOI: 10.1145/1456396.1456397

BehrTech. (2020). *6 Leading Types of IoT Wireless Technologies | BehrTech Blog*. BEHRTECH Technologies Inc. https://behrtech.com/blog/6-leading-types-of-iot-wireless-tech-and-their-best-use-cases/

Bellagarda, J., & Abu-Mahfouz, A. M. (2022). Connect2NFT: A Web-Based, Blockchain Enabled NFT Application with the Aim of Reducing Fraud and Ensuring Authenticated Social, Non-Human Verified Digital Identity. *Mathematics, 10*(21), 3934. DOI: 10.3390/math10213934

Bitcoin.it. (2018). *Weaknesses - Bitcoin Wiki*. Bitcoin.It. https://en.bitcoin.it/wiki/Weaknesses#The_Finney_attack%0Ahttps://en.bitcoin.it/wiki/Weaknesses

Böhme, R., Christin, N., Edelman, B., & Moore, T. (2015). Bitcoin: Economics, technology, and governance. *The Journal of Economic Perspectives, 29*(2), 213–238. DOI: 10.1257/jep.29.2.213

Burhan, M., Rehman, R. A., Khan, B., & Kim, B. S. (2018). IoT elements, layered architectures and security issues: A comprehensive survey. *Sensors (Basel), 18*(9), 1–37. DOI: 10.3390/s18092796 PMID: 30149582

Burks, Z., Morgan, J., & Malone, B. J. S. (2020). *EIP-2981: NFT Royalty Standard.* Ethereum. https://eips.ethereum.org/EIPS/eip-2981

Chaabouni, N., Mosbah, M., Zemmari, A., Sauvignac, C., & Faruki, P. (2019). Network Intrusion Detection for IoT Security Based on Learning Techniques. *IEEE Communications Surveys and Tutorials, 21*(3), 2671–2701. DOI: 10.1109/COMST.2019.2896380

Chiacchio, F., D'urso, D., Oliveri, L. M., Spitaleri, A., Spampinato, C., & Giordano, D. (2022). A Non-Fungible Token Solution for the Track and Trace of Pharmaceutical Supply Chain. *Applied Sciences (Basel, Switzerland), 12*(8), 4019. DOI: 10.3390/app12084019

Chiang, M., & Zhang, T. (2016). Fog and IoT: An Overview of Research Opportunities. In *IEEE Internet of Things Journal* (Vol. 3, Issue 6, pp. 854–864). DOI: 10.1109/JIOT.2016.2584538

Cisco. (2020). Cisco: 2020 CISO Benchmark Report. In *Computer Fraud & Security* (Vol. 2020, Issue 3). DOI: 10.1016/S1361-3723(20)30026-9

Cisco Academy. (2014). *Evolution of Software Defined Networking within Cisco ' s VMDC Challenges within the Data Center SDN Architectural Framework and Solution Characteristics.*

Cryptopedia. (2021). *What Is Tokenization? Blockchain Token Types.* https://www.gemini.com/cryptopedia/what-is-tokenization-definition-crypto-token

Dammak, M., Boudia, O. R. M., Messous, M. A., Senouci, S. M., & Gransart, C. (2019). Token-Based Lightweight Authentication to Secure IoT Networks. *2019 16th IEEE Annual Consumer Communications and Networking Conference, CCNC 2019.* DOI: 10.1109/CCNC.2019.8651825

Davis, S., Diemers, D., & Arsianian, H. G. D. (2019). 4 th ICO / STO Report - A Strategic Perspective. In *PWC Report.* https://www.pwc.ch/en/publications/2019/ch-20190308-strategyand-ico-sto-report-q1-2019.pdf

Deng, W., Huang, T., & Wang, H. (2023). A Review of the Key Technology in a Blockchain Building Decentralized Trust Platform. *Mathematics, 11*(1), 101. Advance online publication. DOI: 10.3390/math11010101

Department of the Army, H. (2006). *Supervisory Control and Data Acquisition (SCADA) Systems for command, control, communications, computer, intelligence, surveillance, and reconnaissance (C4ISR) facilities* (Issue January).

Dorri, A., Kanhere, S. S., Jurdak, R., & Gauravaram, P. (2017). Blockchain for IoT security and privacy: The case study of a smart home. *2017 IEEE International Conference on Pervasive Computing and Communications Workshops, PerCom Workshops 2017*, 618–623. DOI: 10.1109/PERCOMW.2017.7917634

Doshi, R., Apthorpe, N., & Feamster, N. (2018). Machine learning DDoS detection for consumer internet of things devices. *Proceedings - 2018 IEEE Symposium on Security and Privacy Workshops, SPW 2018, Ml*, 29–35. DOI: 10.1109/SPW.2018.00013

Entriken, W., Shirley, D., & Evans, J. N. S. (2018). *EIP-721: Non-Fungible Token Standard.* Ethereum Improvement Proposals. https://eips.ethereum.org/EIPS/eip-721

Eric Binet, R. S. W. R. A. C. P. C. J. T. (2018). "EIP-1155: Multi Token Standard. In *Ethereum Improvement Proposals*. https://eips.ethereum.org/EIPS/eip-1155

Esposito, C., Ficco, M., & Gupta, B. B. (2021). Blockchain-based authentication and authorization for smart city applications. *Information Processing & Management, 58*(2), 102468. DOI: 10.1016/j.ipm.2020.102468

Farooq, U., M., Waseem, M., Mazhar, S., Khairi, A., & Kamal, T. (. (2015). A Review on Internet of Things (IoT). *International Journal of Computer Applications, 113*(1), 1–7. DOI: 10.5120/19787-1571

Ferrag, M. A., Maglaras, L., Derhab, A., & Bernabe, J. B. (2019). Authentication and Authorization for Mobile IoT Devices Using Biofeatures: Recent Advances and Future Trends. *Security and Communication Networks, 2019*, 1–20. DOI: 10.1155/2019/5452870

Ferreira, C. M. S., Garrocho, C. T. B., Oliveira, R. A. R., Silva, J. S., & Cavalcanti, C. F. M. da C. (2021). IoT registration and authentication in smart city applications with blockchain. *Sensors (Basel), 21*(4), 1–23. DOI: 10.3390/s21041323 PMID: 33668415

Finkle, J., & Skariachan, D. (2013). Target cyber breach hits 40 million payment cards at holiday peak. In *Reuters US Edition: Vol. Cyber Crim* (p. https://www.reuters.com/news/technology/article/201). https://www.reuters.com/article/us-target-breach-idUSBRE9BH1GX20131219

Fisher, K. (2007). Jonah liberated by technology. In *Hart's E and P* (Issue AUG.). Uttarakhand Open University, 2017. http://uou.ac.in

Fotiou, N., Pittaras, I., Siris, V. A., Voulgaris, S., & Polyzos, G. C. (2021). *OAuth 2.0 Authorization using Blockchain-based Tokens*. DOI: 10.14722/diss.2020.23002

German Steel Plant Suffers Significant Damage from Targeted Attack - Nouvelles de sécurité - Trend Micro FR. (2015). Nouvelles de Sécurité - Trend Micro. https://www.trendmicro.com/vinfo/fr/security/news/cyber-attacks/german-steel-plant-suffers-significant-damage-from-targeted-attack

Gong, L., Alghazzawi, D. M., & Cheng, L. (2021). Bcot sentry: A blockchain-based identity authentication framework for iot devices. *Information (Basel)*, *12*(5), 1–20. DOI: 10.3390/info12050203

Gope, P., & Sikdar, B. (2019). Lightweight and Privacy-Preserving Two-Factor Authentication Scheme for IoT Devices. *IEEE Internet of Things Journal*, *6*(1), 580–589. DOI: 10.1109/JIOT.2018.2846299

Gubbi, J., Buyya, R., Marusic, S., & Palaniswami, M. (2013). Internet of Things (IoT): A vision, architectural elements, and future directions. *Future Generation Computer Systems*, *29*(7), 1645–1660. DOI: 10.1016/j.future.2013.01.010

Hammi, M. T., Bellot, P., & Serhrouchni, A. (2018). BCTrust: A decentralized authentication blockchain-based mechanism. *IEEE Wireless Communications and Networking Conference, WCNC, 2018-April*, 1–6. DOI: 10.1109/WCNC.2018.8376948

Hasan, H. R., Salah, K., Battah, A., Madine, M., Yaqoob, I., Jayaraman, R., & Omar, M.HASAN. (2022). Incorporating Registration, Reputation, and Incentivization Into the NFT Ecosystem. *IEEE Access : Practical Innovations, Open Solutions*, *10*, 76416–76433. DOI: 10.1109/ACCESS.2022.3192388

Hinrichs, T. (2019). *Centralized vs. Distributed Authorization: The CAP Theorem*. Styra. https://blog.styra.com/blog/centralized-vs.-distributed-authorization-the-cap-theorem

Hriez, S., Obeid, N., & Awajan, A. (2019). User authentication on smartphones using keystroke dynamics. *PervasiveHealth: Pervasive Computing Technologies for Healthcare*, *2–5*, 1–4. Advance online publication. DOI: 10.1145/3368691.3368725

Hussain, F., Hussain, R., Hassan, S. A., & Hossain, E. (2020). Machine Learning in IoT Security: Current Solutions and Future Challenges. *IEEE Communications Surveys and Tutorials*, *22*(3), 1686–1721. DOI: 10.1109/COMST.2020.2986444

Ibrokhimov, S., Hui, K. L., Abdulhakim Al-Absi, A., Lee, H. J., & Sain, M. (2019). Multi-Factor Authentication in Cyber Physical System: A State of Art Survey. *International Conference on Advanced Communication Technology, ICACT, 2019-Febru*, 279–284. DOI: 10.23919/ICACT.2019.8701960

Joost de Kruijff, H. W. (2017). Understanding the Blockchain Using Enterprise Ontology Joost. *Springer International Publishing AG 2017, 10253 LNCS*, 29–43. DOI: 10.1007/978-3-319-59536-8

Kaaniche, N., & Laurent, M. (2017). Data security and privacy preservation in cloud storage environments based on cryptographic mechanisms. *Computer Communications*, *111*, 120–141. DOI: 10.1016/j.comcom.2017.07.006

Kelley, M. B. (2013). The Stuxnet Attack On Iran's Nuclear Plant Was "Far More Dangerous" Than Previously Thought. *Business Insider*, 1. https://www.businessinsider.com/stuxnet-was-far-more-dangerous-than-previous-thought-2013-11

Khalid, U., Asim, M., Baker, T., Hung, P. C. K., Tariq, M. A., & Rafferty, L. (2020). A decentralized lightweight blockchain-based authentication mechanism for IoT systems. *Cluster Computing*, *23*(3), 2067–2087. DOI: 10.1007/s10586-020-03058-6

Khalil, U., Malik, O. A., Hong, O. W., & Uddin, M. (2023). Leveraging a novel NFT-enabled blockchain architecture for the authentication of IoT assets in smart cities. *Scientific Reports 2023 13:1*, *13*(1), 1–26. DOI: 10.1038/s41598-023-45212-1

Khalil, U., Malik, O. A., Uddin, M., & Chen, C.-L. (2022). A Comparative Analysis on Blockchain and Centralized Authentication Architectures for IoT-Enabled Smart Devices in Smart Cities : A Comprehensive Review, Recent Advances, and Future Research Directions. *Sensors (Basel)*, *22*(12), 1–52. DOI: 10.3390/s22145168 PMID: 35890848

Khalil, U., Mueen, U., Malik, O. A., & Hussain, S. (2022). A Blockchain Footprint for Authentication of IoT-Enabled Smart Devices in Smart Cities: State-of-the-Art Advancements, Challenges and Future Research Directions. *IEEE Access : Practical Innovations, Open Solutions*, *10*, 76805–76823. DOI: 10.1109/ACCESS.2022.3189998

Khan, M. A., & Salah, K. (2018). IoT security: Review, blockchain solutions, and open challenges. *Future Generation Computer Systems*, *82*, 395–411. DOI: 10.1016/j.future.2017.11.022

Kraken. (2021). Kraken Report: Non-Fungible Tokens (NFTs): Redefining Digital Scarcity. In *NCFA (National Crowdfunding and Fintech Association) Canada* (Issue September). kraken.com/subscribe/intelligence

Lampson, B., Abadi, M., Burrows, M., & Wobber, E. (1991). Authentication in distributed systems: Theory and practice. *Proceedings of the 13th ACM Symposium on Operating Systems Principles, SOSP 1991*, 165–182. DOI: 10.1145/121132.121160

Lampson, B., Abadi, M., Burrows, M., & Wobber, E. (1992). Authentication in distributed systems. In *ACM Transactions on Computer Systems* (Vol. 10, Issue 4, pp. 265–310). DOI: 10.1145/138873.138874

Lee, I., & Lee, K. (2015). The Internet of Things (IoT): Applications, investments, and challenges for enterprises. *Business Horizons*, *58*(4), 431–440. DOI: 10.1016/j.bushor.2015.03.008

Lewis, A. (2015). Blockchain Technology Explained. In *Blockchain Technologies*. https://www.blockchaintechnologies.com/blockchain-definition

López-Pimentel, J. C., Morales-Rosales, L. A., Algredo-Badillo, I., & Del-Valle-Soto, C. (2023). NFT-Vehicle: A Blockchain-Based Tokenization Architecture to Register Transactions over a Vehicle's Life Cycle. *Mathematics*, *11*(13), 2801. DOI: 10.3390/math11132801

Mateen, A. Q., & Hong, O. W. (2018). Implementation and evaluation of IoT system using cloud storage platform. *ACM International Conference Proceeding Series*, 157–161. DOI: 10.1145/3289430.3289465

Matta, P., & Pant, B. (2019). Internet-of-things: Genesis, challenges and applications. *Journal of Engineering Science and Technology*, *14*(3), 1717–1750.

Mir, O., Roland, M., & Mayrhofer, R. (2020). DAMFA: Decentralized anonymous multi-factor authentication. *BSCI 2020 - Proceedings of the 2nd ACM International Symposium on Blockchain and Secure Critical Infrastructure, Co-Located with AsiaCCS 2020*, 10–19. DOI: 10.1145/3384943.3409417

Monti, M., & Rasmussen, S. (2017). RAIN: A Bio-Inspired Communication and Data Storage Infrastructure. *Artificial Life*, *23*(4), 552–557. DOI: 10.1162/ARTL_a_00247 PMID: 28985116

MORRIS. A., & Ford, B. (2019). Blockchain for Beginners. In *Quill* (Vol. 107, Issue 1). http://search.ebscohost.com/login.aspx?direct=true&db=ufh&AN=135307185&site=eds-live

Mumtaz, M., Akram, J., & Ping, L. (2019). An RSA based authentication system for smart IoT environment. *Proceedings - 21st IEEE International Conference on High Performance Computing and Communications, 17th IEEE International Conference on Smart City and 5th IEEE International Conference on Data Science and Systems, HPCC/SmartCity/DSS 2019*, 758–765. DOI: 10.1109/HPCC/SmartCity/DSS.2019.00112

Musamih, A., Yaqoob, I., Salah, K., Jayaraman, R., Omar, M., & Ellahham, S. (2022a). NFTs in Healthcare: Vision, Opportunities, and Challenges. *IEEE Consumer Electronics Magazine*. Advance online publication. DOI: 10.1109/MCE.2022.3196480

Musamih, A., Yaqoob, I., Salah, K., Jayaraman, R., Omar, M., & Ellahham, S. (2022b). Using NFTs for Product Management, Digital Certification, Trading, and Delivery in the Healthcare Supply Chain. *IEEE Transactions on Engineering Management*, •••, 1–22. DOI: 10.1109/TEM.2022.3215793

NerdWallet. (2023). *11 Best Crypto Wallets of January 2023 - NerdWallet*. https://www.nerdwallet.com/article/investing/best-bitcoin-cryptocurrency-wallet

Odom, W. (2016). *Cisco Cert Guide* (E. B. Bartow, Brett, Sandra Schroeder Senior, Christopher Cleveland, Tonya Simpson, Keith Cline, Chuck Hutchinson, Aubrey Adams (Ed.)). ciscopress.com. https://doi.org/DOI: 1-58720-580-7

Palattella, M. R., Ladid, L., Ziegler, S., Kastner, W., Jung, M., Kofler, M., Drajic, D. D., Krco, S., Nam, G., & Perez, R. M. (2019). *IoT-IPv6 Integration for SMEs*. IoT6 European Project (STREP) of the 7th Framework Program. www.iot6.eu

Perera, C., Zaslavsky, A., Christen, P., & Georgakopoulos, D. (2014). Sensing as a service model for smart cities supported by Internet of Things. *Transactions on Emerging Telecommunications Technologies*, *25*(1), 81–93. DOI: 10.1002/ett.2704

PKtronics: Structure of a wireless sensor node : (2017). http://pktronics.blogspot.com/2017/10/structure-of-wireless-sensor-node.html

Punia, A., Gupta, D., & Jaiswal, S. (2017). A perspective on available security techniques in IoT. *RTEICT 2017 - 2nd IEEE International Conference on Recent Trends in Electronics, Information and Communication Technology, Proceedings, 2018-Janua*, 1553–1559. DOI: 10.1109/RTEICT.2017.8256859

Raible, M. (2017). *What the Heck is OAuth? | Okta Developer*. Okta. https://developer.okta.com/blog/2017/06/21/what-the-heck-is-oauth

Rehman, Z. U., Altaf, S., & Iqbal, S. (2019). Survey of Authentication Schemes for Health Monitoring: A Subset of Cyber Physical System. *Proceedings of 2019 16th International Bhurban Conference on Applied Sciences and Technology, IBCAST 2019*, 653–660. DOI: 10.1109/IBCAST.2019.8667166

Sandoval, K. (2017). *OAuth 2.0 – Why It's Vital to IoT Security*. https://nordicapis.com/why-oauth-2-0-is-vital-to-iot-security/

Sestino, A., Guido, G., & Peluso, A. M. (2022). Non-Fungible Tokens (NFTs). In *Non-Fungible Tokens (NFTs)*. Springer International Publishing., DOI: 10.1007/978-3-031-07203-1

Shepherd, J. (2019). *The Ultimate Authentication Playbook*. Okta. https://www.okta.com/blog/2019/02/the-ultimate-authentication-playbook/

Shiba, K. (2020). *EIP-2615: Non-Fungible Token with mortgage and rental functions*. https://eips.ethereum.org/EIPS/eip-2615

Siddiqui, A. S., Gui, Y., Lawrence, D., Laval, S., Plusquellic, J., Manjrekar, M., Chowdhury, B., & Saqib, F. (2018). Hardware assisted security architecture for smart grid. *Proceedings: IECON 2018 - 44th Annual Conference of the IEEE Industrial Electronics Society, 1*(1566530), 2890–2895. DOI: 10.1109/IECON.2018.8591401

Tahir, M., Sardaraz, M., Muhammad, S., & Khan, M. S. (2020). A lightweight authentication and authorization framework for blockchain-enabled IoT network in health-informatics. *Sustainability (Basel), 12*(17), 6960. Advance online publication. DOI: 10.3390/su12176960

Teicher, J. (2018). *The little-known story of the first IoT device - IBM Industries*. Ibm. https://www.ibm.com/blogs/industries/little-known-story-first-iot-device/

Thomas, Y. C., & Woo, S. S. L. (2014). Distributed Systems. *Distributed Systems, 25*(1), 39–52. DOI: 10.1201/b17224

Underwood, S. (2016). Blockchain beyond bitcoin. *Communications of the ACM, 59*(11), 15–17. DOI: 10.1145/2994581

Vegh, L. (2018). Cyber-physical systems security through multi-factor authentication and data analytics. *Proceedings of the IEEE International Conference on Industrial Technology, 2018-Febru*, 1369–1374. DOI: 10.1109/ICIT.2018.8352379

Verma, S. (2013). Network Topologies in Wireless Sensor Networks: A Review 1. *International Journal of Electronics & Communication Technology, 4*(3), 93–97. https://doi.org/ISSN : 2230-7109 (Online)

Vinet, L., & Zhedanov, A. (2011). A "missing" family of classical orthogonal polynomials. *Journal of Physics. A, Mathematical and Theoretical, 44*(8), 1–11. DOI: 10.1088/1751-8113/44/8/085201

Wang, Z., Dong, X., Li, Y., Fang, L., & Chen, P. (2018). IoT Security Model and Performance Evaluation: A Blockchain Approach. *Proceedings of 2018 6th IEEE International Conference on Network Infrastructure and Digital Content, IC-NIDC 2018*, 260–264. DOI: 10.1109/ICNIDC.2018.8525716

Weiser, M. (1991). The Computer for the 21st Century - Specialized elements of hardware and software, connected by wires, radio waves and infrared, will be so ubiquitous that no one will notice their presence. *Readings in Human–Computer Interaction*, 933–940. https://www.lri.fr/~mbl/Stanford/CS477/papers/Weiser-SciAm.pdf

What Is Token-Based Authentication? (2021). Okta Inc. https://www.okta.com/identity-101/what-is-token-based-authentication/

Wikström, E., & Emilsson, U. M. (2014). Autonomy and Control in Everyday Life in Care of Older People in Nursing Homes. In *Journal of Housing for the Elderly* (Vol. 28, Issue 1). DOI: 10.1080/02763893.2013.858092

Work, O. S. (2020). *A Developer's History of Authentication*. Workos.Com. https://workos.com/blog/a-developers-history-of-authentication

Wright, K. L., Martinez, M., Chadha, U., & Krishnamachari, B. (2018). SmartEdge: A Smart Contract for Edge Computing. *Proceedings - IEEE 2018 International Congress on Cybermatics: 2018 IEEE Conferences on Internet of Things, Green Computing and Communications, Cyber, Physical and Social Computing, Smart Data, Blockchain, Computer and Information Technology, IThings/Gree*, 1685–1690. DOI: 10.1109/Cybermatics_2018.2018.00281

X-Force. I. (2017). *Mirai Botnet Loader Campaign*. IBM X-Force Threat Research. https://exchange.xforce.ibmcloud.com/collection/Mirai-Botnet-Loader-Campaign-7e8131a283d50a0f13d43ae5f1d0058b

Yang, L., Liu, X. Y., & Gong, W. (2020). Secure smart home systems: A blockchain perspective. *IEEE INFOCOM 2020 - IEEE Conference on Computer Communications Workshops, INFOCOM WKSHPS 2020*, 1003–1008. DOI: 10.1109/INFOCOMWKSHPS50562.2020.9162648

Yetis, R., & Sahingoz, O. K. (2019). Blockchain Based Secure Communication for IoT Devices in Smart Cities. *7th International Istanbul Smart Grids and Cities Congress and Fair, ICSG 2019 - Proceedings*, 134–138. DOI: 10.1109/SGCF.2019.8782285

Zhaofeng, M., Jialin, M., Jihui, W., & Zhiguang, S. (2021). Blockchain-Based Decentralized Authentication Modeling Scheme in Edge and IoT Environment. *IEEE Internet of Things Journal*, *8*(4), 2116–2123. DOI: 10.1109/JIOT.2020.3037733

Chapter 2
Decentralization Principles of Blockchain and BC Tokenization (NFTs) in the Era of Smart Cities

Usman Khalil
https://orcid.org/0000-0001-8550-1557
Universiti Brunei Darussalam, Brunei

Owais Ahmed Malilk
https://orcid.org/0000-0002-4888-5448
Universiti Brunei Darussalam, Brunei

ABSTRACT

This chapter delves into the fundamental concepts of distributed and non-distributed systems, laying the groundwork for understanding the intricacies of blockchain technology. A comprehensive overview of public, private, and hybrid blockchain networks is provided, highlighting their unique characteristics and applications. The chapter explores the concept of blockchain tokenization, with a particular focus on non-fungible tokens (NFTs) and their potential to revolutionize security, authentication, and asset digitization. A critical analysis of the challenges and future directions of blockchain technology is presented, followed by an examination of existing NFT-based CPS authentication mechanisms and gaps within the Web2 & Web3 architectures. The chapter concludes with a comparative literature review of NFT-enabled solutions for the cyber-physical environment, highlighting their strengths and weaknesses.

DOI: 10.4018/979-8-3693-8876-1.ch002

INTRODUCTION

This chapter delves into the fundamental concepts of distributed and non-distributed systems, laying the groundwork for understanding the intricacies of blockchain technology. A comprehensive overview of public, private, and hybrid blockchain networks is provided, highlighting their unique characteristics and applications. The chapter explores the concept of blockchain tokenization, with a particular focus on non-fungible tokens (NFTs) and their potential to revolutionize security, authentication, and asset digitization. A critical analysis of the challenges and future directions of blockchain technology is presented, followed by an examination of existing NFT-based CPS authentication mechanisms and gaps within the Web2 & Web3 architectures. The chapter concludes with a comparative literature review of NFT-enabled solutions for the cyber-physical environment, highlighting their strengths and weaknesses.

DISTRIBUTED AND NON-DISTRIBUTED SYSTEMS

The internet inherently poses security risks. Among the myriad services and APIs, certain users are often motivated to breach the layers of established security measures. Jacob Ideskog believes that the "IoT is going to hit us hard if we're not doing anything about it" (Sandoval 2017). Leading this, many mechanisms based on centralized Web2 architectures have been developed and deployed however scope for robust security mechanisms continues. In a non-distributed (or centralized authorization system) the resources are also shared over the interconnected network but the decisions are centrally controlled by a miner machine such as a server in case of client-server computing exhibiting Web2 design. Here any service that needs the authorization to carry out a specific task gets routed to the central server which approves in case all the decision keys meet the criteria or else disapproves in case or vice versa. The concept gained popularity and most of the systems all over the world implemented the centralized/non-distributed system mechanisms as a safety precaution as every request has to be approved every time by the server to stop illegitimate use of the system until Web3 architectures were introduced (Lampson et al. 1991, 1992).

On the other hand, a distributed system (also known as a non-centralized system) consists of hosts that are interconnected by a network. The hosts here refer to the computers in an interconnected computer network. These hosts communicate with each other and other resources in the network such as files and printers with the help of network services provided by servers. These resources are shared over the interconnected network and can be used by distributed authorization systems

(Lampson et al. 1991). The authorization of the services runs for every software that needs it, which means a copy of authorization and authentication results is saved by the resources locally and every request acts as local on the server which in actuality requires no communication on the network layer (Tim Hinrichs 2019). The occasional synchronization with the central service makes it possible to have the updated decision (authorization and authentication decisions) at the edge nodes which authenticates the hosts at the local level contrary to the non-distributed system in which every decision request has to go to a centralized server machine for approval thus making it a centralized system. This attribute of the distributed system poses security problems that are intricate and must be addressed in order to keep the system safe from any sort of attack vector. The decentralization over Web3 architecture however showcases a possible solution for the development of robust protocols as discussed in earlier sections. Several rationales support the adoption of a decentralized system, encompassing attributes like traceability, scalability, security services, platform support, and resource management. These collective aspects contribute to fortifying the overall robustness of the system. Also developing and deploying authentication schemes on different hosts/nodes in smart cities makes the system vulnerable to a variety of adversaries in the form of intruders as well as authentic users of the system. The particular trust assumption necessitates meticulous examination and assessment to ascertain whether the integration of a Web3-based blockchain introduces supplementary value.

BLOCKCHAIN TECHNOLOGY CONCEPTS

The Blockchain concept was realized by a group of researchers in the year 1991 with the intent of timestamping the documents that cannot be changed or tempered. The idea was not used until it was again mentioned in a combination of two words block and chain, originally discussed in the Satoshi Nakamoto original paper (Abideen 2019; Monti and Rasmussen 2017). Since the full BC implementation was observed in the Bitcoin medium the discussion proceeds accordingly. Blockchain technology was the first test run by Bitcoin (a cryptocurrency company) where many investors speculated but received sheer awards as the concept was a huge success (Bitcoin.it 2018). The reason behind Bitcoin's success was blockchain technology which makes a network of blocks connected to other blocks giving it a form of chain hence named "blockchain" (Böhme et al. 2015). People often call it "Blockchain" "Blockchain

Technology" or "Blockchain Concept" but the name blockchain typically refers to Bitcoin blockchain.

Due to the lack of literature initially, and its implementation in the corporate culture, the term Blockchain Technology has often been misinterpreted. People relate it to different terminologies related to it however all the terms and terminologies have a common thread i.e. the distributed ledger technology. In distributed ledger technology the copied transactions are protected on a respective computer (referred to as a verified node) on the network excluding the concept of a central authority being in control (Abideen 2019). In BC when any computer or device connects to the network, it is called a node, which when verified is connected to another verified node. When these verified nodes connect to each other, it is referred to as a "Full node". Bitcoin Core is one of the famous software that implies full nodes in the case of Bitcoin BC. Each full node works independently and stores the validated blocks by that node in the BC. A consensus mechanism triggers when all the full nodes contain the same verified blocks which maintain this consensus with the help of validation rules called "Consensus Rules" (Underwood 2016).

There is a list of records (transactions) that keep growing called blocks and are linked using cryptography. As the records are added and the blocks are linked together, it takes the form of a chain. Each block contains the cryptographic hash of the previous block with the timestamp and the transaction data, generally known as "Merkel Root" (Joost de Kruijff 2017; Monti and Rasmussen 2017).

Figure 1. Bitcoin blockchain blocks structure

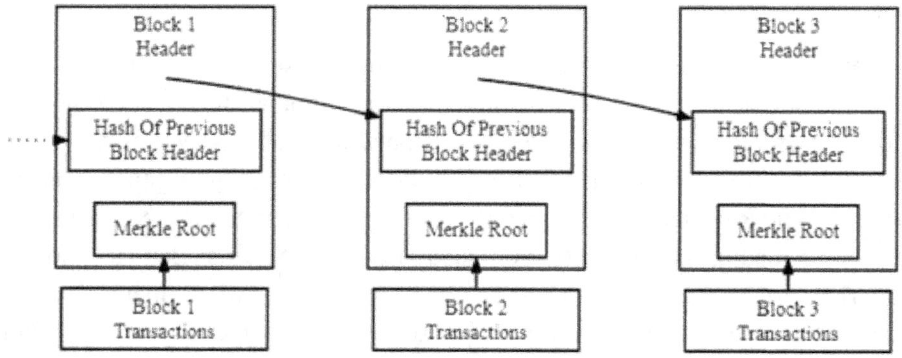

(Joost de Kruijff 2017)

As shown in Figure 1, each block's Merkel Root exists in the header of the respective block. It keeps on updating the hash from the connecting block that has information on transactions from previous blocks. It maintains a chain-like structure that provides robust security by ensuring no modification to the transactions in the linked blocks. This requires no need to download the entire chain for verification of each transaction and results in saving space and processing efficiency (Joost de Kruijff 2017; Monti and Rasmussen 2017).

The blocks contain the transaction information which are also chained to each other and move from transaction to transaction i.e. the input of one transaction is the output of the trailering transaction in respective blocks. Figure 2 shows the concept in which Transaction 0 gets pushed with 100k satoshis (Bitcoin.it 2018) (i.e. Bitcoins are sent as satoshis in Bitcoin Software to and from wallets(Bitcoin.it 2018)) as input 0. Two transactions named TX 1 and TX 2 are further pushed with input 0 of 40k and input 1 of 50k respectively from Transaction 0. These outputs (0,1) from Transaction 0 are chained to TX 1 and TX 2 as input 0 and input 1 respectively. This process clarifies another prospect of the BC transaction; a single input can proceed with multiple outputs to multiple addresses but every transaction (i.e. output) must be used once in the whole process.

Figure 2. Bitcoin triple-entry bookkeeping (TXN to TXN payments) process

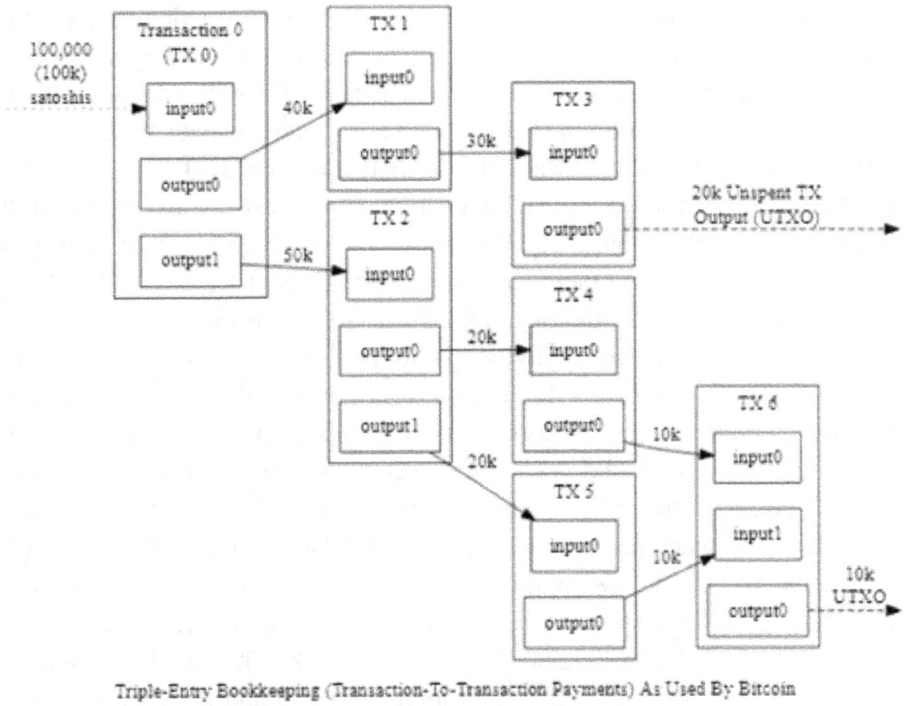

(Joost de Kruijff 2017)

Outputs in the transactions have transaction identifiers i.e. TXID which identifies any validated signed hashes of any transaction. As depicted in Figure 2, there are Unspent Transaction Outputs (UTXOs) referred to as transactions not spent while there are Spent Transactions (STXs) which are the spent transactions. For instance, when Transaction 0 was pushed with 100k satoshis, 10k satoshis were UTXOs while 90k satoshis were STXs in the form of output 0 and output 1. The remaining 10k satoshis are UTXOs for transaction 0 and can further be spent to another address in the BC as desired. Similarly, TX3 & TX6 have 20k and 10k UTXOs receptively. For the transaction to validate, the transactions should be made through UTXOs anyhow if the transaction made is from STXs, it would be rejected. It means the transactions in the ledger system are just not the blocks chained to each other rather all these chained blocks have valuable information which in this case are the Bitcoins. (Bitcoin.it 2018; Dorri et al. 2017; Lewis 2015; Wang et al. 2018).

BC uses SHA-256 hashing and Elliptic Curve Cryptography (ECC) which provides strong encryption for all the transactions being processed. Already discussed aforementioned, there are no centralized bodies like government notary services or Trusted Third Parties (TTP) for the reason that it can be negotiated which weakens the authenticity of the transaction. All of these transactions are verified and validated by the miner nodes by consensus in a shared public ledger. Once the aforementioned process completes, it moves the transactions (block data) into the unerasable, untampered, and intact mode where no more changes to data can be made (Khan and Salah 2018; Lewis 2015; MORRIS and Ford 2019).

Apart from robust encryption, authentication, and access control functionality, the blockchain provides a huge 160-bit address space which has been noticed to be the uppermost limit, any other technology has to offer (Khan and Salah 2018). For instance, the core IP technology since the 1970s i.e. IPv4 is the basis of the current worldwide internet connectivity and offers 32-bit address space. It lasted a couple of decades but ultimately the address space ran out in the year 2010 as there are billions of connected devices as of today whereas each device needs a unique IP address to get identified and to enable packet-switching to transmit and receive the data (Cisco 2020). In order to solve this problem IPv6 was introduced which is 128-bit address space and provides 10,000,000,000,000,000,000,000,000,000 (10^{28}) times as many addresses as IPv4 (Odom 2016). On the contrary, if we look at the sheer sized address space of blockchain, it can generate offline addresses of around 1.46 $*$ 100,000,000,000,000,000,000,000,000,000,000,000,000,000,000,0 00,000 (10^{48}) which means 2^{128} number of unique internet addresses for respective devices (Palattella et al. 2019). Considering this sheer address space, the probability of address duplication is times 10^{48} while it provides 4.3 billion addresses more than IPv6 therefore it is the most suitable choice for industries especially IoT infrastructure as far as future network expansion plans considering smart house, smart office, smart city, smart countries and smart planet is concerned. On top of sheer sized address space, blockchain provides unmatchable security and privacy comparing other technologies (Abideen 2019; Fisher 2007; Khan and Salah 2018; Lewis 2015). Blockchain exists in three forms i.e. Public, Private, and Hybrid blockchain just like its other counterparts in the case of IPv4 and IPv6. Each of these forms shall be discussed one by one in the upcoming sections for clarity.

PUBLIC BLOCKCHAIN

Talking in context to blockchain, we particularly discuss the Bitcoin Blockchain. Public BC is known as an open blockchain form in which the participants can be added by adding the consensus process i.e. Proof of Work (POW) and Proof of Stake (POS) etc. with the help of anonymous node/s. This form eliminates the central authority provisions while everyone in the process does not know the details of the transactions. It means it shall not be a good possibility for businesses like the banking sector to operate without a centralized system where all the transactions are stamped or referred to a central body (i.e. notary or government authority) to avoid any confusion or mishaps. Public blockchain is also referred to as permission-less blockchain (Underwood 2016).

PRIVATE BLOCKCHAIN

A private blockchain is also known as a permissioned blockchain which is or can be restricted to a group of members who are connected through the nodes that are not anonymous means the consensus process i.e. Proof of Work (POW) and Proof of Stake (POS) etc. is performed by the known nodes. This form actually necessitates the central authority provisions while everyone in the process has the right to know the details of the transactions. This blockchain would be more feasible for industries that would not want any anonymous participants while the write permissions are addressed by a centralized body i.e. Government or Notary e.g. the banking sector. This would give industries the power for listing the participants being blacklisted or whitelisted depending on the profile of the user. Comparatively to Public BC, Private BC implies more strict security and privacy rules and that is the reason this BC is the choice of many industries (Deng, Huang, and Wang 2023).

HYBRID BLOCKCHAIN

The Hybrid BC gets its name because of its differentiation of its consensus mechanism which is controlled by a pre-selected group of miners which can be specific software running over servers. The transactions validated by this consensus mechanism do not imply strict security as that of public and private BC mechanisms. Irrespective of the right to read the public, private, or hybrid BC the public members make queries and get cryptographic proof of parts of the blockchain state with the help of Web 3.0 API (Joost de Kruijff 2017; Khan and Salah 2018; Lewis 2015). After the huge success of the technology, the fame made many other cryptocurrency companies and developers come up with alternatives and thus all blockchain alternate solutions are called "Altchain" (Joost de Kruijff 2017). The altchain details and types shall be discussed in the upcoming section. The QoS provided by blockchain has caught the eyes of industries specifically banks to move their business on this technology and get maximum security for their business.

BLOCKCHAIN TOKENIZATION

Based on the literature review, blockchain-based tokenization in the Web3 architecture presents an opportunity for asset identification and authentication schemes in smart city architecture. After a huge appreciation of Token creation in 2018, with over 1,132 Initial Coins Offering/s (ICOs) and Security Token Offering/s (STOs) collected, nearly $20bn (Steve Davis, Daniel Diemers, Henri Arsianian 2019), the concept of tokens has gained wide attention. Tokenization in BC presents the concept of digital representation of an asset on the blockchain or colloquially "programmable asset". There are two models in BC tokenization for transferring values using smart contracts i.e., the UTXO (Unspent Transaction Output)-based model and the Account-based model. Further BC tokenization presents different types of tokens, tangible or intangible, as depicted in Figure 3.

Figure 3. Blockchain tokenization

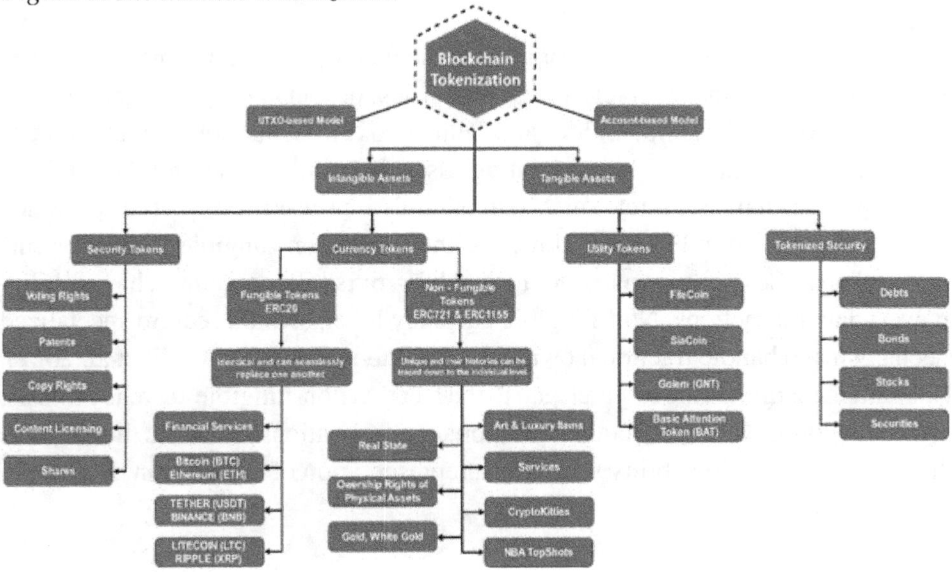

(Khalil et al. 2023)

Among the different types of tokens, Security tokens have been utilized for voting rights, patents, copyrights, etc., and tokenized securities for debts, bonds, stocks, and securities. Utility tokens have been utilized for Filecoin, SiaCoin, Golem network, etc., and Currency tokens have been widely deployed to represent fungible and non-fungible assets (Cryptopedia 2021). The tokens presented by BC tokenization are algorithms implemented as a smart contract on a blockchain. These non-fungible tokens (NFTs) represent the ownership of physical or digital assets, such as physical property, virtual collectibles, or negative value assets. Although the NFTs have been defined under the category of currency tokens (shown in Figure 3), these crypto tokens can be used apart for specified purposes such as Multi Token Standard (ERC-1155) (Eric Binet 2018). This enables the amalgamation of both fungible and non-fungible tokens within a single token, or the utilization of standards that facilitate royalty payments (such as EIP-2981) (Zach Burks, James Morgan, Blaine Malone 2020) and functions related to mortgage/rental (like EIP-2615) (Shiba 2020).

NON-FUNGIBLE TOKENS (NFTS)

Non-fungible tokens, in contrast to fungible tokens, are unique and indivisible. Each token has distinct characteristics, properties, or metadata that differentiate it from other tokens (Sestino, Guido, and Peluso 2022). While non-fungible tokens are typically associated with representing assets like Gold/White gold, digital art, collectibles virtual real estate, etc., they can also be used to represent currency tokens as presented in Figure 3. However, the use of non-fungible tokens for currency tokens is less common due to the need for divisibility and interchangeability in everyday transactions. Non-fungible currency tokens would require specialized mechanisms to handle fractional ownership and divisible units (Khalil et al. 2022). This statement directs the research gap to the fact that non-fungible currency tokens, while less common, would require additional considerations to handle their unique characteristics and divisibility if used as a representation of currency in blockchain tokenization.

NFTS IN SECURITY AND AUTHENTICATION

NFTs can revolutionize security and authentication in the digital world as they offer attributes that are required to attain privacy and robust security such as unique digital identities, immutable recordkeeping, secure access control, enhanced supply chain management, decentralized identity management, etc, while the potential of NFTs for CPS security is undeniable, a gap exists in current research as shown in Table 1. A comprehensive review of the literature reveals a focus on implementing basic functionalities of the ERC721 standard for NFT creation, primarily for asset digitization. Notably, only one study [32] delves into extending the ERC721 functionality for authentication purposes specifically for IoT-enabled smart devices. This highlights a significant research gap in the critical area of leveraging NFTs for robust authentication within CPS environments. The proposed architecture in this work, however, aims to bridge this gap by building upon the foundational security features of NFTs. By extending their capabilities, the aim is to establish a secure and decentralized framework for authentication and access control within CPS.

NFTS FOR ASSETS DIGITIZATION AND REPRESENTATION

Any asset linked to a distinctive cryptographic record refers to an NFT, usually a piece of art and luxury item, services in terms of music, real estate, collectibles, or another presumed valuable object as shown in Figure 3. The asset refers to any physical asset that is a record maintained in the underlying distributed ledger and can be traded through transactions. These records can be bought sold and traded through digital wallets (such as Guarda, MetaMask, Exodus, and Coinbase to name a few (NerdWallet 2023)) in the form of tokens whose ownership can be claimed upon successful purchase by an NFT Creator/seller. Figure 4 depicts the generalized NFT architecture considering the NFT's well-known project of CryptoPunks. The framework encompasses two distinct roles: the NFT owner and the NFT buyer. For the purpose of digitizing an NFT, the owner undertakes an assessment of the file, title, and description for accuracy. If the correct details are found, the raw data is digitized into a proper format through ERC721 standard-defined functions in the smart contract (Kraken 2021). It is important to note here that the ERC721 standard for NFT lacks the ability to support the IoT-enabled smart assets in their current state

The ERC721 standard functions in the NFT smart contract process the creator/owner's request, which stores the raw data in a database external to the BC. However, the owner can also store the raw data in the internal blockchain database, which would be a gas-consuming operation. Once the raw data is stored in the internal blockchain database, the owner signs the transaction, including the NFT data hash. It is then sent to the smart contract, stored in the NFT registry, as depicted in Figure 4. Since NFTs are developed and deployed on BC, their consensus is of much importance in the NFT architecture.

Figure 4. Generalized NFTs architecture

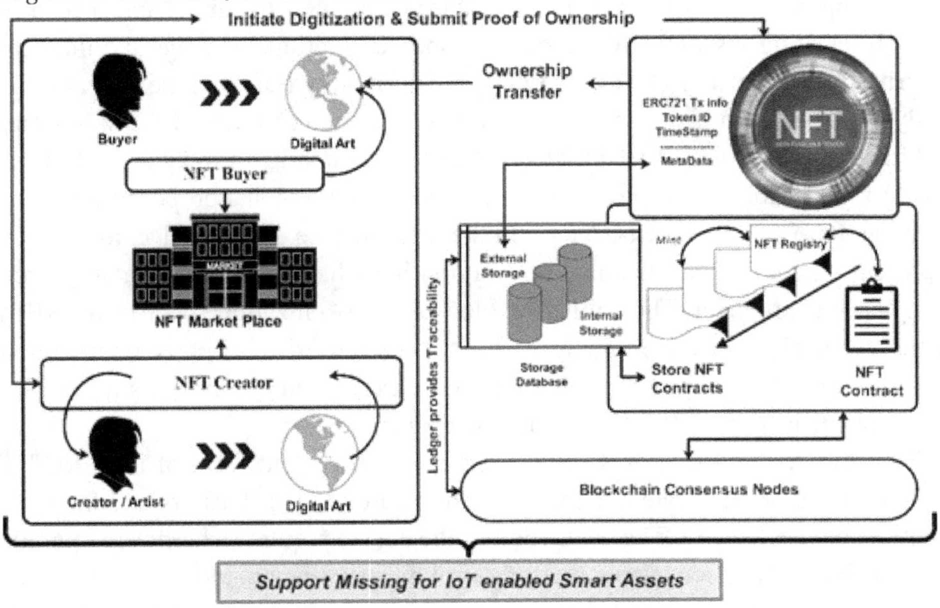

(Khalil et al. 2023)

At this point, the smart contract from the NFT registry receives the NFT data transaction. It is ready for the minting and trading process. Here logic in the form of transactions is processed to the consensus nodes in a P2P network to attain consensus for privacy. Once the logic of the ERC721 Token Standard triggers, the NFT data is minted. The transaction posting confirms the minting process, which can be traced at any time with a unique blockchain address providing traceability of the digital assets on BC. The ledger provides the traceability of NFTs, which provides a physically defined "digital fingerprint" as a unique identifier. The NFT buyers can transfer the proof of ownership after an approved agreement with the NFT Creator.

As depicted in Figure 3 blockchain tokenization has been utilized in many domains whereas the NFT architecture shown in Figure 4 represents the versatile asset tokenization that offers security akin to that of cryptocurrency security, opening up the potential for wide-ranging token applications. Nevertheless, it's important to note that it lacks the possibility of defining attributes for smart city applications considering NFT-based blockchain solutions. Thus, a novel NFT-based blockchain architecture has been proposed through which the smart city applications for underlying cyber-physical systems can be developed and deployed leading to the contributions made in this research.

CHALLENGES AND FUTURE DIRECTIONS

A comprehensive review of the literature (presented in this chapter) reveals a gap in existing research. While many proposed solutions leverage the inherent security mechanisms of Distributed Ledger Technology (DLT), none have specifically explored identification and authentication schemes tailored for smart city architectures. This is further highlighted in the summaries provided in Table 1, (Table 1, and Table 2) Chapter 3. It has also been observed that proposed solutions utilizing non-fungible tokens (NFTs) in the literature are explicitly lacking, which represents crypto tokens as a unique and non-interchangeable unit of data stored on a distributed ledger. Thus, utilizing blockchain tokenization specifically NFTs in the cyber-physical environment without a centralized third-party intervention provides a research gap to digitally define the assets and components to attain a robust identification and authentication mechanism.

The research that proposes the extension in the current form of the ERC721 tokens fails to demonstrate a complete architecture of all IoT assets and their authentication mechanism. The evaluation of the device requires a hardware upgrade for authentication mechanisms that rely on Physical Unclonable Function (PUF) to capture the unique physical characteristics of the devices which leads to computational and time complexity issues. On the contrary, the mechanism proposed in this research focuses on proposing expansion in the NFT standard through ERC721. The expansion enhanced the NFT's capability to establish a decentralized digital identity management system for IoT assets in a cyber-physical system and authenticate unique digital identities, providing stakeholders with control over the data and enhancing security and privacy. By proposing the extension in NFTs, the proposed framework aims to provide users with unique ownership of planning decisions and assets, enhancing transparency and inclusivity in the urban planning domain.

Based on the aforementioned discussion in CHAPTER 1 which presents a detailed overview of issues and their possible elucidation through a novel blockchain-based tokenization approaches for cyber-physical systems in a smart city concept. The proposed mechanisms may be a step towards implementing a blockchain-based tokenization scheme such as non-fungible tokens (NFTs) by proposing an extension in the Ethereum request for comment (ERC-271) standard for token specification (William Entriken, Dieter Shirley, Jacob Evans 2018). NFTs are unique and provably scarce, meaning their histories can be traced down to the individual level which makes this trait feasible for data anonymity in a smart city infrastructure where individual traceability is of immense concern however, some challenges need consideration to develop robust security mechanisms. Scalability is one of the challenges that current blockchain technology can struggle with, potentially impacting transaction processing times and costs for widespread NFT adoption in security and authentication applications. Security Vulnerabilities among other challenges need to be addressed although blockchains are inherently secure, smart contracts used with NFTs can have vulnerabilities. Vigilant development and audits keeping in view the security parameters are crucial to mitigate these risks. Regulation is inevitable as the legal and regulatory landscape surrounding NFTs is still developing. As NFTs become more integrated with security and authentication, clear regulations will be necessary to ensure responsible use and prevent misuse. Conclusively, NFTs provide a powerful set of tools for enhancing security and authentication in various domains. As technology evolves and regulations develop, NFTs can become a keystone of a more secure and transparent digital future.

EXISTING NFT-BASED CPS AUTHENTICATION MECHANISMS

Communication within the Cyber-Physical environment (CPe) relies heavily on secure communication and interaction between physical assets (IoT-enabled smart assets) and the digital world. From smart houses managing actuation to autonomous vehicles navigating streets, robust authentication mechanisms are crucial for ensuring the integrity and trustworthiness of data exchange within Cyber-Physical systems (CPS/s). As discussed earlier in CHAPTER 1, there exists a variety of authentication mechanisms to safeguard data and prevent unauthorized access in traditional Web 2.0 infrastructure for CPS that are beneficial yet pose issues as well. However, Web 3.0 introduces a landscape of unlimited opportunities that will be beneficial in comparison to existing authentication methods used in CPS/s. In this section, established techniques based on emerging solutions utilizing non-fungible tokens for the identification and authentication of IoT-enabled smart assets have been explored. By analyzing the strengths and limitations of these existing mechanisms, the aim is to shed light on the evolving security landscape within CPS/s. Over time, CPS has embraced a diverse array of authentication methods to fortify data security and deter unauthorized access. This introduction aims to delve into the panorama of authentication techniques prevalent in CPS. Through a thorough examination of the merits and limitations associated with these authentication mechanisms, the objective is to shed light on the evolving security landscape within the CPS.

LITERATURE REVIEW COMPARISON ~ NFT-ENABLED SOLUTIONS FOR CYBER-PHYSICAL ENVIRONMENT

By examining the research in the literature, we focus on the goal of gaining insights into the novel and diverse applications of non-fungible token (NFT) enabled solutions in the context of CPSs as shown in Table 1. It will help to identify potential areas of improvement and shed light on the research gap. Nevertheless, among the research examined, we came across one study [32] only that has extended the ERC721 functionality of NFTs for authentication of the IoT-enabled smart devices. The literature (Bellagarda and Abu-Mahfouz 2022; Chiacchio et al. 2022; HASAN et al. 2022; López-Pimentel et al. 2023; Musamih et al. 2022a) primarily focused on implementing the default ERC721 functionality to digitize assets. The review of the literature makes it evident that the digitization of the IoT-enabled smart assets and authentication mechanisms utilizing NFTs is lacking which needs to be explored.

The literature depicts that authors in (Arcenegui et al. 2021) introduced a blockchain tokenization approach for representing unique and indivisible assets, such as IoT-enabled smart devices. This is achieved through non-fungible tokens (NFTs) based on the ERC-721 standard. The integration of physical unclonable functions (PUFs) binds the device's private key and its BCA address to the NFT, ensuring secure authentication and enabling software updates for new owners and users. This linkage is claimed to be unbreakable and traceable throughout the device's lifecycle, assuring the device's trustworthiness from manufacturing to end-use. The NFTs are implemented using Solidity smart contracts, with associated gas consumption provided for comparison. The most resource-intensive function is token creation, as it involves generating comprehensive token information. Conversely, the functions for checking and updating the link with the device are more efficient in terms of gas consumption. However, this mechanism does not comprehensively address all security services (CIA & AAA) and relies on hardware enhancements like Physical Unclonable Functions (PUF). Such upgrades can lead to increased initialization times for IoT-enabled smart assets, causing latency concerns, particularly during Bootloader initialization, stored in the main SoC's internal one-time programmable (OTP) memory. Additionally, on-chip SRAM (SRAM PUF), while unalterable, still presents challenges in terms of time complexity, computational complexity, and latency.

The research in (Bellagarda and Abu-Mahfouz 2022) introduces a framework "*Connect2NFT*" for NFT-based urban planning that emphasizes community engagement and decision-making. The research highlights the potential of NFTs in fostering transparency and inclusivity in urban planning while the framework only utilizes NFT in its current form.

This study (HASAN et al. 2022) investigates the use of NFTs to enhance IoT security in smart cities. The researchers utilize an internally developed blockchain to store reputation values within their system. The research focuses on an identity-based encryption system. The complete implementation details of their system were not disclosed, which leads to ambiguities in system understanding.

The research explores the use and implementation of NFTs for healthcare product management (Musamih et al. 2022b). The authors use the NFT functionality of digital certification to establish and maintain product ownership ensuring ownership integrity, seamless trading, and traceability. However, fails to demonstrate a complete architecture of IoT assets and their authentication mechanism-related expansion in NFTs.

NFT-Vehicle presented in this study (López-Pimentel et al. 2023) are merely an effort to implement and demonstrate the applications and potentials of NFTs in one of the domains of smart city architecture. The author discusses the association of stakeholders such as the manufacturer, owner, government, etc. to its vehicle to enhance security in terms of ownership. However, no mechanism for security services such as Confidentiality, Integrity, and Availability (CIA) has been devised.

The authors in (Chiacchio et al. 2022) merely present the association of pharmaceutical supply chains to attain ownership security and data integrity by minting NFTs on the blockchain's default security mechanism. It's general NFT implementation that fails to demonstrate a complete architecture of IoT assets and their authentication mechanism-related expansion in NFTs. Apart from deployment, the mechanism for security services such as Confidentiality, Integrity, and Availability (CIA) has not been devised which raises security concerns.

The comparison in Table 1 among the NFT-enabled solutions makes it clear that the solutions have implemented the non-fungible tokens in their default form to attain digital identity while the security and privacy of these solutions purely depend on the NFT default mechanism. This can lead to security issues related to unauthorized access, data breaches, and compromised integrity of IoT-enabled smart assets and their digital representations. Secondly, none of the solutions propose components to define the IoT assets and authentication mechanism for enhanced security apart from the research in (Arcenegui et al. 2021) which focuses on device authentication mechanisms and does not offer a complete architecture.

Table 1. Comparison of NFT-enabled solutions with the proposed NFT-expansion

RP	Solution Description	Advantage	Drawbacks
(Arcenegui et al. 2021)	NFT-based Asset Management mechanism utilizing PUF – 2021	Utilizes NFTs for tracking and managing assets in smart cities, providing unique ownership and provenance information. Propose components to extend the NFT to formulate its scope. Proposal of Non-Fungible Tokens (NFTs) has been utilized to bind the IoT assets physically employing PUFs. NFTs were bound to the IoT asset's physical properties utilizing added PUF hardware.	– The proposal is hardware-dependent, requiring a hardware upgrade from the manufacturer, which may incur manufacturing costs. – Authentication mechanisms rely on hardware upgrades. – With hardware upgrades, the IoT assets have been noticed to have increased initialization time, which incurs latency issues such as initializing the Bootloader, located in the main SoC's internal OTP memory. – The coding of the Bootloader cannot be modified since it is the device's Root of Trust (RoT). – Hardware performance issues with startup time, resulting in latency issues. – No support for security Services such as Confidentiality, Integrity, and Availability (CIA) has been provided.
(Bellagarda and Abu-Mahfouz 2022)	Connect2NFT: NFT-driven Urban Planning – 2022	Integrates NFTs to facilitate community participation and decision-making in urban planning and development projects to secure user authentication.	– Framework utilizes NFT in its general form for users to associate social media accounts to authenticate owners. – The framework is dependent on the default NFT standard while security Services such as the CIA have not been taken care of.
(HASAN et al. 2022)	NFT-enabled IoT Security – 2022	Utilizes NFTs to secure Internet of Things (IoT) devices and networks, preventing unauthorized access and ensuring data integrity.	– Complete details of the system are missing. – The framework is dependent on default NFT components which leads to general implementation. – The framework is dependent on the default NFT standard for data integrity while security Services such as the CIA have not been taken care of.

continued on following page

Table 1. Continued

RP	Solution Description	Advantage	Drawbacks
(Musamih et al. 2022b)	NFT-backed Tokenized Services – 2022	Implements NFTs to tokenize and trade healthcare services in smart cities, enabling efficient and transparent service exchange.	– A general association of healthcare assets (i.e., patient's details, medicines, etc.) to the default NFT standard. – No divisibility of components to define IoT assets in a smart city context. – Framework security is dependent on the default NFT security mechanism while security services such as CIA have not been taken care of.
(López-Pimentel et al. 2023)	NFT-Vehicle: NFT-based Digital Representation of vehicle as a smart city asset – 2023	Implements NFTs to create a digital representation of vehicles as smart city assets, enabling real-time monitoring and analysis, and security in the form of associating ownership to the asset.	– NFT-Vehicle involves the general implementation of NFT for the associating stakeholders such as the manufacturer, owner, government, etc. – No architecture is defined for IoT assets in a smart city. – Implementation security is dependent on the default NFT security mechanism through its default ownership mechanism while security services such as the CIA have not been taken care of.
(Chiacchio et al. 2022)	NFT-driven Urban Governance -2022	Integrates NFTs to facilitate transparent and accountable governance processes through the tracking and tracing of the Pharmaceutical Supply Chain for healthcare in smart cities.	– NFT deployment to associate pharmaceutical assets (medicine details) to the default NFT standard. – No divisibility of components to define IoT assets in a smart city context. – Implementation is dependent on the default NFT security mechanism while security services such as the CIA have not been taken care of.

CONCLUSION

The integration of blockchain technology, particularly through NFT-based solutions, offers a promising avenue for enhancing security, authentication, and asset management in cyber-physical systems. By leveraging the decentralized nature, transparency, and immutability of blockchain, it is possible to address the limitations of traditional centralized systems and establish a more secure and efficient digital ecosystem. However, the adoption of blockchain technology also presents challenges, including scalability, interoperability, and energy consumption. Continued research and development are necessary to overcome these obstacles and fully realize the potential of blockchain-based solutions. By addressing these challenges and fostering collaboration between academia, industry, and policymakers, we can pave the way for a future where blockchain-powered cyber-physical systems drive innovation and improve the quality of life.

REFERENCES

Abideen, S. (2019). *Blockchain expert* (Abideen, S., Ed.). CYBROSYS Technologies.

Arcenegui, J., Arjona, R., Román, R., & Baturone, I. (2021). Secure combination of IoT and blockchain by physically binding IoT devices to smart non-fungible tokens using PUFs. *Sensors (Basel)*, *21*(9), 3119. DOI: 10.3390/s21093119 PMID: 33946227

Bellagarda, J., & Abu-Mahfouz, A. M. (2022). Connect2NFT: A web-based, blockchain-enabled NFT application with the aim of reducing fraud and ensuring authenticated social, non-human verified digital identity. *Mathematics*, *10*(21), 3934. DOI: 10.3390/math10213934

Binet, E., Sandford, R., Radomski, W., Cooke, A., Castonguay, P., & Therien, J. (2018). *EIP-1155: Multi-token standard.* Ethereum Improvement Proposals. https://eips.ethereum.org/EIPS/eip-1155

Bitcoin.it. (2018). Weaknesses - Bitcoin Wiki. *Bitcoin.it.* https://en.bitcoin.it/wiki/Weaknesses

Böhme, R., Christin, N., Edelman, B., & Moore, T. (2015). Bitcoin: Economics, technology, and governance. *The Journal of Economic Perspectives*, *29*(2), 213–238. DOI: 10.1257/jep.29.2.213

Burks, Z., Morgan, J., Malone, B., & Seibel, J. (2020). *EIP-2981: NFT royalty standard.* Ethereum. https://eips.ethereum.org/EIPS/eip-2981

Chiacchio, F., D'urso, D., Oliveri, L. M., Spitaleri, A., Spampinato, C., & Giordano, D. (2022). A non-fungible token solution for the track and trace of pharmaceutical supply chain. *Applied Sciences (Basel, Switzerland)*, *12*(8), 4019. DOI: 10.3390/app12084019

Cisco. (2020). *Cisco: 2020 CISO benchmark report* (Vol. 2020). DOI: 10.1016/S1361-3723(20)30026-9

Cryptopedia. (2021). What is tokenization? Blockchain token types. *Gemini.* https://www.gemini.com/cryptopedia/what-is-tokenization-definition-crypto-token

Davis, S., Diemers, D., Arsianian, H., & Dobrauz, G. (2019). *4th ICO/STO report: A strategic perspective.*

de Kruijff, J., & Weigand, H. (2017). Understanding the blockchain using enterprise ontology. In *Proceedings of the International Conference on Advanced Information Systems Engineering* (pp. 29–43). Springer. DOI: 10.1007/978-3-319-59536-8_3

Deng, W., Huang, T., & Wang, H. (2023). A review of the key technology in a blockchain building decentralized trust platform. *Mathematics, 11*(1), 101. DOI: 10.3390/math11010101

Dorri, A., Kanhere, S. S., Jurdak, R., & Gauravaram, P. (2017). Blockchain for IoT security and privacy: The case study of a smart home. In *2017 IEEE International Conference on Pervasive Computing and Communications Workshops (PerCom Workshops)* (pp. 618–623). IEEE. DOI: 10.1109/PERCOMW.2017.7917634

Entriken, W., Shirley, D., Evans, J., & Sachs, N. (2018). *EIP-721: Non-fungible token standard.* Ethereum Improvement Proposals. https://eips.ethereum.org/EIPS/eip-721

Fisher, K. (2007). *Jonah liberated by technology.* Uttarakhand Open University.

Hasan, H. R., Salah, K., Battah, A., Madine, M., Yaqoob, I., Jayaraman, R., & Omar, M. (2022). Incorporating registration, reputation, and incentivization into the NFT ecosystem. *IEEE Access : Practical Innovations, Open Solutions, 10,* 76416–76433. DOI: 10.1109/ACCESS.2022.3192388

Hinrichs, T. (2019). Centralized vs. distributed authorization: The CAP theorem. *Styra Blog.* https://blog.styra.com/blog/centralized-vs.-distributed-authorization-the-cap-theorem

Khalil, U., Malik, O. A., Hong, O. W., & Uddin, M. (2023). Leveraging a novel NFT-enabled blockchain architecture for the authentication of IoT assets in smart cities. *Scientific Reports, 13*(1), 1–26. DOI: 10.1038/s41598-023-45212-1 PMID: 37957161

Khalil, U., Uddin, M., Malik, O. A., & Hussain, S. (2022). A blockchain footprint for authentication of IoT-enabled smart devices in smart cities: State-of-the-art advancements, challenges and future research directions. *IEEE Access : Practical Innovations, Open Solutions, 10,* 76805–76823. DOI: 10.1109/ACCESS.2022.3189998

Khan, M. A., & Salah, K. (2018). IoT security: Review, blockchain solutions, and open challenges. *Future Generation Computer Systems, 82,* 395–411. DOI: 10.1016/j.future.2017.11.022

Kraken. (2021). *Kraken report: Non-fungible tokens (NFTs): Redefining digital scarcity.*

Lampson, B., Abadi, M., Burrows, M., & Wobber, E. (1991). Authentication in distributed systems: Theory and practice. In *Proceedings of the 13th ACM Symposium on Operating Systems Principles* (pp. 165–182). DOI: 10.1145/121132.121160

Lampson, B., Abadi, M., Burrows, M., & Wobber, E. (1992). Authentication in distributed systems. *ACM Transactions on Computer Systems*, *10*(4), 265–310. DOI: 10.1145/138873.138874

Lewis, A. (2015). *Blockchain technology explained.*

López-Pimentel, J. C., Morales-Rosales, L. A., Algredo-Badillo, I., & Del-Valle-Soto, C. (2023). NFT-Vehicle: A blockchain-based tokenization architecture to register transactions over a vehicle's life cycle. *Mathematics*, *11*(13), 2801. DOI: 10.3390/math11132801

Monti, M., & Rasmussen, S. (2017). RAIN: A bio-inspired communication and data storage infrastructure. *Artificial Life*, *23*(4), 552–557. DOI: 10.1162/ARTL_a_00247 PMID: 28985116

Morris, A., & Ford, B. (2019). *Blockchain for beginners* (Vol. 107).

Musamih, A., Yaqoob, I., Salah, K., Jayaraman, R., Omar, M., & Ellahham, S. (2022a). NFTs in healthcare: Vision, opportunities, and challenges. *IEEE Consumer Electronics Magazine*, •••, 21–32. https://ieeexplore.ieee.org/document/9850370

Musamih, A., Yaqoob, I., Salah, K., Jayaraman, R., Omar, M., & Ellahham, S. (2022b). Using NFTs for product management, digital certification, trading, and delivery in the healthcare supply chain. *IEEE Transactions on Engineering Management*, •••, 1–22. DOI: 10.1109/TEM.2022.3215793

NerdWallet. (2023). 11 best crypto wallets of January 2023. *NerdWallet.* https://www.nerdwallet.com/article/investing/best-bitcoin-cryptocurrency-wallet

Odom, W. (2016). *Cisco cert guide* (B. Bartow, S. Schroeder, C. Cleveland, T. Simpson, K. Cline, C. Hutchinson, & A. Adams, Eds.). Cisco Press.

Palattella, M. R., Ladid, L., Ziegler, S., Kastner, W., Jung, M., Kofler, M., Drajic, D. D., Krco, S., Nam, G., & Marin Perez, R. (2019). *IoT-IPv6 integration for SMEs.* IoT6 European Project (STREP) of the 7th Framework Program.

Sandoval, K. (2017). OAuth 2.0 – Why it's vital to IoT security. *Nordic APIs.* https://nordicapis.com/why-oauth-2-0-is-vital-to-iot-security/

Sestino, A., Guido, G., & Peluso, A. M. (2022). *Non-fungible tokens (NFTs).* Springer International Publishing., DOI: 10.1007/978-3-031-07203-1

Shiba, K. (2020). *EIP-2615: Non-fungible token with mortgage and rental functions.* Ethereum Improvement Proposals. https://eips.ethereum.org/EIPS/eip-2615

Underwood, S. (2016). Blockchain beyond Bitcoin. *Communications of the ACM*, *59*(11), 15–17. DOI: 10.1145/2994581

Wang, Z., Dong, X., Li, Y., Fang, L., & Chen, P. (2018). IoT security model and performance evaluation: A blockchain approach. In *2018 6th IEEE International Conference on Network Infrastructure and Digital Content (IC-NIDC)* (pp. 260–264). IEEE. DOI: 10.1109/ICNIDC.2018.8525716

Chapter 3
Cyber-Physical Systems and Security in Smart Cities

Usman Khalil
https://orcid.org/0000-0001-8550-1557
Universiti Brunei Darussalam, Brunei

Adbdulhalim Dandoush
University of Doha for Science and Technology, Qatar

ABSTRACT

This chapter explores the integration of blockchain technology within cyber-physical systems (CPS), focusing on its application in smart houses, smart districts, and federated mechanisms. The chapter delves into the potential of blockchain to enhance security and privacy in IoT-enabled environments, particularly through blockchain-enabled IoT-embedded assets. A thorough examination of the challenges associated with current blockchain-based authentication systems is presented, highlighting issues such as security concerns, communication vulnerabilities, and inadequate authentication mechanisms. To address these limitations, the chapter proposes NFT-enabled solutions for the cyber-physical environment, leveraging permissioned networks and IBFT 2.0 consensus mechanisms to prioritize security services.

DOI: 10.4018/979-8-3693-8876-1.ch003

INTRODUCTION TO BLOCKCHAIN IN CYBER-PHYSICAL SYSTEMS (CPS)

Apart from sensing, actuation, data processing, etc., smart devices have given rise to a network of smart interconnected devices that provide services from self-regulating smart grids to automated factories in automation, monitoring, and intelligent control. However, this complex dance between physical processes and digital data introduces vulnerabilities. Ensuring secure and reliable data exchange within CPS remains a paramount challenge. Here's where blockchain technology steps in, offering a potential revolution for CPS security. Blockchain, renowned for its secure and tamper-proof nature in financial transactions, holds immense promise for securing data and automating processes within these intricate systems. Its fundamental principles of distributed ledger technology and cryptographic security can create a vigorous and transparent infrastructure for CPS. This introduction explores the potential of blockchain to address security vulnerabilities and unlock the full potential of CPS, paving the way for a more secure and efficient future.

Blockchain technology has emerged as a pivotal innovation within the realm of Cyber-Physical Systems (CPS), characterized by its ability to securely integrate computing, communication, and control technologies in environments that interact with the physical world. CPS applications span a variety of sectors, including smart grids, healthcare, and autonomous vehicles, underscoring the importance of ensuring security and reliability in these interconnected systems. The unique properties of blockchain—such as decentralization, consensus mechanisms, and cryptographic security—offer significant advantages in addressing the inherent vulnerabilities of CPS, particularly regarding data integrity and resistance to unauthorized alterations (Keshk et al. 2020; Khalil et al. 2022; Letichevsky et al. 2017).

The integration of blockchain within CPS is notable for its potential to enhance data security, transparency, and operational efficiency. By creating immutable ledgers that securely log transactions across distributed networks, blockchain can safeguard critical data and foster trust among stakeholders, such as consumers, service providers, and regulatory bodies.

Noteworthy applications include peer-to-peer energy trading in smart grids and automated contract execution through smart contracts, both of which demonstrate how blockchain can transform traditional operational paradigms into more resilient and efficient systems (Shi 2011; Syahla and Ogi 2021). However, the implementation of blockchain in CPS is not without challenges. Concerns regarding scalability, interoperability, and security vulnerabilities related to blockchain technologies continue to pose significant hurdles to widespread adoption. Researchers are actively exploring solutions, such as enhanced consensus algorithms and privacy-preserving protocols, to mitigate these issues and ensure that blockchain can meet the rigorous demands of CPS environments. Furthermore, regulatory compliance and ethical considerations regarding data privacy add complexity to the integration of blockchain in these critical systems.

Overall, the intersection of blockchain technology and cyber-physical systems represents a rapidly evolving field that holds promise for addressing critical security challenges while enabling innovative applications. Ongoing research efforts aim to refine these technologies, identify practical use cases, and develop frameworks that support secure and efficient interactions within increasingly interconnected environments.

BLOCKCHAIN-ENABLED SMART HOUSES

A case study for a blockchain-based smart home framework that deploys the IoT security model compared to a cloud-based smart home has been proposed (Dorri et al. 2017). The performance evaluation in terms of fundamental security traits such as confidentiality, integrity, and availability has been performed. The authors define the IoT infrastructure with various components for a smart home using the lightweight blockchain concept for security and privacy issues and discuss the implementation of various transactions and associated procedures. In a smart home, all IoT devices are connected to a miner connected to Blockchain and a local storage device for storing the data from IoT devices has been introduced. The concept discusses how the Blockchain public key authenticates the network traffic and provides security against DDoS and Link Attacks. The experiment showed that Blockchain is a comparatively more reliable solution for a smart home-based IoT infrastructure regarding security and privacy. At the same time, it proved to be quite manageable for low-energy devices.

The authors analyze the limitations of existing centralized approaches in (Yang, Liu, and Gong 2020) and propose a blockchain-enabled solution. The proposed solution can trace every operation on the chain, easily verify device and user identity, and set up multiple-level access control to help build a secure smart home system. The authors demonstrate the design architecture and implementation methods as proof of concept.

A blockchain-based smart home framework that deploys IoT-enabled smart device security has been proposed (Ammi, Alarabi, and Benkhelifa 2021). The performance has been evaluated in terms of fundamental security traits such as confidentiality, integrity, and availability. The solution has been designed to overcome reported security limitations in commonly used permissioned Blockchain approaches. The authors proposed an architecture containing four layers: Cloud storage, Hyperledger Fabric, Hyperledger composer, and a smart home layer. Mapping the attributes of smart home devices to those from the Hyperledger composer has been adopted. It allows for a customized, designed-for-purpose solution that meets IoT-based smart homes' security requirements. The proposed architecture was implemented and tested to improve the authorization and privacy of smart homes and some inherited features, including transparency and interoperability.

The authors discusses the problem of Security Vulnerabilities in Centralized Smart Homes in (Sharma et al. 2024) since the centralized smart home architectures are vulnerable to unauthorized access, data tampering, and single points of failure due to IoT growth. The authors proposes a decentralized blockchain-based system utilizing Ethereum smart contracts and SHA-256 hashing for secure device interactions and tamper-proof data. Real-time data validation over distributed ledgers significantly reduces cyber-attack risks, offering a scalable and safe management strategy for smart homes.

A research problem on conventional transactive energy management (TEM) methods in IoT-aided smart homes shows that it suffers from low efficiency, privacy leakage, and single-point failure (Yang and Wang 2021). The authors develops a novel blockchain-based TEM system for smart homes, enabling vertical (grid interaction) and horizontal (peer-to-peer trading) energy transactions via smart contracts. The testing implements a privacy preserving distributed algorithm for optimal energy usage and demonstrates 25% overall cost reduction through extensive simulations.

The increasing popularity of smart home applications demands improved IT infrastructure for transparency, security, and privacy of user data. The authors in (Moniruzzaman et al. 2020) provides a comprehensive review of blockchain advancements in smart home systems, discussing techniques, prerequisites, applications, and commonly used methods. They identify major challenges such as interoperability protocols, security, privacy, data collection/sharing, data analytics, and latency. Challenges and suggests that the Blockchain-based systems aim to tackle issues such as ensuring data integrity, robust authentication between devices, and data availability in smart homes.

A study (Lakhan et al. 2024) explores security which is a crucial challenge in processing accurate Internet of Energy (IoE) sensor data for energy generation and consumption in smart cities. The authors propose a blockchain-enabled, energy-efficient IoE smart grid architecture with a data scheduling (BEDS) algorithm scheme for smart homes and electric vehicle applications. The simulation results show BEDS achieves 29% less processing time and 41% less power consumption compared to existing blockchain methods in smart grid networks.

A research in inter-connectivity and complexity of smart home systems lead to higher vulnerability to cyberattacks, network congestion, and information leaks. The authors in (Yang et al. 2020) proposes a blockchain-enabled solution to build a secure smart home system, demonstrating its design architecture and implementation methods as a proof of concept. The research aims to improve security and offer intelligent control for smart home systems.

The authors in (Saxena, Sodhi, and Tanwar 2020) discusses a problem of existing smart home security that suffers from privacy and security vulnerabilities, with conventional approaches failing due to IoT's decentralized topology and resource constraints. The authors proposes a novel, decentralized approach using blockchain to enhance the security architecture of smart home networks. The proposed scheme ensures both trustworthiness and user privacy preservation.

Numerous security concerns arise from the exponential increase of smart home IoT devices due to their limited storage and processing power, making them vulnerable to attacks. A study (Arif et al. 2020) examines smart home security through blockchain adoption, exploring proposed architectures, and describing a simple secure smart home framework based on a Consortium blockchain. They highlight both limitations and opportunities of adopting such an architecture, with experimental testbed evaluation.

Research in (Khan et al. 2021) explore achieving secure and private IoT communication which is challenging at scale, and existing blockchain solutions are often computationally demanding for typical IoT applications. The authors propose a resource-efficient, blockchain-based solution for secure and private IoT in smart homes, leveraging computational resources and Deep Extreme Learning Machine (DELM). The simulation results indicate marginal overheads in terms of distribution, processing time, and energy consumption, relative to the significant security and privacy benefits.

A problem of smart home technology often leads to security issues due to vulnerable open internet connections, exposing users to threats, hackers, and confidential information theft. A research in (Nada Ratkovic 2022) presents how blockchain can be effectively used to enhance overall home security. The authors address common smart home vulnerabilities like unauthorized access to door locking passwords by cybercriminals.

BLOCKCHAIN-ENABLED SMART DISTRICT

The authors designed a smart district model in [86], which is the step necessary to build a smart city with the help of IoT smart assets using new technologies, e.g., Block chain (BC). The authors suggest that the role of IoT devices and the BC-based approach would provide an efficient energy management system integrated into a platform. The authors present an architecture for automation, demonstrate how a smart district can be realized, and propose implementing the model to achieve an efficient energy management system, including energy, security, safety, environmental management, communication, information, etc.

Due to the increasing demand for home automation, smart users and houses would add to the concept of a smart city by integrating the smart grid, services, buildings, houses, and appliances that would interact and be connected for better Quality of Living (QoL). The smart district case study was carried out in Bergamo, Italy. The district was designed to be automatically managed by both the inhabitants and the remote users through a control center located on-site for access control to be implemented for authorized uses. The paper conceptualizes how the management system would integrate the subsystem in a smart district. The use of blockchain technology will store, send, and receive information through transactions in a peer-to-peer environment. The authors suggest that blockchain integration would enable application automation, and this technology would be a key element for increased cost competitiveness, leading to smart city deployment.

BLOCKCHAIN-ENABLED FEDERATED MECHANISMS (BEFM)

Blockchain technology and federated learning have emerged as transformative paradigms in the fields of data science and distributed computing. Blockchain is a decentralized, immutable ledger that records transactions in a transparent and tamper-resistant manner, ensuring data integrity and security across multiple participants in a network (Orabi, Emam, and Fahmy 2025; Peng et al. 2024). Each transaction is grouped into blocks that are linked together, creating a secure chain that can only be appended to through consensus mechanisms among network nodes. This structure inherently protects against unauthorized alterations, thereby maintaining the authenticity of the data stored (Boitier et al. 2024; Rapal 2024). On the other hand, federated learning is a machine learning approach that allows multiple entities to collaboratively train a shared model without sharing their raw data. Initially proposed by Google in 2017, federated learning processes data locally on individual devices, which significantly reduces server resource usage and enhances data privacy (Orabi et al. 2025; Ren, Kim, and Lee 2024). By leveraging the computational power of distributed devices, federated learning enables the development of models that cater to the unique needs of each participant while preserving data confidentiality (Hai et al. 2022; Rapal 2024). The intersection of blockchain and federated learning—termed Blockchain-Enabled Federated Learning (BCFL)—holds substantial potential for addressing the challenges associated with traditional centralized systems. The integration of blockchain into federated learning enhances security, ensures fairness, and improves scalability (Hard et al. 2018; Ren et al. 2024). By employing decentralized identity verification and tamper-proof storage for model parameters, BCFL fosters a collaborative environment where participants can contribute to the training process with reduced risks of data breaches and manipulation (Hard et al. 2018; Ren et al. 2024). Moreover, the use of smart contracts in blockchain can automate processes such as registration and model aggregation, streamlining operations within the federated learning ecosystem (Gowda 2025; Ning et al. 2024).

BEFM USE CASES

Blockchain-Enabled Federated Mechanisms (BEFM) has been used in quite a number of cyber-physical system such as healthcare, financial services, IoT, governance compliance etc. The authors in (Esposito, Ficco, and Gupta 2021) shed light on the decentralized management of the security-related information in the smart city ecosystem. They propose a novel solution for distributed management of identity and authorization policies by leveraging blockchain technology to hold a global view of the security policies within the system and integrate it into the FIWARE platform. When such centralized management of policies is unsuitable due to the federated deployment applied to the system of interest or the multi-tenant model, more advanced solutions, such as a federation of databases, are needed. The results showed blockchain as a more beneficial technology when queried rather than implied for data management. The federated database system is faster as the distributed consensus is not needed. Some of them are discussed to provide clarity on federated mechanism that use Blockchain as a framework.

Use Cases in Healthcare

One of the most promising applications of blockchain-enabled federated learning (FL) mechanisms is in the healthcare sector. With the increasing generation of healthcare data across various institutions, federated learning provides a method to analyze this data while maintaining privacy and security. Specifically, federated learning can be applied to electronic health records (EHRs) stored on different blockchain systems, enabling the development of personalized treatment plans based on comprehensive patient data without the need to centralize sensitive information (Boitier et al. 2024) . Research indicates that integrating blockchain with federated learning can enhance data sharing and improve diagnostic accuracy while addressing privacy concerns inherent in healthcare data (Boitier et al. 2024; Ladd 2024).

Financial Services

In the financial domain, blockchain-enabled FL has the potential to revolutionize practices such as credit scoring and fraud detection. By utilizing decentralized models, financial institutions can collaboratively train machine learning models on consumer data while ensuring data privacy and ownership. This approach allows for more accurate and equitable credit assessments that are less prone to bias (Orabi et al. 2025). Moreover, the integration of smart contracts can automate and streamline processes such as loan approvals and compliance checks, thereby enhancing efficiency and reducing operational costs in decentralized finance (DeFi) applications (Ladd 2024).

Internet of Things (IoT)

The IoT landscape is another significant area where blockchain-enabled federated learning can be applied. Smart devices collect vast amounts of data, which can be utilized for various applications, from energy management in smart homes to predictive maintenance in industrial settings. Federated learning allows these devices to collaboratively learn from data patterns while preserving privacy, thereby reducing the need for transferring large datasets to centralized servers (Gowda 2025). For instance, in smart home energy management, federated learning can optimize energy consumption by analyzing data from multiple devices without compromising individual user privacy (Gowda 2025).

Governance and Compliance

Decentralized federated learning networks also present governance and jurisdictional challenges that can be addressed through blockchain technology. By leveraging blockchain's inherent transparency and traceability, organizations can establish robust frameworks for dispute resolution, contract enforcement, and liability management within federated learning ecosystems. Additionally, these frameworks can enhance algorithmic fairness and accountability, ensuring equitable participation and compliance with regulatory standards in decentralized environments (Ladd 2024; Orabi et al. 2025).

BLOCKCHAIN AND ITS APPLICATION IN IOT

The smart city security dimension ranges from data aggregation to confidentiality, integration, availability, and non-repudiation. With the advancement in the computing technologies such as Web3 architectures e.g., distributed ledger technologies, fog computing, and Web2 protocols like IPv6, the authentication mechanisms have evolved but still, it needs a robust security mechanism. Based on the implementation in (Mateen and Hong 2018), a distributed system needs to be developed whose implementation would be more feasible to provide security schemes. These security schemes have already been tested and are in use for a conventional Web2-based system for tasks such as file sharing among computers, printing commands, accessing IP cameras, etc. (Thomas Y.C, Woo 2014). Web3-based blockchain architecture is the underlying technology of Bitcoin for transferring funds from one node to another in a secure and untampered manner. The network of nodes over the blockchain can also be used to transfer information packets securely in the same way. It has ample space with 164 bits to accommodate billions of IoT-enabled smart devices with untampered security. Blockchain is a concept realized by the distributed ledger technology in which the copied transactions are protected on a respective computer (referred to as a verified node) on the network excluding the concept of a central authority being in control. It has three different forms: Public Blockchain, Private Blockchain, and Hybrid Blockchain. Different security mechanisms based on blockchain technology and its robust working mechanism have been proposed recently to attain robustness over Web3 architecture and are discussed in upcoming sections.

BLOCKCHAIN FOR SECURE AUTHENTICATION

The authors in (Khalid et al. 2020), introduced a novel authentication and access control mechanism designed for lightweight IoT devices within a distributed architecture. They assert that this mechanism can be adapted to various scenarios. The approach capitalizes on the advantages of fog computing and public blockchain technologies, which inherently offer a no n-centralized framework due to the decentralized nature of public blockchains. This mechanism comprises an initialization phase for enrolling new IoT systems and a subsequent device authentication phase for registering smart devices via blockchain fog nodes. Additionally, the proposed mechanism includes a phase facilitating direct device-to-device (D2D) communication within the system and access control measures for IoT devices. The utilization of the Elliptic Curve Digital Signature Algorithm (ECDSA) is a pivotal element of this mechanism, responsible for generating public and private keys for both devices and fog nodes. The security attributes, including Confidentiality, Integrity, Identification, Non-Repudiation, Authentication, and Mutual Authentication, were rigorously evaluated using this mechanism. Performance evaluation encompassed assessing the execution time required by IoT nodes for registration requests (ranging from 1.06 ms to 1.25 ms) and the time needed by nodes to transmit data messages (ranging from 0.03 ms to 0.08 ms). Furthermore, the study investigated computational power consumption, measuring the energy consumed by nodes during registration requests (ranging from 7.24 mW to 10.32 mW) and the power utilized by nodes when sending data messages (ranging from 2.91 mW to 4.12 mW). A comprehensive evaluation, comprising 100 experiments, showcased the promising comparative performance of the proposed mechanism.

In (Gong, Alghazzawi, and Cheng 2021), a novel framework named BCoT Sentry (Blockchain of Things Sentry) is introduced, seamlessly integrating blockchain technology into an IoT network. This framework focuses on enhancing network security by analyzing device network traffic patterns derived from blockchain-stored data. A noteworthy aspect of this proposal is its intent to maintain the lightweight nature of IoT devices, which often struggle to meet the computational demands of conventional blockchain-based security models. The core of the BCoT framework involves blockchain nodes referred to as "Gateways." These Gateways host an IoT device security module through a smart contract, effectively enabling the recording of authentication transactions within a blockchain network. Consequently, this mechanism securely stores device identity information within a distributed ledger. A novel approach to feature selection, akin to machine learning's feature selection method utilizing the maximum information coefficient (MIC), is presented. This approach captures IoT device traffic from the network layer and forwards traffic flow features to the Smart Contract through blockchain transactions. The Smart Contract defines the device's identity information and related operations, triggered upon blockchain transactions. The contract also enforces access permission policies, ensuring authorized access to modify or retrieve device identity information via a defined contract in the web3.py interface. Performance evaluation revolves around device identification accuracy and time complexity. The framework demonstrates impressive device identity fraud detection accuracy, surpassing 80%, with 21 instances exceeding 90%. In terms of time complexity, an evaluation was conducted by making 1000 calls to the *Register()* and *Detective()* functions on each BCoT Gateway, yielding an average response time. For the proposed IoT authentication model, identity authentication involves the Register and Fraud Detection functions, with a time complexity denoted as O (m x n) and O (m), considering 'n' as the type of IoT device and 'm' as the number of IoT devices, respectively.

In (Zhaofeng et al. 2021), a blockchain-based distributed authentication model called BlockAuth is introduced. This scheme considers edge devices at the edge layer as nodes to establish a blockchain network. The proposed authentication approach caters to various methods like password-based, certificate-based, biotechnology-based, and token-based authentication. This diversity aims to meet the security needs of high-level systems in Edge and IoT environments. The BlockAuth scheme utilizes the capabilities of blockchain's consensus and smart contracts to develop a distributed authentication protocol. While a client-server-based approach is adopted for blockchain deployment on the server machine, separate registration, and certificate-issuing servers are employed for user authentication and access control based on certificate mechanisms. Evaluation of the BlockAuth scheme is based on authentication initiation response time. Testing is carried out for both centralized and distributed networks with 4-peer, 6-peer, and 8-peer scenarios. The average response time for different peer scenarios in successful and failed authentication scenes is recorded. Comparatively, the centralized authentication scheme exhibits a significantly lower average response time of 1.13 seconds, which can be attributed to network speed and consensus mechanisms in the blockchain scenario. It's worth noting that while the BlockAuth scheme employs smart contracts, specific implementations such as biotechnology-based and token-based password authentication mechanisms are not discussed. Also, the traditional PKI-based implementation in a client-server environment is susceptible to single points of failure.

In (Wright et al. 2018), a cost-effective and efficient approach named SmartEdge, based on Ethereum smart contracts, is presented for edge computing's compute-resource management. The proposed solution outlines a smart contract's design in three main phases, detailed as follows in the context of SmartEdge's design. Firstly, the involved parties within the smart contract are identified. These parties include the compute node, which serves as the host for the Ethereum emulator, and the smart contract itself. Secondly, the data node takes on the responsibility of transmitting and receiving data as defined by the smart contract. This phase also involves identifying critical states within the lifecycle of the smart contract. Thirdly, the five states are Unavailable, Available, Pending, Computing, and Completed, and identifying and defining the methods that trigger state transitions. The performance was evaluated in terms of low overhead delay in executing a job and transaction cost in terms of costs that should not be significant relative to their value. Two factorization jobs were created to evaluate the overhead with input files consisting of 10,000 integers and 100,000 integers using the data node, compute node, and SmartEdge. This job roughly executes in 3 min on a Pi; however, when it was executed using SmartEdge, it only took 8.6 s. There was a noticeable 2-second overhead that included the time it takes to transfer the job to the compute node and the result back to the data node. The execution time of the larger input file was noted as 67s on the compute node, which shows increased latency in terms of larger input files which may affect the time for the Available and Completed states.

SSO (Single Sign-On) is a one-time password authentication scheme that requires a user to authenticate once, which helps avoid the fatigue of adding passwords again and again on the web. It includes a centralized approach with an authorized central body, such as a miner or server, which registers and issues a token for future access to various services and applications (Armando et al. 2008). Alternate to SSO, the authors in (Mir, Roland, and Mayrhofer 2020) proposed a new Distributed Anonymous Multi-Factor Authentication (DAMFA) scheme that uses public blockchain (i.e., Bitcoin and Namecoin). The underlying consensus mechanism improves usability, which builds on a Threshold Oblivious Pseudorandom Function (TOPRF) for resistance to offline attacks. They claim to include a distributed transaction ledger technology such as blockchain to improve usability. It requires no interaction with the identity provider; hence, the user's authentication no longer depends on a trusted third party. Namecoin blockchain is a public ledger blockchain that allows registering names and storing related values in the blockchain, a secure distributed shared database. The performance evaluation of the distributed anonymous authentication system has been carried out in two main steps: the registration and the authentication phases. The total time consumed in the registration phase for generating the credentials was noted at $\approx$703 ms, while the time consumed in the authentication phase for generating the credentials was noted at $\approx$640 ms. The results were achieved by running over 100trials for the authentication and the registration phases.

A framework for the authentication mechanism based on blockchain has been proposed in (Hammi, Bellot, and Serhrouchni 2018) named BCTrust. It has been designed especially for devices with resource constraints such as computational, storage, and energy consumption constraints. Public blockchain Ethereum has been used together with C programming to deploy the mechanism to implement the framework. The robustness claimed by the authors is because of the underlying framework of the public blockchain, distributed ledger technology with no central authority for signing the contracts and principles known as smart contracts. These smart contracts provide access control over the system (SID) authentication mechanisms and User or Device identification (UID). A practical implementation has been carried out on a network composed of two CPANs, while the performance evaluation of the proposed mechanism was measured in terms of execution time and power consumption of the classical association and BCTrust association. The average time and power consumption of the BCTrust association were noted $\approx$ at 14,406 ms and $\approx$0.681 Joule, while that of a Classical association was noted $\approx$ at 34,450 ms and $\approx$2.755 Joule, respectively. It shows that BCTrust was comparatively more robust in terms of saving more than 75.28% of energy.

Blockchain-enabled fog nodes for user authentication schemes have been introduced in (Almadhoun et al. 2019), for user authentication systems. These fog nodes utilize smart contracts to verify user access to IoT devices, as well as manage the registration and oversight of various entities like IoT devices, fog nodes, administrators, and end-users. The deployment of fog nodes offers scalability advantages to the system. These nodes alleviate IoT devices from the burden of resource-intensive tasks associated with authentication and interactions with the public blockchain. The proposed design is based on a distributed system framework, employing public blockchain principles. The implementation leverages Ethereum smart contracts to facilitate large-scale authentication of IoT devices. The smart contract, situated within Ethereum, handles authentication operations, including the addition of end-users and IoT assets. Oversight of the authentication mechanism's overall functionalities and operations is managed by an administrator.

In [29], a decentralized network trust and IoT authentication architecture based on blockchain and public key encryption are introduced. The authors present a Web of Things (WoT) model, which employs web technologies to enhance interoperability and transparency while minimizing the chain of trust. They propose a scalable, decentralized Public Key Infrastructure (PKI) tailored to the IoT context. This approach is integrated with the web-3 authentication and authorization framework, catering to IoT-enabled smart devices.

BLOCKCHAIN-ENABLED IOT EMBEDDED ASSETS

In (Gope and Sikdar 2019), a lightweight two-factor authentication approach is proposed for resource-constrained IoT devices. The method incorporates the physical attributes of the device to enhance authentication and counter physical attacks like impersonation and side-channel attacks. This is achieved through physically unclonable functions (PUFs), unique characteristics resulting from the manufacturing process of Integrated Circuits (ICs). A reverse fuzzy extractor is employed to mitigate noise during PUF operation. The mechanism involves a centralized server, implying a more centralized security model reliant on a central authority for authentication data storage. However, potential vulnerabilities arise due to server compromise and the need for multiple message exchanges between the device and the server, potentially exposing keys to security risks.

Similar approach as aforementioned but not server-dependent on the storage authentication data, the authors in (Aman, Chua, and Sikdar 2017) describe a lightweight authentication mechanism in which there is no need for storing the secret keys in a central server. This is the same problem that has been identified by the authors in (Gope and Sikdar 2019), where the existing mechanism requires authentication credentials to store on a secure centralized miner i.e. server. This mechanism also defines authentication mechanisms based on Physical Unclonable Functions (PUFs), which describe the physical properties of the devices. This property helps the devices to increase security from the attached vector in case of adversaries. The authors present protocols for two scenarios, one that establishes IoT device and server communication and the other for D2D communication when two IoT devices want to establish a session. The proposed mechanism also requires at least 5 exchanges of authentication messages. Moreover, PUF based authentication data is stored on the server node that is prone to single point of failure attack which is not suitable as far as the privacy of the IoT devices is concerned. The literature survey presents the current state-of-the-art security authentication mechanism for IoT-enabled assets in Web3-based IoT architecture. depicts an evaluation summary of the proposed authentication schemes.

Table 1. IoT-Enabled Smart Device Authentication Schemes based on Web3 Architecture for Smart City.

RP	Solution	Scheme	Issues
(Khalid et al. 2020)	BC-based authentication mechanism Ethereum	- Authentication and access control mechanisms for edge devices in an IoT system. - Interoperability among the fog nodes of different IoT systems to operate in smart city infrastructure.	- Security and privacy issues depend on Blockchain PKI-based implementation. - Security data services such as confidentiality and availability concerns have not been taken care of.
(Gong et al. 2021)	BCoT Sentry-Ethereum	- A network security module has been deployed, which analyzes the traffic flow of IoT devices and sends it to Smart Contract. - The maximal Information Coefficient (MIC) method has been used for feature extraction from the device traffic flows, which is used for device identification.	- Security and privacy issues depend on Blockchain PKI-based implementation.
(Zhaofeng et al. 2021)	BlockAuth	- The Client-Server approach has been adopted to deploy blockchain on the server machine. - The registration and certificate-issuing servers have been deployed for user authentication and access control based on a certificate-based security mechanism. - Edge devices build blockchain nodes and provide a distributed, safe, and reliable solution.	- The client-server-based approach has opted for certificate issuance, while communication between RS and edge nodes has not been taken care of. - Claims for the biotechnology-based and token-based password authentication mechanisms have not been seen. - PKI-based implementation in a client-server environment is prone to a single point of failure.

continued on following page

Table 1. Continued

RP	Solution	Scheme	Issues
(Wright et al. 2018)	SmartEdge-Ethereum	- SmartEdge, an Ethereum-based smart contract for edge computing, has been utilized, showing that the solution is a low-cost, low-overhead tool for compute-resource management. - The smart contract has been used to define and deploy the design in three key steps such as, - Identifying the nodes, - Identifying the functions for key states of the nodes, and - Defining the methods that trigger state transitions.	- Identification and authentication of devices have not been taken care of as in the malicious node, the proposed system would be at risk. - No results verification has been involved in verifying that a job was properly performed through the smart contract or not, and - Auctioning contracts such as automatically matching data nodes with the most appropriate compute nodes have not been taken care of. - The communication between the edge node and the distributed platform using the internet poses a threat to the whole system.
(Mir et al. 2020)	DAMFA-Bitcoin and Namecoin	- Blockchain technology to improve usability builds on a Threshold Oblivious Pseudorandom Function (TOPRF) to improve resistance to offline attacks. - Claim to improve usability without any interaction with the identity provider. - The trusted third party is no longer needed for user authentication.	- Depended on Blockchain PKI infrastructure-based implementation.
(Hammi et al. 2018)	BCTrust-Ethereum	- The interoperability of different node registrations in different CPANs has been realized by integrating blockchain (Ethereum), and an evaluation of the proposed mechanism has been carried out.	- Access control and Mutual authentication of sensor nodes are missing. - Depended on Blockchain PKI infrastructure-based implementation.

continued on following page

Table 1. Continued

RP	Solution	Scheme	Issues
(Almadhoun et al. 2019)	User Authentication using Fog Nodes	- The user authentication mechanism for accessing IoT devices using fog nodes. - Fog nodes have been used as Blockchain nodes. - Blockchain-based authentication system.	- Interoperability among the fog nodes in an IoT System is missing. - Data integrity and repudiation security issues have not been effectively handled.
(Yetis and Sahingoz 2019)	Authentication System for IoT Devices	- A Proposal for an authorization system for IoT devices based on Blockchain. - Lightweight communication protocol UDP has been integrated to deploy a simple communication model for lightweight IoT devices. - Integration of the Vigenere cipher encryption method makes the scheme robust in providing data integrity over the blockchain network.	- Smart contracts integration can improve security services by limiting the IoT device availability to unauthorized users, thus increasing confidentiality, which has been missing in the proposal. - Personal BC based on Python was developed, lacking many key security features; hence the proposed solution lacks a public or private BC network deployment and evaluation. - UDP has been employed to achieve a lightweight communication mechanism for IoT devices which may result in data packet loss with no resilience property defined.

CHALLENGES IN CURRENT BLOCKCHAIN-BASED AUTHENTICATION

Based on the literature review presented in this chapter, it has been observed that most of the proposed solutions depend on the internal security mechanism of the distributed ledger technology (DLT) while none of the solutions have explored the identification and authentication schemes keeping smart cities architectures in view as summarized in Table 1.

Several research studies have proposed blockchain-based solutions that introduce default consensus mechanisms which open doors to performance issues of fault tolerance, decentralization, stability, and security. Nevertheless, the use of private blockchain implementation achieves consensus in a matter of hundreds of milliseconds, ensuring minimal latency. This rapid consensus mechanism is essential for constructing IoT networks based on blockchain, which in turn results in reduced communication overhead and enhanced fault tolerance. Apart from the consensus mechanism, none of the solutions manage to deploy all the features of security services (i.e., confidentiality, availability, and integrity), computational costs in terms of Gas consumption, and latency to reduce time complexity.

Hence, lightweight solutions for managing, maintaining, processing, and storing identification and authentication data for smart assets for Web3 architecture are a dire need. This is a step towards realizing cyber-physical systems in a decentralized infrastructure with its implementation on a blockchain tokenization-based authentication mechanism. The adoption of these smart devices expands to different cyber-physical systems in smart city architecture, i.e., smart houses, smart healthcare, smart transportation, smart grid, smart agriculture, etc.

The challenges and insights lead us to explore the smart city assets concerning their digital representation, development, identification, and authentication aspects in a Web3 distributed architecture. Below are the challenges that have been seen in the current literature review and are important from a further research point of view.

SECURITY AND PRIVACY CONCERNS

The current implementation relies heavily on Blockchain Public Key Infrastructure (PKI), raising security and privacy issues. Security triads relating to CIA (Confidentiality, Availability) and AAA (Authorization, Authentication, and Audit) of security data services remain unaddressed.

Lack of Communication Security

The client-server-based approach for certificate issuance neglects secure communication between RS (Registration Server) and edge nodes, potentially compromising data integrity and privacy.

Inadequate Authentication Mechanisms

Biotechnology-based and token-based password authentication mechanisms' divisibility in regard to NFTs are not adequately explored, leaving gaps in authentication reliability and security.

Single Point of Failure

The PKI-based implementation in a client-server environment is vulnerable to a single point of failure, posing a significant risk to system reliability and security.

Absence of Access Control

The absence of access control and mutual authentication mechanisms for sensor nodes increases the risk of unauthorized access and data breaches.

Lack of Interoperability

Interoperability among fog nodes in a Cyber-Physical environment is lacking, hindering seamless communication and data exchange between heterogeneous devices.

Ineffective Handling of Data Integrity

Data integrity and repudiation security issues have not been effectively addressed, leaving vulnerabilities in data integrity assurance and accountability.

Integration of Smart Contracts

Integrating smart contracts can enhance security services by restricting IoT device availability to unauthorized users, thereby improving confidentiality and access control.

Incomplete Security Features

A Python-based personal Blockchain lacks key security features, resulting in a lack of deployment and evaluation of public or private Blockchain networks.

Communication Vulnerabilities

The use of UDP for lightweight communication in IoT devices may lead to data packet loss and lack of defined resilience properties, posing challenges to reliable data transmission and system stability.

SECURITY SERVICES COMPARISON ~ NFT-ENABLED SOLUTIONS FOR CYBER-PHYSICAL ENVIRONMENT

Based on the NFT-enabled solutions explored in this section a comparative evaluation has also been presented. Table 2 shows that NFT has been explored in different domains however, the digital identity attribute that represents IoT assets in smart cities is still a research gap. The analysis compares the proposed architecture and several other NFT-based solutions. The analysis encompassed multiple dimensions, such as blockchain platform, consensus mechanism, domain focus, NFT extension, default NFT mechanism, proposed authentication mechanism, and security services considerations. The comparison also involved a selection of NFT-enabled solutions from distinct domains, each offering unique attributes and functionalities however, none of the solutions provide divisibility in components for the security services (i.e., Confidentiality, Integrity, and Availability) and the authentication mechanism for IoT assets in cyber-physical systems for smart cities.

Table 2. Security Services Comparative Evaluation of NFT-Based Solution

Ref	Year Proposed	Blockchain Platform	Consensus Mech	Domain	Proposed NFT Ext	Default NFT Mech	Proposed Auth Mech	Security Services
(Arcenegui et al. 2021)	2021	Ethereum	*POW*	IoT Security	✓	-	✓	[I]
(Bellagarda and Abu-Mahfouz 2022)	2022	Ethereum	*POW*	Social Media		✓		[I]
(Hasan et al. 2022)	2022	Ethereum	*POW*	NFT and IPFS		✓		[I]
(Musamih et al. 2022)	2022	Ethereum	*POW*	HealthCare		✓		[A]
(López-Pimentel et al. 2023)	2023	Ethereum	*POW*	NFT-Vehicle		✓		[I]
(Chiacchio et al. 2022)	2022	Ethereum	*POW*	Supply Chain HealthCare		✓		[C], [I]
(Khalil et al. 2023)	2022	Hyperledger Besu & Goerli	*IBFT 2.0*	IoT assets security in CPSs	✓	-	✓	[C], [I], [A]

Security Services → [C] Confidentiality, [I] Integrity, [A] Availability,

The comparative evaluation further shows that our proposed extension stands out for its focus on enhancing security services across all three dimensions and the selection of tools and techniques for the proposed framework. An observed pattern is the widespread selection of Ethereum as the favored platform in the studies examined. However, the utilization of the default Proof-of-Work (*PoW*) consensus mechanism is a concern regarding scalability and energy usage. This trend reflects a rising curiosity in alternative platforms featuring more efficient consensus protocols. The proposed framework deviates from this trend by considering Hyperledger Besu with the Goerli testnet. This selection offers several advantages:

PERMISSIONED NETWORK

Hyperledger Besu supports and creates permissioned blockchains, which provide greater control and potentially higher efficiency compared to public blockchains like Ethereum.

IBFT 2.0 CONSENSUS

The adoption of the Istanbul Byzantine Fault Tolerance (IBFT) 2.0 consensus protocol addresses scalability issues associated with PoW. IBFT 2.0 offers faster transaction processing and lower energy consumption, ensuring robustness in managing IoT assets' security within complex smart city infrastructures. The IBFT 2.0 algorithm as shown in Figure 1 depicts the working performance based on below mentioned mechanism.

Awaiting Proposal: The process begins with the system in an "Awaiting Proposal" state, where it expects a new block proposal.
Check Proposal Validity: Upon receiving a pre-prepare message and validating the proposal (RxPre-prepareMsg / ValidateProposal), the system moves to "Check Proposal Validity."
Preparing (Valid Proposal): If the proposal is found to be valid ([Valid] / GossipPrepareMsg), the system transitions to the "Preparing" state.
RoundChange (Invalid Proposal or Timeout): If the proposal is invalid ([Invalid]) while checking its validity, or if a timeout occurs during "Preparing," the system moves to "RoundChange."
Ready: After receiving 2F+1 prepare messages, gossiping a commit message, and locking the block (Rx2F+1PrepareMsgs / GossipCommitMsg; LockBlock), the system enters the "Ready" state.
Check Insert Result: Once 2F+1 commit messages are received and the block is appended to the chain (Rx2F+1CommitMsgs / AppendBlockToChain), the system moves to "Check Insert Result."
Awaiting Proposal (Success): If the block insertion is successful ([Success] / StartRoundTimer), the system returns to the "Awaiting Proposal" state to start a new round.
RoundChange (Failed Insert or Timeout): If the block insertion fails ([Failed] / UnlockBlock) or a timeout occurs during "Ready," the system transitions to "RoundChange."

Awaiting Proposal (from RoundChange): From "RoundChange," upon receiving a RoundChange message with 2F+1 votes (Rx2F+1 RoundChangeMsg), the system can move back to "Awaiting Proposal."
RoundChange (Timeout from Awaiting Proposal): A timeout in the "Awaiting Proposal" state also leads to a "RoundChange.

Figure 1. Working mechanism of the IBFT 2.0 algorithm

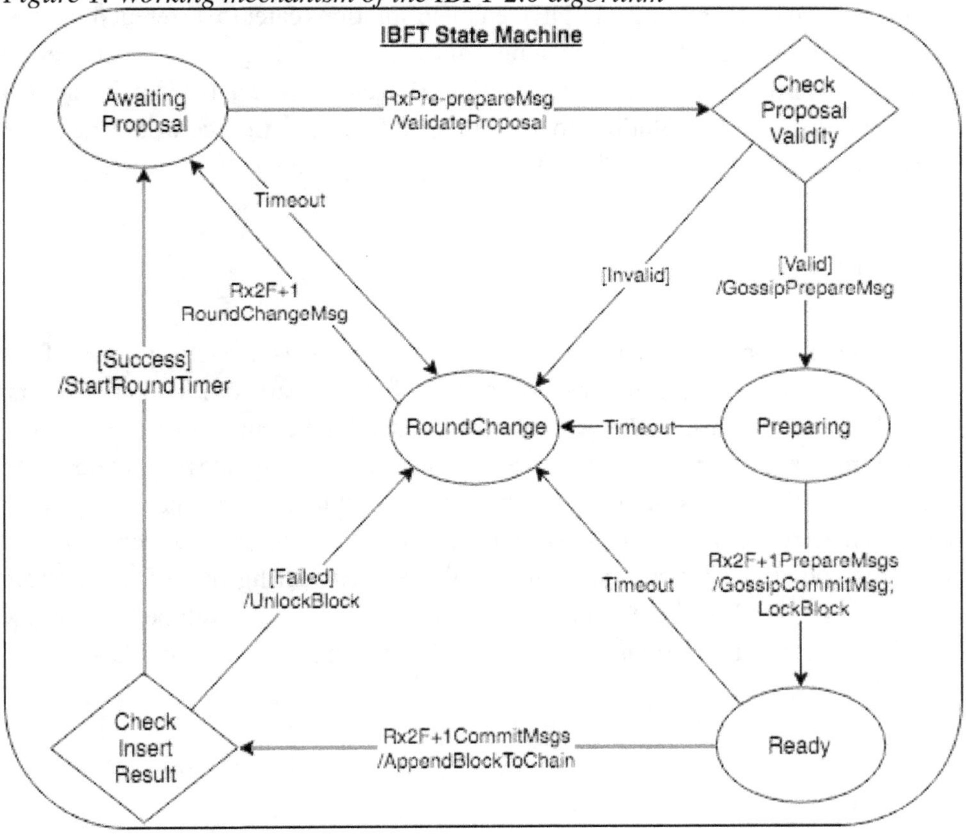

FOCUS ON SECURITY SERVICES

The proposed framework incorporates a wider range of security services (confidentiality, integrity, and access control) denoted by [C], [I], and [A] compared to the reviewed studies which primarily focus on basic NFT implementation or lack mention altogether.

JUSTIFICATION FOR SELECTION

The focus on comprehensive security services positions the proposed frameworks in literature to address a broader range of security concerns within the chosen domain (IoT asset security in CPSs). Unlike other solutions, an NFT extension is specifically tailored to address the security and authentication requirements of IoT assets. Moreover, the proposed extension encompasses all proposed security services—Confidentiality, Integrity, and Availability.

It is evident that while various NFT-enabled solutions cater to different domains, the proposed solution's distinctive features make it a compelling choice for bolstering the security of IoT assets within smart cities. This analysis underscores the significance of tailoring NFT solutions to domain-specific needs, thus contributing to the advancement of secure and efficient smart city ecosystems.

CONCLUSION

The integration of blockchain technology within cyber-physical systems offers massive potential to transform various sectors, including smart homes, smart districts, and federated mechanisms. By leveraging blockchain's inherent security, transparency, and immutability, it is possible to tackle the critical challenges associated with current authentication systems. The chapter has highlighted the specific security services that can be enhanced through NFT-enabled solutions, such as permissioned networks and IBFT 2.0 consensus mechanisms. Considering these factors, more robust, secure, and resilient cyber-physical systems can be developed that allow individuals and organizations to harness the full potential of the digital age.

REFERENCES

Almadhoun, R., Kadadha, M., Alhemeiri, M., Alshehhi, M., & Salah, K. (2019). A user authentication scheme of IoT devices using blockchain-enabled fog nodes. In *Proceedings of IEEE/ACS International Conference on Computer Systems and Applications (AICCSA)* (Vols. 2018–Novem).

Aman, M. N., Chua, K. C., & Sikdar, B. (2017). Mutual authentication in IoT systems using physical unclonable functions. *IEEE Internet of Things Journal*, *4*(5), 1327–1340. DOI: 10.1109/JIOT.2017.2703088

Ammi, M., Alarabi, S., & Benkhelifa, E. (2021). Customized blockchain-based architecture for secure smart home for lightweight IoT. *Information Processing & Management*, *58*(3), 102482. DOI: 10.1016/j.ipm.2020.102482

Arcenegui, J., Arjona, R., Román, R., & Baturone, I. (2021). Secure combination of IoT and blockchain by physically binding IoT devices to smart non-fungible tokens using PUFs. *Sensors (Basel)*, *21*(9), 3119. DOI: 10.3390/s21093119 PMID: 33946227

Arif, S., Khan, M. A., Rehman, S. U., Kabir, M. A., & Imran, M. (2020). Investigating smart home security: Is blockchain the answer? *IEEE Access : Practical Innovations, Open Solutions*, *8*, 117802–117816. DOI: 10.1109/ACCESS.2020.3004662

Armando, A., Carbone, R., Compagna, L., Cuellar, J., & Tobarra, L. (2008). Formal analysis of SAML 2.0 web browser single sign-on: Breaking the SAML-based single sign-on for Google Apps. In *Proceedings of the ACM Conference on Computer and Communications Security* (pp. 1–9). DOI: 10.1145/1456396.1456397

Bellagarda, J., & Abu-Mahfouz, A. M. (2022). Connect2NFT: A web-based, blockchain enabled NFT application with the aim of reducing fraud and ensuring authenticated social, non-human verified digital identity. *Mathematics*, *10*(21), 3934. DOI: 10.3390/math10213934

Boitier, W., Del Pozzo, A., García-Pérez, Á., Gazut, S., Jobic, P., Lemaire, A., Mahe, E., Mayoue, A., Perion, M., Singh, D., Rezende, T. F., & Tucci-Piergiovanni, S. (2024). *Fantastyc: Blockchain-based federated learning made secure and practical.* ArXiv., DOI: 10.1109/SRDS64841.2024.00033

Chiacchio, F., D'Urso, D., Oliveri, L. M., Spitaleri, A., Spampinato, C., & Giordano, D. (2022). A non-fungible token solution for the track and trace of pharmaceutical supply chain. *Applied Sciences (Basel, Switzerland)*, *12*(8), 4019. DOI: 10.3390/app12084019

Dorri, A., Kanhere, S. S., Jurdak, R., & Gauravaram, P. (2017). Blockchain for IoT security and privacy: The case study of a smart home. In *2017 IEEE International Conference on Pervasive Computing and Communications Workshops (PerCom Workshops)* (pp. 618–623). DOI: 10.1109/PERCOMW.2017.7917634

Esposito, C., Ficco, M., & Gupta, B. B. (2021). Blockchain-based authentication and authorization for smart city applications. *Information Processing & Management*, *58*(2), 102468. DOI: 10.1016/j.ipm.2020.102468

Gong, L., Alghazzawi, D. M., & Cheng, L. (2021). BCOT sentry: A blockchain-based identity authentication framework for IoT devices. *Information (Basel)*, *12*(5), 203. DOI: 10.3390/info12050203

Gope, P., & Sikdar, B. (2019). Lightweight and privacy-preserving two-factor authentication scheme for IoT devices. *IEEE Internet of Things Journal*, *6*(1), 580–589. DOI: 10.1109/JIOT.2018.2846299

Gowda, C. (2025, June 4). Emerging trends in federated learning for data science AI. *Voval.Media*. https://vocal.media/education/emerging-trends-in-federated-learning-for-data-science-ai

Hai, T., Zhou, J., Srividhya, S. R., Jain, S. K., Young, P., & Agrawal, S. (2022). BV-FLEMR: An integrated federated learning and blockchain technology for cloud-based medical records recommendation system. *Journal of Cloud Computing (Heidelberg, Germany)*, *11*(1), 1–11. DOI: 10.1186/s13677-022-00294-6

Hammi, M. T., Bellot, P., & Serhrouchni, A. (2018). BCTrust: A decentralized authentication blockchain-based mechanism. In *IEEE Wireless Communications and Networking Conference (WCNC)* (Vol. 2018–April, pp. 1–6). DOI: 10.1109/WCNC.2018.8377413

Hard, A., Rao, K., Mathews, R., Ramaswamy, S., Beaufays, F., Augenstein, S., Eichner, H., Kiddon, C., & Ramage, D. (2018). Federated learning for mobile keyboard prediction. *ArXiv*. https://arxiv.org/abs/1811.03604

Hasan, H. R., Salah, K., Battah, A., Madine, M., Yaqoob, I., Jayaraman, R., & Omar, M. (2022). Incorporating registration, reputation, and incentivization into the NFT ecosystem. *IEEE Access : Practical Innovations, Open Solutions*, *10*, 76416–76433. DOI: 10.1109/ACCESS.2022.3192388

Keshk, M., Turnbull, B., Moustafa, N., Vatsalan, D., & Choo, K. K. R. (2020). A privacy-preserving-framework-based blockchain and deep learning for protecting smart power networks. *IEEE Transactions on Industrial Informatics*, *16*(8), 5110–5118. DOI: 10.1109/TII.2019.2957140

Khalid, U., Asim, M., Baker, T., Hung, P. C. K., Tariq, M. A., & Rafferty, L. (2020). A decentralized lightweight blockchain-based authentication mechanism for IoT systems. *Cluster Computing*, *23*(3), 2067–2087. DOI: 10.1007/s10586-020-03058-6

Khalil, U., Malik, O. A., Hong, O. W., & Uddin, M. (2022). DSCOT: An NFT-based blockchain architecture for the authentication of IoT-enabled smart devices in smart cities. SSRN Electronic Journal. DOI: 10.2139/ssrn.4355848

Khalil, U., Malik, O. A., Hong, O. W., & Uddin, M. (2023). Leveraging a novel NFT-enabled blockchain architecture for the authentication of IoT assets in smart cities. *Scientific Reports*, *13*(1), 1–26. DOI: 10.1038/s41598-023-45212-1 PMID: 37957161

Khan, M. A., Abbas, S., Rehman, A., Saeed, Y., Zeb, A., Uddin, M. I., Nasser, N., & Ali, A. (2021). A machine learning approach for blockchain-based smart home networks security. *IEEE Network*, *35*(3), 223–229. DOI: 10.1109/MNET.011.2000514

Ladd, V. (2024, June 4). Blockchain for AI federated learning and decentralized authentication and privacy. Medium. https://medium.com/@oracle_43885/blockchain-powered-ai-federated-learning-secured-with-decentralized-authentication-and-privacy-ad5812719b1a

Lakhan, A., Mohammed, M. A., Abdulkareem, K. H., Deveci, M., Marhoon, H. A., Memon, S., Nedoma, J., & Martinek, R. (2024). BEDS: Blockchain energy efficient IoE sensors data scheduling for smart home and vehicle applications. *Applied Energy*, *369*, 123535. DOI: 10.1016/j.apenergy.2024.123535

Letichevsky, A. A., Letychevskyi, O. O., Skobelev, V. G., & Volkov, V. A. (2017). Cyber-physical systems. *Cybernetics and Systems Analysis*, *53*(6), 821–834. DOI: 10.1007/s10559-017-9984-9

López-Pimentel, J. C., Morales-Rosales, L. A., Algredo-Badillo, I., & Del-Valle-Soto, C. (2023). NFT-vehicle: A blockchain-based tokenization architecture to register transactions over a vehicle's life cycle. *Mathematics*, *11*(13), 2801. DOI: 10.3390/math11132801

Mateen, A. Q., & Hong, O. W. (2018). Implementation and evaluation of IoT system using cloud storage platform. *ACM International Conference Proceeding Series*, 157–161. DOI: 10.1145/3289430.3289465

Mir, O., Roland, M., & Mayrhofer, R. (2020). DAMFA: Decentralized anonymous multi-factor authentication. BSCI 2020 - Proceedings of the 2nd ACM International Symposium on Blockchain and Secure Critical Infrastructure, 10–19. DOI: 10.1145/3384943.3409417

Moniruzzaman, M., Khezr, S., Yassine, A., & Benlamri, R. (2020). Blockchain for smart homes: Review of current trends and research challenges. *Computers & Electrical Engineering*, *83*, 106585. DOI: 10.1016/j.compeleceng.2020.106585

Musamih, A., Yaqoob, I., Salah, K., Jayaraman, R., Omar, M., & Ellahham, S. (2022). Using NFTs for product management, digital certification, trading, and delivery in the healthcare supply chain. *IEEE Transactions on Engineering Management*, •••, 1–22. DOI: 10.1109/TEM.2022.3215793

Ning, W., Zhu, Y., Song, C., Li, H., Zhu, L., Xie, J., Chen, T., Xu, T., Xu, X., & Gao, J. (2024). Blockchain-based federated learning: A survey and new perspectives. *Applied Sciences (Basel, Switzerland)*, *14*(20), 9459. DOI: 10.3390/app14209459

Orabi, M. M., Emam, O., & Fahmy, H. (2025). Adapting security and decentralized knowledge enhancement in federated learning using blockchain technology: Literature review. *Journal of Big Data*, *12*(1), 1–24. DOI: 10.1186/s40537-025-01099-5

Peng, G., Shi, X., Zhang, J., Gao, L., Tan, Y., Xiang, N., & Wang, W. (2024). BGFL: A blockchain-enabled group federated learning at wireless industrial edges. *Journal of Cloud Computing (Heidelberg, Germany)*, *13*(1), 1–16. DOI: 10.1186/s13677-024-00700-1

Rapal, H. (2024, June 4). Smart contracts and regulatory compliance: Navigating the legal landscape. Legitt AI. https://legittai.com/blog/smart-contracts-and-regulatory-compliance

Ratkovic, N. (2022). Improving home security using blockchain. International Journal of Computations [IJCIM]. *Information and Manufacturing*, *2*(1), 2022. DOI: 10.54489/ijcim.v2i1.72

Ren, S., Kim, E., & Lee, C. (2024). A scalable blockchain-enabled federated learning architecture for edge computing. *PLoS One*, *19*(8), e0308991. DOI: 10.1371/journal.pone.0308991 PMID: 39150937

Saxena, U., Sodhi, J. S., & Tanwar, R. (2020). Augmenting smart home network security using blockchain technology. *International Journal of Electronic Security and Digital Forensics*, *12*(1), 99–117. DOI: 10.1504/IJESDF.2020.103881

Sharma, A. K., Dubey, R. K., Goswami, P., & Sarang, R. P. (2024). Securing smart homes with blockchain-enabled systems. In 2024 IEEE 4th International Conference on ICT in Business Industry and Government (ICTBIG 2024). IEEE. DOI: 10.1109/ICTBIG64922.2024.10911074

Shi, J. (2011). A survey of cyber-physical systems.

Syahla, H. D., & Ogi, D. (2021). Implementation of secure parking based on cyber-physical system using one-time password scheme to overcome replay attack. In 8th International Conference on ICT for Smart Society (ICISS 2021), 1–6. DOI: 10.1109/ICISS53185.2021.9533246

Woo, T. Y. C., & Lam, S. S. (2014). Distributed systems. *Distributed Systems*, *25*(1), 39–52. DOI: 10.1201/b17224

Wright, K. L., Martinez, M., Chadha, U., & Krishnamachari, B. (2018). SmartEdge: A smart contract for edge computing. In *Proceedings of IEEE 2018 International Congress on Cybermatics* (pp. 1685–1690). IEEE. DOI: 10.1109/Cybermatics_2018.2018.00281

Yang, L., Liu, X. Y., & Gong, W. (2020). Secure smart home systems: A blockchain perspective. In IEEE INFOCOM 2020 - IEEE Conference on Computer Communications Workshops (INFOCOM WKSHPS 2020), 1003–1008. DOI: 10.1109/INFOCOMWKSHPS50562.2020.9162648

Yang, Q., & Wang, H. (2021). Privacy-preserving transactive energy management for IoT-aided smart homes via blockchain. *IEEE Internet of Things Journal*, *8*(14), 11463–11475. DOI: 10.1109/JIOT.2021.3051323

Yetis, R., & Sahingoz, O. K. (2019). Blockchain based secure communication for IoT devices in smart cities. In *7th International Istanbul Smart Grids and Cities Congress and Fair (ICSG 2019)* (pp. 134–138). DOI: 10.1109/SGCF.2019.8782285

Zhaofeng, M., Meng, J., Wang, J., & Shan, Z. (2021). Blockchain-based decentralized authentication modeling scheme in edge and IoT environment. *IEEE Internet of Things Journal*, *8*(4), 2116–2123. DOI: 10.1109/JIOT.2020.3037733

Chapter 4
Understanding Non-Fungible Tokens (NFTs) in Smart Cities

Wasswa Shafik
https://orcid.org/0000-0002-9320-3186
Universiti Brunei Darussalam, Brunei

Muhammad Muzamil Aslam
https://orcid.org/0000-0002-8711-2907
Universiti Brunei Darussalam, Brunei

Ali Tufail
https://orcid.org/0000-0003-4871-4080
Universiti Brunei Darussalam, Brunei

ABSTRACT

This chapter depicts the role of Non-Fungible Tokens (NFTs) in the development of smart cities in this digital era, focusing on its perspective to boost urban governance, community engagement, and resource management. A unique digital asset fosters transparent ownership and provenance tracking of urban resources, such as public art, land, and community spaces. The integration of NFTs enhances service delivery and planning as demonstrated in the chapter advance participatory governance, granting citizens to engage in decision-making processes through tokenized voting mechanisms. Moreover, NFTs promote community engagement and tokenized identity expressions, thereby boosting local economies. Finally, the study highlighted the transformative potential of NFTs in creating sustainable, inclusive, and innovative urban environments.

DOI: 10.4018/979-8-3693-8876-1.ch004

INTRODUCTION

Non-Fungible Tokens (NFTs) are unique digital assets that can carry and transfer value, much like cryptocurrencies. However, the individuality and uniqueness of NFTs compared to other fungible cryptocurrencies provide them with a different relevance and purpose in the realm of blockchain applications (Napoli & Gatteschi, 2023). Smart cities are defined as urban areas where various elements such as policies and regulations, experiences, and lifestyles are based and managed through technology to improve or maintain a desired core functional need in delivering a sustainable and high-quality life. In the blockchain world, NFTs could help to yield a new field for city management and urban governance, leading to entirely new options to give city managerial policies stemming from inputs by residents rather than just the city (Venugopalan & Aydt, 2023).

NFTs' seized attributes point to the integral role that they can play beyond entanglement in the world of digital and sometimes physical collectibles and art. This comes as over half the people in the world are living in urban centers, as cities are positions of innovation. Thus, the time is ripe to explore and open the way for conditions to yield a new urban environment. In effect, the term Smart City is slowly becoming more familiar to urban populations and communities across the world. However, as a society, little can be done to inform the population about the importance of designing and governing national and urban infrastructure based on blockchain and NFTs. Therefore, all of us need to have an understanding of both the backgrounds of NFTs and Smart Cities (Khalil et al., 2022). Researchers of cities, security, and blockchain experts are also inclined to have an understanding of these two emerging technologies and bodies of experience to interpret and grapple with issues and concepts related to the new, potential applied, and theoretical variation.

The most referenced definition of a NFT could be "a unit of data stored on a digital ledger called a blockchain that certifies a digital asset to be unique and therefore not interchangeable." However, a more detailed examination of NFT characteristics points to three main features that make NFTs different from other digital assets. The first NFT attribute refers to its uniqueness. This means that no two NFTs are actually the same: each token is different from other tokens and has distinctive features. The second feature refers to the fact that NFTs are not divisible. This means that every NFT is a whole that cannot be further split into smaller units. Instead of having 1 NFT, 2 NFTs, or 3 NFTs, we can talk about 0 or 1, where 1 represents the existence of an intrinsic non-divisible digital asset signed on a blockchain and stored on the network (Khalil et al., 2024). The last feature of NFTs refers to the metadata that could be associated with them. This metadata provides information on the object's authenticity, provenance, and various other characteristics that establish the asset.

With NFTs being tokens based on blockchain technology, a distributed ledger that validates digital transactions and provides transparency, and a system for managing records, any minted, bought, or sold NFT could easily be traced and verified. This allows NFTs to serve as a secure and transparent proof of ownership certificate. In addition, the smart contracts underlying many NFT transactions allow for royalties or income from the secondary sales of an item to be coded into the original item, intuitively allowing creators to profit from the increasing value of their original work when it sells. Despite initial impressions, NFTs can encompass almost anything digital, including recorded music, screen-based art, sponsored brand avatars, and other virtual assets (Ray, 2023). In the few years since NFTs debuted, they have continued to evolve beyond digital art into a wider range of other industry verticals and trading markets.

Figure 1. Smart City domains and application

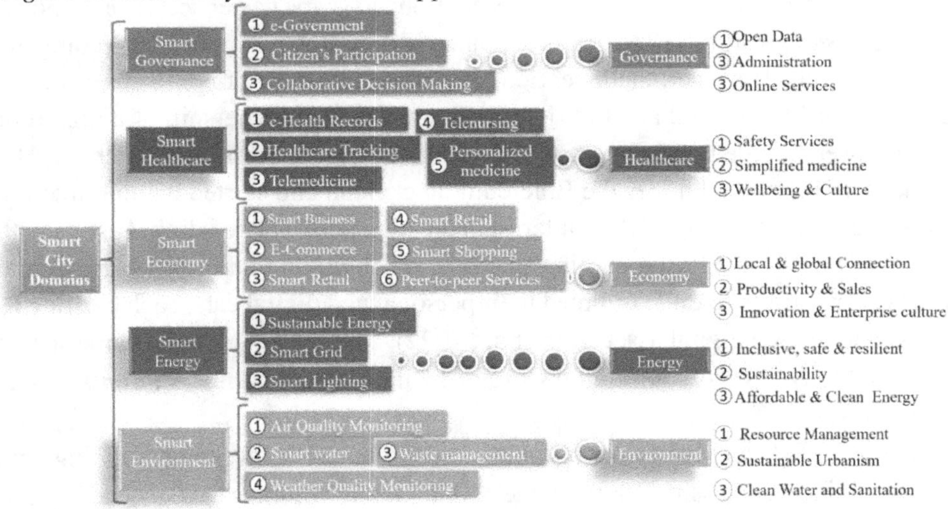

A smart city uses data and advanced technologies to ensure a better quality of living for its residents. The measures covered under the smart cities mission allow city municipalities to focus on their most pressing needs and to provide precise, context-sensitive, and inclusive services, as illustrated in Figure 1. Smart cities represent an innovative response to increasing urbanization by utilizing scarce resources and technology to uplift the standard of living, thereby reducing cultural and economic disparities. This model provides the foundation for the future urban population. A smart city can be categorized into different focus areas, and various components are specified for different levels at which the intervention or initiative is carried out. While the smart city represents an overall composite of multiple aspects, the transformational areas of focus are often characterized by such attributes as economy, environment, mobility, people, living, and governance (Ren et al., 2022). An intelligent transportation system can significantly reduce traffic congestion, enhance people's overall well-being, and reduce travel times and fuel consumption, thereby providing a significant boost to the local economy. Additionally, an environmentally friendly transportation system contributes to smart city initiatives, ensuring long-term protection of environmental quality. Many cities are touting smart cities as a way to address such problems as traffic, water quantity and quality, and low return on tax investment through an open platform. Cities are currently debating the extent to which they want smart cities to be truly open. A smart city focuses not only on technology solutions but also on inclusivity, public safety and security, community engagement, and social equity as part of it (Samuel et al., 2023). Insights into the various components of smart cities and the ways to address urban problems pave the way to understanding how NFTs can be applied to smart cities.

From digital art to smart cities, NFTs continue to shape newer sectors and industries across the world. NFTs became a point of discussion when its parent company renamed itself. However, the inception, origins, and history of NFTs are rooted in the elite world of digital art. In brief, NFTs are proof of ownership of a digital or crypto asset recorded on an interconnected digital ledger known as blockchain. The earliest NFT emerged under the Ethereum blockchain and started gaining traction when digital artists showed their interest in creating personalized digital assets with a unique bit of code. A pioneering platform for digitizing and tokenizing digital assets allows users to trade or breed their personalized digital cats, each existing as a new and unique digital asset (Ren et al., 2022). These NFT assets became scarce to obtain, as NFTs promote 'digital scarcity' by limiting the number of digital assets in the ecosystem.

Digital artists and collectors became more interested in investing, building, and selling digital assets using NFTs. In fact, NFT trading volumes have reached an all-time high. An NFT artwork marked the beginning of NFTs to the masses. Over the years, NFTs have transformed the entire gaming and real estate industries, as they enable gaming organizations to tokenize in-game assets and land over a blockchain network. This provides scarce and unique digital assets to players and gamers. At this point, it is essential to read the line carefully: distinct from cryptocurrencies, NFTs do not represent physical assets and carry a unique piece of digital code beneficial to prove ownership. Later in this paper, we extend NFTs beyond their chasm of crafting digital art and gaming into urban ecosystems, underscoring NFTs to enhance business models, such as a rise in personalization, social commerce, and interactive customer services. Moreover, distinct from fungible tokens carrying the same value as their counterparts, NFTs hold different values (Khalil et al., 2024).

NFTs are created using smart contracts and display all the required digital ownership credentials, including the transaction details and current ownership.

ORIGINS OF NFTS IN THE ART WORLD

Starting from the need for a basic understanding of NFTs and how they have evolved, this study examines the popular discourse around NFTs, including the explosion of NFTs in the digital art community. This explosion led to well-known digital artists and community-driven projects running their digital art residency. The artists who experimented with NFTs in their work included a portrait artist who used the newly formed "NFT" as a step-by-step process, eliminating his signature and background copyright and selling his signed physical portraits, allowing collectors to redeem them for a physical asset. Community experiments like these, as well as more well-known projects such as the decentralized virtual world, have significantly impacted and attracted attention to NFTs (Ray, 2023; Ren et al., 2022).

An online art auction sold a one-of-a-kind NFT by an artist. "The COVID-19 pandemic has been a catalyst for a hugely transformative period in the way that humanity uses, interacts with, and trusts digital technology." Blockchain technology has pushed art into this space, encouraging the audience to buy beyond the digital print and invest in artists who receive royalties for each subsequent physical combined edition they sell. In an age where the market for digital art has been largely crowded and overlooked, NFTs are beginning to foreground a generation that grew up with printing, while blockchain-verified one-to-one digital scarcity has the potential to revolutionize digital image and music monetization. This marking of a paradigm shift includes attracting criticism (Napoli & Gatteschi, 2023). A curator warned that the "market is fully focused on the idea of understanding this exotic new form of asset rather than really critically engaging with the outputs of the technology," echoing a warning that "in the race to own an NFT, the art of creation will become secondary." Despite this critique, NFTs are selling well at auctions. NFT awareness is particularly widespread among mainstream artists (Ray, 2023).

EXPANSION OF NFT USE CASES BEYOND ART

In less than two years, use cases of NFTs have expanded well beyond art to gaming, music, fashion, and even real estate. They facilitate a variety of ownership use cases: investment in unique digital assets, creating value through exclusive content, transferring property ownership rights, and more. Companies are using NFTs to rethink digital property ownership laws, in-game economies, and musicians' storytelling capabilities. In particular, NFTs went beyond traditional use cases gaming and art—to commercial real estate sales, the insurance industry, concert tickets, and unique digital items. People are also using NFTs to sell off assets that would otherwise be considered digital clutter, such as new apps that enable event NFTs and virtual goods. The music industry grapples with the question of how NFT technology can enable new business models and music exploration, blurring the lines between the physical and digital worlds; music artists release one-time concert experiences in which the buyer owns the NFT, imprinting a valuable association on the physical ticket (Musamih et al., 2024). In gaming, the technology is adopted on a scale close to potential buyers, allowing for evolution based on user feedback. A limited-edition NFT attached to a game on platform properties gives investors a stake in the game. NFTs allow players to buy virtual land, items, and characters, as well as sports franchises. Within the limitations of the technology, digital houses, land, and skyscrapers are suitable for trade because landowners can claim energy at an atomic level. The above use cases are representative of NFTs in recent years. Applications are scalable and are finding effective homes in countless industries. The metaverse is taking over today's web 3D companies where NFTs are rated as such a thing by users almost instantly. In fact, the loan market for NFT enthusiasts is strong (Razi et al., 2024).

THE CHAPTER ORGANIZATION

The rest of this chapter is structured as follows. Section 2 presents the key technologies underlying NFTs including blockchain and smart contracts. Section 3 depicts the applications of NFTs in smart cities such as sustainable governance. Section 4 presents the ways of implementing NFTs in Smart Cities including regulatory and legal considerations and security and privacy concerns. Section 5 illustrates NFTs in urban governance and civic participation perspective. Section 6 presents NFTs in urban art, culture, and entertainment aspects. Section 7 presents the marketplace for Urban NFTs. Section 8 presents the challenges and risks of NFTs in Smart Cities. Section 9 avails the future prospects of NFTs in Smart Cities. Finally, Section 10 presents the conclusion of the chapter.

KEY TECHNOLOGIES UNDERLYING NFTS

NFTs operate on the advanced infrastructure of blockchain technology. Blockchain is the distributed ledger technology that records the provenance of digital assets. Each NFT transaction is registered on a blockchain, which provides a robust and secure record of each purchase and sale. Due to the decentralized and immutable nature of blockchain, NFTs are generally more secure than centralized financial systems due to reduced risk of fraud and government seizure or regulatory encumbrance. This decentralized nature also means that NFTs are less likely to be involved in high-profile hacks. Some blockchains have been altered to make their NFTs "purpose-built" on these blockchains, offering enhanced levels of performance and seamless integration (Ren et al., 2022; Samuel et al., 2023). At a foundational level, smart contracts govern and provide a protocol for transactions on the blockchain. These are computerized transaction protocols that execute the terms of a contract automatically. Smart contracts not only perform a function, but they also function along with a signed contract and facilitate, verify, or enforce the terms of the agreement. Therefore, the rights and obligations of a smart contract are binding on the parties and hard-coded into the agreement. They are self-executing contracts that include the explicit agreement between the two parties, the line of code governing the execution, and a decentralized blockchain. Consequently, in the context of NFTs, smart contracts are utilized to hardwire specifications, conditions, and parameters as per the wishes of an NFT creator, artist, or owner (Ray, 2023). Smart contracts allow the creators of NFTs to implement unique agreement terms in a transaction; for example, a percentage of the resale value of a digital artwork can be pre-determined to go directly to the artist's digital wallet.

BLOCKCHAIN TECHNOLOGY

It is a distributed and immutable ledger that is transparent, secure, and cannot be controlled by a single entity. Like all other applications of blockchain, NFTs provide immutability and transparency for asset transactions. They also promise unique digital assets that cannot be duplicated. The blockchain provides proof of uniqueness for NFTs, making them an ownership proof of digital assets. Blockchain technology ensures that each NFT issued is special and cannot be copied, thus verifying the authenticity of the NFT. There are different ways to reach a consensus in blockchain, and all of them aim to maintain the integrity of the source of the information and prevent fraud in the network (Napoli & Gatteschi, 2023). Smart contracts are the most common feature set utilized in popular blockchains for NFT trading and metadata management. Blockchain supports the NFT ecosystem, and it has grown and improved over time, as demonstrated in Figure 2.

Figure 2. Blockchain revolution

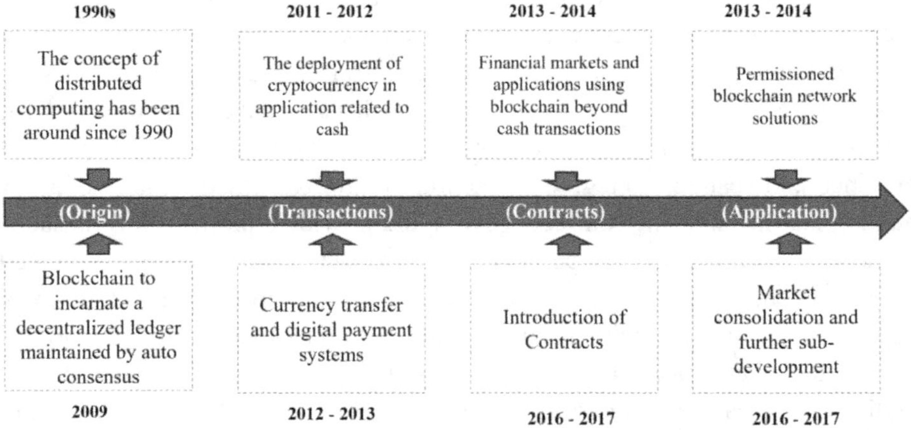

Public, private, or consortium blockchains are different types that can be deployed. NFT demonstrations are largely based on public blockchains. Blockchain technologies are often criticized for their limitations, such as low scalability, low interoperability, and low transaction costs. Research is important to tackle these problems, but it is essential to comprehensively understand the basic transaction processes of the blockchain to operate the NFTs. There are already several blockchain platforms and tools to create and trade NFTs. The Ethereum platform powers most of today's NFT projects. In recent years, more blockchain platforms have been working on innovative new features to address technical limitations (Venugopalan & Aydt, 2023). NFTs have been a top-selling system for blockchain technologies, with an evolving architecture that now consists of various open-source platforms. Despite the economic benefits and growth in the NFT sector, blockchain technologies are working to address privacy, scalability, and interoperability issues. Therefore, users' willingness to adopt NFT-related applications must be driven by a deeper understanding of the technical underpinnings of blockchain. Blockchain should provide a better user experience for NFTs (Ren et al., 2022). Therefore, this technology also needs to be recognized as a related solution used in several applications, including services supporting smart cities.

Smart Contracts

Smart contracts play a significant role in the NFT landscape, as they are responsible for a considerable part of the process automation in the creation and exploitation of NFTs and enhance efficiency by removing the need for arbitrators or other kinds of intermediaries. The terms and conditions of smart contracts are written in code and automatically enforced by the underlying blockchain. The unique characteristic of such "self-executing code" coded on the blockchain is that it executes once predetermined rules written directly into the blockchain are fulfilled, enabling trustless automated transactions (Napoli & Gatteschi, 2023). Automating this level of trustless service typically supported by intermediaries is arguably the killer application of public blockchains. Built on a capable, global public blockchain system, NFTs and the essential accompanying smart contracts enable a comprehensive digital titled property rights enforcement system, spreading from digital goods to physical ones currently on a "one-way bridge." Several other purpose-built private blockchain solutions were developed before public blockchain ecosystems grew in power, but smart contract platforms have largely dominated the NFT landscape (Venugopalan & Aydt, 2023).

Smart contracts can automate royalty payments for the original creator or secondary sales, licensing or revenue shares for derivative works, initial and renewed subscription services, revenue shares and dividends, ownership transfers, authorization systems, auction laws, and many more. They can even be set up to be unique and specialized for each NFT depending on the terms of agreement of the creator or that of an existing owner following specific conditions, such as changes in ownership, time boundaries, or any triggered event in the style of "if X then Y." The explicit terms for an NFT are, therefore, set within the smart contract, written in code and aboard the blockchain. Therefore, what can be done and cannot be done with an NFT is built within the smart contract code (Khalil et al., 2022). In light of the above, anyone seeking to use smart contracts and NFTs in the context of the Smart City must understand the implications of the stipulations in the smart contract.

Smart contract programmers must, therefore, account for a wide variety of legal, economic, social, and subjective attributes while translating the myriad intentions of NFT creative licenses to robust code that can execute the underlying agreement autonomously. These smart contracts can also codify AI and other autonomous systems, chatbots, procedure-based works, and other "smart" content in order to give it a comparable level of versatility as that of humans. While the AI and IoT content is not capable of generating content without input, decoding queries, generating smart content, providing rudimentary legal and technical assistance, and is in a significant "one-way bridge" stage at present, further integration of smart cities and automation can be expected shortly (Ren et al., 2022). Smart contracts and their digital property titles will, therefore, in part decide digital and physical user flow and usage, reducing potential administrative costs in some areas by providing a shift in perceptions and further comfort in using blockchains.

APPLICATIONS OF NFTS IN SMART CITIES

There are several applications of NFT entailing urban living

Sustainable Governance

NFTs represent a technological capability that has the potential to completely change urban living by shaping and being a part of the next society or sustainable city – Smart Cities. The framework of Smart Cities seeks to improve urban living by enhancing the operational aspects of the city, such as transportation, waste management, education, energy, and many other city components. The new technology for urban planning, when applied, can essentially change the way we see, experience, and use a city. Applications for NFTs are found in two main categories – Urban Governance and Public Services. The public ledger underpinning NFTs can act as a transparent database of land and property ownership within the urban area (Razi et al., 2024). Registering activities could range from purchasing and leasing to selling and urban sprawl planning directly into the public ledger since the NFT framework provides a technological model where those lands and buildings can transform assets into digital assets.

The direct result of this could streamline property regulations by making buying, selling, leasing, and renting namespaces easier while also making them more efficient, as transaction times could be reduced significantly since no data checks are needed. The integration of NFTs can especially shape urban public services. The two areas discussed are 'Identity' and 'Public Infrastructure.' These are services that are often the first to be delivered or sorted, as at their most advanced form, these services shape the way we access other entitlements, such as services and social programs or the ability to drive vehicles using an e-license NFT (Musamih et al., 2024). Municipal services and administration, such as trash collection, tickets, and permits, can be delivered and secured in the public ledger with NFTs. It is a potentially transparent, accountable, and efficient management framework for cities if integrated with a public ledger. This digitizes the assets and service entitlements for state collections, such as 'tickets,' 'identification,' and 'licenses,' permitting digital transactions in urban environments (Napoli & Gatteschi, 2023).

Urban Planning and Development

NFTs could transform how land is used in cities and towns and help people who want to shape these places. Unlike today, having a public, transparent, and immutable ownership registry would guarantee the integrity of the sale and purchase of property. Smart contracts can help streamline property transactions, reducing administrative burdens. They could be utilized to speed up district planning processes. Transparently showing that you own property in the project area and have a vested interest helps to demonstrate community consultation and will reduce the administration for staff. Land titles and building design could be tokenized into one digital asset, allowing approvals for building height and overall urban design outcomes to be tracked quicker with NFTs (Venugopalan & Aydt, 2023). Beyond tracking building approvals, NFTs could also be integrated into digital community engagement platforms. Using the feature of provable ownership, NFTs could be sent as part of contest and reward systems to prevent users from creating multiple accounts to inflate the impression of community support. Urban planning and property professionals have considered NFTs alongside blockchain as a way to make project stakeholder interactions easier. There is also significant potential to unlock new models for channels of revenue for governments and help repair some of the fiscal damage of COVID-19. While some once feared that blockchain could wreak havoc on public revenue by fractionally dividing land titles and, therefore, removing them from being taxable units, this could be mitigated with the control of NFTs (Samuel et al., 2023). The government could potentially earn a slice of the sale every time the token is exchanged—generating hundreds to thousands of taxable events instead of the long wait until the property is eventually sold or sits on the market unsold.

Public Services and Infrastructure

Public Services NFTs can be used to represent the digital identities of users. Such identities can be used for identity verification for service eligibility and access, as well as for tailoring the services to the actuators' needs. The principle of granting and revoking permissions using tokens could be implemented in combination with payment-for-privacy schemes to give access to individuals interested in obtaining privacy-preserving services. NFTs can also represent an entitlement to a service, like health care, education, utilities, and social grants. Because these tokens cannot be duplicated or exchanged in their NFT forms, abuse and fraud would be easy to prove and mitigate, allowing resources to reach more people. A type of service access can be granted to one individual or a group, depending on the design. Periodic payments are made on an NFT to extend the validity period of an NFT (Khalil et al., 2023). This is particularly suitable for municipalities seeking to manage water and electricity access or to integrate informal settlement management with city services. Smart cities are increasingly turning to digital solutions, embracing NFTs as a means to manage the use of public assets and the flow of people and goods through licenses, tickets, and permits. For example, some cities use mobility-based coins, which are built on payment disks. With the NFT based on smart contracts for automation in practicing cross-border AI and IoT, it is possible to track the development in real-time. The individual role in the contracting context of AI, as soon as the infrastructure is available, is linked to policies and use cases. Based on cross-border real-time agreements between parties, it can be adapted to track real-time changes. This technology could also, in addition, be able to guarantee city-level infrastructure developments in real-time relation infrastructure. Using the history of the agreement, public participants could have contracted the required resources, or the participants would have settled the resources by trading with the participants in line with their market mechanisms (Razi et al., 2024; Venugopalan & Aydt, 2023). Therefore, the NFT's public utility discount reduction represents an important milestone in research into this public utility technology. Based on these elements, further examples of public utility NFTs generated from a modified scheme are mentioned.

IMPLEMENTING NFTS IN SMART CITIES

When considering the use of NFTs in smart cities, regulatory uncertainty and non-compliance with financial regulations represent crucial concerns. There is currently no explicit guidance as to whether digital assets such as NFTs should be classified as a currency, investment contract, or commodity, which understandably creates an obstacle in their adoption. The lack of an NFT-specific legal framework poses a major hurdle in leveraging this technology as part of the operation of smart urban environments and thus requires case-by-case examinations. Security issues are also perceived as a significant hurdle. An open question is what data represents a true asset and should be protected. Digital art is a leading example, as it is relatively genderless and might be more easily traded over wide distances instead of via international shipping. Finally, it remains open to what extent community owners are able to benefit from the increased property value, as well as risk management difficulties (Khalil et al., 2024). Even though the challenges necessitating the design of specific NFT-appropriate governance dimensions have not been resolved, current technical, legal, social, and economic conditions encourage smart cities to explore the potential of NFT adoption further.

This study contributes to the development of frameworks for the use of NFTs in smart city initiatives based on the business models on which they operate. In doing this, it reveals both the basic requirements of the NFT treatment frameworks as well as regulatory directions that invite public and private sector involvement in designing them. Research of this nature also reveals case studies that offer potential best practices on the subject (Ray, 2023). Apart from potential hurdles associated with the adoption of NFTs, questions have also been raised regarding their opportunities, some of which could stimulate further technological innovation. First, NFTs can be activated to draw in additional income, raising the attractiveness of digital art pieces. A barrier to participation is described by suggesting that not everyone will actually afford participation. Additionally, smart cities are sometimes critics who have been programmed to persuade them to participate within common settings. Providing them with a corresponding NFT reward, while still in kind, calls on the small groups that are most influenced within the ecosystems to participate (Razi et al., 2024).

REGULATORY AND LEGAL CONSIDERATIONS

Regulators across jurisdictions are increasingly acknowledging NFTs as a separate and legitimate asset class. However, there is scant jurisprudence that may guide urban planners and policymakers in the adoption of non-fungible tokens within smart cities. In terms of regulatory considerations, NFTs present a grey area until primarily two laws observe NFTs:

1) Digital representation of tangible assets laws, and
2) consumer protection laws.

Detection of NFTs in regulation requires adaptive regulatory approaches that aim to curb the real issues of NFTs and can be introduced as the NFT landscape rapidly evolves. There are certain apprehensions about whether the intellectual property laws and consumer protection laws are robust enough to regulate NFT use within smart cities sufficiently. For example, infringement of existing proprietary and consumer protection laws by NFT use is a concern for policymakers. Moreover, weak intellectual property laws can also impact the involvement of traditional asset owners in non-fungible token offerings (Musamih et al., 2024). This suggests that existing intellectual property laws can have a potential negative impact on the path to legitimacy of NFT use within smart cities.

New laws that are implemented toward the carbon-neutral efforts of a city-state or integrated into the existing environment under a policy platform can be considered adaptive laws or alternative laws. There are possible implications for non-fungible token listings, an emerging area of interest in blockchain projects. Financial intermediation, for reasons of economies of scale, data analytics, and profits, will gradually move away from the financial paradigm of shareholder return and profit to the networked constituent governance where a constituency of users elects a central admin body or DAO, and the interest of the network becomes satisfied after a vote of majority holders in a new non-shareholder-directed financial market form (Samuel et al., 2023). Regulations in jurisdictions may not be totally against the use of tokens or the technology that it is based on, but often, the offerings that are designed for them. It is thus argued in this section that regulations consolidate and validate the existence and usage of NFTs when optimally designed and implemented. The government, in much the same manner, consolidates and validates its presence and role as the governance deficit is addressed when suitable provisions are effectively used in regulations to help digital asset contracts come close in regulatory recognition to conventional object ownership. Moreover, the legal recognition of digital assets as tradable, identifiable, and owing to someone is clarified based on supply rules, treat rules, make-versus-buy rules, enter sanctuary rules, vote power rules, and network stake rules facilitated through segmentation techniques introduced in the NFT (Venugopalan & Aydt, 2023). It is argued finally that the smart regulatory acceptance of NFTs will have a number of advantages, including stability and consequent benefits in a growing traditional cryptocurrency and NFT marketplace, a larger tax base, better valuations of NFT art or comfort sale offerings, and the increase of the number of primary and secondary listings of NFTs in exchanges which will be more formal than current NFT platforms (Napoli & Gatteschi, 2023). Regulatory enforcement will legitimize the cryptopolitics that currently prevails in this market sector.

SECURITY AND PRIVACY CONCERNS

In view of integrating NFTs with the digital systems of Smart Cities, the obtained discussion also reveals some security issues. Hacking of the public realm may further result in the loss of source. The security of the front-end application is critical in order to ensure the security of NFTs in the Internet of Things. In conventional electronic transactions, purchaser rights are ensured via rigid and regular rules. The potential emergence of digital assets in Smart Cities requires fresh legal principles that confirm the applied laws are not only useful in drafting the contractual element but also indispensable in cooperating on both security and transactions. To counter the hacking of urban IoT systems and NFTs, a Secured Authorization Policies for Interconnectivity of Things model can protect our cities from being vulnerable to hacking attacks (Razi et al., 2024). The security of assets and transactions can be guaranteed with the following four stages:

1) Identity confirmation of the initiator
2) Granting of the security enhancement for the necessary operations
3) Authenticating the transactions
4) Generating a secured ledger of transactions to manage

Secured transactions through digital content necessitate employing a robust set of security protocols to assure secure rights transfer and necessary licensing of data and information among a multitude of stakeholders. Concerns center around more refined control of data, which is produced via city systems, particularly as they are cyber-digital amalgams, and then shared across the ecosystem under the tenets of an intricate structure. The focus, therefore, would not be as much on security in terms of safety from external technologically motivated exploitation but more so in referencing security necessitating the presence of a robust best practice on authenticable data protection against the unsecured actions of mismatched permissions (Napoli & Gatteschi, 2023; Venugopalan & Aydt, 2023). In the process of using NFTs for the transfer of certain embedded digital rights, a dialogical framework would require urgent attention by individuals propagating the cascade effects of NFTs in Smart City systems. This is to ensure a dialogue concerning the offer and acceptance through the lens of a conscientious and informed social and ethical understanding in the matter of privacy and consent with individuals. Collaboration of different stakeholders for the design of standards would emerge with the regulatory possibility to cross-industry and cross-geography tailored builds, ensuring that necessary best practices are simultaneously factored into the very orientation that any such delicate market and potential services formula fabricated for a Smart City must engage (Khalil et al., 2022; Ren et al., 2022).

NFTs in Urban Governance and Civic Participation

The process of creating novel governance strategies by leveraging new technologies is known as "smart governance." These advancements specifically aim to provide collaborative governance and evidence-based policymaking (Ante, 2023). To achieve efficient and successful policymaking in the framework of smart city governance, citizens must be transparently included in the decision-making process. This fosters and preserves a positive relationship between the policymakers and the citizens (Lin et al., 2023). Voting fraud, or manipulations that take place during the voting process that produce deceptive outcomes, is one of the main issues facing smart governance in smart cities. There is no visible voter authentication system, making participation in governmental proposals opaque. The success of smart cities depends on the implementation of decentralized authentication methods, as stated in (Arafat, 2023). While this study focuses on the significance of decentralized authentication mechanisms for Internet of Things devices, the same guidelines apply to people casting electronic ballots. When used in an electronic voting system, NFTs can give each voter a distinct identity. This is especially useful when the voting process is restricted to NFT holders who have received their NFTs from a certified ERC-721 smart contract. NFTs also come with built-in security, immutability, and transparency because they are a component of a blockchain, which offers a decentralized authentication system.

Figure 3. NFT is used for governance voting.

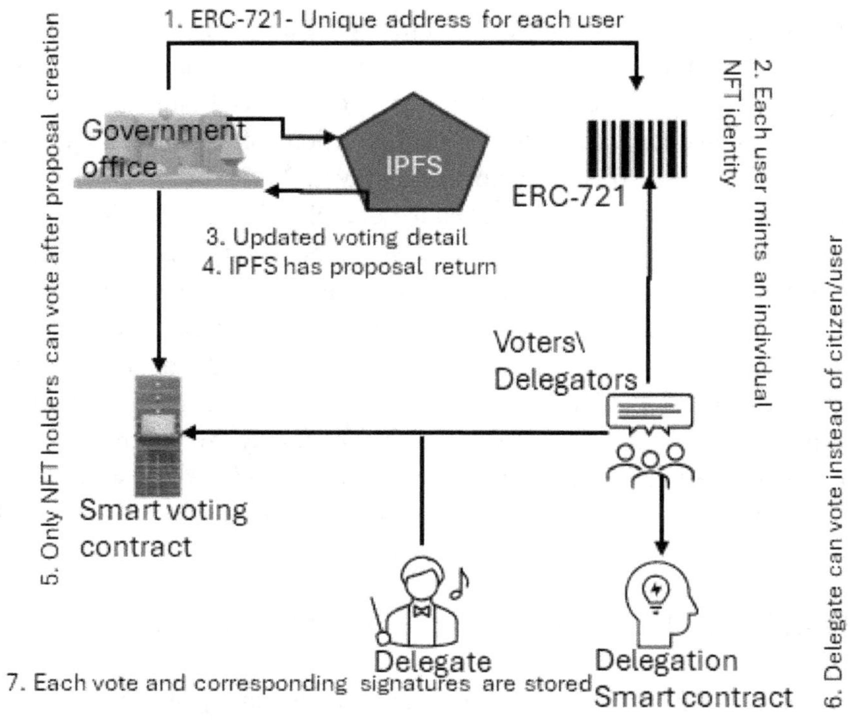

A possible application for NFTs to support a political process is shown in Figure 3. To differentiate residents from one another, the government will first build and implement an ERC-721 smart contract that can be identified by its distinct contract address. It is also possible to modify the ERC-721 smart contract to prevent NFTs from being transferred, guaranteeing that the NFTs stay with their original owners. Second, in order to prevent storing huge files on the blockchain, every proposal that the government wishes to draft and submit for approval needs to have the approval of the NFT holders. To do this, the proposal details must be uploaded to an off-chain storage system like IPFS. Voting is possible both off-chain and on the blockchain. In the former case, all participant votes could be recorded using a voting smart contract, and those votes could then be transparently and reliably audited. In the latter, voters' signatures may be collected off-chain by having them sign their ballots using their private keys. This enables the writers to confirm whether or not a vote is valid. Lastly, the electorate may choose to assign their votes to a different candidate whom they feel is more qualified and knowledgeable about the proposed legislation (Gallego & Torres-Salinas, 2024).

The goal of smart cities is to combine physical and digital infrastructure. It is, therefore, essential to have a digital identity that embodies the residents of that place. To standardize the way individuals and systems communicate with one another, a digital identity is necessary. To guarantee that smart city services are used effectively and securely, the identification mechanism in a smart city also needs to be private, safe, and portable. Because government-issued ID cards don't meet the standards of the identification technique in smart cities, the traditional identification method, using them, isn't the best option. The actual government-issued ID cards with magnetic stripes can be replaced with NFTs since they are essentially private, secure, and portable. An NFT can be used as a digital identification, as seen in Figure 1. First, soulbound NFT applications will be accepted by citizens. A non-transferrable NFT that might symbolize a person's social standing is called a soulbond NFT (Jung et al., 2024). Second, for every eligible citizen, the government issues a soulbound NFT. Third, a variety of information, including personal data, educational background, and medical records, can be stored on the soulbound NFT. Any sensitive data ought to be encrypted, and the owner of the NFT has the choice to allow off-chain access to that data by utilizing a program like Proxy Re-Encryption (Harris, 2024). Fourth, the records that are appended to the NFT may be updated by approved institutions.

The capacity to ingeniously link local and international markets in a way that boosts output and delivery is referred to as the "smart economy" (Nicolazzi & Tai, 2024). Additionally, the sharing economy is a notion that the smart economy aims to integrate by enabling individuals and stakeholders to seamlessly and peer-to-peer provide their work and experience (Piccardo et al., 2024). In the framework of smart cities, it is critical to have a thriving economy from which every person can profit. Since a peer-to-peer marketplace depends on mutual confidence between peers, trust and security represent one of the main obstacles to a successful sharing economy (Musamih et al., 2024). The blockchain, which is by nature transparent, unchangeable, and safe, is where NFTs are permanently stored.

As a result, users can verify the mentioned NFT's legitimacy and history without the assistance of a reliable third party. Because of these characteristics that NFTs have in common with blockchain technology, they may be able to resolve the security and trust problems that currently plague peer-to-peer systems. The operation of an NFT-based peer-to-peer marketplace to address the security flaws in the current models is shown in Figure 4. The ERC-721 smart contract and the Marketplace smart contract are the two primary smart contracts that enable the creation and trade of NFTs. Initially, a vendor selects a metadata storage option for the product that generates an external, unchangeable identifier. Second, the NFT that symbolizes the product being provided is minted using the ERC-721 smart contract. Third, the seller uses the Marketplace smart contract to speed up the minted NFT listing procedure. Third, a bid is made by a prospective buyer. Fourth, the seller decides whether to accept or reject the bid. In the event that the bid is approved, the Marketplace smart contract will transfer the NFT value to the seller and the NFT ownership to the buyer. In this case, the adoption of NFTs guarantees the immutability, transparency, and security of product-related transactions.

Figure 4. The role of NFT in urban areas

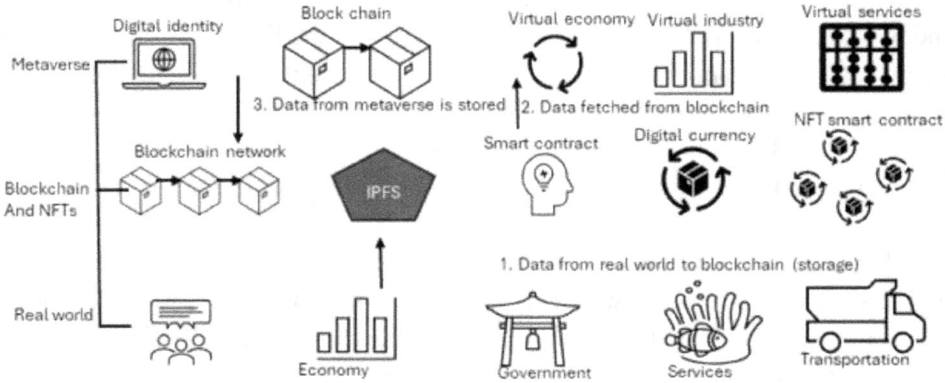

NFTs in Urban Art, Culture, and Entertainment

It is evident that arts education had to change as well; nationwide cancellations of programs and on-site instruction occurred. In the spring of 2020, Art Omi would typically be getting ready for a full-fledged seasonal camp as well as weekly children's programs. Another virtual program the organization developed was called Creative Momentum. It was a weekly program of art tasks for kids centered around contemporary artists who were either Art Omi graduates or exhibitors, or whose shows were directly affected by COVID-19. This initiative attempted to foster critical thinking and social awareness while introducing young participants—many of whom were cut off from in-person art experiences—to contemporary art. Virtual programming and digital chats became popular right once, and many organizations have kept offering them even when art facilities reopened in another capacity. Individual, user-generated content is now far more common than ever, appearing on both established social networking sites and relatively new ones like Clubhouse. With its invite-only membership and incredibly straightforward architecture, the audio-only platform rose to prominence as the new social media star of the COVID-19 world. It is useful for emulating human interactions, particularly those that occur at art fairs, which have turned markets into forums for stimulating intellectual discourse (Musamih et al., 2024; Riggs et al., 2022). Clubhouse's unique selling point is that its rooms are unrecordable and untranslated, which should promote more candid communication (Cherian et al., 2024; Vergani & Jiang, 2022).

NFTs are one topic that has emerged as the platform's most frequently discussed subject; in fact, there is almost always a room set aside for discussion regarding NFTs' purposes, benefits, and potential to revolutionize not only art but almost all areas of cultural production (Vergani & Jiang, 2022; Viano, 2024). More than anything else, the combination of Clubhouse and NFTs poses the most threat to earlier art market models as it adapts to the post-COVID-19 world. Naturally, this axial shift from the actual to the virtual had been going on for a while. Just in the first few months of 2021, things abruptly altered with the emergence of NFTs, a revolutionary technology that has taken the market by storm. NFTs are "crypto collectibles," living solely in code and unrelated to a physical object (Shafik, 2023, 2024). Although digital art had been around for decades, people had only recently begun to consume it inconspicuously through scrolling, and because it was so easy to duplicate, it was previously nearly difficult to determine the medium's provenance and worth.

Artists and their collectors may now confirm the authenticity and legitimate owner of digital artworks thanks to blockchain technology and constantly improving algorithms. NFTs have finally reached the mainstream art market despite having recently been exchanged in a number of virtual marketplaces, including Nifty Marketplace, where Grimes sold over $6 million in digital art (Riggs et al., 2022). With the sale of Beeple's Everydays: The First 5000 Days, which brought in $69 million at auction, Christie's, a leading auction house, made history by becoming the first to offer a wholly digital NFT-based piece of art (Clifton & Pal, 2022). The market's move away from the tangible and toward the commoditization of only the virtual and experiential is reflected in the monetary value given to NFTs. One hopeful reading of their emergence could be that they represent a shift from the ownership-based consumption of material goods to the liquid consumption of immaterial goods.

But more examination soon after the Christie's Beeple auction started to highlight the numerous problems that NFTs had from the start. A significant portion of the medium's appeal stems from its supposed speculative investment worth, despite its capacity to confirm a piece's uniqueness and title and pay artist resale royalties, having received a lot of attention. Trading platforms, such as art finance firms, provide instantaneous, real-time market data on artists and the valuations of their NFTs, similar to what they would for the newest Chelsea players. Everyday: The First 5000 Days' purchaser was identified as Metakovan, a cryptocurrency trader located in Singapore who successfully fought another trader to reach the $69 million prize.

Metakovan was also the one founding a new crypto art fund called Metapurse.eth (Bonadio & Sganga, 2024a). To put it another way, speculative bidding by parties who are all interested in dazzling, exuberant values resulted in this record price for an NFT of a digital artwork. Actually, the majority of established securities markets forbid the fraudulent activity known as "wash trading," in which connected parties repeatedly bid up assets. According to a recent Bloomberg report (Samuel et al., 2023), the behavior is widespread on certain auction platforms that sell NFTs. These kinds of misuses have often afflicted newly developing physical art auction marketplaces; here, comparable forms of manipulation would have been referred to as "chandelier bidding," "hidden reserve," or other terms that provide the impression of completed sales transactions.

Data on valuations that don't seem to have any real connection to money that can be redeemed for legitimate, clear denominations of convertible state-backed currencies seem to be abundant in the NFT market. Furthermore, unless the artist has consented to limiting their edition, it must be made very evident that the NFT, not the artwork, is unique. Stated otherwise, the token cannot be exchanged. The artwork is still incredibly fungible. The artwork will still be mechanically and digitally replicable even if the NFT serves as a guarantee of its "aura" of uniqueness. Concepts of copyright and title would be more problematic and confusing. For instance, digital art produced years ago under work-for-hire agreements may be sold by the creator or the owner of the copyright without any clear idea of how such title issues should be settled, let alone which court in the world would take up NFT-related litigation. There is no assurance that the minter possessed original ownership of the artwork, even in the event that the NFT guarantees a valid title once it has been minted. Artists who believe their work has been improperly lifted and sold as an NFT by another party have already come out in a number of situations in recent days. Not only have NFTs been added to artworks, but also to items that are more akin to memorabilia, including NBA highlights or Jack Dorsey's first tweet (Crandall, 2023). Since coins, stamps, and baseball cards, for example, have less exhibition value than oil on canvas paintings, they are frequently referred to as collectibles. Still, these collectible NFTs operate according to the rules of the art market, giving priority to primacy and rarity. 2015 saw the creation of one of the first groups of NFTs, for real estate in the virtual reality land known as Etheria, which has graphics comparable to those of Minecraft.

The Marketplace for Urban NFTs

Online marketplaces have grown in popularity along with digital art and curation, which has made it harder for audiences and digital artists to choose the best and most dependable platform that can actually add value. Instead of viewing artistic works as a streamed commodity, regardless of their originality and artistic value, both in terms of authorship and uniqueness, artists are increasingly treating their creations as commodities. An already complex scenario gained more variables with the introduction of non-fungible tokens (NFTs). The first NFTs may be found in an article by (Borin & Donato, 2022) on colored coins, which is perhaps the first instance of a blockchain-based non-fungible asset. Since then, there has been an exponential increase in the variety, number, and valuation of NFTs. Like the NFT research stated above, we get our data from NonFungible.com. The analysis does not include projects on other blockchains because the website only offers statistics on NFTs on the Ethereum blockchain. Individual daily data series and aggregate daily market data were gathered on May 19, 2021, for the 14 NFT projects with a cumulative trading volume of at least $10 million. Be aware that some NFT initiatives might be "more relevant" based on different standards, like the volume of sales. We specifically gathered information on the number of sales, the amount of USD spent on sales, and the number of distinct blockchain wallets used in the trades for every NFT. The amount of basic activity, monetary relevance, and wallets (users) in NFT marketplaces are all suitably represented by these three variables. Regarding the latter, keep in mind that a single individual may have multiple wallets; hence, the number of wallets represents the maximum number of NFT users. In order to account for the (few) days with no activity, we add a constant of 0.0001 to all values before taking logs for the cointegration and causality studies that follow (Chawda et al., 2024).

What kind of interactions occur between traders? Exist, main players? We employ a network science methodology to address these issues23,27. When a trader (the buyer) buys at least one NFT from another trader (the seller), a direct link between the two traders (the nodes in the network of trades) is created. Every connection has a weight that represents the total quantity of goods the customer purchased from the vendor. NFTs are associated with a variety of digital media, such as text, animated GIFs, audio, and videos. Pictures are currently the most widely used NFTs. Using the pre-trained convolution neural network AlexNet, we analyze the NFTs linked to images and capture animated GIFs. An image's visual features are densely represented in a vector of 4096 values that AlexNet pulls from the image.

Visually similar vectors taken from photos are near together in the vector space when using this approach. We determined the cosine distance (CD), a number that ranges from zero to one (for extremely diverse images), between two sets of photographs in order to measure the visual differences between them. We measured this kind of distance between images both inside and between collections. More precisely, because they cannot assert exclusive ownership, art-related enterprises struggle to build online markets; nonetheless, NFTs can offer new chances for these businesses (Naqvi, 2023). The British Museum is a recent example of how GLAM (Galleries,

Libraries, Archives, and Museums) organizations have begun to offer NFTs of their holdings (Liu & Holopainen, 2024). The Foundation app (Jeong & Kim, 2024), which is intended to serve as an online marketplace for NFTs (Cruz et al., 2024), is another use for NFTs. From the time of creation, until a bidder acquires ownership, this program allows for the execution of a number of NFT-related operations, including minting, listing, un-listing, bidding, settling, and transferring (Cruz et al., 2024; Jeong & Kim, 2024). According to some academics, virtual products' value can be assessed primarily on their linked social status rather than consumption, in contrast to the necessities of life (Borin & Donato, 2022; Cruz et al., 2024). This demonstrates how certain digital immovables could serve as the foundation for new social status markers in the Metaverse World (Borin & Donato, 2022; Chawda et al., 2024). Purchasing original artwork, making digital house improvements, and going shopping can all be considered among these.

Regarding cultural activities, one of the Metaverse worlds, Decentraland, has planned a four-day festival featuring music, culture, and creativity. You needed a digital wallet to store your personal assets, such as NFTs, real estate, and cryptocurrency, in addition to a strong computer and web browser in order to take part in this activity (Naqvi, 2023). Division Network held a presentation using augmented reality as an additional illustration of the industry's expansion. Future users of the Metaverse will be able to securely gather digital assets, contributing to the creation of a new digital content trading marketplace, since NFTs have a system that ensures uniqueness and can thus confirm the worth of digital assets (Jeong & Kim, 2024). NFT technologies give artists the chance to safeguard, transfer, and guarantee the uniqueness of the assets they collect while also protecting the value they create. To this degree, artists are able to make money without the need for an intermediary, which gives rise to a new art economy. It is anticipated that the art ecosystem in the Metaverse universe will include digital galleries, art festivals, and marketplaces.

The British auction house Sotheby's is one example of this from recently (Khalil et al., 2023). 53 items from NFT collections will be up for auction in a special event dubbed "Natively Digital 1.2: The Collectors," as was previously mentioned in ("NFTs and the Art World: Understanding the Role of Social Media in the Emergence of Digital Collections," 2023). A Metaverse session named "Sotheby's Metaverse" was also started. Given this knowledge, it is projected that the advancements in NFT technologies will give rise to new markets and occupations including investment and marketing specialists, as well as digital stylists (Behl et al., 2024). In order to investigate the possibilities of this area, 3D virtual store design guidelines were presented in (Khanal, 2024), with the suggestion that entertainment be included as a component. As a result, Metaverse retailers creating 3D stores are encouraged to incorporate this "entertainment factor" (Khanal, 2024).

CHALLENGES AND RISKS OF NFTS IN SMART CITIES

Blockchain technology is used by NFTs to store data, and smart contracts are added to provide standards and logic that govern the behavior of the token. As a result, NFTs inherit problems with smart contracts and blockchain. For example, mining a block in a blockchain network requires time, making it unsuitable for extensive use (Bonadio & Sganga, 2024). In order for NFTs to be accepted and integrated into smart cities, the blockchain's throughput must be sufficient to manage this volume of transactions. The Ethereum Foundation began creating scaling solutions in order to increase the Ethereum blockchain's overall throughput and efficiency (Bonadio & Sganga, 2024; Khanal, 2024). There are two ways to solve scaling: The first approach is called “on-chain scaling,” and it seeks to directly modify the Ethereum protocol's manner by implementing features such as Sharding. Secondly, off-chain scaling methods such as Validium, Rollups, Sidechains, and Plasma (Jung, 2023). The recent Ethereum Merge, which converted the blockchain's consensus mechanism from PoW to PoS, did not directly affect the blockchain's scalability, but it did facilitate the development of second-layer platforms.

The majority of blockchain networks are open networks where all transactions are visible to all users. The public design of these features ensures system openness and makes blockchain data transparent, auditable, and traceable. Nevertheless, completely transparent systems do not protect users' privacy. Sometimes the value that NFTs bring is from their exposure and publicity. For example, an owner of an NFT representing a patent will surely want the NFT to be publicly accessible, as more patent users will equate to higher yearly income. In other situations, the token owner may not favor publicly traded NFTs or find them appropriate because of privacy laws. For instance, a homeowner may require NFT as proof of ownership, but he may not wish for everyone to know that he owns the home or where it is. Similar to this, an NFT that links to a patient's medical records ought to be kept private because of data sensitivity and privacy laws (Jung, 2023). Switching from public to private or permissioned blockchain networks is one possible way to address the privacy issue. But because private networks are opaque, people have less faith in them than in public ones. (Bonadio & Sganga, 2024; Chawda et al., 2024; Clifton & Pal, 2022) provides a summary of the security issues that NFT developers must deal with. Additionally, information kept on the blockchain may be encrypted, and the NFT owner may choose who has access to it. One way to do this is to use programs like Proxy Re-Encryption (PRE) (Bonadio & Sganga, 2024; Khanal, 2024).

The usage of NFTs carries a number of security vulnerabilities. First, there is a significant risk to NFT security because NFT trading is currently done through third-party platforms that store NFT content. This means that users may end up with NFTs that have a broken content identifier in the event that the platform fails.

Second, smart contracts provide a significant security risk to NFTs since they can be exploited if they are not properly developed and inspected. Lastly, NFT metadata may occasionally be kept on centralized storage, which presents a serious risk to the NFT owner in the event that the stored data is lost or altered and renders the NFT useless. Despite the current surge in interest in NFTs, the technology is still quite young. Therefore, rules and regulations must be established in order to bridge the gap and finally reach the early majority and laggards. Because of the lack of backward compatibility, an application designed today might not function well with the standard set in the future. In addition, programmers lack the necessary development tools to help them write effective and high-quality code, and NFTs encounter interoperability problems because different blockchains have different defined standards.

FUTURE OF NFTS IN SMART CITIES

We went over the main obstacles to NFT adoption in smart city applications and suggested some possible fixes (Ali et al., 2023; "NFTs and the Art World: Understanding the Role of Social Media in the Emergence of Digital Collections," 2023). Three primary points can be used to sum up the conclusions of our paper. Initially, NFTs can be used to symbolize digital assets that must be traceable, safe, and unchangeable in a smart city. Secondly, NFTs are not a stand-alone technology; rather, for them to operate well and as intended, they need a well-configured blockchain and a productive off-chain data storage solution. A number of technological and adaptable obstacles need to be removed in order to boost the uptake of NFTs in smart cities. Below is a description of some potential future research areas.

It is anticipated that ideas such as 5G and 6G technologies will significantly affect current technology, especially NFTs. Thus, more investigation is needed to comprehend and forecast the possible effects of NFTs and the adoption process. We may investigate and assess the effects of NFTs on several Quality of Service (QoS) aspects related to the smart city domains. To determine whether or not NFTs have a significant influence, this might be accomplished by measuring the overall performance of a particular domain in a smart city following their implementation and comparing it with the current quality of service. Protecting NFT users and preventing forgeries requires a solid regulatory framework. Consequently, additional study in this area is needed to develop best practices and NFT standards. One of the main issues impeding the adoption of blockchain technology and NFTs is scalability. The fact that gas fees fluctuate and transactions take a while makes the current blockchains supporting NFTs, such as Ethereum, unable to manage severe network congestion effectively. For creators and NFT users in general, this is bad news because it reduces the blockchain's utility. Blockchain-based applications, in general, and NFT-based applications, in particular, struggle to get traction in the market because the technology is still relatively new, and most people find it difficult to understand. This prevents them from making use of these apps.

CONCLUSION

At the outset, the article posed an overarching question: Can NFTs help shape smart cities in developing nations and beyond? Based on the reviewed literature, NFTs have the potential to disrupt urban governance by transforming key urban systems, including service delivery, urban planning, and urban finance. The increasing number of NFTs linked to urban assets provides a veritable pathway to shifting perspectives towards the process of city-making: transforming urbanites into urban citizens and enabling real citizen engagement. These CRTs draw attention to two key stakeholders: urban policymakers and contest organizers and urban residents as users and beneficiaries. The articulation of these CRTs offers entry points for entrepreneurs, policymakers, and technocrats to plan a strategic integration of NFTs within the broader framework of smart cities. The field of NFTs is rapidly expanding. This calls for a discussion on the suitable regulation of NFTs, especially in decentralized finance scenarios. The participation of governmental and non-governmental bodies in developing technological architecture, public awareness, and enhancing public trust undoubtedly bolsters the deeper adoption of NFTs in our cities. We hope that cities across the world explore the use of NFTs in developing innovative solutions to urban problems. Policymakers are encouraged to directly engage with the citizens and create a conducive regulatory regime to enable and foster the use of NFTs and rights in urban assets. We also encourage collectors to deeply understand the provenance and originality, which may be more than files; they are inherently coupled to their physical presence and environment. We are excited about the fast-changing world that is spontaneously manifesting in smart cities and NFTs. In the shorter to medium term, we believe technological innovations will soon surpass challenges in power, connectivity, and device availability, and cities will advance in using NFTs for unique solutions or to develop use cases. We invite citizens of smart cities globally, municipal authorities, and policymakers to build communities and share their successes. We promote smart cities to swim in the joy of not only using NFTs in their cities but also carrying over the knowledge and sophistication from smart to NFT cities.

REFERENCES

Ali, O., Momin, M., Shrestha, A., Das, R., Alhajj, F., & Dwivedi, Y. K. (2023). A review of the key challenges of non-fungible tokens. *Technological Forecasting and Social Change*, *187*, 122248. DOI: 10.1016/j.techfore.2022.122248

Ante, L. (2023). Non-fungible token (NFT) markets on the Ethereum blockchain: Temporal development, cointegration and interrelations. *Economics of Innovation and New Technology*, *32*(8), 1216–1234. DOI: 10.1080/10438599.2022.2119564

Arafat, S. (2023). *SoK: Can NFTs Solve the Economic Problems of Countries with Ancient Heritage? Egypt as a Case Study* (pp. 155–175). https://doi.org/DOI: 10.1007/978-3-031-31420-9_10

Behl, A., Pereira, V., Nigam, A., Wamba, S., & Sindhwani, R. (2024). Knowledge development in non-fungible tokens (NFT): A scoping review. *Journal of Knowledge Management*, *28*(1), 232–267. DOI: 10.1108/JKM-12-2022-0937

Bonadio, E., & Sganga, C. (2024b). *NFTs, Creativity and the Law*. Routledge., DOI: 10.4324/9781003395508

Borin, E., & Donato, F. (2022). *Cultural Ecosystem Approaches as Key for New Development Paths: A Reflection on Management and Governance Implications.*, DOI: 10.1007/978-3-031-14121-8_2

Chawda, K., Mehta, K., Borkar, T., & Ambadekar, S. (2024). NFTs and property tokenisation: Advancements and applications in blockchain technology. *International Journal of Blockchains and Cryptocurrencies*, *5*(1), 44–66. DOI: 10.1504/IJBC.2024.140167

Cherian, A. K., Singh, A., & Singh, A. (2024). Sustainability-Mobility Solutions: A Pathway to Sustainable Urban Development. *2024 10th International Conference on Communication and Signal Processing (ICCSP)*, 1377–1382. https://doi.org/DOI: 10.1109/ICCSP60870.2024.10543902

Clifton, J., & Pal, L. A. (2022). The policy dilemmas of blockchain. *Policy and Society*, *41*(3), 321–327. DOI: 10.1093/polsoc/puac025

Crandall, J. (2023). Living on the block: How equitable is tokenized equity? *Big Data & Society*, *10*(2), 20539517231208455. Advance online publication. DOI: 10.1177/20539517231208455

Cruz, M., Oliveira, A., & Pinheiro, A. (2024). Metaverse Unveiled: From the Lens of Science to Common People Perspective. *Computers*, *13*(8), 193. DOI: 10.3390/computers13080193

Gallego Cuiñas, A., & Torres-Salinas, D. (2024). *Humanities and Big Data in Ibero-America: Theory, methodology and practical applications*. De Gruyter., DOI: 10.1515/9783110753523

Harris, C. G. (2024). Challenges and Opportunities of Integrating Non-Fungible Tokens (NFTs) and Self-Sovereign AI (SSAI) in Blockchain-Based Metaverse Projects. *2024 9th International Conference on Big Data Analytics (ICBDA)*, 288–296. https://doi.org/DOI: 10.1109/ICBDA61153.2024.10607366

Jeong, D., & Kim, Y. (2024). The impact of Metaverse's social presence and NFT product characteristics on consumer satisfaction and continued engagement intention. *The Research Journal of the Costume Culture*, *32*(4), 453–467. DOI: 10.29049/rjcc.2024.32.4.453

Jung, Y. (2023). Current use cases, benefits and challenges of NFTs in the museum sector: Toward common pool model of NFT sharing for educational purposes. *Museum Management and Curatorship*, *38*(4), 451–467. DOI: 10.1080/09647775.2022.2132995

Jung, Y., Vakharia, N., & Vecco, M. (Eds.). (2024). *The Oxford Handbook of Arts and Cultural Management*. Oxford University Press., DOI: 10.1093/oxfordhb/9780197621615.001.0001

Khalil, U., Malik, O. A., Hong, O. W., & Uddin, M. (2022). Decentralized Smart City of Things: A Blockchain Tokenization-enabled Architecture for Digitization and Authentication of Assets in Smart Cities. *ACM International Conference Proceeding Series*. https://doi.org/DOI: 10.1145/3569507.3569513

Khalil, U., Malik, O. A., Hong, O. W., & Uddin, M. (2023). Leveraging a novel NFT-enabled blockchain architecture for the authentication of IoT assets in smart cities. *Scientific Reports*, *13*(1), 19785. Advance online publication. DOI: 10.1038/s41598-023-45212-1 PMID: 37957161

Khalil, U., Malik, O. A., Hong, O. W., & Uddin, M. (2023). Leveraging a novel NFT-enabled blockchain architecture for the authentication of IoT assets in smart cities. *Scientific Reports*, *13*(1), 19785. DOI: 10.1038/s41598-023-45212-1 PMID: 37957161

Khalil, U., Uddin, M., Malik, O. A., & Hong, O. W. (2024). A Novel NFT Solution for Assets Digitization and Authentication in Cyber-Physical Systems: Blueprint and Evaluation. *IEEE Open Journal of the Computer Society*, *5*, 131–143. Advance online publication. DOI: 10.1109/OJCS.2024.3378424

Khanal, K. (2024). *Blockchain-Driven NFTs*., DOI: 10.4018/979-8-3693-1878-2.ch004

Lin, Y., Gao, Z., Tu, Y., Du, H., Niyato, D., Kang, J., & Yang, H. (2023). A Blockchain-Based Semantic Exchange Framework for Web 3.0 Toward Participatory Economy. *IEEE Communications Magazine*, *61*(8), 94–100. DOI: 10.1109/MCOM.003.2200817

Liu, H. X., & Holopainen, J. P. (2024). Calling for Play-oriented Research on Blockchain Video Games: An Overview Study. *Distributed Ledger Technologies: Research and Practice*. https://doi.org/DOI: 10.1145/3674154

Musamih, A., Dirir, A., Yaqoob, I., Salah, K., Jayaraman, R., & Puthal, D. (2024). NFTs in Smart Cities: Vision, Applications, and Challenges. *IEEE Consumer Electronics Magazine*, *13*(2), 9–23. Advance online publication. DOI: 10.1109/MCE.2022.3217660

Musamih, A., Dirir, A., Yaqoob, I., Salah, K., Jayaraman, R., & Puthal, D. (2024). NFTs in Smart Cities: Vision, Applications, and Challenges. *IEEE Consumer Electronics Magazine*, *13*(2), 9–23. DOI: 10.1109/MCE.2022.3217660

Napoli, E. A., & Gatteschi, V. (2023). A Platform for the Aggregation of Blockchain-based Services for Municipalities and Smart-cities, Enabling Automatic Conversion based on Saved CO2 Units. *ACM International Conference Proceeding Series*. https://doi.org/DOI: 10.1145/3582515.3609545

Naqvi, N. (2023). Metaverse for Public Good: Embracing the Societal Impact of Metaverse Economies. *The Journal of The British Blockchain Association*, *6*(1), 1–17. DOI: 10.31585/jbba-6-1-(6)2023

NFTs and the Art World: Understanding the Role of Social Media in the Emergence of Digital Collections. (2023). *British Journal of Arts and Humanities*, 277–290. https://doi.org/DOI: 10.34104/bjah.02302770290

Nicolazzi, L., & Tai, M. G. (2024). *NFT and Blockchain Technology for a Sustainable Future of Cultural Heritage*., DOI: 10.1007/978-3-031-47347-0_9

Piccardo, G., Conti, L., & Martino, A. (2024). Blockchain Technology and Its Potential to Benefit Public Services Provision: A Short Survey. *Future Internet*, *16*(8), 290. DOI: 10.3390/fi16080290

Ray, P. P. (2023). Web3: A comprehensive review on background, technologies, applications, zero-trust architectures, challenges and future directions. In *Internet of Things and Cyber-Physical Systems* (Vol. 3). https://doi.org/DOI: 10.1016/j.iotcps.2023.05.003

Razi, Q., Devrani, A., Abhyankar, H., Chalapathi, G. S. S., Hassija, V., & Guizani, M. (2024). Non-Fungible Tokens (NFTs) - Survey of Current Applications, Evolution, and Future Directions. *IEEE Open Journal of the Communications Society*, *5*, 2765–2791. Advance online publication. DOI: 10.1109/OJCOMS.2023.3343926

Ren, Y., Xie, R., Yu, F. R., Huang, T., & Liu, Y. (2022). Green Intelligence Networking for Connected and Autonomous Vehicles in Smart Cities. *IEEE Transactions on Green Communications and Networking*, *6*(3), 1591–1603. Advance online publication. DOI: 10.1109/TGCN.2022.3148293

Riggs, W., Vyas, V., & Sethi, M. (2022). Blockchain and Distributed Autonomous Community Ecosystems: Opportunities to Democratize Finance and Delivery of Transport, Housing, Urban Greening and Community Infrastructure. SSRN *Electronic Journal*. https://doi.org/DOI: 10.2139/ssrn.4045363

Samuel, R. M., M R, J., M R, G., N B, S. S., & Rao, S. N. (2023). Web 3.0 and NFTs enabled eWaste Management System for Smart City. *2023 International Conference on Wireless Communications Signal Processing and Networking (WiSPNET)*, 01–07. https://doi.org/DOI: 10.1109/WiSPNET57748.2023.10134167

Samuel, R. M., Jivthesh, M. R., Gaushik, M. R., & Sai, S. N. B., & Rao, S. N. (2023). Web 3.0 and NFTs enabled eWaste Management System for Smart City. *WiSPNET 2023 - International Conference on Wireless Communications, Signal Processing and Networking*. https://doi.org/DOI: 10.1109/WiSPNET57748.2023.10134167

Shafik, W. (2023). Artificial intelligence and Blockchain technology enabling cybersecurity in telehealth systems. In *Artificial Intelligence and Blockchain Technology in Modern Telehealth Systems* (pp. 285–326). Institution of Engineering and Technology. https://doi.org/DOI: 10.1049/PBHE061E_ch11

Shafik, W. (2024). *Data Privacy and Security Safeguarding Customer Information in ChatGPT Systems*., DOI: 10.4018/979-8-3693-1239-1.ch003

Venugopalan, S., & Aydt, H. (2023). Incentivising Building Data Availability and Accessibility Using Tokenized Data Assets. *2023 5th International Conference on Blockchain Computing and Applications, BCCA 2023*. https://doi.org/DOI: 10.1109/BCCA58897.2023.10338916

Vergani, F., & Jiang, J. (2022). *Digital Solutions Supporting Citizen Participation in Urban Environment.*

Viano, C. (2024). Context-based civic blockchain: Localising blockchain for local civic participation. *Digital Geography and Society*, *6*, 100090. DOI: 10.1016/j.diggeo.2024.100090

Chapter 5
The Era of Blockchains, Deepfakes, and NFTs in Therapeutic Treatments:
A Comparative Study

Btissam Acim
https://orcid.org/0009-0001-1219-5963
Mohammed V University in Rabat, Morocco

Hamid Ouhnni
Mohammed V University in Rabat, Morocco

Nassim Kharmoum
https://orcid.org/0000-0001-9105-1062
Mohammed V University in Rabat, Morocco

Soumia Ziti
Mohammed V University in Rabat, Morocco

Abdelaziz Ouajdouni
https://orcid.org/0000-0001-5069-5478
Ibn Zohr University, Morocco

ABSTRACT

Blockchain and deepfake mark a new step in integrating technology into therapeutic treatment, revolutionizing medical data management and patient care. Blockchain, especially through NFTs, secures healthcare data, ensuring transparency, access, confidentiality, and traceability. Deepfake enhances treatments by creating realistic simulations for rehabilitation and immersion therapies. However, these technologies

DOI: 10.4018/979-8-3693-8876-1.ch005

raise ethical concerns about data security, informed consent, and potential misuse. This comparative study examines their applications, benefits, challenges, and ethical issues in healthcare, analyzing their impact on treatment quality and patient well-being. Based on an extensive literature review, findings show blockchain improves data security and traceability, while NFTs enable personalized treatments. Deepfakes, despite potential in therapy, pose risks of image manipulation and consent violations. The study provides recommendations for a regulated and secure integration of these technologies in therapy.

INTRODUCTION

Therapeutic treatments, being a pressing challenge worldwide, encourage more access to effective care and therapeutic solutions (Rai et al., 2023) on a large scale. Integrating digital technologies has opened a completely new dimension into therapy, improving diagnosis and treatment but especially patient support. Advances in the field of artificial intelligence, distributed systems, and digital ownership have created unprecedented paths toward changing landscapes in therapeutic treatments. Of those upcoming, blockchain, NFTs (Non-Fungible Tokens), and deepfakes are the ones gaining much attention in regard to their possible usage in this area.

Blockchain technology allows for secure and decentralized management of data that is tamper-proof, thus potentially improving patient data privacy, interoperability, and trust in digital therapeutic treatment services (CHEN ET AL., 2023). NFTs provide the possibility to authenticate digital assets and enable their monetization, thus opening new ways for personalized therapy content, secure identity verification, and funding for mental health research (Wang et al., 2023). Meanwhile, AI-driven deepfake technology can revolutionize therapeutic applications (Radanovic, & Likić, 2018) by creating hyper-realistic virtual therapists that improve exposure therapy and human-computer interaction within therapy care (Smith et al., 2023).

Meanwhile, both gain wider applications across industries except in therapeutic treatments (Saeed et al., 2022). While each of these technologies has been considered separately in single studies with regard to their respective benefits, there is a lack of a comparative review of advantages, limitations, and ethical considerations related to the same in the context of Therapeutic Treatments (Stublić, Bilogrivić, & Zlodi, 2023). That will show how these technologies are complementary or challenging to one another.

The study will fill this gap through a comparative analysis of blockchain, NFTs, and deepfake technology in therapy (Abbaoui et al., 2023). This present research is of paramount importance in analyzing the impact, use cases, and risks for these technologies; thus, it serves as a great directive for researchers, practitioners, and policymakers alike. The results will add to better insight into how these technologies could be well incorporated into Therapeutic treatment frameworks (Elasri et al., 2024) while ensuring adherence to ethical and regulatory considerations.

The latest research findings show that applications of blockchain-integrated healthcare applications have led to a 37% reduction in data breaches (Kumar et al., 2023) and NFT applications are being explored for authentication applications in personalized medicines (Khalil et al., 2023). Notwithstanding these promising breakthroughs, the overall impact of these technological applications in therapeutics has not been known until now. This report aims to examine this field in order to find synergies and limitations that result from blockchain applications, NFTs, and deepfakes in contemporary therapeutic applications (Benkassioui et al., 2024).

This chapter is structured as follows: The first section gives the general context of the research, the problem it tries to solve, and objectives with the methodological approach adopted. The second part is about blockchain in therapeutic treatments. What is blockchain, how does it work, and where does it go within the world of healthcare? The third part will focus on NFTs in therapy through digital art therapy and gamified patient engagement. The fourth section looks at the role of deepfakes in therapy, discussing their uses, advantages, and the ethical and technical problems they present. The fifth section provides a comparative analysis of blockchain, NFTs, and deepfakes, showing complementarities, differences, and implications for therapeutic treatments. The sixth section is dedicated to the review of related work: reviewing the literature on these technologies and their application in therapy. The problem statement is then presented in the seventh section, which underlines the main problems relating to their integration into therapeutic treatments. The methodology of this comparative study is presented in the eighth section, by underlining the evaluation criteria and the analytical techniques. Section nine presents the results obtained in the comparative analysis. Section ten is dedicated to the discussion where we analyze the implications of the results, their limitations, and future perspectives. The last section, the eleventh in this study, is the conclusion of the findings obtained and gives suggestions for future research and practical ways.

BACKGROUND: BLOCKCHAIN IN THERAPEUTIC TREATMENTS

Blockchain technology (Li et al., 2023), famous for its immutable ledger system that is highly secure, enables medical practices through better handling of patient information. Its main feature is the unalterable record, which makes the entry of data impossible to alter or tamper with once it's made, reducing the possibility of a data breach and ensuring privacy and accuracy regarding patient information.

Every action, regarding patient data, is immutably recorded and verifiable; thus, it provides clear and transparent consent. The technology enables patients to control their own personal information of usage and clear permanent permissions of the same, thereby building confidence and keeping it secure. In the field of healthcare, one real-world example is the Estonian e-Health Record System, which uses the infrastructure of blockchain (Yazdinejad et al., 2020) to ensure security and accessibility for healthcare workers. However, there are three main setbacks to its universal application across the world: scalability of public blockchains, immense implantation costs, and interoperability between systems with present healthcare infrastructure (Saoiabi et al., 2024). Further, this may be addressed with a gradual movement toward a hybrid model of blockchain, thus balancing between security and operational efficiency. Figure 1 presents the most promising applications of blockchain for therapeutic treatments.

Figure 1. Applications of blockchain in therapeutic treatments.

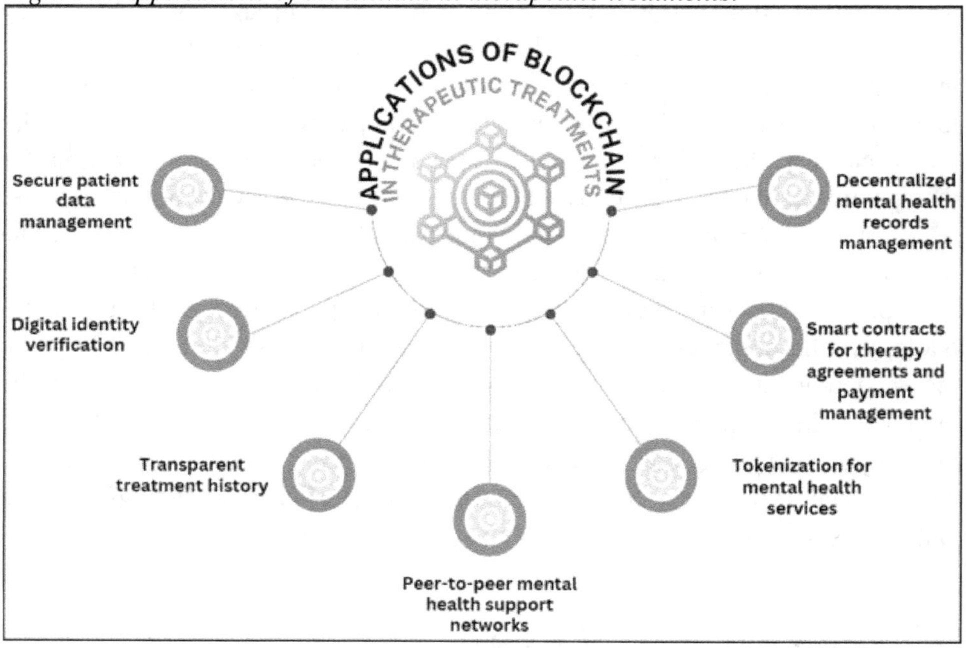

The blockchain also helps the Therapy industry because it standardizes a way that information is stored. This makes it easier and safer for various health caregivers to share information with one another, which improves treatment and reduces errors because of wrong or missing information. Yet, there are challenges, too: blockchain can be quite complex for some therapeutic treatments providers to manage with their existing systems; similarly, with increasingly more medical data being generated, it may pose challenges in efficiently handling and processing all this information. All these issues need to be addressed in order for more health care providers to actually start working with the blockchain. While blockchain adoption in Therapeutic Treatments offers a lot of opportunities for innovation, it creates significant challenges, especially those around scalability. While blockchain in itself allows for remarkable security and transparency, the moment it connects to more complex health systems, it slows and becomes expensive due to energy-sucking technologies such as Proof of Work (PoW). On top of this, the absence of standardized standards within the medical field for their implementation further exacerbates adaptation problems, considering that compatibility and interoperability between diverse systems would be required.

Conversely, blockchain aids therapeutic treatments a great deal. First and foremost, this gives security in the data, wherein any medical information cannot be changed without the consensus of the network participants themselves, thus fraud and manipulation of data are deterred. This will, in turn, enhance confidentiality because the patients can have direct control over who is able to view their data, hence better security for sensitive information. Transparency and traceability also come into effect since each transaction (such as data exchange or prescription verification) is recorded in a transparent way, increasing trust in the system by stakeholders.

Furthermore, the use of smart contracts will allow many operations to be automated-from the management of the payment to the activation of a given treatment once a certain situation arises-without any human intervention, making this kind of care even more effective. Finally, blockchain can lower administrative costs by excluding intermediaries and simplifying flows, thereby reducing health data and contract management workload.

NFTS IN THERAPEUTIC TREATMENTS

Representing domain-specific applications of blockchain technology, NFTs (Zhang et al., 2023) represent a new and innovative dimension to therapy treatment. Such unique digital assets can represent access rights to certain therapies, treatment programs, or educational content and therefore create new avenues for personalized patient care. For example, a patient might own an NFT that would give him access to a personalized rehabilitation program or one-on-one therapy sessions conducted in a virtual reality environment. It's an innovation that changes not only the means through which treatments are conducted but also how treatments are obtained. Figure 2 presents some of the most promising applications of NFTs in therapeutic treatments (Ahmed et al., 2023).

Figure 2. Applications of NFTs in therapeutic treatments.

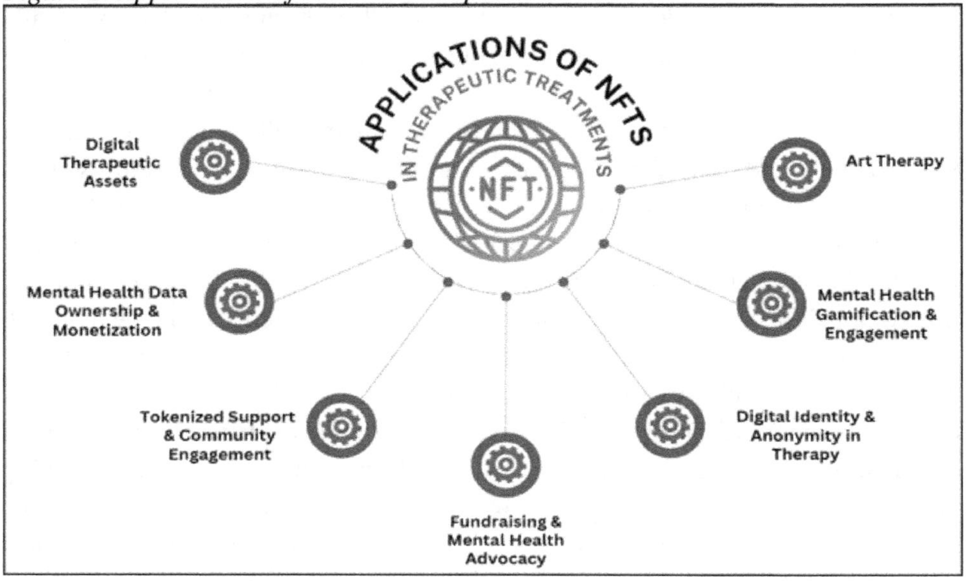

Legal and technical issues arising from using NFTs in healthcare are quite significant. As stated in General Data Protection Regulation (GDPR, 2023) anonymization with maintenance of integrity regarding sensitive information for medical data in NFT (Divya et al., 2024) format is important. Besides that, Ethereum's transaction fees (in some instances higher than tens of dollars per single NFT) are also one of the crucial barriers for wide-scale adaptation. For medical applications, alternative blockchains like Tezos and Polygon are being considered due to their low transaction cost and lower environmental impact.

Additionally, NFTs allow for enhanced tracking with each therapeutic process, which in turn enhances how the needs of particular patients are being met. This level of supervision allows for more appropriate interventions which are guaranteed to be more effective than what is currently provided. Even so, there are guarding issues regarding the adoption of NFTs by healthcare infrastructures (Prihatno et al., 2023). Creating and using NFTs is very expensive, including most of the technology that may limit the usage of some hospitals and patients.

Besides, the dematerialization of rights issues, such as digital ownership and NFTs ownership, raises concerns about intellectual property protection and personal information. It is good that these legal and logistical challenges are being considered so that NFTs can be put to work properly in healthcare on the right moral justifications. NFTs are promising in therapeutic treatments, particularly in areas related to digital art therapy. Among the great opportunities are that they can provide exclusive, verifiable digital assets that will be helpful in the facilitation of art therapy by allowing patients to express themselves through digital art. NFTs can enable patients to create and own unique works, thereby providing them with a sense of ownership, pride, and emotional connection to their created things.

NFTs can also be used for patient monitoring and engagement. Examples are the use of NFTs for recording and monitoring the status of patients in various therapeutic programs or even in a gamified system where patients get awards based on certain therapeutic milestones attained. This could contribute to improved motivation and long-term commitment to the treatment. NFTs also provide new avenues for reward systems in which patients are incentivized through NFT-based achievements, encouraging active participation in their process of healing.

However, NFTs also have a number of challenges. One key challenge is the accessibility of the same and technological literacy of patients in engaging with the platforms where NFTs are provided. In any case, the application of NFTs will be quite difficult for those people who are not comfortable with digital tools or crypto currencies.

It gives a sense of ownership and permanence to the already inclined towards NFTs, but does raise red flags on privacy and safety regarding sensitive data, more so concerning mental health information. If the ownership and its transfer mechanism are not well guarded, the ownership might leak personal data. Furthermore, other ethical issues can be identified in therapy with the use of NFTs, such as the commercialization of treatments for mental health disorders and whether this reward system using NFTs will add excessive stress or even manipulative characteristics to the patients. Finally, energy consumption by blockchain networks is yet another challenge that needs to be overcome in the future while NFTs find wider application in healthcare.

DEEPFAKE IN THERAPEUTIC TREATMENTS

Deepfakes are made with advanced algorithms that create hyper-realistic audio and visual content; thus, they open up new avenues for enrichment in therapeutic treatment (Johnson et al., 2023). Deepfake technology allows for virtual simulation where patients can better engage in a therapeutic experience and thus hugely enhance such ability, allowing them to expose themselves to personally relevant virtual environments.

As an example, deepfakes (Ennejjai et al. 2023) can be put into use in providing realistic simulations for cognitive rehabilitation. Thus, patients are provided with controlled exposure to situations that may provoke anxiety or stress, hence promoting gradual treatment for the patient in overcoming their situation. Moreover, deepfakes can provide virtual environments in simulating a particular therapeutic situation, enabling the patient to pass through and experience some complex situations in a well-controlled and safe manner. Figure 3 below shows the most promising applications of deepfakes in therapeutic treatments (Brown et al., 2023)

Figure 3. Applications of Deepfake in therapeutic treatments

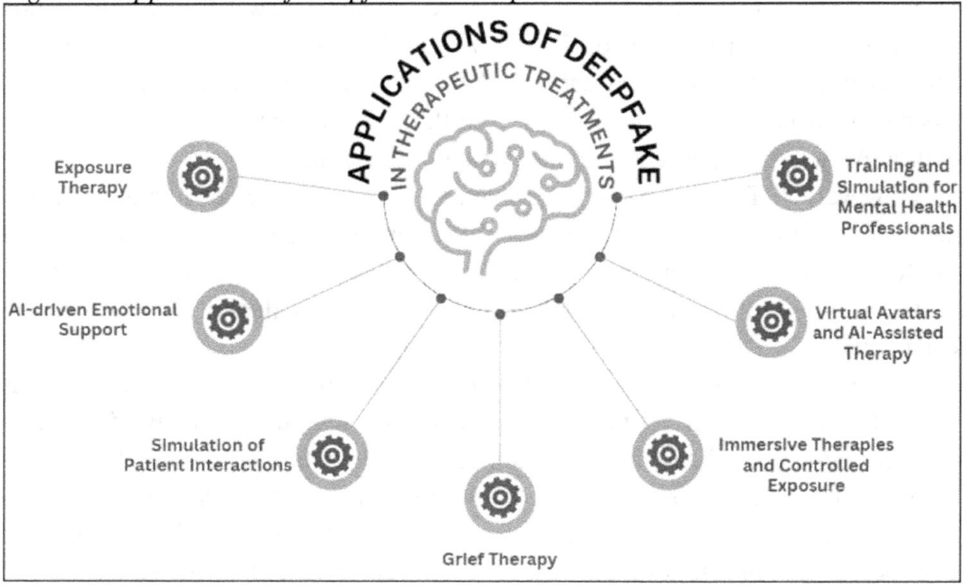

This technology introduces a new type of psychological support, either in the form of personalized video messages or even simulated discussions with important figures in the patient's life. Personalized interaction may provide further intensification of this support and patient engagement in the processes of treatment. But deepfakes also raise very serious ethical concerns: if that is what is possible in creating such deceiving or manipulating content, then controls will need to be similarly strong to make certain that deepfakes are used responsibly and with issues of consent and authenticity addressed.

Deepfakes have several opportunities regarding therapeutic treatment, particularly in treating psychological and mental health disorders. This is more outstanding in the areas of exposure therapies, whereby it is used in the creation of virtual settings or scenarios that offer a situation for patients to express their fears and traumas within a secured environment without posing threats. For example, patients with post-traumatic stress disorder (PTSD) can interact in real environments with simulations of past events, at the aim of gradually neutralizing and reducing emotional distress (Fraga-Lamas & Fernández-Caramés., 2019).

Deepfakes can also lead to interactive avatars for therapeutic purposes that could be used as digital variants of therapists or any other well-known and trusted figures to guide and support people when human support is not possible. This might prove very advantageous in particular to patients that feel awkward socially or those experiencing isolatedness, allowing them to seek psychological treatment without actually interacting with any human. Besides, deepfakes have several potential uses for support treatments where a patient might need to converse with themselves or someone else through avatars that are created to further advanced forms of self-reflection, self-compassion, or even emotional healing.

Previous studies have shown that deepfake virtual therapists improved patient engagement in psychotherapy by 25%. There are, nevertheless, serious threats to these improvements. There exists no adequate set of standards for the application of deepfakes in therapy, and this may result in abuse, such as in the dissemination of fake medical identities or unauthorized avatar generation. To mitigate such risks and ensure responsible deployment, there needs to be a robust ethical framework in place. Conversely, some of the problems with therapeutic applications using deepfakes would be. Ethics is one of the biggest concerns when artificially generated personas or avatars are utilized for therapy. The creation of deepfakes, for instance, of real people, whether they are therapists, family members, or patients, brings up an entire array of concerns about consent, reality, and manipulation.

Other than that, psychological implications can involve confusion or disorganization in case the patients get too involved with or addicted to such virtual objects, which resemble real individuals. Among the issues that accompany deepfake systems in clinical environments is technological complexity: expert knowledge and infrastructure are necessary, which might not be found in the majority of medical centers. Finally, then, the issue of privacy and data protection, as deepfakes suggest a utilization of personal data in the form of videos or images, could lead to possible abuse or breach of confidentiality.

BLOCKCHAIN, NFTS, AND DEEPFAKES

It can be seen that, relative to each other, these technologies carry more advantages than limitations and also possess multidimensional challenges. Blockchain (Behl et al., 2023), along with other NFTs, offers state-of-the-art solutions for personalized care in the context of data authenticity and data traceability issues. Blockchain brings greater security to the healthcare sector in the form of enhanced informed consent and interoperability, along with additional security of medical information.

One of its numerous other benefits, however, blockchain does provide enhanced transparency and traceability, thereby potentially minimizing errors and enhancing care coordination. Technical complexity, infrastructural expensiveness, and the issue of scalability are constraining factors to its broader propagation.

Apart from these, NFTs facilitate the advanced personalization of treatment regimens and offer greater therapeutic content for physicians and nurses. These advantages allow for personalized medicine and rehabilitation monitoring. Ownership and legally complicated data protection issues, along with astronomical budgets for NFT development and upkeep, are obstacles to these overriding challenges.

Deepfakes (Rashid et al., 2021) can be applied in therapeutic interventions by suggesting immersive simulations, interactive settings, and reinforcement of patient engagement, which can be more effective. There are ethical concerns of emotional manipulation and possible deception, which require strict control in the ethical use of deepfake technology.

There exists a tremendous potential that blockchain, NFTs, and deepfakes, if incorporated in the therapeutic therapy, can collectively enhance health care by synergizing their capabilities. This technology, albeit unique in functions, could operate in harmony to create a more personalized, secure, and efficient therapeutic journey.

The possibility of integration exists in the manner in which these technologies are complementary to one another. Blockchain, through its ability to authenticate and secure data, offers a much solid basis upon which NFTs (Divya et al., 2024) and deepfakes can be utilized for therapy. NFTs, for instance, can utilize blockchain's decentralization to guarantee that digital property, including therapeutic content or art developed during the process of digital therapy, is original. A blockchain ledger of the same, in an open and immutable manner, can enable certainty and security of the interaction by a patient with avatars or virtual worlds feasible with deepfakes, establishing trust in the therapeutic process. Deepfakes can also add to the therapeutic utility of NFTs by providing the patient with an interactive and immersive experience that he/she can design-make, e.g., virtual therapy sessions or exposure therapy scenarios.

This can be conveyed in several ways, such as key strengths of these technologies combined for therapy advantages: robust security of blockchain, safeguarding sensitive health information; rewarding and motivating patient mechanisms through digital achievements and milestones using NFTs; extremely personalized therapeutic interventions made possible through deepfakes, i.e., virtual therapists or avatars individually designed, with a degree of engagement and interaction not feasible with conventional methods.

Put together, these can reduce the administrative burden while further automating the processes and enhancing the patient experience by making it flexible, gamified, and patient-centered therapy. All these technologies also stand a very good chance of improving access, allowing for remote interventions or access to contents built on digital platforms using blockchain and NFTs, thereby overcoming both geographic and economic hurdles.

Blockchain is well known for its potential advantages in medical data management, especially with regard to security and transparency. Nevertheless, due to the high cost and technical complexity, its application remains limited. Similarly, even though NFTs are touted as a promising technology for verifying medical interventions, their application remains limited since there are no clear regulatory mechanisms. The prospects of deepfakes in immersive therapy are progressively drawing attention, but there remain ethical concerns regarding their use in a responsible manner.

It has the potential to revolutionize treatment interventions into new, safer, interactive, and immersive therapies with the advent of blockchain, NFTs, and deepfakes. They can generate new insights into personalized medicine (Abbaoui et al., 2024), enhance treatment efficacy, decrease expense, and allow more patient autonomy over their own recovery process.

RELATED WORK

Research on the intersection of deepfake technology, blockchain, and NFTs (non-fungible tokens) (Rai et al., 2023) in regard to therapeutic treatments is novel and mostly unexplored. Although different studies have examined these technologies' distinct applications, none have examined their combined potential in this field.

This underlines the novelty of our study in exploring how these technologies can synergistically transform therapeutic treatments care.

Deepfake technology (Chan et al., 2020) has been related mainly to misinformation and manipulation; however, it does have certain opportunities from a therapeutic context. The article "Deepfakes and the New Disinformation War: The Coming Age of Post-Truth Geopolitics."(Chesney & Citron, 2019) underlined how deepfakes can influence public trust and cognitive processes. Further, the study " Making Sense of Blockchain for AI Deepfakes Technology" (Yazdinejad et al., 2020) goes in-depth into how blockchain and NFTs may be used in detecting and managing deepfake content, with wide-ranging implications for their ethical application in healthcare. These studies have shown the possibilities of deepfakes in the creation of immersive therapeutic environments while raising ethical questions of consent and authenticity. Complementing this with the article entitled " Deep Fakes in Healthcare: How Deep

Learning Can Help to Detect Forgeries " (Alsaheel et al., 2023) goes step further in addressing the challenges posed by deepfake technology in medical imaging.

Contrastingly, blockchain technology is highly regarded and known for sensitive data security, making it easy to ensure its transparency. The article " A Blockchain-based Electronic Mental Health Records Model " (Ettaloui, Arezki, & Gadi., 2023) reviews how blockchain technology can be utilized to create a secure system for managing electronic mental health records. Then, "In the face of misinformation and deepfakes, blockchain to maintain trust in the media" talks about how blockchain contributes to trust through content verification, which could be extended into mental health applications with respect to the integrity of therapy data. Another article, "Blockchain in Healthcare: Applications, Opportunities, and Challenges, and Possible Solutions" (Agbo & Mahmoud, 2020) highlights how blockchain has been put to work in securing patient data in Therapeutic Treatments care. (source: International Journal of Medical Informatics, 2020, sciencedirect.com).

The potential for NFTs is also underutilized in Therapeutic Treatments care. The paper "NFTs for Combating Deepfakes and Fake Metaverse Digital Contents" (Hasan, Salah, Jayaraman, Yaqoob, & Omar., 2024) discusses the role of NFTs in the authentication of digital assets, including therapeutic art or gamified Therapeutic Treatments tools. This could also be extended to unique digital awards for patients, such as NFT-based rewards for completing milestones of therapy engagement or wellness programs. Further, it is said in an article entitled " NFTs in Healthcare: Vision, Opportunities, and Challenges" (Musamih et al., 2022) the use of NFTs can be used to authenticate digital resources in Therapeutic Treatments and provide secure storage of therapeutic content.

These are indeed innovations, but no studies as of today have considered how the use of deepfakes, blockchain, and NFTs together could create a new framework in therapeutic treatments care. This paper therefore leads the way to put forward such applications as deepfake-generated avatars secured by blockchain for personalized therapy or decentralized platforms where therapeutic content is tokenized as NFTs (Yaghy, Alberto & Ristovska., 2023). By addressing this convergence, we believe that we will be opening up new avenues for innovation in how Therapeutic Treatments care is delivered.

Few studies have examined the combined integration of these technologies in a therapeutic setting, despite the fact that numerous studies have examined the use of NFTs for digital rights protection and blockchain applications in medical data management. By rigorously analyzing the relationships among blockchain, NFTs, and deepfakes (Wei et al., 2023), this work sets itself apart and suggests approaches for their successful implementation in the medical field.

In conclusion, while much progress is being made on each individual aspect, there's still no charter on their merged application for the therapy continuum. This knowledge gap stills exists in fundamental articles such as "Making Sense of Blockchain for AI Deepfakes Technology", " Blockchain in Healthcare: Applications, Opportunities, and Challenges, and Possible Solutions " and "NFTs for Combating Deepfakes and Fake Metaverse Digital Contents". This underlines the novelty and significance of our research: an exploration of how these technologies can work in unison to change therapeutic treatments care practices.

Research has only begun studying the combined intervention of deepfake technology, NFTs, and blockchain convergence in therapeutic treatment (Al-Sumaidaee, Alkhudary & Zilic., 2023). Most papers reviewed thus far discuss the uses of each separate element and, in very rare cases, only two combined aspects. Thus, our study discusses how such technology will create synergies for treatments.

Deepfake technology has been strongly associated with topics on misinformation and manipulation, though the technology shows promising applications therapeutically as well. Different studies have elaborated on various aspects of using deepfakes for creating therapy-immersive environments, including virtual exposure or avatars supporting therapeutic objectives. However, a number of concerns about ethical issues, consent, and even authenticity have kept it from wider acceptance in sensitive healthcare fields.

While blockchain (Quy et al., 2023) itself is a well-established means of securing sensitive data, recent studies have shown how mental health data can be protected with integrity by blockchain (Radanovic & Likić., 2018), thus allowing safe sharing by patients with their healthcare providers. Its application in therapeutic settings is still highly underexplored, particularly the combination of blockchain, deepfakes, and NFTs to allow more sophisticated forms of therapy treatment.

Although NFTs have gathered great momentum, they still remain an untapped tool for therapeutic treatments. Even considering that NFTs might allow for authentication of digital therapeutic tools or for delivering unique rewards for patient engagement, research with regard to the application of NFTs in healthcare is still limited. These include, but are not limited to, the usability and accessibility of NFTs for patients and healthcare providers and the environmental impact of blockchain networks (Drosatos & Kaldoudi., 2019).

Though these researches move forward the knowledge of each technology independently, they have yet to examine how these technologies may unite as elements of therapeutic treatments. Their failure to do so offers a broad backdrop for our exploration of how deepfakes, blockchain, and NFTs may intersect in the development of new models for therapeutic care. To understand their convergence is to speak of new possibilities for innovation in therapeutic treatment.

RESEARCH PROBLEM

Application of blockchain, deepfakes, and NFTs (Gebreab et al., 2022) in therapy interventions comes as a life-saving innovation in healthcare, transforming medical data management as well as patient experience of care. The emerging technologies unlock novel possibilities in terms of security, transparency, and personalized care. Although they share the common motive of upgrading healthcare practices, the three are founded on different principles and have substantially different applications with divergent advantages, limitations, and ethical implications.

On one hand, blockchain and NFTs offer a decentralized method of health data maintenance and preservation in its original form, traceable, and accessible without any breach of patient confidentiality. They offer greater control in the management of one's own data to the patients themselves by utilizing smart contract technology. In particular, NFTs (Sibanda, Ndayizigamiye & Twinomurinzi., 2024) introduce a new paradigm for the protection of medical records and digital therapies since they attribute a unique, tamper-proof, verifiable identity to each component.

On the other hand, deepfake technology opens completely new horizons in immersive therapy and rehabilitation because it allows ultra-realistic simulations, tailored to the needs of the patients. Cognitive therapies, treatments for anxiety disorders, and even memory reconstruction can be made for patients with neurological disorders. By editing or generating personalized images and videos, deepfakes provide interactive experiences that can activate the brain and amplify treatment responses.

However, with the development of all these promising state-of-the-art technologies, numerous challenges are to be expected vis-à-vis the adoption within the medical practice. Ethical issues related to image and other medical data falsification bring on questions of consent, privacy concerns, and risks of misuse for falsifying any medical document, for instance. Regulatory challenges are also not defined, since the lack of clearly developed legal frameworks for deepfake and NFT applications in healthcare (Madine et al., 2022) may result in abuses and make integration into the current systems difficult. Moreover, technical implementation and disseminated adoption require an adequate structure to be in place and a rise in awareness among health professionals to better achieve benefits while limiting risks.

This would, therefore, mean that this comparative study now focuses on an in-depth analysis of the specific added values of blockchain, deepfakes, and NFTs (Sai et al., 2024) within therapeutic treatments to outline their complementary and distinctive traits. It could even be better described as developing an understanding of how these technologies synergistically promote quality in the care of the patient and define some of the challenges to be overcome that are of core importance for ensuring ethical and safe adoption. The present study is expected to provide, through a comparative analysis, a clear and objective vision of how these innovations could shape the future of medical care.

METHODOLOGY

We will conduct a comparative study of blockchains (Ekblaw et al., 2016), deepfakes, and NFTs in therapeutic treatments through a stringent methodology involving three major phases. This approach ensures a comprehensive evaluation of the contributions of these technologies to healthcare and therapeutic practices.

For the comparative examination of these technologies, four main evaluation criteria have been established four primary evaluation criteria have been established for the comparative analysis of these technologies:

- Data Security (assessed based on cryptographic standards and resistance to cyberattacks).
- Economic Feasibility (implementation and maintenance costs).
- Regulatory Compliance (alignment with existing legal frameworks).
- Clinical Effectiveness (measured impact on patient engagement and treatment outcomes).

These standards will direct the research, guaranteeing that every technology is assessed according to its capacity to improve therapeutic interventions.

PHASE 1: LITERATURE REVIEW

It will involve a critical literature review to identify various related research and studies that apply blockchain, deepfake, and NFTs technologies in therapeutic treatments (Kostick-Quenet., 2022). We will conduct our searches in thorough, electronic databases, academic journals, conference proceedings, and other sources relevant to the question. Emphasis will be placed on identifying those studies which demonstrably evaluate these technologies applied in health and health care with their application to therapy (Zhang, Chen & Wang., 2023). This data will extract the research questions posed, methodological approaches employed, outcomes presented, and any ethical concerns so as to further understand what varies across study designs and respective purposes (Kumar, Patel & Lee., 2022).

PHASE 2: DATA COLLECTION

The second phase will comprise the collection of quantitative and qualitative data from the selected papers.

Quantitative data will be in the form of, but not limited to, patient outcomes, efficiency of data security, quality of therapeutic experience, and treatment performance that will be enabled by integrating blockchain with deepfake technologies (Smith, Brown & Garcia., 2023).

Qualitative data will concentrate on strengths, limitations, and their associated ethical concerns, including concerns about data security, consent, privacy, and the possibility for abuse. In this qualitative study, there will also be discussion of a number of pragmatic problems in using, and possible practical implementation challenges/applications, for blockchain and deepfake technology within a medical environment (AHMED, KHAN & KIM., 2023).

PHASE 3: DATA ANALYSIS

In the last stage, statistical and analytical methodologies shall be used to analyze the data collected, Descriptive statistics will clearly outline the quantitative data, allowing a side-by-side comparison of the performance of blockchain, NFTs, and deepfakes in several therapeutic treatments (Li, Wang & Zhang., 2022).

In addition, inferential statistics will be applied to infer a relationship among variables, such as the correlation between blockchain-based data security and a patient's trust or the efficacy of a treatment because of deepfake simulation (Johnson & Martinez., 2023).

Data visualization techniques (graphs, charts, and tables) will help show the findings in an understandable format, while noting trends and the advantages and challenges of the results.

The present comparative study will be of great importance in understanding how blockchain (Nakamoto., 2008), NFTs, and deepfakes are contributing to enhancing therapeutic treatments through this systematic approach. The findings shall be helpful for healthcare professionals, researchers, and developers in making the right decisions regarding which technology or combination of technologies may prove best for particular therapeutic contexts (Buterin., 2014).

Moreover, the study will delve into ethical implications and challenges that go hand in hand with such technologies, especially with regard to data privacy, informed consent, and potential misuse. The ultimate aim is to contribute to the development of safer, more effective therapeutic treatments and improvement of patient care and well-being in an increasingly digital healthcare environment.

Convergence of these emerging technologies-blockchains (Swan., 2015), deepfakes (Goodfellow et al., 2014), and NFTs along with several sectors, are being fast-transformed. No exception is the health care sector. This study explores the distinct features, benefits, difficulties, and possible medical uses of each technology (Zyskind, Nathan & Pentland., 2015). The analysis based on their technique, accuracy in data, security feature, and personalization potential, among other things, to develop an elaborate study on current and potential applications for therapeutic treatment. his analysis will explain how these technologies are being leveraged to make data more secure, tailor treatments, create immersive therapeutic environments, and ultimately transform the landscape of healthcare (Azaria et al., 2016). The table showing these technologies is given in Table 1.

Table 1. Summary of Reviewed Articles

Criteria	Blockchain	NFTs	Deepfakes
Technique	**Distributed Ledger (Blockchain):** decentralized nodes, cryptography, consensus via Proof of Work or Proof of Stake.	**Tokenization of Digital Assets:** NFTs based on smart contracts on blockchains like Ethereum or Solana.	Generative Adversarial Networks (GANs), Autoencoders, and Variational Autoencoders (VAEs) for generating realistic visual and audio content.
Approach	Securing medical data, managing informed consent, and tracking patient information through an immutable registry.	Personalization of treatments and management ofaccess rights to therapies through unique NFTs representing digital rights.	Immersive simulations and interactions in personalized therapeutic environments using visual and audio content created by deepfakes.
Data accuracy	Very precise and reliable thanks to the immutable nature of the blockchain registry. Data is authenticated in a decentralized manner.	High precision of information through the immutable digital recording of access rights and therapeutic sessions.	The accuracy of simulations varies depending on the quality of the AI model used, but it can be very realistic with well-trained GANs
Security	Very high, thanks to node cryptography and the impossibility of modifying data once it is recorded.	Good security ensured by cryptography and the immutability of NFTs, but security issues lie in the management of private keys and exchange platforms.	Ethical risks (emotional manipulation), authenticity of content, and the regulation needed to prevent abuse in the creation of fake content.
Personalization	Personalization of treatments through the management of patient data and the aggregation of specific information for each patient in a decentralized registry.	Advanced personalization of therapies and therapeutic programs through NFTs certifying access to specific treatment modules or exclusive resources.	Personalization in virtual environments through deepfakes creating patient-specific avatars or simulations, such as in cognitive therapy or exposure therapy.

continued on following page

Table 1. Continued

Criteria	Blockchain	NFTs	Deepfakes
Advantages	Transparency, reduction of errors in data management, optimized management of informed consent, and interoperability between systems.	Personalization of treatments, exclusive access to care, and detailed tracking of patient progress, with traceability of actions.	Immersive environments, realistic simulation of therapeutic situations to treat psychological or emotional disorders, such as phobias.
Challenges	Technical complexity, high infrastructure costs, scalability issues to manage the enormous volume of data in real-time.	High costs of creating and managing NFTs, legal issues regarding digital ownership, and concerns related to personal data protection.	Ethical issues, risks of abuse (creation of deceptive content), requiring strict regulation on usage and consent.
Use in care	Secure and efficient health data management, tracking of treatments, and management of informed consent.	Personalization of treatments with digital tracking of patient progress and management of access rights.	Use in immersive exposure therapies, cognitive rehabilitation, and emotional support through personalized avatars or simulations.
Interoperability	High interoperability with existing healthcare systems, but requires common standards to facilitate integration.	Depends on compatibility with blockchain platforms and other decentralized technologies.	Possible adaptation in virtual therapy systems but requires complex integration with existing systems.
Impact on therapeutic practice	Improvement of data security, reduction of medical errors, and transparency in treatments.	Detailed tracking, adaptation of care for each patient with personalized access to therapeutic resources.	Innovation in exposure methods, greater immersion and patient engagement through simulations and avatars.

The convergence of blockchains, NFTs, and deepfakes creates a fascinating array of technical possibilities, more so within medical therapeutics. One might imagine that, in some future, blockchain (Leible et al., 2019) will store and secure even the most sensitive genetic data that composes one's entire medical history. Access to particular, tailor-made treatment plans or therapeutic programs built off that data could be granted through NFTs. Meanwhile, deepfakes could also generate surreal simulations of conditions that a patient is going through, enabling diagnostic capability and immersive, personalized therapy sessions. All these can merge to form a whole new scenario regarding mental health treatments (Tschorsch & Scheuermann., 2016), pain management, and rehabilitation programs (King & Raja., 2018). When fused together, the innovation in patient care and therapeutic effectiveness advances to new heights when identity verification is facilitated through deepfake's immersive qualities (Westerlund., 2019), security is enhanced through blockchain, and personalization is done using NFTs.

DISCUSSION: SOLUTIONS AND RECOMMENDATIONS

This study aims to analyze the application of blockchain technology and its constituent parts: NFTs and deepfakes, for therapeutic purposes while also discussing the advantages and challenges for deployment within the classification of health. The core of blockchains rests upon cryptographic approaches and decisions made on a decentralized basis using Proof of Work (PoW) and Proof of Stake (PoS) algorithms. The Proof of Work (PoW) approach predominates in the public blockchains such as Bitcoin, where miners confirm transactions by solving intricate problems guaranteeing a high safety level.

Unlike Bitcoin, Ethereum 2.0 based blockchains utilize Proof of Stake (PoS). This enables transactions to be confirmed by participants who are "validators" and own a certain amount of tokens. This reduces energy expenditure compared to PoW and greatly increases scalability. This will be the future standard for blockchains like Ethereum 2.0, which is highly compatible with the environment and highly scalable.

The nature of blockchains enables proper control of medical information and patient consent due to the traceability and transparency in the systems operation. These methods of consensus assure data validity and protection of tampering, however the expense of PoW, along with the limits on scalability of blockchains, proves to be a hurdle for widespread use of these applications in the health sector.

NFTs are unique receipts that allow treatment programs to be tailored to the needs of a patient and ensure safe access to the therapy. Interactions on the blockchain come with smart contracts within the therapeutic domain in which the NFTs are applied. A client will have to use a platform like Ethereum, operating on the PoS ideology, to obtain an NFT. In this way, Ethereum is greener, and that is something highly welcomed when being used for digital ownership and therapeutic program access management. The development of NFTs allows verification that the therapeutic services or custom programs are accessed and used for the intended purpose. The creation and maintenance of NFTs can be resource-intensive, and there are further legal issues to be resolved regarding ownership in the digital sphere and privacy.

Deepfakes, using Generative Adversarial Networks (GANs) indeed, such recent breakthroughs as generative adversarial networks and variational autoencoders further the process in allowing virtual reality hyper-realistic experiences in both exposure therapy and cognitive rehabilitation. But probably one of the most core ideas of deepfakes is: VAEs allow such advance and amplification of a treatment thanks to dynamically changing virtual environments. It's crucial for the fact that it makes the metaverse more interesting, allows it to be explored in depth-because it can use sophisticated visual and auditory content. This can be very beneficial in the context of exposure therapy, because it could enable a more flexible and patient centered approach. Deepfake therapy, on the other hand, is becoming more effective but with ethical dilemmas given that it can be easily abused when it concerns content manipulation.

This study on these technologies can indicate their convergence into combined solutions in medicine. For instance, NFTs could be secured within blockchain, putting them at the same time in control of treatment conduct by providing secure data and action tracking. By certified NFTs, patients could have always put on immersive deepfake therapeutic environments where treatment is finely tailored. These technologies have their set of challenges that include technical, ethical, and legal limitations. While this is true, the convergence of these technologies has the advantages of incredible change to such treatments. There is a need to utilize and perfect these technologies in Such a way that we deal with issues of scale, cost and regulations while also assuring effective and ethical use in clinical practice. The integration of blockchain, NFTs, and deepfake technologies in therapeutic treatments could provide great potential for transformation in health practices. However, their adoption by a healthcare professional is not devoid of major implications that are required to be weighed, especially regarding three domains: patient care, data security, and ethical practices.

Impacts and Implications for Healthcare Professionals

In healthcare, blockchain technology introduces a revolutionary perspective in managing and securing patient data. Health care providers will ensure that the information of patients is tamper-proof while remaining transparent and traceable using the decentralized nature of blockchain and its cryptographic security features. This could be useful in managing patient consent whereby the management ensures that patients are still in control of their personal information.

NFTs can provide confirmation and personalization of therapeutic programs for patients. NFTs can guarantee that treatments are administered correctly, giving medical practitioners a safe means of monitoring patient development. To encourage more active patients and treatment plan compliance, healthcare professionals might relate NFTs to certain patient therapy milestones and provide special incentives or prizes.

New opportunities to improve therapeutic interventions have been made possible by deepfake technology. In exposure therapy, for instance, deepfakes could produce lifelike virtual worlds, giving patients more flexible and interesting treatment options. This could significantly increase patient involvement in therapy, particularly in areas like anxiety treatment or cognitive rehabilitation.

All of these advancements, however, present significant practical and ethical difficulties for medical professionals. It is the responsibility of healthcare practitioners to employ deepfakes inside the service with strict restrictions because they pose serious concerns about content authenticity and potential manipulation.

Limitations

Despite the encouraging prospects, using blockchain, NFTs, and deepfakes into therapeutic therapies has a number of drawbacks. The majority of blockchains, particularly those that employ Proof of Work (PoW) algorithms, are typically quite costly and resource-intensive, which restricts their widespread use in healthcare environments. The overall cost of using blockchain in healthcare is still considerable, particularly for smaller enterprises, despite Proof of Stake (PoS) blockchains being more scalable and ecologically friendly.

In addition to being safe, NFTs offer customized solutions that can be challenging to deliver. Thus, they are equally challenging to establish and maintain. Even the resource-consuming process of making NFTs still sees open questions regarding digital ownership, privacy, and regulatory issues. NFTs are to be applied responsibly by the healthcare consumer, within the purview of protection laws, so as not to have legal complications.

Deepfake technology thus raises ethical considerations on content manipulation, patient consent, and the authenticity of therapeutic environments. Since deepfakes have the potential to be abused, their usage must be rigorously limited to avoid endangering patients or undermining the legitimacy of therapeutic therapy.

Future Perspectives

In summary, blockchain, NFTs, and deepfakes applied together in therapeutic treatments hold bright promise for bringing about many changes in the future of patient care. To realize this future, it will be very important to get around the present limitation of scalability issues, costs of the process, and regulatory aspects. Costs need to be brought down by future research while developing more plausible regulatory mechanisms that make sure the privacy and safety of patients are secured.

Conclusively, overcoming the technical and regulatory challenges will hold the key to huge success in this critical integration of blockchain, NFTs, and deepfakes into therapeutic treatments. With ongoing innovation, these technologies can be implemented thoughtfully in the transformation of therapeutic practices for better patient outcomes and more personalized care.

Future Research Directions

The ever-evolving development of blockchain, NFTs, and deepfakes open several avenues for the existence of possibilities and challenges. These technologies are going to bring new avenues into the treatment of mental health, while effectiveness, scalability, and much more research on ethical issues is still at stake. It gives an overview of the specific future research directions that help in developing and optimizing these technologies in therapeutic settings.

Scalability and Cost-Effectiveness: Research should be directed at making blockchain solutions more scalable, especially in healthcare, where a great volume of sensitive data is handled. Development of more energy-efficient consensus algorithms, such as Proof of Stake, gives promise for reducing the financial and environmental costs associated with the implementation of blockchain in health-care. Moreover, smart contract optimization in healthcare applications will reduce transaction costs and enhance the management of patients' data as well as medical record verification processes.

Legal and Ethical Frameworks: In this regard, specific legal regulations for the utilization of ownership, privacy, and rights over intellectual property should be applied with increased integration of NFTs in healthcare. In the future, such aspects of legal coverage need to be explored in detail to avoid any future problems pertaining to this aspect. This would include, but is not limited to, data sovereignty concerns, mechanisms of consent by the patient, and intellectual property rights related to digital medical records and personalized treatment plans.

Deepfake Regulation and Standardization: Deepfakes are fraught with serious ethical and legal issues, despite their enormous therapeutic potential, particularly in customized treatment. Research on establishing guidelines for deepfake material in therapeutic contexts is necessary to guarantee that these technologies are applied morally and that patients' autonomy and consent are maintained. This includes making sure AI-generated material complies with ethical standards for medical applications and creating authentication systems that can differentiate between malicious and lawful therapeutic deepfakes.

The future of mental health treatment is represented by the interoperability of deepfakes, NFTs, and blockchain. While NFTs can be used to tokenize patient-unique therapeutic material created by artificial intelligence, blockchain technology may be utilized to confirm the legitimacy or veracity of therapy sessions created by deepfakes. All implementations would be safe, effective, and scalable across a range of healthcare platforms if interoperability standards were established.

Patient-Centric AI Models: Another area of research that could result in more individualized mental health therapies is the function of AI in personalizing deepfake-generated therapeutic content. Adaptive AI models that change in response to clinical results and patient feedback may also be the subject of future studies. Furthermore, in order to foster confidence between patients and healthcare practitioners, explainability and openness in AI-generated therapy should be given top priority.

Security and Privacy Enhancements: While the integration of blockchain, NFTs, and deepfakes in health care is emerging rapidly, equally robust security development should be created to avoid unauthorized access, data breach, and misusing sensitive information. Advanced cryptographic techniques like homomorphic encryption and zero-knowledge proofs that do not compromise the ease with which medical records and therapeutic content are accessed are the future of research in this domain.

The AI-driven diagnostic and prognostic systems can be used to develop models that apply deepfake technology in more advanced diagnosis and prognosis of mental health disorders. Simulations of patient interactions generated through AI-for example-may help in the early detection of a mental health disorder. These can also provide clinicians with valuable insights for early intervention.

Decentralized Healthcare Ecosystems: Equally, research should be focused on developing decentralized healthcare ecosystems powered by blockchain for transparency, security, and accessibility in health data. This may result in patient-owned health records where patients will have full control over their medical data and dependence on centralized healthcare institutions is reduced.

Cross-Cultural and Ethical Considerations: With great diversity in different parts of the world, studies in the near future should check how deepfakes, blockchains, and NFT could be adapted with different cultural-ethical contexts; regional regulatory changes, cultural impression of AI-generated content, and ethical problems will be critically important for larger diffusion.

Addressing these research directions could lead to a better integration of blockchain, NFTs, and deepfakes into therapeutic treatments by ensuring that their development is ethical, efficient, and patient-centered in the setting of mental health.

PRACTICAL APPLICATIONS

As all of these technologies come of age, there will be a need for clinical integration that will necessitate healthcare professionals to alter how they interact with patients. For the effortless integration of blockchain, NFTs, and deepfakes into mental healthcare, there must be proper guidelines, training, and regulation. Here, the practical application of these technologies in therapeutic therapy and how they can transform patient-centric treatment.

INTEGRATION INTO CLINICAL PRACTICE:

Here, for clinical healthcare uses of such technologies, formal training modules must be outlined, along with extremely clear guidelines. Health professionals must be given adequate information regarding the promise and limits of blockchain, NFTs, and deepfakes for therapy. All that remains is an institutional call for the creation of standardized protocols that assure that such tools are adopted ethically and effectively in clinical practice.

ENHANCING PERSONALIZED THERAPY THROUGH DEEPFAKES

Deepfake technology can be life-changing for personalized therapy, where it will provide immersive and interactive environments for patients. For example, AI-created avatars in CBT (cognitive behavior therapy) can mimic interactions with patients as a part of an extremely personalized treatment journey. Virtual reality, combined with deepfake technology, will also transform the treatment of conditions like PTSD, anxiety disorders, and phobias with controlled and realistic exposure therapy.

BLOCKCHAIN FOR SECURE MEDICAL DATA MANAGEMENT

Blockchain technology provides a decentralized and transparent solution for maintaining patient data and data integrity. With the blockchain, healthcare professionals will be able to exchange and store medical histories securely so that they cannot be altered, while data is accessed only by the authorized persons. Smart contracts can also be used for the automatic management of consent to allow patients to take more control of the use of their medical data.

NFTS FOR DIGITAL OWNERSHIP AND PATIENT RIGHTS

NFTs may be a means of creating ownership of a digital healthcare asset, including but not limited to, individualized therapy schedules, AI-driven treatment plans, and mental health evaluation. Patients, for instance, might store medical records as NFTs, so that patients have ownership and complete control over who can access their healthcare data. This can reduce administrative burdens significantly, simplify medical record management processes, and give patients more control over treatment.

INTEROPERABILITY FOR A UNIFIED HEALTHCARE SYSTEM

Some of the most significant challenges in healthcare include institutional and systematic information fragmentation. Integration of blockchain, NFTs, and deepfakes contributes to a unified, interoperable healthcare system. Blockchain offers an accredited, secure sharing of data with service providers. NFTs introduce unique and verifiable medical records, while deepfakes offer AI-driven therapeutic intervention personalized to every patient's need.

ETHICAL AND REGULATORY CONSIDERATIONS IN IMPLEMENTATION

Their successful adoption necessitates a proper setting of ethical and regulatory standards. It would be the health providers' job to ensure that deepfake-generated content is produced in an ethical manner, solutions comply with protection-of-data requirements, and NFTs are implemented in such a way that no legal complexities with patient ownership rights arise. This requires regulatory bodies to engage with healthcare institutions and technology developers in the light of establishing industry-wide best practices.

CONCLUSION

This study aims to assess how blockchain, deepfake, and NFT technologies can be implemented into therapeutic practice and develop its potential further while considering the possible barriers that could be posed. Each of these has their advantages and disadvantages. Medical blockchain could improve the workflow in the hospital's and practitioners' office with a well-designed system of medical data and informed consent management. However, issues of system complexity and insufficient scalability remain a problem. Contrarily, innovation therapies involving personalization as well as access restriction to copyrighted NFT materials poses no problem. Though, this does require great legal investment. Deepfakes can heighten the therapeutic value of healthcare services through immersive and tailored simulation, however, the ethics of creating and using such simulation technologies requires strict regulation.

The corrective measures for data supervision and artificial intelligence misuse must be dealt with first in order to implement these novel technologies, as well as ensure that the therapeutic processes in the clinics are actually optimized and enhanced. It is important to separate each technology's potential problems and ways to solve them in order to come up with a solution that will make it possible to have an ethical healthcare system.

The current review, therefore, highlights the aspects of blockchain, NFTs, deepfake technologies, and their likely revolutionary impact on medical practices. Their actual use in practice, however, requires careful consideration because there are existing problems related to scalability, ethics, and regulations. More research is needed to devise ways of addressing these issues with the aim of maximizing therapeutic effectiveness and improving the efficiency, cost-effectiveness, and ethical validation of healthcare delivery.

REFERENCE

Abbaoui, W., Retal, S., El Bhiri, B., Kharmoum, N., & Ziti, S. (2024). Towards revolutionizing precision healthcare: A systematic literature review of artificial intelligence methods in precision medicine. *Informatics in Medicine Unlocked, 46*, 101475. DOI: 10.1016/j.imu.2024.101475

Abbaoui, W., Retal, S., Kharmoum, N., & Ziti, S. (2023). Artificial intelligence in the service of precision medicine. In J. Kacprzyk, M. Ezziyyani, & V. E. Balas (Eds.), International Conference on Advanced Intelligent Systems for Sustainable Development. AI2SD 2022 (Vol. 713, pp. 145-157). Springer, Cham. DOI: 10.1007/978-3-031-35248-5_9

Agbo, C. C., & Mahmoud, Q. H. (2020). Blockchain in Healthcare: Opportunities, Challenges, and Possible Solutions. [IJHISI]. *International Journal of Healthcare Information Systems and Informatics, 15*(3), 82–97. DOI: 10.4018/IJHISI.2020070105

Ahmed, F., Khan, S., & Kim, D. (2023). NFTs as a tool for digital rights management in healthcare. *Blockchain in Healthcare Today, 6*, 1–12. DOI: 10.3099/bht.2023.0007

Ahmed, F., Khan, S., & Kim, D. (2023). NFTs as a tool for patient data ownership and consent management in healthcare. *Blockchain in Healthcare Today, 6*, 1–12. DOI: 10.3099/bht.2023.0007

Al-Sumaidaee, G., Alkhudary, R., & Zilic, Z. (2023). Non-fungible tokens (NFTs) as a means for blockchain networks integration in healthcare. 2023 5th Conference on Blockchain Research & Applications for Innovative Networks and Services (BRAINS), 1-2.

Alsaheel, A., Alhassoun, R., Alrashed, R., Almatrafi, N., Almallouhi, N., & Albahli, S. (2023). Deep fakes in healthcare: How deep learning can help to detect forgeries. *Computers, Materials & Continua, 76*(2), 2461–2482. DOI: 10.32604/cmc.2023.040257

Azaria, A., Ekblaw, A., Vieira, T., & Lippman, A. (2016). MedRec: Using blockchain for medical data access and permission management. *2nd International Conference on Open and Big Data*, 25-30. DOI: 10.1109/OBD.2016.11

Bansal, G., Rajgopal, K., Chamola, V., Xiong, Z., & Niyato, D. (2022). Healthcare in Metaverse: A Survey on Current Metaverse Applications in Healthcare. *IEEE Access : Practical Innovations, Open Solutions, 10*, 119914–119946. DOI: 10.1109/ACCESS.2022.3219845

Behl, A., Pereira, V., Nigam, A., Wamba, S., & Sindhwani, R. (2023). Knowledge development in non-fungible tokens (NFT): A scoping review. *Journal of Knowledge Management.*

Benkassioui, B., Retal, S., Kharmoum, N., Hadi, M. Y., & Rhalem, W. (2024). Information extraction for biomedical literature using artificial intelligence: A comparative study. In M. Ezziyyani, J. Kacprzyk, & V. E. Balas (Eds.), International Conference on Advanced Intelligent Systems for Sustainable Development (AI2SD'2023). AI2SD 2023. Lecture Notes in Networks and Systems (Vol. 904, pp. 211-225). Springer, Cham. DOI: 10.1007/978-3-031-52388-5_6

Brown, K., Wilson, L., & Taylor, M. (2023). Ethical considerations of deepfake technology in healthcare. *Journal of Medical Ethics*, *49*(5), 321–330. DOI: 10.1136/medethics-2022-108567

Buterin, V. (2014). A next-generation smart contract and decentralized application platform. https://ethereum.org/en/whitepaper

Cao, B., Li, Y., Zhang, L., Zhang, L., Mumtaz, S., Zhou, Z., & Peng, M. (2019). When Internet of Things Meets Blockchain: Challenges in Distributed Consensus. *IEEE Network*, *33*(6), 133–139. DOI: 10.1109/MNET.2019.1900002

Chan, C. C. K., Kumar, V., Delaney, S., & Gochoo, M. (2020). Combating deepfakes: Multi-LSTM and blockchain as proof of authenticity for digital media. 2020 IEEE / ITU International Conference on Artificial Intelligence for Good (AI4G), 55-62.

Chen, R. J., Lu, M. Y., Chen, T. Y., Williamson, D. F. K., & Mahmood, F. (2021). Synthetic data in machine learning for medicine and healthcare. *Nature Biomedical Engineering*, *5*(6), 493–497. DOI: 10.1038/s41551-021-00751-8 PMID: 34131324

Chen, Y., Li, X., & Zhang, Q. (2023). Blockchain-based secure data sharing for healthcare applications: A comprehensive review. *IEEE Transactions on Biomedical Engineering*, *70*(4), 1234–1245. DOI: 10.1109/TBME.2023.3234567 PMID: 36288237

Chesney, R., & Citron, D. (2019). Deepfakes and the New Disinformation War: The Coming Age of Post-Truth Geopolitics. *Foreign Affairs*, *98*(1), 147–155. https://www.jstor.org/stable/26798018

Divya, N., Dhawan, E., Sundar, H. S., Jain, H., & Dinakar, R. (2024). NFTGenesis - An NFT generation and authentication system with market intelligence using deep learning-based steganography. 2024 IEEE International Conference on Contemporary Computing and Communications (InC4), 1-6.

Drosatos, G., & Kaldoudi, E. (2019). Blockchain applications in the biomedical domain: A scoping review. *Computational and Structural Biotechnology Journal, 17*, 229–240. DOI: 10.1016/j.csbj.2019.01.010 PMID: 30847041

Ekblaw, N.. (2016). A case study for blockchain in healthcare: "MedRec" prototype for electronic health records and medical research data. *Open Journal of Blockchains, 1*(1), 44–56.

Elangovan, D., Long, C. S., Bakrin, F. S., Tan, C. S., Goh, K. W., Hussain, Z., Al-Worafi, Y. M., Lee, K. S., Kassab, Y. W., & Ming, L. C. (2020). Application of Blockchain Technology in Hospital Information System. Dans CRC Press eBooks (p. 231-246). DOI: 10.1201/9781003038399-12

Elasri, C., Kharmoum, N., Saoiabi, F., Boukhlif, M., Ziti, S., & Rhalem, W. (2024). Applying graph theory to enhance software testing in medical applications: A comparative study. In M. Ezziyyani, J. Kacprzyk, & V. E. Balas (Eds.), International Conference on Advanced Intelligent Systems for Sustainable Development (AI2SD'2023). AI2SD 2023. Lecture Notes in Networks and Systems (Vol. 904, pp. 227-242). Springer, Cham. DOI: 10.1007/978-3-031-52388-5_7

Ennejjai, I., Ariss, A., Kharmoum, N., Rhalem, W., Ziti, S., & Ezziyyani, M. (2023). Artificial intelligence for fake news. In J. Kacprzyk, M. Ezziyyani, & V. E. Balas (Eds.), International Conference on Advanced Intelligent Systems for Sustainable Development. AI2SD 2022 (Vol. 637). Springer, Cham. DOI: 10.1007/978-3-031-26384-2_8

Ettaloui, N., Arezki, S., & Gadi, T. (2023). A blockchain-based electronic mental health records model. In Proceedings of the 2023 10th International Conference on Information Technology, Computer, and Electrical Engineering (ICITACEE) (pp. 320–325). IEEE. DOI: 10.1109/ICITACEE58587.2023.10277507

Fraga-Lamas, P., & Fernández-Caramés, T. (2019). Fake news, disinformation, and deepfakes: Leveraging distributed ledger technologies and blockchain to combat digital deception. *IT Professional, 22*(2), 53–59. DOI: 10.1109/MITP.2020.2977589

Gebreab, S. A., Hasan, H. R., Salah, K., & Jayaraman, R. (2022). NFT-based traceability and ownership management of medical devices. *IEEE Access : Practical Innovations, Open Solutions, 10*, 126394–126411. DOI: 10.1109/ACCESS.2022.3226128

Goodfellow, I., Pouget-Abadie, J., Mirza, M., Xu, B., Warde-Farley, D., Ozair, S., Courville, A., & Bengio, Y. (2014). Generative adversarial nets. *Advances in Neural Information Processing Systems, 27*, 2672–2680.

Hasan, H. R., Salah, K., Jayaraman, R., Yaqoob, I., & Omar, M. (2024). NFTs for combating deepfakes and fake metaverse digital contents. *Internet of Things : Engineering Cyber Physical Human Systems*, *25*, 101133. DOI: 10.1016/j.iot.2024.101133

Hasan, H. R., Salah, K., Jayaraman, R., Yaqoob, I., & Omar, M. (2024). NFTs for combating deepfakes and fake metaverse digital contents. *Internet of Things : Engineering Cyber Physical Human Systems*, *25*, 101133. DOI: 10.1016/j.iot.2024.101133

Johnson, E., & Martinez, R. (2023). Deepfake avatars in virtual reality therapy: Opportunities and risks. *Journal of Medicine and Virtual Reality : Computers, Imagery, Photonics and Robotic Applications*, *14*(4), 210–225. DOI: 10.1093/jmvr/2023.00456

Johnson, E., & Martinez, R. (2023). Deepfake avatars in virtual reality therapy: Opportunities and risks. *Frontiers in Digital Health*, *5*, 78–92. DOI: 10.3389/fdgth.2023.00567

Khalil, U., Malik, O. A., Lai, D. T. C., & King, O. S. (2023). Profiling obese subgroups in national health and nutritional status survey data using machine learning techniques: A case study from Brunei Darussalam. *Biomedical Journal of Scientific & Technical Research*, *48*(3), 39629–39643. DOI: 10.26717/BJSTR.2023.48.007641

King, N., & Raja, V. (2018). Protecting privacy in medical data: A blockchain-based approach. *Journal of Medical Systems*, *42*(8), 1–9.

Kostick-Quenet, K. (2022, April 19). What if our medical records became NFTs? LADN.

Kumar, S., Patel, R., & Lee, T. (2022). Blockchain-based secure data sharing for therapeutic applications: A review. *Health Informatics Journal*, *28*(4), 1–15. DOI: 10.1177/14604582221123456

Kumar, S., Patel, R., & Lee, T. (2023). A blockchain-based framework for secure and private health data sharing. *Health Informatics Journal*, *29*(2), 146–160. DOI: 10.1177/14604582231123456

Leible, S., Schlager, S., Schubotz, M., & Gipp, B. (2019). A review on blockchain technology and blockchain projects fostering open science. *Frontiers in Blockchain*, *2*, 16. DOI: 10.3389/fbloc.2019.00016

Li, X., Wang, Y., & Zhang, Q. (2022). A blockchain-based framework for authenticating digital therapeutic assets. *IEEE Transactions on Biomedical Engineering*, *69*(5), 1789–1801. DOI: 10.1109/TBME.2022.3145678

Li, X., Wang, Y., & Zhang, Q. (2023). Integrating blockchain and AI for secure and efficient healthcare data management. *IEEE Journal of Biomedical and Health Informatics*, *27*(6), 2890–2901. DOI: 10.1109/JBHI.2023.1234567

Madine, M., Salah, K., Jayaraman, R., Battah, A., Hasan, H. R., & Yaqoob, I. (2022). Blockchain and NFTs for time-bound access and monetization of private data. *IEEE Access : Practical Innovations, Open Solutions*, *10*, 94186–94202. DOI: 10.1109/ACCESS.2022.3204274

Musamih, A., Salah, K., Jayaraman, R., Yaqoob, I., Puthal, D., & Ellahham, S. (2023, July 1). NFTs in Healthcare: Vision, Opportunities, and Challenges. *IEEE Consumer Electronics Magazine*, *12*(4), 21–32. DOI: 10.1109/MCE.2022.3196480

Nakamoto, S. (2008). Bitcoin: A peer-to-peer electronic cash system. https://bitcoin.org/bitcoin.pdf

Oladoyinbo, T. O., Olabanji, S. O., Olaniyi, O. O., Adebiyi, O. O., Okunleye, O. J., & Alao, A. I. (2024). Exploring the Challenges of Artificial Intelligence in Data Integrity and its Influence on Social Dynamics. *Asian Journal Of Advanced Research And Reports*, *18*(2), 1–23. DOI: 10.9734/ajarr/2024/v18i2601

Prihatno, A. T., Suryanto, N., Oh, S., Le, T.-T.-H., & Kim, H. (2023). NFT image plagiarism check using EfficientNet-based deep neural network with triplet semi-hard loss. *Applied Sciences (Basel, Switzerland)*, *13*(5), 3072. DOI: 10.3390/app13053072

Quy, T. L., K. V., Huong, H. L., Khiem, H. G., P. N., N. K., T. N., B. K., Trong, D. P. N., Hieu, M. D., Bao, Q. T., & Khoa, D. T. (2023). Decentralized management of medical test results utilizing blockchain, smart contracts, and NFTs. *International Journal of Advanced Computer Science and Applications*.

Radanovic, I., & Likić, R. (2018). Opportunities for the use of blockchain technology in medicine. *Applied Health Economics and Health Policy*, *16*(5), 583–590. DOI: 10.1007/s40258-018-0412-8 PMID: 30022440

Radanovic, I., & Likić, R. (2018). Opportunities for use of blockchain technology in medicine. *Applied Health Economics and Health Policy*, *16*(5), 583–590. DOI: 10.1007/s40258-018-0412-8 PMID: 30022440

Rai, S., Chaurasia, B., Gupta, R., & Verma, S. (2023). Blockchain-based NFT for Healthcare System. 2023 IEEE 12th International Conference on Communication Systems and Network Technologies (CSNT), 12, 700-704.

Rai, S., Chaurasia, B., Gupta, R., & Verma, S. (2023). Blockchain-based NFT for healthcare system. 2023 IEEE 12th International Conference on Communication Systems and Network Technologies (CSNT), 700-704.

Rashid, M. M., Suk, H. L., & Kwon, K. R. (2021). Blockchain technology for combating deepfake and protecting video/image integrity.

Saeed, H., Malik, H., Bashir, U., Ahmad, A., Riaz, S., Ilyas, M., Bukhari, W. A., & Khan, M. I. A. (2022). Blockchain technology in healthcare: A systematic review. *PLoS One*, *17*(4), e0266974. DOI: 10.1371/journal.pone.0266462 PMID: 35404955

Sai, S., Hassija, V., Chamola, V., & Guizani, M. (2024). Federated learning and NFT-based privacy-preserving medical-data-sharing scheme for intelligent diagnosis in smart healthcare. *IEEE Internet of Things Journal*, *11*(4), 5568–5577. DOI: 10.1109/JIOT.2023.3308991

Saoiabi, F., Kharmoum, N., Elasri, C., Boukhari, M. E., Ziti, S., & Rhalem, W. (2024). Agile software engineering in medical environments: Challenges and opportunities. In M. Ezziyyani, J. Kacprzyk, & V. E. Balas (Eds.), International Conference on Advanced Intelligent Systems for Sustainable Development (AI2SD'2023) (Vol. 904). Springer, Cham. DOI: 10.1007/978-3-031-52388-5_8

Sibanda, K., Ndayizigamiye, P., & Twinomurinzi, H. (2024). Non-fungible tokens (NFTs) in healthcare: A thematic analysis and research agenda. *Frontiers in Digital Health*, *6*, 6. DOI: 10.3389/fdgth.2024.1377531 PMID: 38919876

Smith, J., Brown, A., & Garcia, M. (2023). Ethical and therapeutic implications of deepfake technology in mental health interventions. *Frontiers in Digital Health*, *5*, 78–92. DOI: 10.3389/fdgth.2023.00567

Smith, J., Brown, A., & Garcia, M. (2023). Ethical implications of deepfake technology in virtual reality therapy. *Journal of Medical Ethics and Technology*, *15*(3), 112–125. DOI: 10.1093/jmet/2023.00345

Stublić, H., Bilogrivić, M., & Zlodi, G. (2023). Blockchain and NFTs in the cultural heritage domain: A review of current research topics. *Heritage*, *6*(1), 256–274. DOI: 10.3390/heritage6040202

Swan, M. (2015). *Blockchain: Blueprint for a new economy*. O'Reilly Media.

Tschorsch, F., & Scheuermann, B. (2016). Bitcoin and beyond: A technical survey on decentralized digital currencies. *IEEE Communications Surveys and Tutorials*, *18*(3), 2084–2123. DOI: 10.1109/COMST.2016.2535718

Wang, H., Liu, J., & Zhang, L. (2023). NFTs for medical data ownership: A new paradigm in healthcare. *Journal of Medical Internet Research*, *25*(3), e45678. DOI: 10.2196/45678

Wei, X., Zhang, W., Bai, G., & Li, B. (2023). Research on technology against deepfake. 2023 3rd International Conference on Mobile Networks and Wireless Communications (ICMNWC), 1-5.

Westerlund, M. (2019). The emergence of deepfake technology: A review. *Technology Innovation Management Review*, *9*(11), 39–52. DOI: 10.22215/timreview/1282

Yaghy, A., Alberto, N. R., & Ristovska, L. (2023). The potential use of non-fungible tokens (NFTs) in healthcare and medical research. *PLOS Digital Health*, *2*(7), 2. DOI: 10.1371/journal.pdig.0000312 PMID: 37498836

Yazdinejad, A., Parizi, R., Srivastava, G., & Dehghantanha, A. (2020). Making sense of blockchain for AI deepfakes technology. 2020 IEEE Globecom Workshops (GC Wkshps), 1-6.

Yazdinejad, A., Parizi, R., Srivastava, G., & Dehghantanha, A. (2020). Making sense of blockchain for AI deepfakes technology. 2020 IEEE Globecom Workshops (GC Wkshps), 1-6.

Yli-Huumo, J., Ko, D., Choi, S., Park, S., & Smolander, K. (2016). Where is current research on blockchain technology? — A systematic review. *PLoS One*, *11*(10), 11. DOI: 10.1371/journal.pone.0163477 PMID: 27695049

Zhang, L., Chen, Y., & Wang, H. (2023). The role of NFTs in digital art therapy: A new frontier for mental health interventions. *Journal of Digital Psychology*, *8*(2), 45–60. DOI: 10.1016/j.jdp.2023.100123

Zhang, L., Chen, Y., & Wang, H. (2023). The role of NFTs in digital art therapy: A new frontier for mental health interventions. *Journal of Digital Psychology*, *8*(2), 45–60. DOI: 10.1016/j.jdp.2023.100123

Zyskind, G., Nathan, O., & Pentland, A. (2015). Decentralizing privacy: Using blockchain to protect personal data. IEEE Security and Privacy Workshops, 180-184.

Chapter 6
NFT Innovation:
Past the Fad

Ganesh Kumar
https://orcid.org/0000-0002-0098-0948
Universiti Teknologi PETRONAS, Seri Iskandar, Malaysia

Pooja Singhal
ABES Engineering College, India

Deepak Aneja
ABES Engineering College, India

Ritu Gupta
Bhagwan Parshuram Institute of Technology, India

Abdullahi Abubakar Imam
Universiti Brunei Darusalam, Brunei

ABSTRACT

People can purchase, sell, and trade the NFTs (non-fungible tokens) on an NFT marketplace. NFTs are one-of-a-kind digital assets recorded on the Blockchain. The market facilitates the buying and selling of digital commodities by individuals from all over the globe and allows artists to tokenize their creations to prove their legitimacy. Secondary sales and royalties provide creators with a reliable source of cash. At its core, the NFT ecosystem revolves around NFT marketplaces. Blockchain technology used to guarantee transparency and security, increase visibility for artists and collectors, and encourage community involvement. Incorporating community and social features, ensuring strong security measures, optimizing scalability and performance, adhering to regulations, and continuously improving are all tasks that need to be completed for an NFT marketplace. To ensure security and transparency, boost artists' and collectors' visibility, and inspire community interaction.

DOI: 10.4018/979-8-3693-8876-1.ch006

1. INTRODUCTION

NFTs, or non-fungible tokens, have completely changed the way that digital assets are valued by making it possible to prove things like ownership, legitimacy, and uniqueness. NFTs, as opposed to replaceable cryptocurrencies, are unique and cannot be duplicated (Batra, Singh, & Gandhi, 2023). Through the use of Blockchain technology, they keep track of ownership and transactional information, enabling creators to tokenize their digital works and offer them for sale directly to customers. NFT marketplaces have evolved as venues for creatives to sell their products and demonstrate their talents, while consumers can gather and acquire these rare digital goods. In the rapidly developing digital world, NFTs have spurred a fresh wave of digital ownership and expression. NFTs (non-fungible tokens) make it possible to create, trade, and possess distinctive digital goods, they have challenged the traditional art, collectibles, and gaming industries. NFTs are a brand-new method of proving ownership and authenticity for digital information, including everything from in-game objects to virtual homes and music. A dependable and effective NFT market is increasingly necessary as the demand for NFTs rises. An NFT marketplace provides a venue for buyers to find and buy rare digital assets as well as for creators to mint and sell their NFTs. The marketplace uses Blockchain technology to guarantee transparency, immutability, and authenticity while providing features like safe transactions, secondary market assistance, and community interaction (Thottungal Valapu et al., 2023).

In this regard, planning and creating a successful NFT marketplace necessitates a thorough comprehension of the requirements and preferences of both creators and consumers, as well as the technical and legal facets of Blockchain-based platforms. The planning and implementation of our strategy, as well as the results of our testing and evaluation of the functio1.nality and usability of this application, will all be covered in the sections that follow. The future directions for study and development in this area will also be discussed. We will also discuss the results of our performance analysis of our application

1.1 NFT Marketplaces

The evolution and rise of NFT marketplaces have been nothing short of remarkable. NFTs, or non-fungible tokens, have transformed the digital asset landscape by providing a way to tokenize and trade unique digital items.

Table 1. Classification of various NFT Marketplaces

Marketplace	Launch Year	Main Features	Supported Blockchain(s)	Transaction Fees	Supported Currencies	Actions Supported	Royalties	Traders
OpenSea	2017	Largest NFT marketplace with broad asset support	Ethereum, Polygon	2.5% on primary sales, 2.5% on secondary sales	ETH, USDC, DAI	Buy, sell, auction, bundle	Up to 10%	Over 1 million
Rarible	2020	Community-owned marketplace with low fees	Ethereum	2.5% on primary sales, 2.5% on secondary sales	ETH, RARI	Buy, sell, create, auction	Up to 15%	Over 700,000
SuperRare	2017	Curated marketplace for high-quality artworks	Ethereum	3% on primary sales	ETH	Buy, sell, auction	10%	Over 200,000
Foundation	2021	Invitation-only marketplace for creators	Ethereum	10% on primary sales, 0% on secondary sales	ETH	Buy, sell, auction, create	Up to 10%	Invitation-only
NBA Top Shot	2020	Officially licensed NBA collectibles marketplace	Flow	5% on primary sales, 5% on secondary sales	USD, CAD, EUR, GBP	Buy, sell, trade, pack openings	Up to 5%	Over 2 million
Axie Marketplace	2018	Marketplace for trading Axie Infinity assets	Ethereum	4.25% on primary sales, 4.25% on secondary sales	ETH	Buy, sell, auction	4.25%	Over 500,000
Mintable	2018	User-friendly platform for creating and selling NFTs	Ethereum, Polygon	2.5% on primary sales, 2.5% on secondary sales	ETH, USDC, DAI			

While the concept of NFTs has been around for several years, it was in recent times that they gained mainstream attention and adoption. The launch of platforms like Open Sea, Rarible, and Super Rare provided the necessary infrastructure and marketplaces for creators and collectors to engage in NFT transactions (Sree Kumar et al., 2023; Ranjbar Alvar et al., 2023; Pelechrinis et al., 2023). These differentiations of NFT marketplaces shown in Table 1 that enabled artists, musicians, and even athletes to tokenize and sell their digital creations directly to a global audience, eliminating the need for intermediaries. This newfound ability to authenticate and prove ownership of digital assets revolutionized the art and collectibles industries.

2. DESIGN & IMPLEMENTATION

The NFT marketplace involves creating a straightforward and intuitive platform for the trading of digital assets. The design must focus on providing a visually appealing and engaging interface that emphasizes the unique attributes of each NFT (Deshpande, Sangitrao, & Panchal, 2023; Kazi et al., 2023). Establishing a reliable infrastructure that facilitates seamless transactions and protects users' digital assets is essential for implementing the marketplace. The marketplace must include Blockchain technology to ensure the authenticity, permanence, and transparency of NFT ownership as depicted in Figure 1.

2.1 Wallet Connect

As shown in Figure 1, a marketplace for NFTs is established with Wallet Connect. Users can securely link their cryptocurrency wallets and interact with the marketplace by including Wallet Connect into the marketplace's frontend application. This connection enables users to authorize transactions, explore their NFT collections, and engage in sales or auctions without revealing their private keys. Wallet Connect establishes an encrypted communication channel between the wallet and the marketplace, safeguarding user data's safety and integrity, hence enhancing the entire user experience and fostering trust in the NFT marketplace ecosystem (Konagari et al., 2023; Kamble et al., n.d.; White, Mahanti, & Passi, 2022).

2.2 NFT Generation

Developers frequently utilize smart contracts on blockchain systems such as Ethereum to create NFTs. The method for an NFT involves specifying its distinct attributes, data, and ownership regulations. These smart contracts provide the framework for generating new NFTs and documenting their ownership history on the Blockchain (Kireyev, 2022; Das et al., 2022; Vasan, Janosov, & Barabási, 2022a). Developers may utilize standards like as ERC-721 or ERC-1155 to ensure compatibility and interoperability among various platforms and wallets. Transaction fees, which users are required to pay to execute transactions on the Blockchain, are an additional consideration in the creation of NFTs as illustrated in Figure 1. NFT marketplaces facilitate the generation of unique and unequivocally rare digital assets, allowing artists, creators, and collectors to engage in the flourishing market for digital art, collectibles, and singular digital assets.

2.3 NFT Minting

NFT marketplaces might also include extra services like community involvement, promotion, and curation. Companies might offer creators resources like social media integration and analytics to help them promote their work and engage with customers. For buyers and collectors, some markets may include curated or exclusive collections, celebrity or brand relationships, and other benefits (La Morgia et al., 2022). In general, NFT marketplaces function as a decentralised platform for sellers and buyers to interact when it comes to the ownership and exchange of distinctive digital assets.

2.4 Work Flow

Figure 1. Work Flow for NFT Marketplace

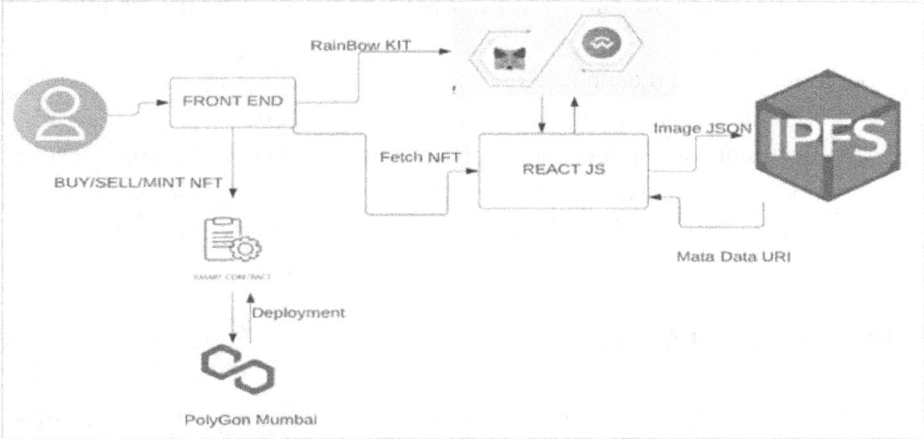

1. Conceptualization and Planning
    - Perform detailed market research to understand past trends and current market conditions.
    - Establish long-term goals centred on innovation and sustainable value creation.
    - Ensure plans adhere to regulatory standards and ethical considerations.
2. Platform Development
    - Choose a technology stack that ensures scalability, security, and interoperability.
    - Create secure, reliable, and verifiable smart contracts.
    - Design a user-friendly interface and experience.
3. Integration and Testing
    - Facilitate integration with various cryptocurrency wallets seamlessly.
    - Support diverse payment methods, including decentralized finance (DeFi) protocols.
    - Perform extensive testing, including stress and security tests, to ensure robustness.
4. Deployment
    - Launch smart contracts on a trustworthy and secure blockchain network.
    - Implement a phased rollout strategy, beginning with a beta version for feedback and adjustments.
5. Marketing and User Acquisition

- Develop a marketing strategy to attract both early adopters and the general public.
- Build and nurture a strong, engaged community.
- Form strategic partnerships with established brands, creators, and influencers.

6. Operations and Maintenance
   - Offer responsive, multi-channel customer support.
   - Continuously update and improve the platform based on user feedback and technological advancements.
   - Utilize advanced analytics tools to monitor performance and user behaviour.

2.5 Mathematical Model

1. User Activity: Define the number of users (U_t) at time (t) using a growth model. A common choice is the logistic growth model:

U_t = L / (1 + exp (-k (t - t0))) ....(i)

where U_t is the number of users at time t, L is the limiting number of users, k is the growth rate, and t0 is the inflection point in time.

2. Transaction Metrics: To calculate transaction volume (TV_t) over time:

TV_t = ∫[0, t] (Number of Transactions per unit time) dt ....(ii)

Average transaction fee (ATF_t) can be estimated as:

ATF_t = Total Transaction Fees / Total Number of Transactions.........(iii)

3. Marketplace Efficiency: The time required to list an NFT (T_list) can be represented as a function dependent on various factors, but a mathematical expression would depend on platform-specific data.
4. Liquidity Metrics: Bid-ask spread (BAS_t) can be calculated as the difference between the highest bid and the lowest ask prices at a given time (t).
5. User Engagement: Calculate the user retention rate (RR_t) over time as:

RR_t = (Number of Users at time (t+1)) / (Number of Users at time (t)) ...(iv)

6. Transaction Fee Revenue (TRF_t) is the primary source of income for a market, and it may be computed as follows:

TRF_t = [0, t] (Transaction Fees per unit time). dt.............(v)

The listing revenue function (LRF_t) is defined as follows:

LRF_t = [0, t] (Listing Fees per unit time) dt..................(vi).

These formulas give a framework for measuring the effectiveness of an NFT market on a variety of KPIs. To use these equations effectively, you'll need to gather data particular to the target market and modify the equations accordingly.

3. RESEARCH METHODOLOGY

Studying the NFT market requires a solid grounding in research technique. Quantitative examination of market trends and statistics and qualitative studies of user experiences and motives are only two of the many possible approaches to this area of study. Among the most typical approaches is to conduct interviews, focus groups, and surveys of NFT market participants. Researchers can gain a deeper insight into user behaviour, preferences, and attitudes towards NFTs by taking a qualitative approach (Chaparala et al., 2022; Agarwal, Singh, & Verma, 2022; Deshpande, Sangitrao, & Panchal, 2023). Analysing market data from different NFT platforms to spot trends in sales, pricing, and popularity is another common method. Researchers are able to better understand market behaviour and spot new patterns and opportunities thanks to this quantitative method. Case studies of completed NFT projects, content analysis of online discourse, and ethnographic studies of NFT groups round out the available research methodologies. Researchers need to weigh the benefits and drawbacks of available research methods in order to select the most suitable strategy for achieving their study aims (Pawelzik & Thies, 2022; Caxton et al., 2022). In order to keep up with the current trends and changes in the NFT sector, it may be necessary to adopt new research approaches.

4. RESULT

4.1 NFT Creation Process

The NFT Creation home page serves as a gateway for users to mint and customize their unique digital assets, facilitating the creation and issuance of non-fungible tokens (NFTs) as shown in Figure 2.

Figure 2. Home Place for NFT Creation

The landing page built in react. At the top right, in the navbar, it shows a login/logout button to connect to the user's wallet. This button uses a rainbow kit in the background to give the functionality. Other than this, the user's address and the network is also shown in the navbar depicted in Figure 3.

Figure 3. Landing Page

This page employs the Ether.js library to retrieve and display a comprehensive list of NFTs currently available for purchase from smart contracts shown in Figure 4, providing users with real-time access to the marketplace.

Figure 4. Retrieve &Display NFT

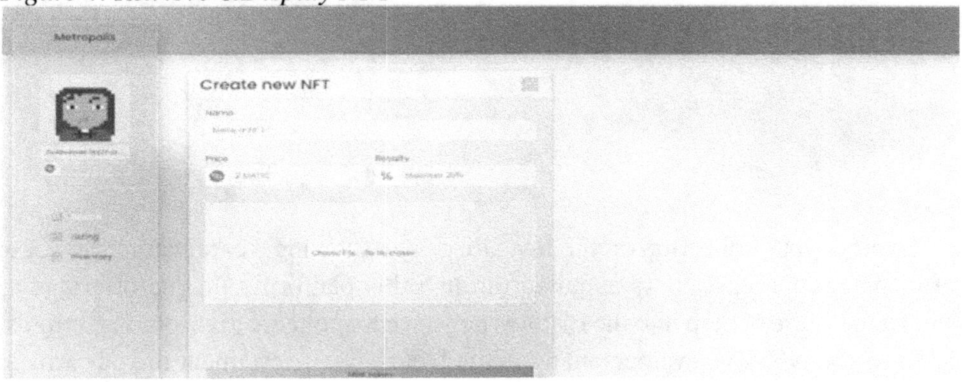

Figure 5. Minted NFT's

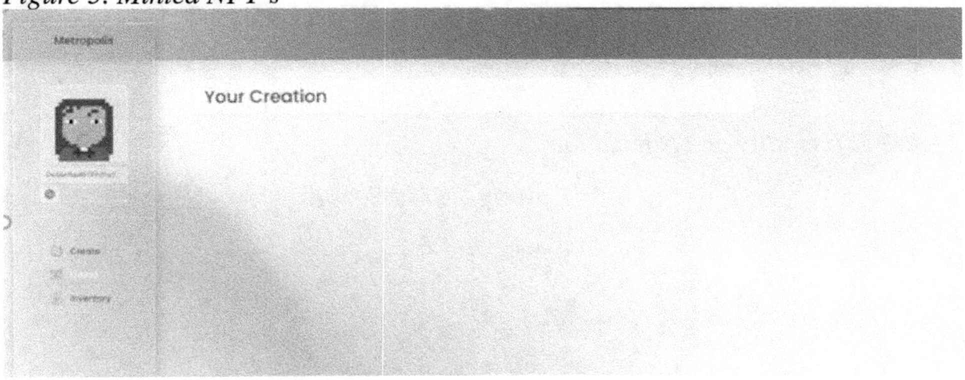

This is the minting page from where any user can mint NFTs. These minted NFTs goes to smart contracts as shown in Figure 5. Users can set different NFT attributes here such as Name, Price, Royalty % and the image for the NFT. Uploaded images are stored in IPFS using web3.js.

Figure 6. Inventory Page

Explore your collection on the Inventory page showing a captivating showcase of all your cherished NFTs acquired through this platform's unique offerings as shown in Figure 6. Step into the Listings page, where your creative journey unfolds. Witness the NFTs you've personally minted, each one a testament to your artistic expression in the digital realm.

4.2 Performance Evaluation

H1: How simple was it to use and navigate the marketplace?

Figure 7. Usability and Navigation

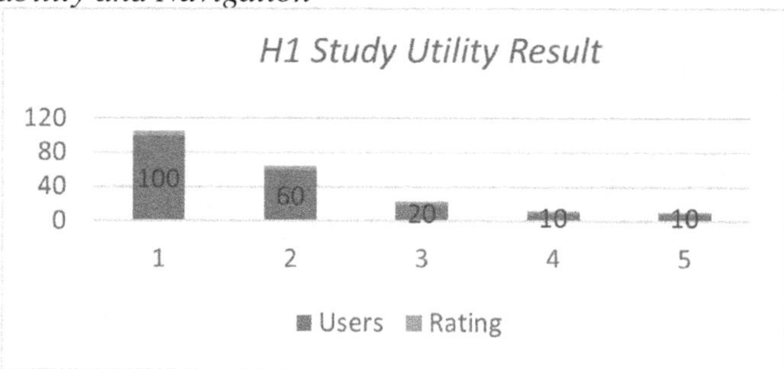

Average (*H1*) = (Sum of ratings for Q1) / (Number of responses for Q1)

Average (*H1*) = (90) / (20) =4.5

In this case, the average rating for *H1* is 4.5 shown in Figure 7, indicating that users find the marketplace relatively easy to use and navigate.

H2: When rated from 1 to 5, How simple is it to produce NFT without problems?

Figure 8. NFT Creation Ease

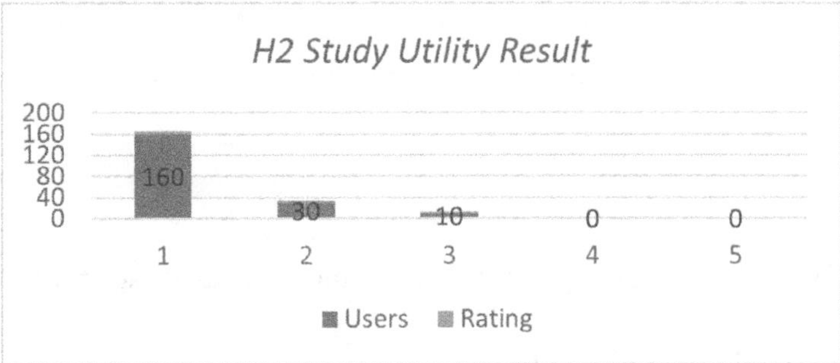

Average (*H2*) = (Sum of ratings for Q2) / (Number of responses for Q2)

Average (*H2*) = (110) / (25) =4.4

Standard Deviation (*H2*) = Calculate the standard deviation to understand the variability in responses. The average rating for Q2 is 4.4, and the standard deviation can provide insights into the consistency of user experiences depicted in Figure 8.

H3: What level of interactivity would you say NFT Marketplace has on a scale of 1 to 5?

Figure 9. Interactivity Level

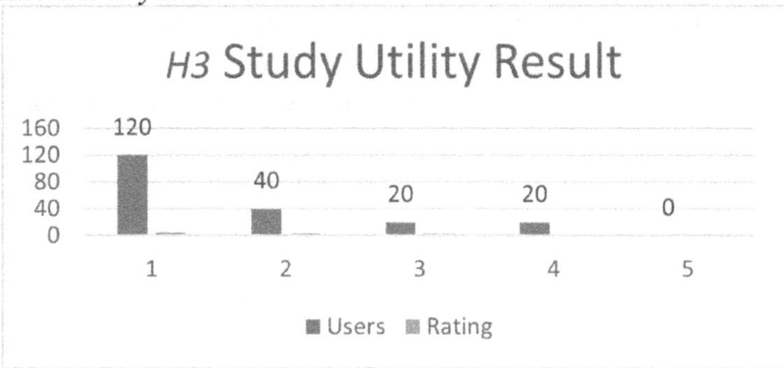

Average (*H3*) = (Sum of ratings for Q3) / (Number of responses for Q3)

Average (*H3*) = (120) / (30) =4.0

The average rating for *H3* is 4.0 shown in Figure 9, suggesting that users perceive a moderate level of interactivity on the NFT marketplace.

H4: How simple was trading NFT, rated from 1 to 5?

Figure 10. NFT Trading Ease

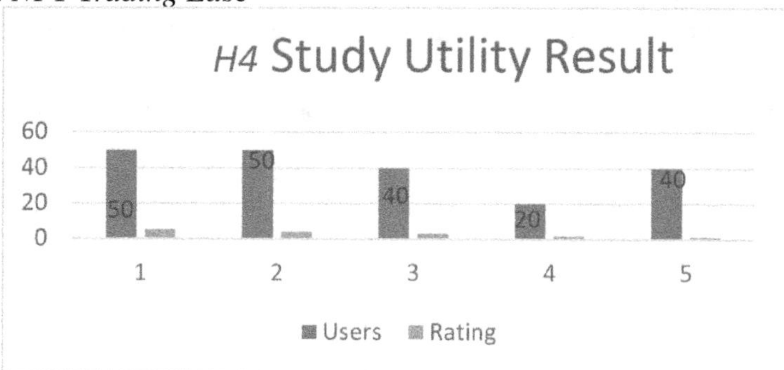

Average (*H4*) = (Sum of ratings for Q4) / (Number of responses for Q4)

Average (*H4*) = (60) / (15) = 4.0

Standard Deviation (*H4)* = Calculate the standard deviation to assess the variability in user responses.The average rating for Q4 is 4.0 shown in Figure 10, with standard deviation information for additional insights.

H5: How interactive is the dashboard for your profile?

Figure 11. Dashboard Interactivity

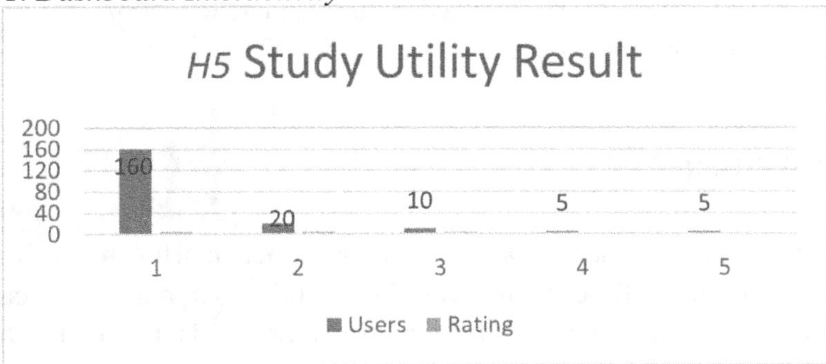

Average (*H5*) = (Sum of ratings for Q5) / (Number of responses for Q5)

Average (*H5*) = (80) / (20) = 4.0

The average rating for *H5* is 4.0 depicted in Figure 11, indicating a moderate level of interactivity in user profiles.

H6: What would you say the entire experience was like?

Figure 12. Overall Experience

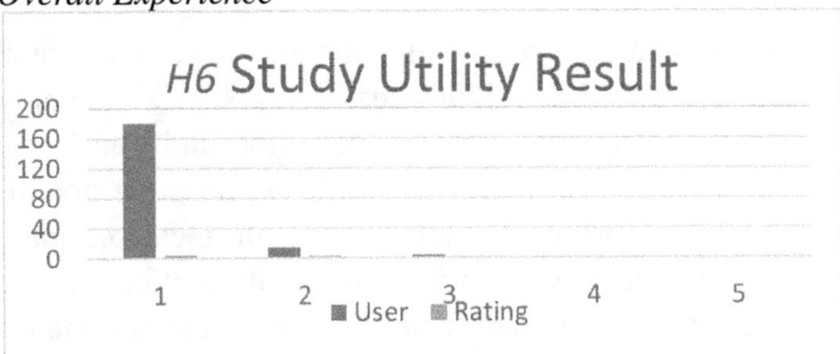

Average (*H6*) = (Sum of ratings for Q6) / (Number of responses for Q6)

Average (*H6*) = (140) / (35) = 4.0

The average rating for H6 is 4.0 as shown in Figure 12, suggesting that users had a consistent overall experience.

These computations provide a quantitative analysis of user feedback based on the questionnaire responses. The average ratings offer insights into user perceptions of different aspects of the NFT marketplace, while standard deviations can help assess the level of consensus among users.

5. FUTURE SCOPE

The future of the NFT marketplace holds immense potential for growth, innovation, and transformation. As Blockchain technology continues to mature, we can expect NFT marketplaces to become more diverse, specialized, and integrated with existing platforms. Artists, creators, and collectors will find an expanding array of niche marketplaces catering to specific interests, ranging from art and music to gaming and virtual real estate. The integration of NFTs with social media, e-commerce, and gaming platforms will make it easier for users to showcase and trade their digital assets seamlessly. Efforts towards interoperability and standardization will enable NFTs to move fluidly across different Blockchain networks, promoting a more connected and accessible ecosystem. Environmental concerns will drive sustainability initiatives, pushing for eco-friendly alternatives and carbon offset solutions within NFT marketplaces. The future of the NFT marketplace is an exciting realm of possibilities, where creativity, technology, and digital ownership converge to reshape the way we perceive and engage with digital assets.

6. CONCLUSION

NFT marketplace represents a ground-breaking shift in how we perceive and engage with digital assets. While still in its early stages, the future of NFT marketplaces holds immense potential for growth, innovation, and transformation. As the technology continues to evolve, we can expect to see an expansion of specialized marketplaces catering to various interests, along with increased integration with existing platforms. Interoperability and standardization efforts will enhance the fluidity of NFTs across different Blockchain networks, while sustainability and environmental concerns will drive the adoption of eco-friendly solutions. As regulatory frameworks are established, consumer protection and trust within the marketplace will be prioritized. The versatility of NFTs will lead to the exploration of new use cases beyond art, enabling digital identity verification, decentralized finance, and more. The NFT marketplace is an exciting and dynamic landscape that has the potential to revolutionize ownership, creativity, and digital interactions for years to come.

REFERENCES

Agarwal, U., Singh, K., & Verma, R. (2022). An Overview of Non-Fungible Tokens (NFT). International Journal of Advanced Research in Science, Communication and Technology (IJARSCT, 2(1).

Batra, P., Singh, G. R., & Gandhi, R. (2023). NFT Marketplace. arXiv preprint arXiv:2304.10632.

Caxton, S. V. M., Naveen, K., Karthik, R., & Bama, S. S. (2022, July). User-Centered Evaluation and Design Suggestions for NFT Marketplaces. In *2022 International Conference on Inventive Computation Technologies (ICICT)* (pp. 1214-1221). IEEE. DOI: 10.1109/ICICT54344.2022.9850815

Chaparala, H. K., Doddala, S. V., Showail, A., Singh, A., Gazzaz, S., & Nawab, F. (2022, August). Liftchain: A scalable multi-stage nft transaction protocol. In *2022 IEEE International Conference on Blockchain (Blockchain)* (pp. 362-369). IEEE. DOI: 10.1109/Blockchain55522.2022.00057

Das, D., Bose, P., Ruaro, N., Kruegel, C., & Vigna, G. (2022, November). Understanding security issues in the NFT ecosystem. In *Proceedings of the 2022 ACM SIGSAC Conference on Computer and Communications Security* (pp. 667-681). DOI: 10.1145/3548606.3559342

Deshpande, I., Sangitrao, R., & Panchal, L. (2023, January). Study of NFT Marketplace in the Metaverse. In International Conference on Data Management, Analytics & Innovation (pp. 855-862). Singapore: Springer Nature Singapore. DOI: 10.1007/978-981-99-1414-2_59

Deshpande, I., Sangitrao, R., & Panchal, L. (2023, January). Study of NFT Marketplace in the Metaverse. In International Conference on Data Management, Analytics & Innovation (pp. 855-862). Singapore: Springer Nature Singapore. DOI: 10.1007/978-981-99-1414-2_59

Kamble, M., Chaudhari, T., Korewar, M., & Umale, A. NFT MARKETPLACE WEB APPLICATION.

Kazi, S., Kazi, A., D'souza, L., & Loke, A. (2023, April). NiftyPlace: An NFT Marketplace Using Blockchain. In International Conference on Soft Computing for Security Applications (pp. 299-314). Singapore: Springer Nature Singapore.

Kireyev, P. (2022). NFT marketplace design and market intelligence.

Konagari, A., Kusuma, H. P., Chetharasi, S., Kuchipudi, R., Babu, P. R., & Murthy, T. S. (2023, June). NFT Marketplace for Blockchain based Digital Assets using ERC-721 Token Standard. In *2023 International Conference on Sustainable Computing and Smart Systems (ICSCSS)* (pp. 1394-1398). IEEE. DOI: 10.1109/ICSCSS57650.2023.10169350

La Morgia, M., Mei, A., Mongardini, A. M., & Nemmi, E. N. (2022). Nft wash trading in the ethereum blockchain. arXiv preprint arXiv:2212.01225.

Pawelzik, L., & Thies, F. (2022). Selling digital art for millions-a qualitative analysis of NFT art marketplaces. In *Proceedings of the Thirtieth European Conference on Information Systems (ECIS 2022)*, Timisoara, Romania.

Pelechrinis, K., Liu, X., Krishnamurthy, P., & Babay, A. (2023). Spotting anomalous trades in NFT markets: The case of NBA TopShot. *PLoS One*, *18*(6), e0287262. DOI: 10.1371/journal.pone.0287262 PMID: 37319178

Ranjbar Alvar, S., Akbari, M., Yue, D., & Zhang, Y. (2023, August). NFT-Based Data Marketplace with Digital Watermarking. In *Proceedings of the 29th ACM SIGKDD Conference on Knowledge Discovery and Data Mining* (pp. 4756-4767).

Sree Kumar, C., Lenka, A. K., Dora, S. A., Sharma, A., Fiore, U., & Roy, D. S. (2023, June). TokenFuse: A Versatile NFT Marketplace. In International Conference on Computational Science and Its Applications (pp. 179-192). Cham: Springer Nature Switzerland.

Thottungal Valapu, S., Sarkar, T., Coleman, J., Avyukt, A., Embrechts, H., Torfs, D., . . . Krishnamachari, B. (2023, September). DARSAN: A Decentralized Review System Suitable for NFT Marketplaces. In International Conference on Blockchain (pp. 3-20). Cham: Springer Nature Switzerland. DOI: 10.1007/978-3-031-44920-8_1

Vasan, K., Janosov, M., & Barabási, A. L. (2022). Quantifying NFT-driven networks in crypto art. *Scientific Reports*, *12*(1), 2769. DOI: 10.1038/s41598-022-05146-6 PMID: 35177628

Vasan, K., Janosov, M., & Barabási, A. L. (2022). Quantifying NFT-driven networks in crypto art. *Scientific Reports*, *12*(1), 2769. DOI: 10.1038/s41598-022-05146-6 PMID: 35177628

White, B., Mahanti, A., & Passi, K. (2022, April). Characterizing the OpenSea NFT marketplace. In Companion Proceedings of the Web Conference 2022 (pp. 488-496). DOI: 10.1145/3487553.3524629

Chapter 7
Blockchain Integration for Smart City Infrastructure:
Advancing Urban Connectivity and Security

Vasima Khan
https://orcid.org/0000-0002-6903-9910
Department of Computer Science and Engineering, Sagar Institute of Science and Technology, Bhopal, India

R. Nithin Kumar
https://orcid.org/0009-0001-7672-1475
Department of Computer Science and Engineering, Velammal Institute of Technology, Tiruvallur, India

Senthil Kumar Chandrasekaran
https://orcid.org/0000-0001-6137-1858
School of Computer Science Engineering and Information Systems (SCORE), Vellore Institute of Technology, Vellore, India

K. Chokkanathan
Department of Artificial Intelligence, Madanapalle Institute of Technology and Science, Madanapalle, India

D. K. Singh
https://orcid.org/0000-0001-5618-9752
Department of Fire Engineering, National Fire Service College, Nagpur, India

J. K. Periasamy
https://orcid.org/0000-0002-2065-6539
Department of Computer Science and Engineering, Sri Sai Ram Engineering College, Chennai, India

ABSTRACT

Blockchain technology is being integrated in smart city architecture to enhance urban connectivity and safety. The intention of this article is to compare Smart Cities to create that of the 'Quality of Life' through the adoption of digital technology and data, overcoming interoperability, security and data management issues. Here, blockchain offers a solution as it assures security, data integrity, and

DOI: 10.4018/979-8-3693-8876-1.ch007

transparency. It could transform data governance, public services, transportation, and energy management. Decentralized energy grids also engage in peer-to-peer energy trade that helps reduce dependency on centralized power systems. To increase communication security between vehicles and infrastructure in the presented paper, blockchain technology has been successfully used. This can enable people to make better decisions without disrupting the system. It can also enhance public services by providing secure platforms for voter registration, identity verification and public records management.

INTRODUCTION

Due to issues like urbanization, population growth, and sustainable development, metro areas are being developed into smart cities. They leverage state-of-the-art technologies within the sectors of IoT and artificial intelligence, but also big data analytics, to spur economic growth, effective urban services delivery, and livability. These systems are still vulnerable to compatibility, security, and data management issues. For these issues, blockchain technology brings optimistic solutions (Li, 2018).

These features lead to the use of blockchain for smart city applications because it is decentralized, secure, and transparent. It can do this while ensuring data integrity, providing full transparency at public service points, and enabling smooth interchange between city systems. This chapter investigates the potential contribution of blockchain technology to the built environment of smart cities in terms of data governance, public services, energy management, and transportation. At its core, it reviews existing case studies and implementations to give an overall view of the advantages and challenges to the implementation of blockchains in smart cities, as well as potential future use cases. We now have case studies and real-world applications (Singh et al., 2020).

Blockchain technology can greatly enhance energy management by establishing decentralized energy networks, reducing dependence on centralized power systems, and facilitating renewable energy sources. This is where peer-to-peer energy trading is so vital—people and companies are buying and selling excess energy to each other directly in order to increase energy efficiency and promote smart city initiatives for a more sustainable future. It saves events in a distributed manner, which takes out the problem of trust between different networks or organizations. In doing this, it can enable more accurate and reliable data interchange between infrastructure and cars. Combining autonomous vehicles and smart traffic management systems can make urban roads more efficient, less congested, and safer (Rotună et al., 2019).

With the integration of blockchain technology, public services can be significantly enhanced to provide stronger security, transparency, and reliability. It has the potential to reduce the risk of fraudulent activities, protect the privacy of citizens' data, and boost public confidence in digital governance. Integration of blockchain technology with smart city infrastructure, however, is fraught with challenges of scalability, regulatory compliance, and cross-sector cooperation. This chapter will address these challenges and present proposals to solve them, allowing blockchain technology to realize its full potential (Xihua & Goyal, 2022).

Blockchain technology is already being integrated into the infrastructure of smart cities to enhance efficiency, security, and connectivity. Blockchain and Resilience in Urban Development for 2050 Examples are ICT and IoT when cities use cutting-edge technology to collect, analyze, and process data from urban systems. This integration allows for real-time resource management and monitoring, enhancing efficiency in public safety, energy, transportation, and waste management services. This chapter illustrates the potential of blockchain for urban sustainable development by investigating the applications, benefits, and challenges of the technology in smart cities (Abbas et al., 2021).

A smart city aims to optimize its use of municipal resources, reduce waste, and have as little environmental impact as possible through the use of smart energy grids, efficient water management systems, and sustainable waste disposal. It improves the quality of life for residents by providing smart transport systems, reducing congestion, and facilitating alternative transport options such as bike-sharing and electric vehicles. It enhances public safety and security through predictive analytics, emergency response technologies, and surveillance systems. Thanks to e-governance portals, citizens can engage more effectively with local authorities, be part of the decision-making process, and obtain government services online (Bommu et al., 2023).

Nonetheless, there are significant barriers to the rapid deployment of smart city technology, including interoperability, security, and data privacy. This huge amount of data that is collected and processed is subject to abuse and cyberattacks." The backbone of smart cities is based on the seamless sharing of information. Upgrading existing infrastructure can be an expensive and complicated financial and logistical challenge, which is to say it requires advanced planning and funding (Theodorou & Sklavos, 2019).

The chapter also offers a structured approach for creating a business model that incorporates blockchain technology into smart city infrastructure. This paper discusses the ways blockchain protocol can provide improved urban connectivity and security, paving the way for sustainable, efficient, and secure urban ecosystems. This is a great resource for entrepreneurs, policymakers, and urban planners striving to forge ahead and lead the future of smart cities.

Objectives of the Chapter

To find out how blockchain technology can implement its features in smart city infrastructure across areas such as energy management, transportation, public services, and data governance.

Investigate the potential benefits of implementing blockchain technology in smart cities, such as enhanced data integrity, transparency, and decentralization, and discuss the challenges that need to be overcome, such as scalability and regulatory compliance.

Facilitate the demonstration of successful and emerging implementations of blockchain in smart cities, applying lessons of early adopters to inform the next generation of urban infrastructure innovation.

BLOCKCHAIN TECHNOLOGY FUNDAMENTALS: THE ROLE OF BLOCKCHAIN IN URBAN DEVELOPMENT

Blockchain technology, being decentralized and irreversible, can provide a secure, transparent, and tampering-resistant means for managing data and transactions and hence addresses the challenges that can be encountered in smart cities. It enhances urban systems' reliability and efficiency, particularly in processing the large volumes of data generated by sensors and other devices. It secures data authenticity and integrity with the help of blockchain technology, shaping protection against any manipulation or unauthorized access. Critical systems such as public safety networks and energy grids looking for this is especially important (Alasbali et al., 2022).

Blockchain technology can therefore enhance energy management through decentralized energy markets, promotion of renewable energy source utilization, and reduced dependence on centralized power grids. This enables smart cities to meet their sustainability goals. In transportation networks, blockchain tech may improve vehicle/equipment connections and enable driverless vehicles as well as smart traffic management. Data reliability of this secured platform means less traffic, better traffic flow, and safer roads. Blockchain technology, all up in the grand scheme of things, is greatly beneficial to the smart city transportation and energy sector (Alnahari & Ariaratnam, 2022).

Implementing blockchain technology within public services could streamline voter processes, confirm identification, and if needed, manage public records. It reduces the chances of digital fraud, protects data privacy, and enhances public trust in digital governance. As a result, citizens are more engaged with urban development processes, and services are delivered more efficiently. Blockchain and smart city – Blockchain technology can improve all of this by creating decentralized networks that enhance the integrity and reliability of data in addition to reducing the overall costs of city management. With cities transforming toward the objective of smart urban development, integrating blockchain tech in smart city infrastructure will also become imperative.

Concepts of Blockchain

Blockchain is a Distributed Ledger Technology, which saves data on several computer nodes with a guarantee of permissionless security, transparency, and immutability. In the blockchain, each block holds a linked list of transactions. This means, to alter a single block's cryptographic hash, timestamp, and transaction data without changing the contents of the other blocks, a majority of the network users must agree (Bommu et al., 2023). Three fundamental elements of the blockchain are transactions, miners (or validators), and nodes. The machinery behind it includes nodes, which keep the blockchain from being tampered with, transactions — records that are counted in blocks — and miners who validate those transactions through consensus mechanisms (e.g., Proof of Work or Proof of Stake)). It is a riskless transaction, as no central authority is required to record the transactions.

Decentralization and Immutability

A key feature of blockchain, decentralization distributes power among every node (these nodes have a complete copy of the entire blockchain). And thankfully no one single failure point will ever determine the value of the net, because for any changes to take effect a consensus of just over 51% of the nodes must agree with the change. In contrast, while the data in the block is linked using the chaining mechanism, and each block links back using the cryptographic hash mechanism, it is impossible to lose or modify it (blockchain's immutability). The hash for each block is computed from the content of the current block, but also the hash from the previous block. Thus everyone on the network set that anything between the data and the chains is the sign of any changes in the hash of a block of the data, hence interrupting the chain (Rahamathunnisa et al., 2023; Srinivas et al., 2023).

Smart Contracts and Their Applications

Smart contracts refer to self-executing agreements with the terms of the agreement between the buyer and seller directly written into lines of code which, in the absence of intermediaries, automatically execute the provisions of the contracts when predetermined conditions have been met and verified. They provide features such as immutability, transparency, and security powered by blockchain networks. Their use cases are vast and include automating financial operations such as insurance claims and loan payments, which lowers fraud risk. By digitizing the flow of commodities, verifying product authenticity, and reinforcing contractual obligations, smart contracts enhance transparency and efficiency in supply chain management. Those features also reduce costs and delays. Overall, smart contracts are a potential solution for many industries (Maguluri, Arularasan, et al., 2023).

Smart contracts enable peer-to-peer energy trading, automated invoicing, and energy distribution management in smart cities. A blockchain-based system enables residents to sell surplus energy while ensuring timely payments and accurate record-keeping. Smart contracts also optimize public services, such as by enabling secure identity verification, verified voting platforms, and public records management. They enhance public trust in digital public administration, speed up administrative procedures, and reduce the risk of fraud and error. It implements smart contracts on a decentralized ledger that results in better efficiency, transparency, and security in multiple categories. From supply chain management to banking, and smart cities, the disruptive potential of blockchain in reengineering traditional processes and creating a secure digital future is well documented.

SMART CITY INFRASTRUCTURE

Despite obstacles such as data management, interoperability, security, and funding, smart cities can improve citizens' quality of life and support sustainable development by investing in state-of-the-art communication networks and robust cybersecurity measures. This creates a more seamless, practical, and secure urban setting (Sundaramoorthy et al., 2024).

Components of Smart City Infrastructure: Information and Communication Technology (ICT) Infrastructure

A well-established data infrastructure integrates data into different elements of smart cities, such as buildings, roads, transport, and energy, encouraging intelligent reactions to developments in one or more systems. This infrastructure enables the collection, transmission, and analysis of data, thereby allowing for the real-time monitoring and management of urban systems. It integrates cloud-based platforms, smart sensors, and Internet of Things devices to offer application-based solutions, including traffic controls and environmental monitoring (Malathi et al., 2024). Figure 1 depicts the various components of Smart City Infrastructure.

Figure 1. Components of Smart City Infrastructure

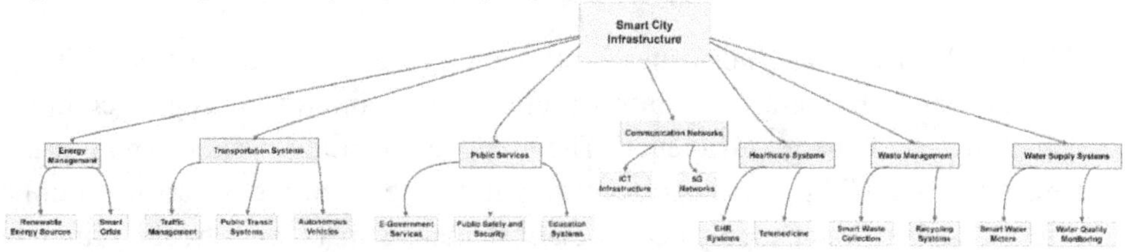

Internet of Things (IoT) Devices

Smart cities demand more Internet of Things (IoT) devices, including sensors, cameras, and smart meters, to collect information about the urban environment air quality, temperature, humidity, traffic flow, and energy consumption. This optimizes traffic, reduces congestion , and also synchronizes with the current traffic light status (Boopathi et al., 2022; Subha et al., 2023).

Smart Energy Systems

The foundation of smart city infrastructure is energy management, which improves urban energy efficiency and sustainability by leveraging smart grids, renewable energy sources, and energy storage solutions. Smart grids facilitate the needed demand response and integration of distributed energy resources like wind turbines and solar panels. Because they balance demand and supply, batteries and other energy storage technologies provide a constant and steady energy supply (Syamala et al., 2023; Venkateswaran, Vidhya, Ayyannan, et al., 2023).

Intelligent Transportation Systems

Smart cities put transport at the forefront for sustainable, reliable, and safe urban mobility. Intelligent transportation systems (ITS) use data from various sources to manage traffic, public transport, and other transportation systems. This includes adaptive traffic signal control, intelligent parking solutions, real-time observation, and unified public transport systems. ITS can reduce commuting time, enhance the quality of urban life, and clean up air (Boopathi et al., 2021; Gopal et al., 2024).

Smart Buildings and Infrastructure

Using advanced materials, energy-efficient systems and Internet of Things technology, smart buildings and infrastructure seek to improve occupant comfort, sustainability, and energy efficiency. They reduce operating costs by monitoring and manipulating HVAC systems according to the needs of the occupants. Public utilities — such as water supply networks, trash management, and street lighting — also use IoT technologies to enable higher sustainability and efficiency (Sharma et al., 2024).

E-Governance and Citizen Services

E-governance platforms such as e-services provide many key benefits such as improving communication between citizens and municipalities by allowing online access to government services including permit applications and public documents. By making government data more available, they promote accountability and transparency. Smart cities are harnessing digital platforms to engage citizens in the decision-making processes, which not only enhances social engagement but also increases public trust in government.

Data Management and Analytics

For smart city initiatives to gather meaningful insights from the millions of data generated each day due to IoT devices, they call for dynamic analytics and data management. This data is analyzed through AI, Machine Learning , and Advanced Analytics, enabling proactive decision-making, resource management, and predictive maintenance. Data analytics improves the effectiveness and efficiency of urban management by helping local authorities identify trends, monitor performance, and react to emerging challenges. Smart city infrastructure integrates information and communication technologies (ICT), the Internet of Things (IoT), smart energy systems, intelligent transportation, smart buildings, e-governance, and advanced data analytics to form a connected, efficient, and sustainable city ecosystem that enhances residents' quality of life and addresses the challenges of urbanization in an innovative way.

CURRENT CHALLENGES IN SMART CITIES

While smart cities have the potential to fundamentally change urban living, several challenges plague them. Cities generate massive amounts of data from a multitude of sensors and systems, resulting in a substantial data management challenge. Still, many of them are missing the required tools and knowledge, which leads to data silos and unused data. Interoperability is yet another primary challenge in smart city systems as they often include diverse technologies from multiple vendors, all of whom tend to use their standards and protocols. These diverse solutions are integrated within a complex `internet of Things (IoT) layer, and drive the deployment of a smart city program However, the complexity and fragmentation stemming from establishing multiple IoT systems but lacking a layered IoT approach results in reduced efficiency and effectiveness of overall smart city programs (Sonia et al., 2024).

Since smart cities are Networked, provide significant security and privacy issues. Threats to one system could endanger citizens or disrupt city operations. Cyberattacks on critical infrastructure — things that are essential for the country to work, such as hospitals, waterworks, etc. Due to the fact that a lot of personal data is collected, developers and administrators must take care to prevent its abuse and unauthorized access. These technologies can be expensive, and funding can often require complex public-private partnerships. Return on investment can be difficult to quantify, making it challenging to justify expenses to stakeholders and decision-makers.

The Need for Enhanced Connectivity and Security

A greater focus on secure and connected environments is critical for smart cities to deliver on their promise. Connectivity is the bedrock of any infrastructure allowing for seamless transfer of data among systems, devices, and stakeholders. Real-time integration, analysis, and response to data from multiple sources Your IP: 5G and other next-generation communication networks, that provide fast speeds, low latency, and increased capacity, are critical for the real-time integration, analysis, and response to data from numerous sources IP (Nanda et al., 2024; Srinivas et al., 2023).

Examples of IoT devices integrated into cities to support connectivity and the real-time observation and control of urban processes are smart traffic signals and environmental sensors. This allows inhabitants to live in higher quality of life while achieving higher efficiency and cost savings. Hyper-intelligent control systems monitor and optimize traffic movements, while intelligent energy grids balance supply and demand, reducing energy loss, benefiting the environment, and speeding up sustainability. Intelligent city infrastructure needs strong security measures to ensure data is kept private and systems are kept operational. This includes the use of tentative encryption algorithms, the updating of hardware and software for bug corrections, and deep risk assessments to identify and eradicate potential risks (Sharma et al., 2024).

Blockchain in Energy Management

The potential of blockchain technology is revolutionizing the energy sector by supplying innovative solutions to age-old dilemmas. Its distributed and immutable ledger can revolutionize energy management practices and build more transparent, sustainable, and efficient systems. This section analyses two of the significant applications of blockchain in the energy management sector (Kumar et al., 2023; Maguluri, Arularasan, et al., 2023). Figure 2 depicts the use of blockchain technology in energy management.

Figure 2. Blockchain in Energy Management

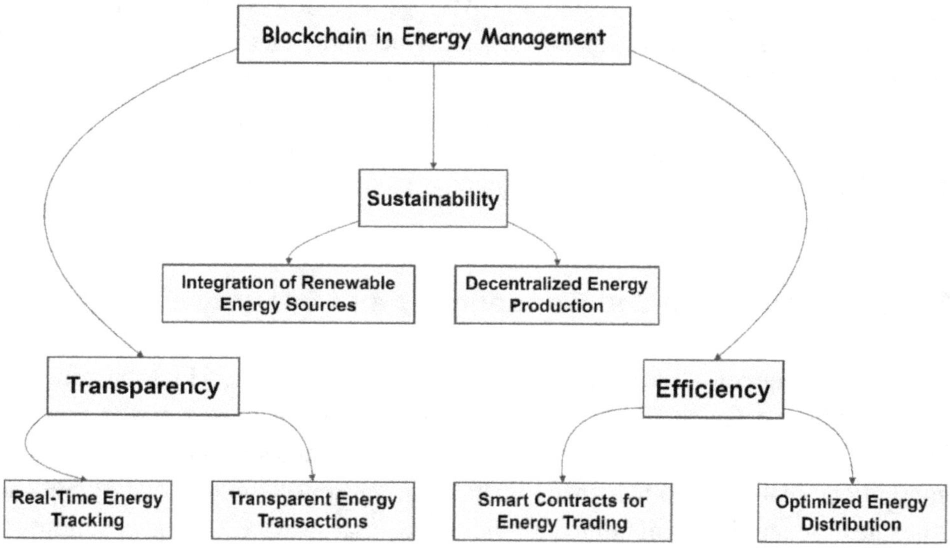

Decentralized Energy Grids

Because traditional energy systems depend on large power plants, they are inefficient and vulnerable to trespass. Decentralized energy blockchain networks decentralize energy generation and energy storage into networked nodes/kWh. On top of that, using renewable energy sources at various locations, like solar panels and wind turbines, generates electricity closer to consumption and decreases the necessity for long-distance transmission. Un-utilized additional energy generated by these DERs can enhance the performance of other nodes or can be retained in batteries when not used. Instead, this alternative offers a sustainable solution as opposed to traditional energy systems (Kavitha et al., 2023). Decentralized energy systems based on blockchain technology offer several benefits by dispersing energy generation and distribution.

Decentralized grids are much more resilient and reliable when disruptions occur, whether from cyberattacks, natural disasters, or equipment failures. Because energy is produced and stored close to where it is needed, grid disruptions in one part are less likely to affect the entire system.

Efficiency and cost savings — Decentralized grids can reduce energy losses and lower operating costs by removing the need for long-distance transmission. That translates into a net gain in productivity. Consumers also benefit from lower energy costs and more control over energy use.

Sustainability: Decentralized networks promote the use of renewable energy sources such as solar and wind power to mitigate the impacts of climate change by reducing greenhouse gas emissions. By allowing users to generate their clean energy, decentralized grids help facilitate the transition to a more sustainable energy future.

Peer-to-Peer Energy Trading

Blockchain technology is revolutionizing peer-to-peer (P2P) energy trade in there being a transaction directly between the energy provider and consumer without intermediaries. This innovative application of blockchain helps to maintain the authenticity and reliability of information as it provides a public (open), secure (transparent and tamper-proof), and trustworthy (reliable) recording of energy transactions. Smart contracts automate this trading, allowing energy producers to sell surplus energy on-the-spot pricing to customers. Customers can now access locally sourced renewable energy, generating new revenue for energy producers in the process. There are really a few advantages of P2P energy trading (Agrawal et al., 2023; Kavitha et al., 2023; Venkateswaran, Vidhya, Ayyannan, et al., 2023).

Flexibility and Choice: Customers can choose energy suppliers based on price, percentage of renewable energy, and proximity. This fosters innovation and competition among energy providers, ultimately serving customers.

Efficiency and Optimization: By matching supply and demand in real-time, P2P energy trading lends efficiency to energy distribution. This waste reduction maximizes the use of renewable energy resources, creating a sustainable energy system.

Empowerment and Community Engagement: Peer-to-peer energy trading empowers customers to produce and consume their desired amount of energy. It encourages community engagement and experience to empower customers to engage with local renewable energy initiatives and help drive the transition to a cleaner, more sustainable energy future.

Indeed, blockchain technology could completely transform the energy management industry by facilitating peer-to-peer trade and decentralized energy grids. By enabling effective coordination and optimization of energy resources, it enables a better, non-shadowy, and sustainable energy system. As the energy industry evolves, so too does its management, and blockchain represents the technology that could prove pivotal in its future development. Energy trading is one area where blockchain technology really shines as a disruptive option, providing solutions to management challenges such as peer-to-peer trade and decentralized energy grids. Here we see its many applications in energy management and the benefits it brings to the industry.

Decentralized Energy Grids

Utility companies concentrate on traditional energy-wheel systems that often lead to costs of costs, inaccuracies, and weaknesses towards disruption. Blockchain as an alternative model to enable peer-to-peer energy trading by a decentralized energy Grid, where Networked nodes are monitored by the Pay Generation and Distribution of Energy. In addition, blockchain provides a transparent and safe platform to record zero transactions, enabling users to use renewable energy such as wind or solar power to sell direct surplus energy zones to their neighbors. Smart contracts automate trade, eliminate intermediate parties, promote sustainable energy zoning consumption, and reduce dependence on central energy room structures (Bikash Chandra Saha, 2022).

Peer-to-Peer Energy Trading

Blockchain technology enables peer-to-peer energy trading, allowing customers to purchase and sell energy directly from each other, cutting out intermediaries. This paradigm enables users to quickly control their energy consumption and production which would encourage energy self-sufficiency and self-sufficiency. The smart agreement enables customers to limit the parameters and values surrounding consumption through negotiations, implementation, and payment of energy zones. This automatic approach has made the energy business more accessible and efficient for a wide range of players, reduces transaction costs, and eliminates the need for third-party mediators. The use of distributed pay generation and renewable energy sources is encouraged with peer-to-peer blockchain-based energy trade. This descent from the decentralized strategy reduces the emissions of greenhouse gas and reduces the effects of climate change while driving energy production to be durable and elastic to supply. Blockchain allows the monetization of more energy production, promoting renewable energy sources such as solar and wind turbines.

REAL-WORLD APPLICATIONS

Blockchain technology has shown promise in both Management, both real-world programs, and pilot programs. For example, the Brooklyn Microgrid project in New York allows residents with solar panels to sell more energy zones to nearby neighbors, and a power platform in Estonia can token their output to renewable Energy. Peer-to-Peer Trading during Solar Generation with Power Ledger in Apartment Buildings in Australia These case studies showcase how blockchain technology will be able to provide people with the power and ability to harness renewable energy resources (Revathi et al., 2024).

Case Study

As urban areas become more connected, the integration of advanced technologies like blockchain in smart city infrastructure is pivotal for enhancing both connectivity and security. This case study examines a real-world application of blockchain technology in the smart city of Dubai, focusing on how it has advanced urban connectivity and security (Ravisankar et al., 2024; Venkateswaran, Vidhya, Naik, et al., 2023).

Background

Dubai launched the Dubai Blockchain Strategy with the aim of becoming the first fully blockchain-powered government by 2020. The strategy aims were to: ensure efficient government, enable blockchain innovation, and lead global thinking on the technology. The project was a joint effort between the Smart Dubai Office and the Dubai Future Foundation.

Implementation

Dubai has focused on many key blockchain projects in its smart city infrastructure such as government services, real estate transactions, digital identities, smart contracts, and healthcare. For example, the Dubai Land Department brought a blockchain to real estate for safe, transparent transactions and the Project was designed to serve as a secure digital identification platform. Within the finance and healthcare industries, smart contracts were deployed to run transactions and increase efficiency. This integration reduces the care and administrative load of a better patient.

Benefits

This provides a variety of benefits for improved security and efficiency, increased transparency and confidence in the consolidation of blockchain in Smart City Infrastructure in Dubai, and reduction of cyber and fraud. This reduces the need for physical documents as it automates processes through a smart agreement. Blockchain promotes interoperability, which allows improved collaboration and data sharing in fields and institutions.

Challenges and Solutions

However, many challenges were faced: Dubai addressed scalability challenges through the adoption of multiple blockchain protocols, challenged complex regulatory frameworks by testing innovative regulations, and introduced training programs to educate the local talent pool to help with investments in blockchain projects, where the supply of skilled professionals was lacking.

The Case Study of Dubai Blockchain has immensely contributed to the enhancements of urban connectivity and security in Dubai through security, efficiency, transparency, and interoperability. Though Dubai, like any decentralized city, is not without its challenges, the proactivity adopted by Dubai's government shows the way for the rest of the decentralized cities to adopt this technology, moving towards smart city evolution powered by blockchain technology.

Blockchain in Transportation

Blockchain technology is likely to completely transform the transport industry by increasing efficiency, security, and connectivity, such as communication between autonomous vehicles, traffic management and communication between autonomous vehicles, traffic management, and vehicles and infrastructure. Figure 3 depicts the implementation of blockchain technology in the transportation sector.

Figure 3. Blockchain In Transportation

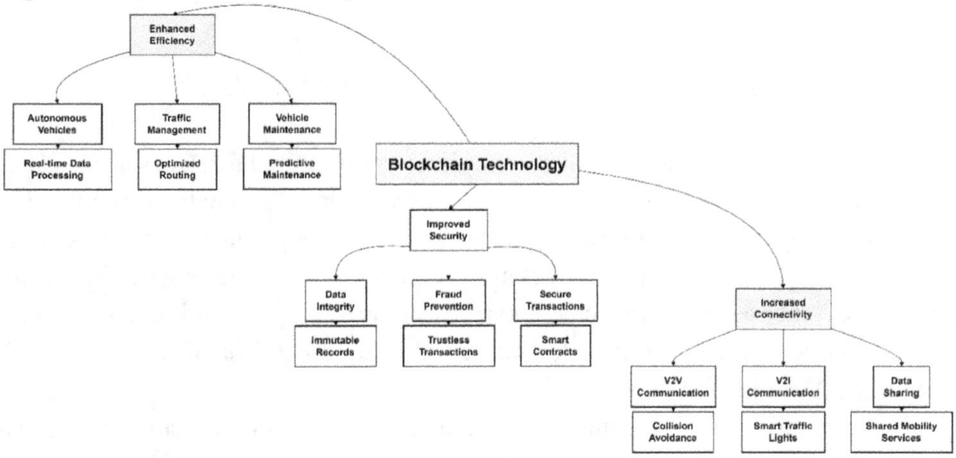

Vehicle-to-Infrastructure (V2I) Communications

Vehicle-to-infrastructure (V2I) communications enable vehicles to communicate with roadside infrastructure, resulting in improved traffic flow, safety, and efficiency. Blockchain tech helps to improve this by providing a decentralized safe environment to share data. Recording transactions on an unbreakable ledger reduces the risk of cyber by guaranteeing blockchain data integrity and honesty. Smart contracts automate traffic light adjustments due to accidents or congestion and other measures that improve traffic flow and eliminate delays. This makes the communication between vehicles and infrastructure more reliable (Godwin Immanuel et al., 2024; Maguluri, Ananth, et al., 2023).

Vehicle-to-Vehicle (V2V) Communications

Blockchain technology facilitates secure and transparent data exchange, which improves Vehicle-to-Vehicle (V2V) interactions. With the use of V2V communication, the data will be logged in a distributed ledger using blockchain, thus providing a guarantee of the validity and integrity of data and reducing the chances of data manipulation and tampering. This enhances trust and dependability by allowing automobiles to make decisions based on accurate and up-to-the-minute data. The smart contract also improves road safety by meaningfully enhancing vehicle coordination through vehicle negotiation and execution automation. Decentralized reputation systems - a crucial feature of blockchain technology -will help cars trust each other based on previous contacts, encouraging cooperation and coordination between vehicles.

Enhancing Traffic Management and Autonomous Vehicles

Blockchain provides a safe and decentralized environment for data sharing- Harbinger of Traffic Management and Autonomous Vehicles. This enables optimization and Monitoring of Traffic in Real-Time, thereby increasing productivity and reducing traffic jams. Smart contracts drive behavioral changes by automating traffic control procedures such as congestion charges and dynamic pricing, incentivizing drivers to adjust their behavior and route selection (Babu et al., 2022; Chandrika et al., 2023; Maguluri, Ananth, et al., 2023).

The integration of this technology, combined with its inherent security and transparency, allows for an easy implementation of autonomous vehicles. V2X technology allows road traffic sensors and. road infrastructure to communicate, significantly improving situational awareness and decision-based abilities of autonomous vehicles on the road. Blockchain technology will also be a revolutionary answer to multiple issues arising from transportation which includes traffic management, autonomous car technology along with V2I and V2V communication connectivity, security as well and efficiency (Godwin Immanuel et al., 2024; Reddy et al., 2024).

BLOCKCHAIN IN PUBLIC SERVICES

Blockchain technology provides creative answers to current problems and has the ability to completely transform public services by improving openness, security, and efficiency in government processes, including voter registration, identity verification, and public record management. Figure 4 depicts the implementation of blockchain technology in various public services (Domakonda et al., 2022).

Figure 4. Blockchain in Public Services

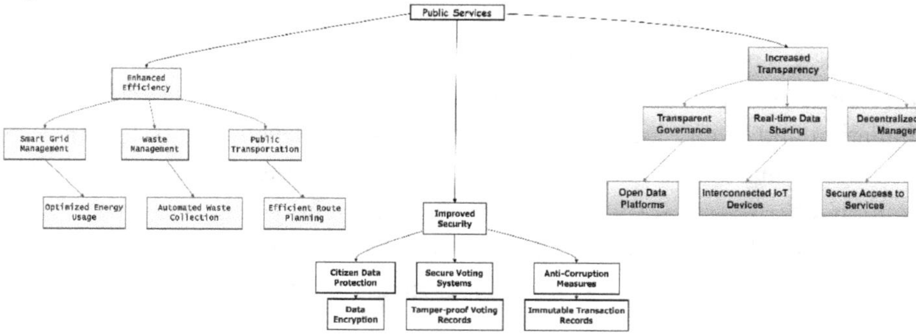

Identity Verification Systems

Organizations that deliver public services, from voting to banking, as well as healthcare, all rely on identity verification. Traditional systems are concentrated and susceptible to attacks. Blockchain technology offers people a decentralized platform on which they can safely control and manage their digital identity. Everyone on the blockchain has a unique cryptographic identity that can verify their identity without disclosing intelligence. This allows you to share information more securely and privately. Blockchain authentication reduces the theft of fraud and identity by maintaining integrity and integrity of records. This helps to increase the reliability and integrity of identification verification processes by changing information without contract or cleverly in the network.

Voting Systems and Digital Democracy

Blockchain technology solves problems such as voting, forcing, and compromising by providing transparent and safe platforms for elections. Election results are less reliable due to the problems of traditional voting processes. Voters can cast anonymously and safely using blockchain-based voting systems, as each vote is registered with tampering on the blockchain. This guarantees the transparency and integrity of the voting process and enables voters to confirm the validity of their ballots (Godwin Immanuel et al., 2024; Reddy et al., 2024). Election officials, observers, and voters can accuse and verify voting activities attributed to blockchain technology, making the election process transparent. This increases the confidence of the voters in the voter process and ensures that the results are appropriate, transparent, and unclear.

Public Records Management

Blockchain technology offers a decentralized, unchangeable platform for safe and effective public records administration. It allows government organizations to securely store, manage, and share various documents on a tamper-proof ledger, including birth certificates, property deeds, business licenses, and land titles. This reduces the risk of fraud, corruption, and data tampering, ensuring the integrity and validity of public records. Blockchain technology carries revolutionary answers for public services: it increases the performance, safety, and transparency of voting, and manages public records and identity verification systems. It streamlines the paper, reduces red tape, and automates procedures such as licensing and testing the integrity of the documents. Using blockchain technology, governments can deliver the services necessary for the public, create more reliable institutions, and open the process of democracy for its people (Chandrika et al., 2023; Dhanalakshmi et al., 2024; Maguluri, Ananth, et al., 2023).

Data Governance and Security

Blockchain assures technology integrity, privacy, and secure distribution and solves interoperability difficulties in industries such as healthcare, banking, and government, especially when providing novel solutions for data governance and security in the digital age (Kumar et al., 2023; Maguluri, Arularasan, et al., 2023; Sundaramoorthy et al., 2024).

Ensuring Data Integrity and Privacy

When it comes to sensitive data — whether that be financial transactions or personal health information — data governance is critical to maintaining data integrity and privacy. It utilizes consensus mechanisms and cryptographic hash functions to provide a decentralized, immutable ledger that makes transaction records virtually tamper-proof. This increases data governance by ensuring integrity and reducing fraud, manipulation, and unauthorized access. Advanced Data Privacy: Blockchain enables customers to protect and control their data. Each user has a cryptographic key that provides their data. They are still preserving privacy and can only do those who allow their data access (Boopathi, 2024).

Secure Data Sharing Among Stakeholders

In areas such as government services, supply chain management, healthcare, and research, blockchain technology, which securely shares data with stakeholders, securely sharing data, has led to innovation and cooperation. Provides an effective way to automate data-sharing contracts, without the use of smart contracts, or moderators, to reduce the issue of privacy and inaccuracy, without the use of smart contracts, or moderators. With blockchain, users enjoy specific control over their distribution permission - what to determine who can cause access to their data and under what conditions. It added to accountability and trail of data-sharing activities and ensured privacy and data protection laws (Boopathi & Khang, 2023).

Addressing Interoperability Issues

Interoperability is a crucial challenge in data governance, especially when it involves dealing with multiple systems and formats. In response, blockchain technology offers a unified platform for data exchange and integration. By leveraging standardized protocols and data formats, it also promotes innovation and collaboration across industries, simplifying system and stakeholder integration. This drives competition and innovation in the market because more communication will take place across platforms and services, safely transferring data via blockchain technology. Besides ensuring data integrity, privacy, and secure sharing between parties, it also solves interoperability problems. Organizations can leverage the technology in order to create more transparent and trustworthy data ecosystems, enable consumers to control how they use their data and foster cross-industry collaboration—leading to greater innovation and collaboration.

INTEGRATING BLOCKCHAIN FOR SMART CITY INFRASTRUCTURE FOR BUILDING A BUSINESS MODEL

It highlights the advantages, challenges, and practical implications of blockchain adoption in smart city scenarios, highlighting its potential to attract governments, technology vendors, and urban residents. Value Proposition and Innovation: The chapter highlights how blockchain provides unique value for smart cities, including immutable data, enhanced security, and improved operations. Arguably the key features of such a business model, address urban challenges like data breaches, inefficiencies, and opacity, and also illustrate the value proposition for deploying a model of blockchain. Smart contracts enable automated and secure transactions, resulting in cost savings while increasing trust between citizens and service providers.

Engagement of customer segments and stakeholders: The key is to know your goal customers and stakeholders. Chapter blows major parts such as municipalities, urban organizers, utilities, and citizens. Focusing on cases of use such as energy management, transportation, and public safety, it gives a sample to include these groups. This enables customized marketing strategies and services that meet certain requirements, leading to the acceptance and adoption of blockchain solutions.

Revenue flow, economic impact: Conversations regarding the economic benefits of blockchain, e.g. Cost-saving is obtained by preventing fraud or achieving operational efficiency, helping to understand income trends. These income opportunities may include subscription models for blockchain-based solutions, data exchanges producing transactions for secure exchanges, and savings from efficient resource management. It also discusses potential funding sources (government grants and private investments), giving a holistic outlook on financial stability.

Important activities and partnerships: Cooperation of companies in other fields is required to implement blockchain in smart cities for corporations. It highlights the crucial need to create long-term winners with tech companies, research and development centers, and government agencies. White paper emphasizes pilot activities as a crucial element for adherence to ecosystems such as pilot projects, public-private partnerships, and community connection initiatives that promote innovative solutions as well as splitting. Like other techniques of risk management and security, smart cities face security challenges. Blockchain will not only improve the protection of data, but also facilitate the integrity of the system, and be used to show regulatory compliance, this chapter investigates more closely. This is a critical component of the business model that serves to establish trust with stakeholders and limits potential liabilities. Also, it tackles the complexities associated with blockchain integration, including scalability and interoperability, providing strategies to overcome these hurdles.

Challenges and Considerations

Figure 5 can provide valuable insights into the challenges and considerations of integrating blockchain into smart city infrastructure for improved urban connectivity and security.

Scalability Issues

Scalability poses a major challenge for blockchain technology, especially since its applications and transactions volume increase rapidly. This challenge motivates developers to experiment with layer 2 protocol, off-chain scaling, or sharing. The goal of these solutions is to maintain decentralization and protection when the transaction throughput, reduces network congestion and increases user experience. It can lead to more cost and low-quality user experience.

Regulatory and Legal Considerations

A large number of legal and regulatory systems are not integrated into the blockchain technology ecosystem, which makes it challenging to apply blockchain technology to places such as government, healthcare, and banking. Irregular regulatory structures and burdens of compliance with data protection law such as hinder investment and innovation. To cope with these issues, designers should join legislators and regulators to advance clear, consistent frameworks, that protect customers, promote innovation, and ensure adherence to existing rules and laws.

Figure 5. Challenges and considerations of integrating blockchain into smart city infrastructure

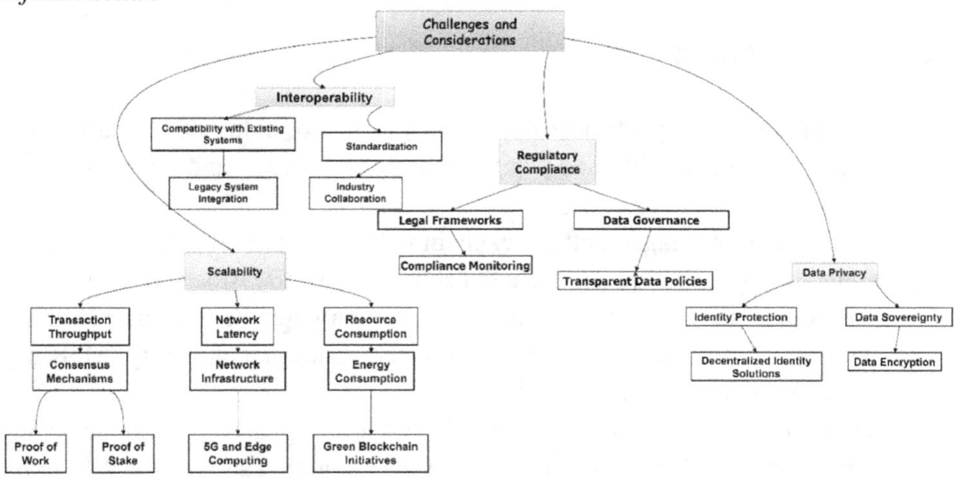

Cross-Sector Collaboration

Blockchain technology deals with a wide range of participants, including government departments, business partners, technology providers, and academic institutions, making cross-sector collaboration essential for successful deployment. On the other end, differences in organizational cultures, incentives, and priorities posed challenges. These challenges require building consensus and fostering trust. Industry consortia, standards bodies, and public-private partnerships can facilitate this by sharing information, resources, and best practices."

Technological and Social Barriers

Often, social and technical barriers resist the adoption of blockchain techniques. There are experimental issues with technical issues of implementation such as scalability, and interoperability, as well as how the lack of technical will hinder innovation. Social barriers such as dislike and resistance to change can also cause a barrier to adoption. Education, awareness, and involvement of the community are needed to overcome obstacles. Working in the concert, technology, legislators and social enthusiasts can be sure that blockchain technology fulfills its promise and is widely adopted (Mohanty, Jothi, et al., 2023). Lack of technological and social sanity issues, the hesitance of cross-sector collaboration, legal- and regulatory-related circumstances, and scalability-related deny the potential of blockchain technology.

Overcoming those hurdles comes with potential game-changing advantages and can stimulate innovation across a variety of sectors and industries.

Real-World Applications

Blockchain technology has been applied in a variety of industries and use cases, demonstrating its adaptability and potential to spur efficiency and creativity.

Supply Chain Management: Blockchain reduces fraud, fake, and inaccuracy by enabling transparent and detected supply networks. Blockchain technology is being used by businesses like IBM to guarantee the customer from the manufacturer to trace and trace the products, honesty, and quality (Mohanty, Venkateswaran, et al., 2023; Verma et al., 2024).
Financial & Banking: By facilitating faster, less expensive, and more secure transactions, blockchain will advance installed banking and financial systems. Traditional banks are investigating blockchain for trade finance, identification verification, and cross-border payments, while cryptocurrencies such as Bitcoin and Ethereum use blockchain for smart contracts and peer-to-peer payments.
Healthcare: Blockchain technology provides safe and relevant ways to originate drugs, manage electronic health records (EHRS), and safety of the patient's data. Blockchain is being used by initiatives such as medical-chain to increase the patient's privacy, data management, and healthcare delivery (Boopathi & Khang, 2023; Ramudu et al., 2023; Satav et al., 2023).
Identity management: Reduces identity theft and fraud by providing a decentralized, secure platform to manage blockchain digital identity. Blockchain is being used by initiatives such as providing self-identification solutions that allow users to charge and operate their identity data.
Real estate: Land registrations, title transfer, and transparent property transactions are made possible by all blockchain technology, which is completely replacing the real estate sector. Blockchain is being used by a bit-proprietary platform to buy, rent, and ease the sale of real estate assets while reducing transaction costs and paper.
Government Services: Voting, managing public records, identification verification, and other government functions can now be transparently controlled and attributed to blockchain technology. Blockchain is being used to enhance the efficiency, security, and transparency of government operations through initiatives such as WhatsApp and Estonia's e-residency program.
Supply Chain Finance: Transparent and datable records of transactions and wealth provided by blockchain make supply chain finance solutions possible. Blockchain is being used to accelerate liquidity by businesses, speeding up

trade finance processes, and seeing the risk of low suppliers and buyers (Pasumarthy et al., 2024).
Digital Rights Management: In the field of media and entertainment, blockchain technology offers options for digital rights and royalties. Blockchain is being used to trace the use of digital materials by the platform and mycelia, guarantee a reasonable return for artists, and stop piracy (Maguluri, Arularasan, et al., 2023; Sundaramoorthy et al., 2024).

As the use of blockchain technology increases and matures, it will lead to creativity, transparency, and efficiency in different fields, showing the possibility of changing different industries and fields.

CONCLUSIONS

Implementation of blockchain technology in smart city infrastructure is a transformative opportunity to enhance urban alliance and security. It not only solves interoperability challenges but also ensures data integrity, privacy, and secure data sharing. The unchanging and distributed nature of blockchain technology fully financed the efficiency and transparency of government processes such as voter registration, identity, and public record services. Blockchain reduces admin costs on scalability, increases trust and responsibility, and enables safe, transparent, unchanging transactions. This can lead to public engagement, improved regimes, and more elastic urban systems.

Therefore, some very important challenges need to be attention for the responsible benefit of blockchain in smart cities: scaling, regulatory challenges, cross-sectoral cooperation, and social and technical challenges. In order to cope with these issues and create a favorable environment for innovation and development, governments, industry participants, and technologies need to collaborate. Blockchain technology, which increases productivity, security, and connectivity, is likely to revolutionize the atmosphere of smart cities. It applies to many areas, such as real estate, banking, healthcare, and supply chain management. Using blockchain technology, cities can generate better accountability, transparency, and a citizen-centric environment, thereby laying the foundations for a smarter, more sustainable future. The ecosystem is still maturing, and we are only at the starting point to fully adopt blockchain for our cities, much work is needed in order to be able to provide the full potential.

REFERENCES

Abbas, K., Tawalbeh, L. A., Rafiq, A., Muthanna, A., Elgendy, I. A., & Abd El-Latif, A. A. (2021). Convergence of blockchain and IoT for secure transportation systems in smart cities. *Security and Communication Networks*, *2021*(1), 5597679. DOI: 10.1155/2021/5597679

Agrawal, A. V., Shashibhushan, G., Pradeep, S., Padhi, S., Sugumar, D., & Boopathi, S. (2023). Synergizing Artificial Intelligence, 5G, and Cloud Computing for Efficient Energy Conversion Using Agricultural Waste. In *Sustainable Science and Intelligent Technologies for Societal Development* (pp. 475–497). IGI Global.

Alasbali, N., Azzuhri, S. R. B., Salleh, R. B., Kiah, M. L. M., Shariffuddin, A. A. A. A., & Kamel, N. M. I. (2022). bin N. M., & Ismail, L. (2022). Rules of smart IoT networks within smart cities towards blockchain standardization. *Mobile Information Systems*, (1), 9109300.

Alnahari, M. S., & Ariaratnam, S. T. (2022). The application of blockchain technology to smart city infrastructure. *Smart Cities*, *5*(3), 979–993. DOI: 10.3390/smartcities5030049

Babu, B. S., Kamalakannan, J., Meenatchi, N., Karthik, S., & Boopathi, S. (2022). Economic impacts and reliability evaluation of battery by adopting Electric Vehicle. *IEEE Explore*, 1–6.

Bikash Chandra Saha, M. S., Deepa, R., Akila, A., & Sai Thrinath, B. V. (2022). *Sampath Boopathi *, J. Ramya*. IOT BASED SMART ENERGY METER FOR SMART GRID.

Bommu, S., Babburu, K. N. S., Thalluri, L. N., Gopalan, A., Mallapati, P. K., Guha, K., & Mohammad, H. R. (2023). Smart city IoT system network level routing analysis and blockchain security based implementation. *Journal of Electrical Engineering & Technology*, *18*(2), 1351–1368. DOI: 10.1007/s42835-022-01239-4 PMID: 37521954

Boopathi, S. (2024). Balancing Innovation and Security in the Cloud: Navigating the Risks and Rewards of the Digital Age. In *Improving Security, Privacy, and Trust in Cloud Computing* (pp. 164–193). IGI Global.

Boopathi, S., Arigela, S. H., Raman, R., Indhumathi, C., Kavitha, V., & Bhatt, B. C. (2022). Prominent Rule Control-based Internet of Things: Poultry Farm Management System. *IEEE Explore*, 1–6.

Boopathi, S., Gavaskar, T., Dogga, A. D., Mahendran, R. K., Kumar, A., Kathiresan, G., N., V., Ganesan, M., Ishwarya, K. R., Ramana, G. V., & others. (2021, August 4). *Emergency medicine delivery transportation using unmanned aerial vehicle (Patent Grant).*

Boopathi, S., & Khang, A. (2023). AI-Integrated Technology for a Secure and Ethical Healthcare Ecosystem. In *AI and IoT-Based Technologies for Precision Medicine* (pp. 36–59). IGI Global. DOI: 10.4018/979-8-3693-0876-9.ch003

Chandrika, V., Sivakumar, A., Krishnan, T. S., Pradeep, J., Manikandan, S., & Boopathi, S. (2023). Theoretical Study on Power Distribution Systems for Electric Vehicles. In *Intelligent Engineering Applications and Applied Sciences for Sustainability* (pp. 1–19). IGI Global. DOI: 10.4018/979-8-3693-0044-2.ch001

Dhanalakshmi, M., Tamilarasi, K., Saravanan, S., Sujatha, G., Boopathi, S., & Associates. (2024). Fog Computing-Based Framework and Solutions for Intelligent Systems: Enabling Autonomy in Vehicles. In *Computational Intelligence for Green Cloud Computing and Digital Waste Management* (pp. 330–356). IGI Global.

Domakonda, V. K., Farooq, S., Chinthamreddy, S., Puviarasi, R., Sudhakar, M., & Boopathi, S. (2022). Sustainable Developments of Hybrid Floating Solar Power Plants: Photovoltaic System. In *Human Agro-Energy Optimization for Business and Industry* (pp. 148–167). IGI Global.

Godwin Immanuel, D., Solaimalai, G., Chandrakala, B. M., Bharath, V. G., Singh, M. K., & Boopathi, S. (2024). Advancements in Electric Vehicle Management System: Integrating Machine Learning and Artificial Intelligence. In *Advances in Web Technologies and Engineering* (pp. 371–391). IGI Global. DOI: 10.4018/979-8-3693-1487-6.ch018

Gopal, M., Lurdhumary, J., Bathrinath, S., Priya, A. P., Sarojwal, A., & Boopathi, S. (2024). Energy Harvesting and Smart Highways for Sustainable Transportation Infrastructure: Revolutionizing Roads Using Nanotechnology. In *Principles and Applications in Speed Sensing and Energy Harvesting for Smart Roads* (pp. 136–165). IGI Global. DOI: 10.4018/978-1-6684-9214-7.ch005

Kavitha, C., Varalatchoumy, M., Mithuna, H., Bharathi, K., Geethalakshmi, N., & Boopathi, S. (2023). Energy Monitoring and Control in the Smart Grid: Integrated Intelligent IoT and ANFIS. In *Applications of Synthetic Biology in Health, Energy, and Environment* (pp. 290–316). IGI Global.

Kumar, P. R., Meenakshi, S., Shalini, S., Devi, S. R., & Boopathi, S. (2023). Soil Quality Prediction in Context Learning Approaches Using Deep Learning and Blockchain for Smart Agriculture. In *Effective AI, Blockchain, and E-Governance Applications for Knowledge Discovery and Management* (pp. 1–26). IGI Global. DOI: 10.4018/978-1-6684-9151-5.ch001

Li, S. (2018). Application of blockchain technology in smart city infrastructure. *2018 IEEE International Conference on Smart Internet of Things (SmartIoT)*, 276–2766. DOI: 10.1109/SmartIoT.2018.00056

Maguluri, L. P., Ananth, J., Hariram, S., Geetha, C., Bhaskar, A., & Boopathi, S. (2023). Smart Vehicle-Emissions Monitoring System Using Internet of Things (IoT). In *Handbook of Research on Safe Disposal Methods of Municipal Solid Wastes for a Sustainable Environment* (pp. 191–211). IGI Global.

Maguluri, L. P., Arularasan, A., & Boopathi, S. (2023). Assessing Security Concerns for AI-Based Drones in Smart Cities. In *Effective AI, Blockchain, and E-Governance Applications for Knowledge Discovery and Management* (pp. 27–47). IGI Global. DOI: 10.4018/978-1-6684-9151-5.ch002

Malathi, J., Kusha, K., Isaac, S., Ramesh, A., Rajendiran, M., & Boopathi, S. (2024). IoT-Enabled Remote Patient Monitoring for Chronic Disease Management and Cost Savings: Transforming Healthcare. In *Advances in Explainable AI Applications for Smart Cities* (pp. 371–388). IGI Global.

Mohanty, A., Jothi, B., Jeyasudha, J., Ranjit, P., Isaac, J. S., & Boopathi, S. (2023). Additive Manufacturing Using Robotic Programming. In *AI-Enabled Social Robotics in Human Care Services* (pp. 259–282). IGI Global. DOI: 10.4018/978-1-6684-8171-4.ch010

Mohanty, A., Venkateswaran, N., Ranjit, P., Tripathi, M. A., & Boopathi, S. (2023). Innovative Strategy for Profitable Automobile Industries: Working Capital Management. In *Handbook of Research on Designing Sustainable Supply Chains to Achieve a Circular Economy* (pp. 412–428). IGI Global.

Nanda, A. K., Sharma, A., Augustine, P. J., Cyril, B. R., Kiran, V., & Sampath, B. (2024). Securing Cloud Infrastructure in IaaS and PaaS Environments. In *Improving Security, Privacy, and Trust in Cloud Computing* (pp. 1–33). IGI Global. DOI: 10.4018/979-8-3693-1431-9.ch001

Pasumarthy, R., Mohammed, S., Laxman, V., Krishnamoorthy, V., Durga, S., & Boopathi, S. (2024). Digital Transformation in Developing Economies: Forecasting Trends, Impact, and Challenges in Industry 5.0. In *Convergence of Human Resources Technologies and Industry 5.0* (pp. 47–68). IGI Global. DOI: 10.4018/979-8-3693-1343-5.ch003

Rahamathunnisa, U., Subhashini, P., Aancy, H. M., Meenakshi, S., & Boopathi, S. (2023). Solutions for Software Requirement Risks Using Artificial Intelligence Techniques. In *Handbook of Research on Data Science and Cybersecurity Innovations in Industry 4.0 Technologies* (pp. 45–64). IGI Global.

Ramudu, K., Mohan, V. M., Jyothirmai, D., Prasad, D., Agrawal, R., & Boopathi, S. (2023). Machine Learning and Artificial Intelligence in Disease Prediction: Applications, Challenges, Limitations, Case Studies, and Future Directions. In *Contemporary Applications of Data Fusion for Advanced Healthcare Informatics* (pp. 297–318). IGI Global.

Ravisankar, A., Shanthi, A., Lavanya, S., Ramaratnam, M., Krishnamoorthy, V., & Boopathi, S. (2024). Harnessing 6G for Consumer-Centric Business Strategies Across Electronic Industries. In *AI Impacts in Digital Consumer Behavior* (pp. 241–270). IGI Global.

Reddy, P. Y., Madan, B. S., Anandaram, H., Rathod, P., Vasanthaseelan, S., & Boopathi, S. (2024). Analyzing Fuel Cell Vehicles Through Intelligent Battery Management Systems (BMS): AI and ML Technologies for E-Mobility. In *Advances in Web Technologies and Engineering* (pp. 335–355). IGI Global. DOI: 10.4018/979-8-3693-1487-6.ch016

Revathi, S., Babu, M., Rajkumar, N., Meti, V. K. V., Kandavalli, S. R., & Boopathi, S. (2024). Unleashing the Future Potential of 4D Printing: Exploring Applications in Wearable Technology, Robotics, Energy, Transportation, and Fashion. In *Human-Centered Approaches in Industry 5.0: Human-Machine Interaction, Virtual Reality Training, and Customer Sentiment Analysis* (pp. 131–153). IGI Global.

Rotună, C., GHEORGHI Ă, A., Zamfiroiu, A., & SMADA ANAGRAMA, D. (2019). Smart City Ecosystem Using Blockchain Technology. *Informatica Economica, 23*(4).

Satav, S. D., Hasan, D. S., Pitchai, R., Mohanaprakash, T., Sultanuddin, S., & Boopathi, S. (2023). Next generation of internet of things (ngiot) in healthcare systems. In *Sustainable Science and Intelligent Technologies for Societal Development* (pp. 307–330). IGI Global.

Sharma, M., Sharma, M., Sharma, N., & Boopathi, S. (2024). Building Sustainable Smart Cities Through Cloud and Intelligent Parking System. In *Handbook of Research on AI and ML for Intelligent Machines and Systems* (pp. 195–222). IGI Global.

Singh, S., Sharma, P. K., Yoon, B., Shojafar, M., Cho, G. H., & Ra, I.-H. (2020). Convergence of blockchain and artificial intelligence in IoT network for the sustainable smart city. *Sustainable Cities and Society*, *63*, 102364. DOI: 10.1016/j.scs.2020.102364

Sonia, R., Gupta, N., Manikandan, K., Hemalatha, R., Kumar, M. J., & Boopathi, S. (2024). Strengthening Security, Privacy, and Trust in Artificial Intelligence Drones for Smart Cities. In *Analyzing and Mitigating Security Risks in Cloud Computing* (pp. 214–242). IGI Global. DOI: 10.4018/979-8-3693-3249-8.ch011

Srinivas, B., Maguluri, L. P., Naidu, K. V., Reddy, L. C. S., Deivakani, M., & Boopathi, S. (2023). Architecture and Framework for Interfacing Cloud-Enabled Robots. In *Handbook of Research on Data Science and Cybersecurity Innovations in Industry 4.0 Technologies* (pp. 542–560). IGI Global. DOI: 10.4018/978-1-6684-8145-5.ch027

Subha, S., Inbamalar, T., Komala, C., Suresh, L. R., Boopathi, S., & Alaskar, K. (2023). A Remote Health Care Monitoring system using internet of medical things (IoMT). *IEEE Explore*, 1–6.

Sundaramoorthy, K., Singh, A., Sumathy, G., Maheshwari, A., Arunarani, A., & Boopathi, S. (2024). A Study on AI and Blockchain-Powered Smart Parking Models for Urban Mobility. In *Handbook of Research on AI and ML for Intelligent Machines and Systems* (pp. 223–250). IGI Global.

Syamala, M., Komala, C., Pramila, P., Dash, S., Meenakshi, S., & Boopathi, S. (2023). Machine Learning-Integrated IoT-Based Smart Home Energy Management System. In *Handbook of Research on Deep Learning Techniques for Cloud-Based Industrial IoT* (pp. 219–235). IGI Global. DOI: 10.4018/978-1-6684-8098-4.ch013

Theodorou, S., & Sklavos, N. (2019). Blockchain-based security and privacy in smart cities. In *Smart cities cybersecurity and privacy* (pp. 21–37). Elsevier. DOI: 10.1016/B978-0-12-815032-0.00003-2

Venkateswaran, N., Vidhya, K., Ayyannan, M., Chavan, S. M., Sekar, K., & Boopathi, S. (2023). A Study on Smart Energy Management Framework Using Cloud Computing. In *5G, Artificial Intelligence, and Next Generation Internet of Things: Digital Innovation for Green and Sustainable Economies* (pp. 189–212). IGI Global. DOI: 10.4018/978-1-6684-8634-4.ch009

Venkateswaran, N., Vidhya, R., Naik, D. A., Raj, T. M., Munjal, N., & Boopathi, S. (2023). Study on Sentence and Question Formation Using Deep Learning Techniques. In *Digital Natives as a Disruptive Force in Asian Businesses and Societies* (pp. 252–273). IGI Global. DOI: 10.4018/978-1-6684-6782-4.ch015

Verma, R., Christiana, M. B. V., Maheswari, M., Srinivasan, V., Patro, P., Dari, S. S., & Boopathi, S. (2024). Intelligent Physarum Solver for Profit Maximization in Oligopolistic Supply Chain Networks. In *AI and Machine Learning Impacts in Intelligent Supply Chain* (pp. 156–179). IGI Global. DOI: 10.4018/979-8-3693-1347-3.ch011

Xihua, Z., & Goyal, S. (2022). Security and privacy challenges using IoT-blockchain technology in a smart city: Critical analysis. *Int. J. Electr. Electron. Res*, *10*(2), 190–195. DOI: 10.37391/ijeer.100224

Chapter 8
NFT Security in Smart Cities:
An Exploration of Challenges, Countermeasures, and Emerging Trends

Kassim Kalinaki
https://orcid.org/0000-0001-8630-9110
Islamic University in Uganda, Uganda

Owais Ahmed Malik
https://orcid.org/0000-0002-4888-5448
Universiti Brunei Darussalam, Brunei

Gusti Ahmad Fanshuri Alfarisy
https://orcid.org/0000-0002-0689-7002
Institut Teknologi Kalimantan, Indonesia

Jalia Nassanga
Islamic University in Uganda, Uganda

ABSTRACT

The fusion of blockchain technologies and non-fungible tokens (NFTs) into smart city ecosystems presents new security challenges, impeding the widespread adoption of NFT in urban settings. Accordingly, this study comprehensively reviews the cybersecurity aspects surrounding NFTs within smart city environments. Firstly, a discussion of the various applications of NFTs in smart cities is provided. This is followed by an exploration of the unique cybersecurity vulnerabilities emanating from implementing NFTs in smart city ecosystems, including data privacy issues,

DOI: 10.4018/979-8-3693-8876-1.ch008

smart contract vulnerabilities, token theft, and the potential for market manipulation, etc. Moreover, various countermeasures and best practices to negate NFTs' cybersecurity concerns and vulnerabilities have been detailed. Finally, emerging trends in NFT security are equally also analyzed. This review study provide urban planners, policymakers, technologists, students, and researchers with a refined understanding of the cybersecurity concerns of NFT in smart cities.

INTRODUCTION

By definition, NFTs are unique digital assets representing ownership or proof of authenticity of a specific item or piece of content using blockchain technology (S. Yang et al., 2023). NFTs, whose structure is decocted in Figure 1, gained mainstream attention in 2021 with high-profile sales like Beeple's "Everydays: The First 5000 Days" artwork selling for $69 million[1] (Jenkins, 2024). While the initial hype has settled, NFTs continue to be used for digital ownership, community building, access passes, and various Web3 applications. However, integrating NFTs with smart city frameworks marks the point of intersection at which technological advancement meets smart city planning, presenting a lot of opportunities while also introducing complex security issues (Musamih et al., 2024; Razi et al., 2024). NFTs seem to present viable instruments for managing digital assets, property ownership, and public participation in the environment of a smart city within the context of Smart City initiatives globally adopting digital transformation. However, this integration presents many security concerns that need to be deeply analyzed and supported by innovative solutions (Ali et al., 2023). Smart cities, characterized by integrated systems and data-driven functions, are increasingly researching the applicability of NFTs in various domains, such as digital identity management, property tokenization, public services, and cultural heritage preservation (Kalinaki et al., 2023; Kuznetsov et al., 2024). These unique digital tokens, verified using blockchain technology, provide tamper-proof proof of ownership and authenticity and are thus highly sought after for application in governance and service provision in smart city settings (Kalinaki, 2024; Khalil et al., 2022; Shafik et al., 2024). Incorporating NFTs into smart city systems, nonetheless, brings with it a complicated security environment that intersects with critical infrastructure, safeguarding of personal information, and public safety concerns (Ali et al., 2023).

The security considerations that accompany the utilization of NFTs in smart cities extend outside the conventional cybersecurity frameworks. Although blockchain technology inherently delivers security advantages due to its decentralization and cryptography, the broader ecosystem facilitating NFTs, such as marketplaces, wallet frameworks, and smart contracts, is fraught with numerous potential weaknesses that may be susceptible to exploitation by malicious entities (Ali et al., 2023; Mollajafari & Bechkoum, 2023). The implication of such vulnerabilities is greatly amplified in the context of smart cities where the compromise of NFT systems can have a negative impact on essential services, property rights, or citizens' privacy (Khalil et al., 2022). Recent publications that have revealed security breaches relating to NFTs in the context of smart cities highlight the urgent necessity of the implementation of robust security frameworks. As an example, phishing attacks that resulted in the theft of non-fungible tokens (NFTs) accounted for draining 67,188 NFTs, which were worth over $20 million (J. Yang et al., 2024). There were also issues with smart contracts, such as floating pragma, delegate calls, insecure self-destruct functions, and integer overflow/underflow, among many others (Kushwaha et al., 2022), as well as exploits in marketplaces (Al Shamsi et al., 2023). These incidents have intensified concerns about the efficacy of current security measures in securing valuable digital assets held within smart city ecosystems. Moreover, these challenges are further accentuated by the rapid development of NFT technologies and their diverse applications within smart cities, often outpacing the development of related security measures and regulatory frameworks. Besides, integrating NFTs with smart cities gives rise to unique challenges around scalability issues (Al Shamsi et al., 2023), interoperability, and governance.

As the number of smart cities adopting NFT-based solutions such as transportation accessibility, e-building permits, or other services increases, so does the integration challenge while maintaining security. That pressing need to balance innovation with security directives creates friction between speeding up implementation and thorough protective measures, especially in essential smart city infrastructure contexts. As such, this study explores the various use cases of NFTs in smart cities, explains the security issues faced while deploying NFTs, and discusses recent countermeasures, best practices, and future trends. This chapter provides highly relevant information to smart city planners, security professionals, blockchain developers, and decision-makers involved in smart city projects. Thus, we will contribute recent knowledge to developing more secure and resilient NFT implementations in smart city environments by examining current challenges, evaluating existing solutions, and exploring future trends.

Figure 1. NFT structure

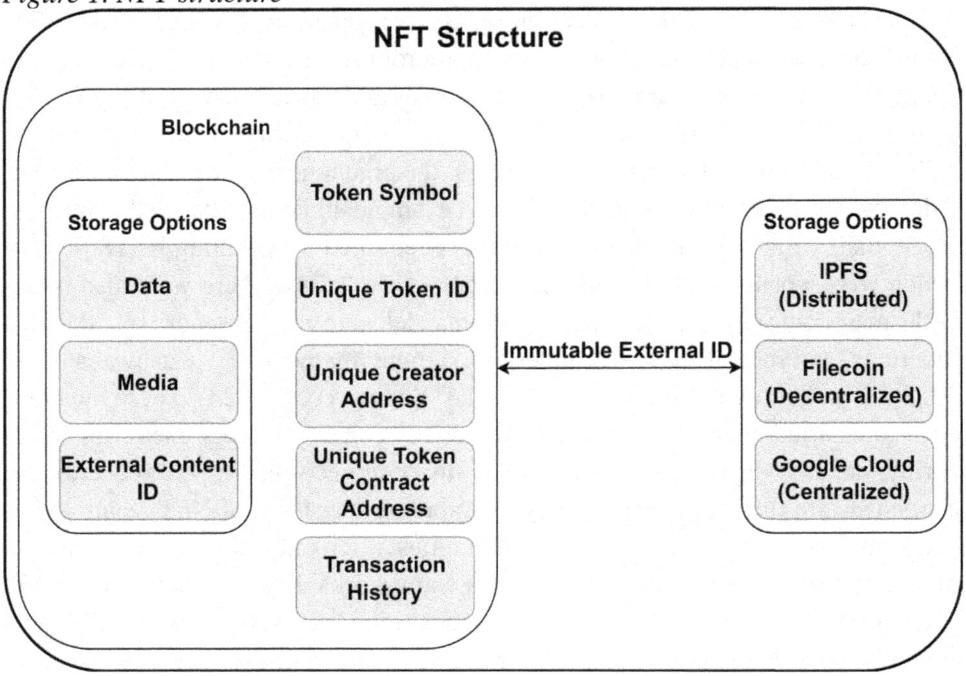

(Musamih et al., 2024)

Chapter Contributions

The main contributions of the chapter are highlighted below:

- Provision of a comprehensive overview of NFT applications in smart city digital infrastructure.
- Analysis of the unique cybersecurity vulnerabilities associated with NFT implementation in smart city ecosystems.
- Exploration of the various countermeasures and best practices designed to mitigate cybersecurity concerns and vulnerabilities related to NFTs.
- Examination of emerging trends in NFT security within smart city contexts.

Chapter Roadmap

After the introductory section in Section 1, the other sections of the chapter are structured as follows: Section 2 presents a comprehensive review of the applications of NFTs in the context of smart cities. Section 3 assesses the various cybersecurity threats related to the use of NFTs in smart city ecosystems. Section 4 explores the various countermeasures and best practices aimed at mitigating the vulnerabilities of NFTs in smart cities. Section 5 elaborates on the ethical frameworks for NFT security. Section 6 puts forward the developing trends in NFT security in smart cities. Lastly, the conclusion is drawn in section 7.

APPLICATIONS OF NFTS IN SMART CITY ECOSYSTEMS

The next section discusses the different innovative applications of NFTs within smart city ecosystems, as depicted in Figure 2, proving how these cryptographic tokens could change the face of traditional urban systems.

Figure 2. Applications of NFTs in smart cities

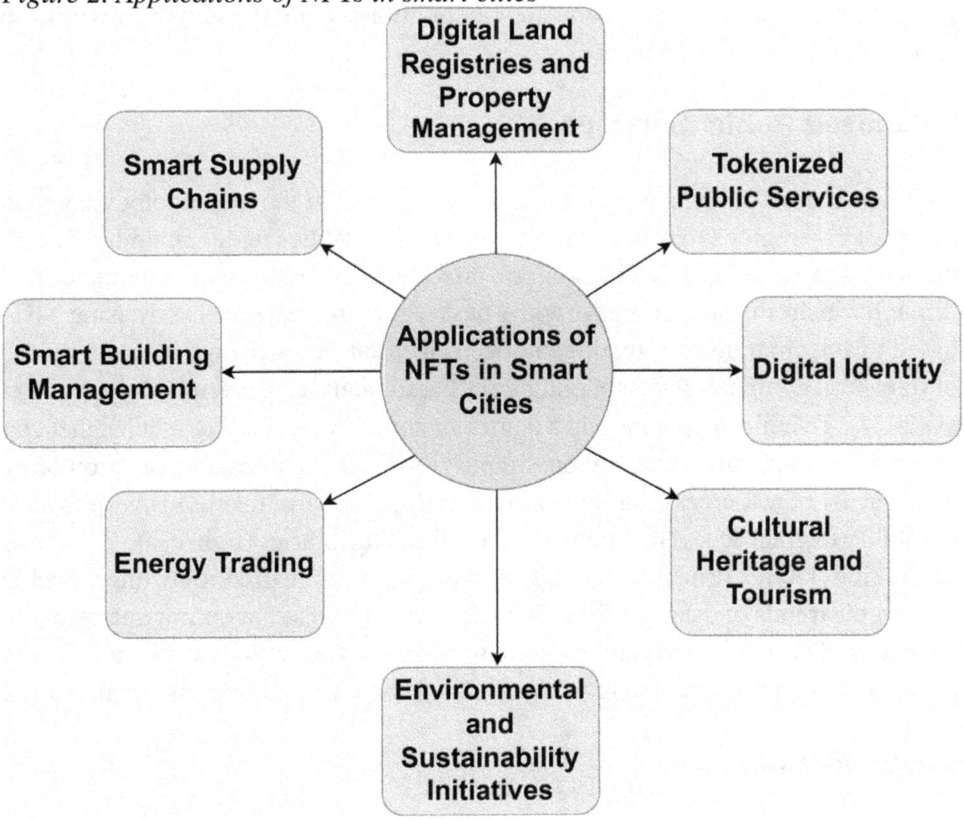

Digital Land Registries and Property Management

In the area of smart city property management, NFTs are changing traditional systems by setting up an irreversible digital framework for real estate transactions and records of ownership (Chawda et al., 2024; Tien et al., 2024). Each property is assigned a unique digital identifier that comes with a complete set of attributes: history of ownership, structural changes, zoning permissions, and rights related to it (Khanh et al., 2024). Such digital transformation shines particularly in handling complex property arrangements, such as multi-owner buildings, whereby smart contracts automatically manage shared spaces and utilities (Oza et al., 2024). One study proposed a property management system using blockchain and NFTs to improve real estate transfers (Sharma et al., 2024)The system automatizes ownership verification and transfers via smart contracts on Ethereum; NFTs represent tamper-proof digital property deeds. Compared to traditional registry systems, this aims to reduce fraud, costs, and delays.

Tokenized Public Services

Tokenization of civic facilities is a paradigm shift in the methodology adopted by smart city regions to provide and govern civic facilities under an umbrella program (Rubino et al., 2024). The program provides a unified system of digital access through which citizens can engage with a basket of municipal services by using NFT-based tokens. In transport, intelligent tokens facilitate easy change between modes of transport, computing and charging fares based on usage patterns (Meneguzzo et al., 2024). Tokenized systems add a degree of complexity in utility management by efficiently monitoring consumption, simplifying payment processes, and promoting efficient use of resources (Kanimozhi et al., 2023). The same tokens in question have the ability to grant access to communal facilities like libraries (Behl et al., 2024) and sports clubs (Ayres Principe et al., 2024), while at the same time collecting valuable data on the trends of usage of these facilities, which will aid in optimizing resource allocation. This inclusion includes waste management systems, whereby tokens can track recycling programs and reward sustainable behavior (Bułkowska et al., 2023).

Digital Identity

NFT-based digital identity systems offer a secure and privacy-oriented foundation for the identification of citizens and their participation in civic activities. Each token of a digital identity holds authenticated credentials without invading user privacy through sophisticated encryption methods (Agarkhed et al., 2023; Banaeian Far & Hosseini Bamakan, 2023).

This system allows for secure electronic voting within the scenario of local elections and referenda, thus providing accessibility and integrity of the democratic process (Bang et al., 2025).

Cultural Heritage and Tourism

The application of non-fungible tokens (NFTs) in cultural heritage preservation and tourism has novel aspects regarding how individuals engage with and conserve cultural heritage (Nicolazzi & Tai, 2024; Stublić et al., 2023). Historic locations are now accompanied by digital twins on the back of non-fungible tokens (NFTs), containing rich historical data, architectural data, and restoration history (M. Wang & Lau, 2023). The digital representations have twin functions of preservation and education, enabling remote access to locations while keeping precise records for conservation activities. Tourism services can be augmented through deep digital passes that grant access to several destinations, along with personalized guides and augmented reality tours (Onder, 2023). Event ticketing is made more effective and safer since NFTs cannot be forged and allow for regulated secondary market resale (Jiang & Zhou, 2022).

Environmental and Sustainability Initiatives

Environmental initiatives gain improved transparency and effectiveness through NFT implementation. For instance, carbon credit trading has grown in sophistication with tokens representing validated carbon offsets tradable in the smart city ecosystem (Razi et al., 2024; Vilkov & Tian, 2023). The tokens fully and accurately account for the reduction in emissions and the production of renewable energy sources, including their environmental effects (Babel et al., 2022). Waste management systems also use NFTs to track recycling efforts from source to processing, rewarding individuals and businesses for sustainable practices (Bułkowska et al., 2023; Souza et al., 2024).

Energy Trading

Blockchain technologies transform the method through which customers buy, sell, and track clean energy. Literature like (Trung et al., 2024) explores the use of blockchain, NFT, and IPFS in developing a secure renewable energy trading platform. The system, therefore, facilitates peer-to-peer direct transactions and stores information optimally via IPFS. To decrease transactional costs and boost the adoption of the market, the platform avoids utilizing the Ethereum mainnet and utilizes less expensive chains like Fantom and Polygon for business activities. Further, another group of researchers introduced TokenGreen, an innovative blockchain-based system for energy trading among electric vehicle charging stations, which employs NFTs and smart contracts to establish an open market (Naik et al., 2024). The test outcome was successful execution with a transaction time of approximately 10-12 seconds and reasonable utilization of resources, outperforming existing implementations.

Intelligent Building Management

Smart building systems use NFTs to create digital management frameworks. Access control, in this scenario, is optimized through tokens that are assigned with special rights according to time, location, and user identity. Such tokens would be integrated with building automation systems for the control of elevator access control and parking lot reservation (Bai et al., 2024).

Smart Supply Chains

NFTs are becoming an attractive instrument in supply chain management, providing distinctive digital identifiers capable of tracing specific items throughout their journey from production to delivery (Narayanan et al., 2024). In contrast to other forms of tracking, NFTs allow for tamper-proof and transparent documentation on blockchain networks and hence find applicability in domains where stringent authentication and traceability are needed.

Each NFT serves as a digital passport for an item, documenting the complete history and ownership trail. One of the interesting applications of this technology is in the pharmaceutical industry where researchers propose the use of NFTs and blockchain for making pharmaceutical supply chain tracing more advanced than conventional serialization approaches (Chiacchio et al., 2022). As Industry 4.0 brings about smart business-customer interactions, this solution provides an improvement in drug safety and authenticity verification within the supply chain network. The strategy is explained using a sample application, illustrating how decentralized monitoring has the potential to fulfill stringent regulatory requirements while furthering transparency in parallel.

CYBERSECURITY THREATS OF NFT IN SMART CITY ENVIRONMENTS

As NFTs are becoming more and more part of the smart city digital fabric, a complex ecosystem of cybersecurity threats is endangering the seemingly impenetrable blockchain-based networks. The growth of NFT technology in smart city ecosystems heralds an advanced range of possible security threats undermining the vital smart city digital services' functionality, privacy, and integrity. It thus discusses, in this section, sophisticated threats that can undermine these emerging digital assets. In contrast to the traditional digital systems, NFTs introduce certain vulnerabilities brought about by the decentralization, composite smart contract models, and intersection of blockchain technologies with digital infrastructure in smart cities.

Smart Contract Vulnerabilities

Inherent vulnerabilities of smart contracts pose a serious security issue in NFT-based smart city environments. Automation of various services and transactions in smart cities is dependent on these contracts, which can contain coding flaws that can be exploited by attackers (Kushwaha et al., 2022). One of the most dangerous among them are reentrancy attacks, where an attacker exploits the order of contract execution to repeatedly replay an unauthorized transaction (Al-E'mari & Sanjalawe, 2025). This can impact essential services like control of utilities and property transactions within the environment of smart cities. A genuine threat can also emerge from integer underflow or overflow conditions, wherein computation by mathematics in smart contracts results in unforeseen outputs (Kanimozhi et al., 2023). This can extend to computations by tokenized public services in calculating various factors ranging from transport rate calculations to energy consumption figure measurements.

Second, visibility issues can turn the internal contractual arrangements that are meant to be private into public knowledge, thereby compromising the operational integrity of municipal services (Fang et al., 2023).

Theft of Tokens and Unauthorized Entry

Smart cities also have the problem of NFT token theft and unauthorized access to tokenized services (JY Tan, 2024). Recovery of stolen NFTs is extremely difficult compared to other digital assets since blockchain technology is immutable. This presents an issue when the tokens are used to represent access rights to critical infrastructure or basic services. Another critical weakness pertains to the digital wallet security, since compromised wallets would be able to provide attackers with access to other municipal services in parallel. Such a weakness increases in settings where single tokens regulate access to a variety of essential systems and, as such, introduce possible points of failure (Watanabe et al., 2024). TokenPatronus devises the solution to the issue of NFT theft through its decentralized security protocol for implementation in ERC-721 tokens (Cao et al., 2022). This security system functions prior to, during, and subsequent to attempted thefts via four primary components: Decentralized Access Control, Risk Management, Arbitration, and an ERC-721G contract. Already deployed by Turtlecase NFT on the Ethereum blockchain, this token-based security system is setting its sights on other blockchains.

Market Manipulation Risks

The tokenization process of smart city assets and services also carries the risk of a manipulative market. Bad actors may attempt to manipulate prices of tokenized real estate or services through some misleading buying and selling patterns (Bhujel & Rahulamathavan, 2022). This problem becomes more serious in the cases that involve partial ownership of common property or even utility credits trading (Bose et al., 2023). In addition, front-running attacks in NFT markets could allow malicious actors to exploit pending transactions in the city's service marketplace (Zhang et al., 2023). For instance, in the Bancor network attack, attackers exploited the price calculation mechanism by front-running transactions during token conversions (Russell, 2018). Lastly, Market manipulation, mainly wash trading, poses significant risk, where a recent systematic analysis revealed wash trading comprised 94.5% of LooksRare's volume and 84.2% of X2Y2's volume (Niu et al., 2024).

Security and Privacy Risks

Blockchain networks typically operate with complete transparency; every transaction is kept visible to all members, thereby creating an auditable and traceable system. While this transparency is fundamental to blockchain's integrity, it creates privacy challenges for NFT users (Musamih et al., 2024). The visibility of NFTs can be beneficial or problematic, depending on their purpose. In some cases, public exposure is advantageous. For example, an NFT representing a patent benefits from maximum visibility, as broader awareness can increase licensing revenues and overall value. However, privacy concerns arise in many other scenarios. For example, a homeowner using an NFT to verify property ownership may not want their address and ownership status publicly available. Equally, NFTs containing sensitive medical records need very strong privacy protection to keep healthcare regulations (Uribe, 2020).

Oracle Vulnerabilities

Smart city infrastructures often rely on oracles to provide external data that is needed by smart contracts. Such oracles, which may provide information about meteorological conditions, traffic patterns, or market valuations, are potential points of failure (Tjiam et al., 2021). Oracle manipulation attacks could potentially allow compromised oracles to inject false information into NFT-based systems, and thereby affect automated decision-making and service provisioning. In order to deal with such an attack, and consequently minimize its associated threats, approaches like SecPLF have been introduced (Arora et al., 2024).

Regulatory Compliance Challenges

The constantly evolving regulatory landscape around NFTs and blockchain technology poses additional security risks. A very careful reconciliation of compliance obligations related to data protection, financial transactions, and public service provision is needed with the intrinsic characteristics of blockchain technology (Kafteranis et al., 2023). Changes in regulations might require changes to existing security measures, leading to the temporary appearance of vulnerabilities. Lastly, absence of regulations exposes participants to market manipulation like wash trading, where traders artificially inflate NFT prices through internal buying and selling (Upadhyay & Upadhyay, 2025).

Scalability and Performance Issues

Constraints on scalability can give rise to security weaknesses in blockchain networks. Growing pains come with the surging popularity of NFTs. The blockchain networks that power these digital assets can only handle so many transactions simultaneously—imagine a highway with a limited number of lanes. When too many users try to buy, sell, or mint NFTs simultaneously, the network gets congested, much like rush hour traffic (Bhujel & Rahulamathavan, 2022). This constraint results in two major issues: the duration for completing transactions increases, and associated fees escalate dramatically. Such challenges become especially pronounced during high-demand periods, such as eagerly awaited NFT launches or intense buying surges in marketplaces. Table 1 summarizes the NFT security vulnerabilities discussed above.

Table 1. Summary of the NFT security vulnerabilities

Vulnerability	Summary	References
Smart Contract Vulnerabilities	- Coding errors can be exploited by malicious actors. - Reentrancy attacks allow replaying illicit transactions. - Integer overflow/underflow conditions cause erroneous calculations. - Visibility issues can expose internal contract functions	(Al-E'mari & Sanjalawe, 2025; Fang et al., 2023; Kanimozhi et al., 2023; Kushwaha et al., 2022)
Token Theft & Unauthorized Entry	- Recovery of stolen NFTs is difficult due to blockchain immutability. - Hacked wallets can provide access to multiple municipal services. - Single tokens controlling multiple systems create potential points of failure	(JY Tan, 2024; Watanabe et al., 2024)
Market Manipulation	- Price manipulation through misleading buying/selling patterns. - Affects tokenized real estate and service markets. - Front-running attacks can exploit pending transactions	(Bhujel & Rahulamathavan, 2022; Bose et al., 2023; Zhang et al., 2023)
Security & Privacy Risks	- Blockchain transparency creates privacy challenges. - Sensitive information (e.g., property ownership, medical records) becomes publicly visible. - Trade-off between transparency and privacy protection	(Musamih et al., 2024; Uribe, 2020)
Oracle Vulnerabilities	- Oracles providing external data are potential points of failure. - Manipulation attacks can inject false information. - Affects automated decision-making and service provisioning	(Arora et al., 2024; Tjiam et al., 2021)
Regulatory Compliance Challenges	- Evolving regulatory landscape creates security risks. - Need for reconciliation between compliance obligations and blockchain technology. - Regulatory changes may create temporary vulnerabilities	(Kafteranis et al., 2023)
Scalability & Performance Issues	- Network congestion during high demand periods. - Increased transaction completion times- Escalating fees during network congestion	(Bhujel & Rahulamathavan, 2022)

Strategies and Best Practices For Securing NFTs in Smart City Settings

As cities increasingly adopt blockchain technology for asset tokenization, digital identity management, and secure transactions across various urban services, the security of NFTs becomes very important. This section covers the different countermeasures to NFT vulnerabilities in the ecosystem of smart cities. The countermeasures are grouped into technical, infrastructure, operational, and market security.

Technical Security Measures

Smart Contract Security

As indicated earlier, the safety of smart contracts is the foundation of NFT protection in smart cities. To begin with, formal verification and specification should be conducted before deployment to ensure mathematical proofs of the correctness of contract behaviors (Tolmach et al., 2021). Moreover, regular security audits incorporating automated tools and expert manual reviews could be systematically conducted to detect vulnerabilities (Rameder et al., 2022; Zhu et al., 2024). In addition, the usage of standardized contract templates, which are carefully reviewed and audited, reduces the chances of common vulnerabilities (Sebastian-Cardenas et al., 2022). Finally, to tackle reentry attacks in smart contracts, BlockWatchdog—a static analysis tool for detecting reentrancy attacks in smart contracts—was proposed (S. Yang et al., 2024). This tool decompiles bytecode to an intermediate representation, builds cross-contract control and call graphs, and performs taint analysis to find possible attack paths. The tool identifies attacker and vulnerable victim contracts by analyzing external calls and dataflow patterns.

Access Control and Authentication

Highly restrictive access control systems comprise an essential security infrastructure for NFT-based services. For instance, multi-factor authentication is required for all critical operations (Jose Diaz Rivera et al., 2024). In addition, the deployment of role-based access control systems allows finer-grained permission administration complemented with biometric authentication for high-security operations (Norta et al., 2024). Ultimately, it is recommended to apply the concepts of zero-trust architecture to ensure that every access attempt is authenticated regardless of its source and previous authentication state (Jose Diaz Rivera et al., 2024).

Data Privacy Protection

NFT-based systems demand sophisticated technical approaches for privacy protection. Advanced encryption is used to protect sensitive off-chain data, such as in healthcare, and schemes like hOCBS have been successfully implemented (Miyachi & Mackey, 2021). Zero-knowledge proofs are a tool for making transactions and credentials verification possible while preserving privacy (X. Yang & Li, 2020). Another measure is to apply data minimization principles, where only necessary information is stored and processed (Lax et al., 2024). Routine assessments of privacy impacts systematically identify and address potential vulnerabilities; strict policies related to data retention and deletion are further reinforced. Secure multiparty computation enables collaborative functions without disclosure of sensitive information, while mechanisms designed with privacy preservation maintain the utility of data without compromising on security (Kalinaki, Alli, et al., 2024; Kalinaki, Malik, et al., 2024; Shafik et al., 2024).

Infrastructure Security

Network Security

Network infrastructure requires comprehensive protection through multilayer segregated networks for different security levels (Pajooh et al., 2021). In addition, performing regular security assessments is essential to identify potential vulnerabilities (Leong et al., 2024), while advanced intrusion detection and prevention systems provide real-time threat monitoring (Shalabi et al., 2024). Moreover, the use of secure communication protocols, such as B-HAS, ensures data security when transmitted from one system to another (Dwivedi et al., 2023). Finally, the use of redundant systems helps to ensure continuity of service during various types of incidents (Khan & Anjum, 2023), and secure cross-chain communication protocols, such as CrossDeFi, protect multi-chain operations (Mohammed Abdul et al., 2024).

Oracle Security

Oracle systems, being a critical element in the operations of smart cities, require custom security protocols. It is recommended that several independent oracle sources be implemented, as it provides data redundancy and validation (J. Wang et al., 2024), while the consensus mechanism guarantees data precision (Xie et al., 2023).

Operational Security

Incident Response

Comprehensive incident response plans provide structured approaches to dealing with security incidents. Clear communication channels enable effective collaboration during incidents (Dwivedi et al., 2023), while regular testing evaluates the effectiveness of the response (Kaushik & Madhoun, 2023). Automated threat detection mechanisms provide initial notifications of potential incidents (Putz & Pernul, 2020), which are complemented by secure key backup and recovery protocols, such as KeyScrub (Jeong et al., 2023). Containment strategies, such as Rearguard, prevent the escalation of incidents (Elsayed, 2021), and the institution of clear escalation procedures ensures appropriate response levels (Rajeswari & Magesh, 2024).

Surveillance and Identification

Real-time monitoring mechanisms provide seamless security oversight of NFT activities. Automated notifications help in the detection of anomalous behaviors, such as identifying unauthorized accounts involved in illicitly acquired NFTs, while regular log analyses reveal potential security threats (Kim et al., 2023). The maintenance of detailed audit records ascertains an accountability framework (Liu et al., 2024).

Market Security

Trading Security

It protects the integrity of NFT-based transactions in the ecosystem of smart cities by market security. Mechanisms against manipulations disallow market abuse (Barczentewicz et al., 2023). Any suspicious trading patterns are detected through market monitoring systems (Sifat et al., 2024). Circuit breakers prevent the market from turning extremely sour (Liao et al., 2024), whereas secure price discovery mechanisms ensure that the tokenized assets and services are well-valued (Kräussl & Tugnetti, 2024; Marin et al., 2023).

Value Protection

Value protection mechanisms preserve the economic stability of NFT-based systems. Secure custody techniques_ safeguard token holdings (Kaisto et al., 2024), while insurance mechanisms provide protection against losses. The latter depends on the fact that value stability mechanisms avoid excessive price volatility by being supported with clear valuation guidelines of tokenized assets. Anti-fraud measures protect from unauthorized transactions (Sechting & Raschke, 2024), while secure trading mechanisms ensure transaction integrity. Regular monitoring should be conducted on token values and market conditions. Table 2 summarizes the countermeasures to NFT vulnerabilities in smart cities.

Table 2. Summary of the countermeasures to NFT vulnerabilities in smart cities.

Security Aspect	Security Measures	Summary	References
Technical Security	Smart Contract Security	• Formal verification before deployment. • Regular security audits. • Use of standardized contract templates. • Implementation of BlockWatchdog for reentrancy attack detection	(Rameder et al., 2022; Sebastian-Cardenas et al., 2022; Tolmach et al., 2021; S. Yang et al., 2024)
	Access Control and Authentication	• Multi-factor authentication. • Role-based access control. • Biometric authentication. • Zero-trust architecture implementation	(Jose Diaz Rivera et al., 2024; Norta et al., 2024)
	Data Privacy Protection	• Advanced encryption for off-chain data. • Zero-knowledge proofs. • Data minimization principles. • Secure multiparty computation. • Privacy impact assessments	(Kalinaki, Alli, et al., 2024; Miyachi & Mackey, 2021; X. Yang & Li, 2020)
Infrastructure Security	Network Security	• Multilayer segregated networks. • Regular security assessments. • Intrusion detection systems. • Secure communication protocols. • Redundant systems. • Cross-chain communication protection	(Leong et al., 2024; Mohammed Abdul et al., 2024; Pajooh et al., 2021; Shalabi et al., 2024)
	Oracle Security	• Multiple independent oracle sources. • Data redundancy and validation. • Consensus mechanism for data precision	(J. Wang et al., 2024; Xie et al., 2023)

continued on following page

Table 2. Continued

Security Aspect	Security Measures	Summary	References
Operational Security	Incident Response	• Comprehensive response plans. • Clear communication channels. • Regular testing. • Automated threat detection. • Secure key backup protocols. • Containment strategies	(Dwivedi et al., 2023; Elsayed, 2021; Jeong et al., 2023; Kaushik & Madhoun, 2023)
	Surveillance and Identification	• Real-time monitoring. • Automated notifications. • Regular log analysis. • Detailed audit records	(Kim et al., 2023; Liu et al., 2024)
Market Security	Trading Security	• Anti-manipulation mechanisms. • Market monitoring systems. • Circuit breakers. • Secure price discovery mechanisms	(Barczentewicz et al., 2023; Kräussl & Tugnetti, 2024; Liao et al., 2024; Sifat et al., 2024)
	Value Protection	• Secure custody solutions. • Insurance mechanisms. • Value stability mechanisms. • Anti-fraud measures. • Regular market monitoring	(Kaisto et al., 2024; Sechting & Raschke, 2024)

Ethical Frameworks for NFT Security

The intersection of NFTs, security, and AI raises important ethical considerations that can be examined through frameworks as described below;

Fairness

In NFT security, fairness involves equal access to ensure all participants have similar opportunities to create, buy, and sell NFTs without technical barriers. This includes protection against price manipulation through practices like wash trading or shill bidding (Tahmasbi et al., 2024). Fair distribution mechanisms are essential in designing mint processes that don't unfairly advantage wealthy participants or automated bots (Liddell, 2024). AI-powered systems supporting NFT platforms should be designed to avoid perpetuating existing biases in creative markets or unfairly advantaging certain groups of creators (Serada, 2022).

Accountability

Accountability frameworks for NFT security establish clear ownership of failures and determine who is responsible when NFTs are compromised. This includes providing meaningful recourse for victims through methods to recover lost assets or receive compensation. Maintaining transparent audit trails of transactions and security incidents creates a record that supports accountability (Lohachab & Urovi, 2024). Legal frameworks are evolving to develop regulations that hold platform developers accountable for security. When AI systems are used for security, there must be clear lines of responsibility between AI developers, platform operators, and users.

Transparency

Transparency in NFT security encompasses open security protocols that make protective measures understandable to all users (Bhujel & Rahulamathavan, 2022). Platforms should practice thorough disclosure of risks by clearly communicating potential vulnerabilities to participants (Otoni et al., 2023). Smart contract verification enables public auditing of code, building trust in the system (Permenev et al., 2020). When AI systems are employed for security or fraud detection, making their decision processes interpretable is important for maintaining trust and allowing oversight.

EMERGING TRENDS IN NFT SECURITY FOR SMART CITIES

The following section highlights the emerging security aspects of NFT security in smart city ecosystems.

Advanced Cybersecurity Protocols

Today's urban blockchain ecosystems face increasingly sophisticated threats, necessitating the rapid evolution of cybersecurity protocols that extend far beyond conventional security measures. The current technological landscape has embraced multi-factor authentication, decentralized identity verification frameworks, and advanced encryption methodologies that form the foundation of modern digital protection systems (Jose Diaz Rivera et al., 2024). What distinguishes these contemporary approaches is their proactive nature, incorporating cutting-edge capabilities such as real-time threat detection algorithms and specialized blockchain forensics tools that not only respond to existing vulnerabilities but can anticipate and neutralize potential security breaches before they materialize, creating a more resilient and adaptive security infrastructure for our increasingly interconnected digital urban environments (Atlam et al., 2024; Khoa et al., 2024).

AI-Driven Threat Detection

Artificial intelligence has become a game-changing component in NFT security strategies by integrating sophisticated machine learning algorithms across multiple security dimensions. These systems leverage advanced pattern recognition to analyze blockchain transactions in real time, detecting anomalous behaviors that might indicate fraud or theft attempts before damage occurs (Soori et al., 2023). These systems effectively combat wash trading, counterfeit NFTs, and smart contract exploitations for NFT marketplaces while continuously improving through adaptive learning mechanisms that enhance detection capabilities with each identified threat. This protection extends to smart city applications, where AI security systems safeguard digital infrastructure assets, verify digital identities, and secure blockchain-based municipal services thereby creating a comprehensive security framework that evolves alongside emerging threats to maintain robust protection for valuable digital assets in increasingly complex blockchain ecosystems (Kalinaki, Yahya, et al., 2024).

Interoperability and Cross-Platform Security

Interoperability is one of the most important factors for creating robust security frameworks of NFTs. In smart cities, there are efforts to establish a homogeneous security protocol that would operate seamlessly across different blockchain networks and yield secure and smooth transactions of digital assets (Ali et al., 2023; Khalil et al., 2024; Razi et al., 2024). This approach requires developing holistic identity management systems along with verification mechanisms that can operate within a technological contour (Han et al., 2024). To this end, the authors proposed MetaOpera, a generalized cross-metaverse interoperability protocol that enables seamless interaction between users and digital objects across diverse metaverse platforms (Li et al., 2023). By establishing wireless communication links with MetaOpera, entities from both centralized server-based and decentralized blockchain-powered metaverses can engage with one another, transcending previously established ecosystem boundaries.

Regulatory Compliance and Privacy Protection

Privacy protection and regulatory compliance remain paramount. Emerging NFT security frameworks implement zero-knowledge proof technologies, such as Zk-Auction, that protect sensitive information while maintaining transparency (Tran et al., 2024). These approaches balance the need for secure, verifiable transactions with stringent data protection principles, ensuring that smart city blockchain ecosystems remain innovative and legally compliant.

Quantum-Resistant Encryption

Quantum-resistant encryption represents a proactive cybersecurity approach as smart cities prepare for the threat quantum computing poses to current cryptographic methods (Muda et al., 2024; Zheng, 2024). While large-scale quantum computers don't yet exist, their eventual development could break widely-used encryption algorithms like Rivest-Shamir-Adleman (RSA) and Elliptic Curve Cryptography (ECC) through quantum algorithms such as Shor's algorithm (Albuainain et al., 2022; Kute et al., 2024). In response, urban planners and security experts are implementing solutions including lattice-based cryptography, hash-based methods, code-based systems, multivariate polynomial approaches, and quantum-resistant blockchain architectures (Muda et al., 2024; Zheng, 2024). These implementations face challenges like increased computational requirements, standardization needs, and legacy system integration issues. However, this forward-thinking strategy exemplifies smart cities' evolution toward adaptive, resilient systems that anticipate technological threats years before they materialize which is essential given the long lifecycle of urban digital infrastructure and the potentially catastrophic consequences of compromised systems controlling critical utilities and services.

CONCLUSION

In a nutshell, this chapter has presented a wide-based analysis of NFT security in smart city ecosystems, highlighting the transformative possibilities and the fundamental challenges associated with this emerging technology. Through an in-depth investigation of different applications, from digital land registries to environmental projects, this chapter will exemplify how NFTs are redefining smart city governance and service delivery while emphasizing the critical need for robust security frameworks. The diverse applications explored throughout the chapter reveal NFTs' potential to revolutionize smart city operations with greater transparency, efficiency, and citizen engagement. Digital land registries and property management systems have shown promise in simplifying smart city administration, while tokenized public services have opened new avenues for citizen interaction with city infrastructure. It is further exemplified by the implementation of NFT-based solutions in digital identity systems, cultural heritage preservation, and environmental initiatives. On the other hand, the identified security vulnerabilities, ranging from weaknesses in smart contracts to risks of market manipulation, have shown the need for advanced security protocols in the implementation of smart cities. The above challenges are of specific significance owing to the interdependent nature of smart city systems, where security breaches can spread through different municipal services, thus negatively impacting citizens' well-being. The countermeasures described above provide a comprehensive framework for securing NFT applications in smart cities. With the continued development of smart cities, the trends identified highlight a future where enhanced security measures, security based on artificial intelligence, and interoperability will become critical to successfully integrating NFTs. The underlying focus of this research on NFT security in the smart city scenario reflects the need for proactive security policies, continuous monitoring, and adaptable strategies in a rapidly evolving technological landscape. As cities move toward the embracing of digital innovation, the various findings presented in this chapter provide critical guidance for policymakers, developers, and smart city planners in developing secure, efficient, and resilient ecosystems of smart cities through NFT technology.

REFERENCES

Agarkhed, J., Patil, S. S., Raza, S. Y., & Patil, V. (2023). Secure Digital Identity using Non-Fungible Tokens. *Proceedings of the 5th International Conference on Inventive Research in Computing Applications, ICIRCA 2023*, 1196–1201. DOI: 10.1109/ICIRCA57980.2023.10220854

Al-E'mari, S., & Sanjalawe, Y. (2025). A Review of Reentrancy Attack in Ethereum Smart Contracts. *Lecture Notes in Networks and Systems, 977 LNNS*, 53–70. DOI: 10.1007/978-981-97-2671-4_5

Al Shamsi, M., Smith, D., & Gleason, K. (2023). Space transition and the vulnerabilities of the NFT market to financial crime. *Journal of Financial Crime, 30*(6), 1664–1673. DOI: 10.1108/JFC-09-2022-0218

Albuainain, A., Alansari, J., Alrashidi, S., Alqahtani, W., Alshaya, J., & Nagy, N. (2022). Experimental Implementation of Shor's Quantum Algorithm to Break RSA. *Proceedings - 2022 14th IEEE International Conference on Computational Intelligence and Communication Networks, CICN 2022*, 748–752. DOI: 10.1109/CICN56167.2022.10008287

Ali, O., Momin, M., Shrestha, A., Das, R., Alhajj, F., & Dwivedi, Y. K. (2023). A review of the key challenges of non-fungible tokens. *Technological Forecasting and Social Change, 187*, 122248. DOI: 10.1016/j.techfore.2022.122248

Arora, S., Li, Y., Feng, Y., & Xu, J. (2024). SecPLF: Secure Protocols for Loanable Funds against Oracle Manipulation Attacks. *ACM AsiaCCS 2024 - Proceedings of the 19th ACM Asia Conference on Computer and Communications Security*, 1394–1405. DOI: 10.1145/3634737.3637681

Atlam, H. F., Ekuri, N., Azad, M. A., & Lallie, H. S. (2024). Blockchain Forensics: A Systematic Literature Review of Techniques, Applications, Challenges, and Future Directions. *Electronics 2024, Vol. 13, Page 3568, 13*(17), 3568. DOI: 10.3390/electronics13173568

Ayres Principe, V., da Silva, G. C. P. S. M., de Souza Vale, R. G., & Moreira Nunes, R. de A. (. (2024). Blockchain and sports industry: A systematic literature review of Fan Tokens and their implications. *Retos, 60*, 823. DOI: 10.47197/retos.v60.107125

Babel, M., Gramlich, V., Körner, M. F., Sedlmeir, J., Strüker, J., & Zwede, T. (2022). Enabling end-to-end digital carbon emission tracing with shielded NFTs. *Energy Informatics, 5*(1), 1–21. DOI: 10.1186/s42162-022-00199-3 PMID: 35252758

Bai, H., Li, Z., Chen, K., & Li, X. (2024). Blockchain-Based Responsibility Management Framework for Smart City Building Information Modeling Projects Using Non-Fungible Tokens. *Buildings (Basel, Switzerland), 14*(11), 3647. DOI: 10.3390/buildings14113647

Banaeian Far, S., & Hosseini Bamakan, S. M. (2023). NFT-based identity management in metaverses: Challenges and opportunities. *SN Applied Sciences, 5*(10), 1–12. DOI: 10.1007/s42452-023-05487-5

Bang, L. K., Khanh, H. V., Triet, M. N., Hung, N. N., Trinh, P. D., Bang, H. N., Anh, N. T., & Ngan, K. T. N. (2025). *Enhancing Election Security Through Blockchain: An In-Depth Study of Encrypted NFTs and Smart Contracts* (pp. 21–36). DOI: 10.1007/978-3-031-77153-8_3

Barczentewicz, M., Sarch, A., & Vasan, N. (2023). Blockchain Transaction Ordering as Market Manipulation. *Ohio State Technology Law Journal, 20*. https://heinonline.org/HOL/Page?handle=hein.journals/isjlpsoc20&id=7&div=&collection=

Behl, A., Pereira, V., Nigam, A., Wamba, S., & Sindhwani, R. (2024). Knowledge development in non-fungible tokens (NFT): A scoping review. *Journal of Knowledge Management, 28*(1), 232–267. DOI: 10.1108/JKM-12-2022-0937

Bhujel, S., & Rahulamathavan, Y. (2022). A Survey: Security, Transparency, and Scalability Issues of NFT's and Its Marketplaces. *Sensors 2022, Vol. 22, Page 8833, 22*(22), 8833. DOI: 10.3390/s22228833

Bose, P., Das, D., Gritti, F., Ruaro, N., Kruegel, C., & Vigna, G. (2023). *Exploiting Unfair Advantages: Investigating Opportunistic Trading in the NFT Market*. https://arxiv.org/abs/2310.06844v1

Bułkowska, K., Zielińska, M., & Bułkowski, M. (2023). Implementation of Blockchain Technology in Waste Management. *Energies 2023, Vol. 16, Page 7742, 16*(23), 7742. DOI: 10.3390/en16237742

Cao, Z., Zhen, Y., Fan, G., & Gao, S. (2022). *TokenPatronus: A Decentralized NFT Anti-theft Mechanism*. https://arxiv.org/abs/2208.05168v1

Chawda, K., Mehta, K., Borkar, T., & Ambadekar, S. (2024). NFTs and property tokenisation: Advancements and applications in blockchain technology. *International Journal of Blockchains and Cryptocurrencies, 5*(1), 44–66. DOI: 10.1504/IJBC.2024.140167

Chiacchio, F., D'Urso, D., Oliveri, L. M., Spitaleri, A., Spampinato, C., & Giordano, D. (2022). A Non-Fungible Token Solution for the Track and Trace of Pharmaceutical Supply Chain. *Applied Sciences (Basel, Switzerland), 12*(8), 4019. DOI: 10.3390/app12084019

Dwivedi, S. K., Amin, R., Vollala, S., & Khan, M. K. (2023). B-HAS: Blockchain-Assisted Efficient Handover Authentication and Secure Communication Protocol in VANETs. *IEEE Transactions on Network Science and Engineering*, •••, 1–14. DOI: 10.1109/TNSE.2023.3264829

Elsayed, M. A. S. (2021). Rearguard: A Novel Blockchain-based Automatic Worm Containment System. *2021 International Telecommunications Conference (ITC-Egypt)*, 1–8. DOI: 10.1109/ITC-Egypt52936.2021.9513932

Fang, Y., Wu, D., Yi, X., Wang, S., Chen, Y., Chen, M., Liu, Y., & Jiang, L. (2023). Beyond "Protected" and "Private": An Empirical Security Analysis of Custom Function Modifiers in Smart Contracts. *ISSTA 2023 - Proceedings of the 32nd ACM SIGSOFT International Symposium on Software Testing and Analysis*, 1157–1168. DOI: 10.1145/3597926.3598125

Han, Y., Wang, C., & Wang, H. (2024). Research on Blockchain Cross-Chain Model Based on "nFT + Cross-Chain Bridge.". *IEEE Access : Practical Innovations, Open Solutions, 12*, 77065–77078. DOI: 10.1109/ACCESS.2024.3401405

Jenkins, B. (2024). NFTs and the financialization of art. *Cultural Studies*. Advance online publication. DOI: 10.1080/09502386.2024.2329873

Jeong, W., Park, H., & Park, C. (2023). KeyScrub: A Reliable Key Backup and Recovery Method for Blockchain. *IEEE Access : Practical Innovations, Open Solutions, 11*, 91747–91755. DOI: 10.1109/ACCESS.2023.3308208

Jiang, Y. Y., & Zhou, J. T. (2022). Ticketing System Based On NFT. *2022 IEEE 24th International Workshop on Multimedia Signal Processing, MMSP 2022*. DOI: 10.1109/MMSP55362.2022.9948706

Jose Diaz Rivera, J., Muhammad, A., & Song, W. C. (2024). Securing Digital Identity in the Zero Trust Architecture: A Blockchain Approach to Privacy-Focused Multi-Factor Authentication. *IEEE Open Journal of the Communications Society, 5*, 2792–2814. DOI: 10.1109/OJCOMS.2024.3391728

Kafteranis, D., Unozkan, H., & Turksen, U. (2023). Know Your NFTs: Compliance and Enforcement Challenges in Trading of Non-Fungible Tokens. *International Journal of Law in Changing World, 2*. https://heinonline.org/HOL/Page?handle=hein.journals/inljlolwic2&id=145&div=&collection=

Kaisto, J., Juutilainen, T., & Kauranen, J. (2024). Non-fungible tokens, tokenization, and ownership. *Computer Law & Security Review*, *54*, 105996. DOI: 10.1016/j.clsr.2024.105996

Kalinaki, K. (2024). IoT and Blockchain Integration for Enhanced AI-Driven Business Intelligence. In *Intersection of AI and Business Intelligence in Data-Driven Decision-Making* (pp. 21–52). IGI Global., DOI: 10.4018/979-8-3693-5288-5.ch002

Kalinaki, K., Alli, A. A., Asuman, B., & Zakari, R. Y. (2024). Secure federated learning in the Internet of Health Things for improved patient privacy and data security. In *Federated Learning for Digital Healthcare Systems* (pp. 387–408). Elsevier., DOI: 10.1016/B978-0-443-13897-3.00003-5

Kalinaki, K., Malik, O. A., Yahya, U., & Lai, D. T. C. (2024). Federated learning challenges and risks in modern digital healthcare systems. In *Federated Learning for Digital Healthcare Systems* (pp. 283–300). Elsevier., DOI: 10.1016/B978-0-443-13897-3.00004-7

Kalinaki, K., Thilakarathne, N. N., Mubarak, H. R., Malik, O. A., & Abdullatif, M. (2023). Cybersafe Capabilities and Utilities for Smart Cities. In *Cybersecurity for Smart Cities* (pp. 71–86). Springer., DOI: 10.1007/978-3-031-24946-4_6

Kalinaki, K., Yahya, U., Malik, O. A., & Lai, D. T. C. (2024). A Review of Big Data Analytics and Artificial Intelligence in Industry 5.0 for Smart Decision-Making. In *Human-Centered Approaches in Industry 5.0* (pp. 24–47). Human-Machine Interaction, Virtual Reality Training, and Customer Sentiment Analysis., DOI: 10.4018/979-8-3693-2647-3.ch002

Kanimozhi, P., Jayasri, A. R., Ananth Kumar, T., & Arunmozhiselvi, S. (2023). *Smart Contracts for Enhanced Water Resource Management.*, DOI: 10.4018/979-8-3693-0497-6.ch011

Kaushik, S., & El Madhoun, N. (2023). Analysis of Blockchain Security: Classic Attacks, Cybercrime and Penetration Testing. *Proceedings of the 2023 8th International Conference on Mobile and Secure Services, MobiSecServ 2023.* DOI: 10.1109/MobiSecServ58080.2023.10329210

Khalil, U., Malik, O. A., Hong, O. W., & Uddin, M. (2022). Decentralized Smart City of Things: A Blockchain Tokenization-enabled Architecture for Digitization and Authentication of Assets in Smart Cities. *ACM International Conference Proceeding Series*, 38–47. DOI: 10.1145/3569507.3569513

Khalil, U., Uddin, M., Malik, O. A., & Hong, O. W. (2024). A Novel NFT Solution for Assets Digitization and Authentication in Cyber-Physical Systems: Blueprint and Evaluation. *IEEE Open Journal of the Computer Society*, *5*, 131–143. DOI: 10.1109/OJCS.2024.3378424

Khan, A., & Anjum, A. (2023). Optimizing Data Distribution to Balance Scalability-Redundancy Trade-off for Collaborative Blockchain Storage. *2023 IEEE International Conference on Pervasive Computing and Communications Workshops and Other Affiliated Events, PerCom Workshops 2023*, 249–255. DOI: 10.1109/PerComWorkshops56833.2023.10150226

Khanh, B. L. Phung, Trinh. D., Nguyen, T. M., Vo, H. K., Dang, K. T., Trong, P. N., Kim, N. N. T., & Kha, N. H. (2024). *Property and Pixels: Redefining Real Estate in the Digital Era* (pp. 162–177). DOI: 10.1007/978-3-031-65154-0_10

Khoa, T. V., Son, D. H., Hoang, D. T., Trung, N. L., Thuy Quynh, T. T., Nguyen, D. N., Ha, N. V., & Dutkiewicz, E. (2024). Real-time Cyberattack Detection with Collaborative Learning for Blockchain Networks. *IEEE Wireless Communications and Networking Conference, WCNC*. DOI: 10.1109/WCNC57260.2024.10571103

Kim, H., Cui, J., Jang, E., Lee, C., Lee, Y., Chung, J.-W., & Shin, S. (2023). *DRAINCLoG: Detecting Rogue Accounts with Illegally-obtained NFTs using Classifiers Learned on Graphs*. DOI: 10.14722/ndss.2024.24888

Kräussl, R., & Tugnetti, A. (2024). Non-Fungible Tokens (NFTs): A Review of Pricing Determinants, Applications and Opportunities. *Journal of Economic Surveys*, *38*(2), 555–574. DOI: 10.1111/joes.12597

Kushwaha, S. S., Joshi, S., Singh, D., Kaur, M., & Lee, H. N. (2022). Systematic Review of Security Vulnerabilities in Ethereum Blockchain Smart Contract. *IEEE Access : Practical Innovations, Open Solutions*, *10*, 6605–6621. DOI: 10.1109/ACCESS.2021.3140091

Kute, S., Desai, C., & Jadhav, M. (2024). Analysis of RSA and Shor's algorithm for cryptography: A quantum perspective. *AIP Conference Proceedings*, *3156*(1), 040004. Advance online publication. DOI: 10.1063/5.0227773

Kuznetsov, O., Frontoni, E., Kuznetsova, K., Shevchuk, R., & Karpinski, M. (2024). NFT Technology for Enhanced Global Digital Registers: A Novel Approach to Tokenization. *Future Internet 2024, Vol. 16, Page 252*, *16*(7), 252. DOI: 10.3390/fi16070252

Lax, G., Canino, A., & Musarella, L. (2024). A Blockchain-Based Approach for Certifying Information at Different Levels of Granularity According to the Data Minimization Principle of the GDPR. *Proceedings - 2024 8th International Conference on Computer, Software and Modeling, ICCSM 2024*, 31–35. DOI: 10.1109/ICCSM63823.2024.00014

Leong, W. Y., Leong, Y. Z., & Leong, W. S. (2024). Enhancing Blockchain Security. *2024 IEEE Symposium on Wireless Technology & Applications (ISWTA)*, 108–112. DOI: 10.1109/ISWTA62130.2024.10651753

Li, T., Yang, C., Yang, Q., Lan, S., Zhou, S., Luo, X., Huang, H., & Zheng, Z. (2023). Metaopera: A Cross-Metaverse Interoperability Protocol. *IEEE Wireless Communications*, *30*(5), 136–143. DOI: 10.1109/MWC.011.2300042

Liao, X., Li, Q., Chan, S., Chu, J., & Zhang, Y. (2024). Interconnections and contagion among cryptocurrencies, DeFi, NFT and traditional financial assets: Some new evidence from tail risk driven network. *Physica A*, *647*, 129892. DOI: 10.1016/j.physa.2024.129892

Liddell, F. (2024). THE DISTRIBUTED MUSEUM: Using Smart Contracts and NFTs to Find Financial Equity in Co-produced Exhibitions. *Financial Management in Museums: Theory, Practice, and Context*, 314–329. DOI: 10.4324/9781003308003-26

Liu, Z., Zhang, X., Li, G., Cui, H., Wang, J., & Xiao, B. (2024). A Secure and Reliable Blockchain-based Audit Log System. *ICC 2024 - IEEE International Conference on Communications*, 2010–2015. DOI: 10.1109/ICC51166.2024.10623012

Lohachab, A., & Urovi, V. (2024). A Blockchain-Based Approach for Model Card Accountability and Regulatory Compliance. *Lecture Notes in Business Information Processing*, *521*, 37–48. DOI: 10.1007/978-3-031-61003-5_4

Marin, O., Cioara, T., Toderean, L., Mitrea, D., & Anghel, I. (2023). Review of Blockchain Tokens Creation and Valuation. *Future Internet 2023, Vol. 15, Page 382, 15*(12), 382. DOI: 10.3390/fi15120382

Meneguzzo, S., Selabi, E. G. K., Favenza, A., Gatteschi, V., & Schifanella, C. (2024). Enabling Citizen Sustainable Behaviors in Urban Mobility through Blockchain and Tokenization. In *Blockchain Technology in the Automotive Industry* (pp. 245–279). CRC Press., DOI: 10.1201/9781003450306-17

Miyachi, K., & Mackey, T. K. (2021). hOCBS: A privacy-preserving blockchain framework for healthcare data leveraging an on-chain and off-chain system design. *Information Processing & Management*, *58*(3), 102535. DOI: 10.1016/j.ipm.2021.102535

Mohammed Abdul, S. S., Shrestha, A., & Yong, J. (2024). CrossDeFi: A Novel Cross-Chain Communication Protocol. *Future Internet*, *16*(9), 314. DOI: 10.3390/fi16090314

Mollajafari, S., & Bechkoum, K. (2023). Blockchain Technology and Related Security Risks: Towards a Seven-Layer Perspective and Taxonomy. *Sustainability 2023, Vol. 15, Page 13401*, *15*(18), 13401. DOI: 10.3390/su151813401

Muda, I., Santosh, K., Aarif, M., Natrayan, L., Kaliappan, S., & Muthuperumal, S. (2024). Innovative Blockchain Protocol for Enhancing Transaction Security and Integrity in Decentralized Financial Ecosystems. *2nd IEEE International Conference on Data Science and Network Security, ICDSNS 2024*. DOI: 10.1109/ICDSNS62112.2024.10691288

Musamih, A., Dirir, A., Yaqoob, I., Salah, K., Jayaraman, R., & Puthal, D. (2024). NFTs in Smart Cities: Vision, Applications, and Challenges. *IEEE Consumer Electronics Magazine*, *13*(2), 9–23. DOI: 10.1109/MCE.2022.3217660

Naik, M., Singh, A. P., Pradhan, N. R., Kumar, N., Nayak, A., & Guizani, M. (2024). TokenGreen: A Versatile NFT Framework for Peer-to-Peer Energy Trading and Asset Ownership of Electric Vehicles. *IEEE Internet of Things Journal*, *11*(8), 13636–13646. DOI: 10.1109/JIOT.2023.3340155

Narayanan, G., Cvitić, I., Peraković, D., & Raja, S. P. (2024). Role of Blockchain Technology in Supplychain Management. *IEEE Access : Practical Innovations, Open Solutions*, *12*, 19021–19034. DOI: 10.1109/ACCESS.2024.3361310

Nicolazzi, L., & Tai, M. G. (2024). *NFT and Blockchain Technology for a Sustainable Future of Cultural Heritage*., DOI: 10.1007/978-3-031-47347-0_9

Niu, Y., Li, X., Peng, H., & Li, W. (2024). Unveiling Wash Trading in Popular NFT Markets. *WWW 2024 Companion - Companion Proceedings of the ACM Web Conference*, 730–733. DOI: 10.1145/3589335.3651580

Norta, A., Udokwu, C., & Craß, S. (2024). Real-World Asset Identity Authentication in Blockchain Enabled Inter-Organizational Process-Aware Systems Involving Adjustable Challenge-Response Evaluation Sets. *SN Computer Science*, *5*(7), 1–16. DOI: 10.1007/s42979-024-03265-7

Onder, I. (2023). ENHANCING SUSTAINABLE TOURISM THROUGH BLOCKCHAIN-BASED TOKENIZATION. *Blockchain for Tourism and Hospitality Industries*, 105–121. DOI: 10.4324/9781003351917-8

Otoni, R., Marescotti, M., Alt, L., Eugster, P., Hyvärinen, A., & Sharygina, N. (2023). A Solicitous Approach to Smart Contract Verification. *ACM Transactions on Privacy and Security, 26*(2), 1–28. Advance online publication. DOI: 10.1145/3564699

Oza, V. J., Nikte, A., Bhanushali, V., & Rote, U. (2024). Smart Contracts and Tokenization: Revolutionizing Real Estate Transactions with Blockchain Technology. *2024 International Conference on Inventive Computation Technologies (ICICT)*, 1598–1604. DOI: 10.1109/ICICT60155.2024.10544886

Pajooh, H. H., Rashid, M., Alam, F., & Demidenko, S. (2021). Multi-Layer Blockchain-Based Security Architecture for Internet of Things. *Sensors 2021, Vol. 21, Page 772, 21*(3), 772. DOI: 10.3390/s21030772

Permenev, A., Dimitrov, D., Tsankov, P., Drachsler-Cohen, D., & Vechev, M. (2020). VerX: Safety verification of smart contracts. *Proceedings - IEEE Symposium on Security and Privacy, 2020-May*, 1661–1677. DOI: 10.1109/SP40000.2020.00024

Putz, B., & Pernul, G. (2020). Detecting Blockchain Security Threats. *Proceedings - 2020 IEEE International Conference on Blockchain, Blockchain 2020*, 313–320. DOI: 10.1109/Blockchain50366.2020.00046

Rajeswari, M., & Magesh, R. (2024). Hierarchical Escalations of Incidents in Block Chain Technology. *Organization, Purpose and Values: Integrating Diversity, Equity and Inclusion*, 327–344. DOI: 10.4324/9781003501374-24

Rameder, H., di Angelo, M., & Salzer, G. (2022). Review of Automated Vulnerability Analysis of Smart Contracts on Ethereum. *Frontiers in Blockchain, 5*, 814977. DOI: 10.3389/fbloc.2022.814977

Razi, Q., Devrani, A., Abhyankar, H., Chalapathi, G. S. S., Hassija, V., & Guizani, M. (2024). Non-Fungible Tokens (NFTs) - Survey of Current Applications, Evolution, and Future Directions. *IEEE Open Journal of the Communications Society, 5*, 2765–2791. DOI: 10.1109/OJCOMS.2023.3343926

Rubino, F., Agostino, D., & Spallazzo, D. (2024). Strategizing blockchain adoption in public cultural services: a comprehensive scoping review. *International Journal of Public Sector Management, ahead-of-print*(ahead-of-print). DOI: 10.1108/IJPSM-12-2023-0383

Russell, J. (2018). *The crypto world's latest hack sees Bancor lose $23.5M*. https://techcrunch.com/2018/07/10/bancor-loses-23-5m/

Sebastian-Cardenas, D. J., Gourisetti, S. N. G., Wang, P., Smith, J. J., Borkum, M. I., & Mukherjee, M. (2022). *Smart Contract Architectures and Templates for Blockchain-based Energy Markets (V.1.0)*. DOI: 10.2172/1987264

Sechting, C., & Raschke, P. (2024). A Taxonomy of Anti-Fraud Measures within Token Economy: Insights from Rug Pull Schemes. *2024 6th Conference on Blockchain Research & Applications for Innovative Networks and Services (BRAINS)*, 1–9. DOI: 10.1109/BRAINS63024.2024.10732222

Serada, A. (2022). Fairness by Design: The Fair Game and the Fair Price on a Blockchain-Based Marketplace. *Lecture Notes in Networks and Systems*, *382*, 63–75. DOI: 10.1007/978-3-030-93780-5_6

Shafik, W., Kalinaki, K., & Zakari, R. Y. (2024). Blockchain's Motivation for IoT-Enabled Smart City. *Secure and Intelligent IoT-Enabled Smart Cities*, 195–221. DOI: 10.4018/979-8-3693-2373-1.ch010

Shalabi, K., Al-Haija, Q. A., & Al-Fayoumi, M. (2024). A Blockchain-based Intrusion Detection/Prevention Systems in IoT Network: A Systematic Review. *Procedia Computer Science*, *236*, 410–419. DOI: 10.1016/j.procs.2024.05.048

Sharma, A., Sharma, A., Tripathi, A., & Chaudhary, A. (2024). Real Estate Registry Platform Through NFT Tokenization Using Blockchain. *2024 2nd International Conference on Disruptive Technologies (ICDT)*, 335–340. DOI: 10.1109/ICDT61202.2024.10488945

Sifat, I., Tariq, S. A., & van Donselaar, D. (2024). Suspicious trading in nonfungible tokens (NFTs). *Information & Management*, *61*(1), 103898. DOI: 10.1016/j.im.2023.103898

Soori, M., Dastres, R., & Arezoo, B. (2023). AI-powered blockchain technology in industry 4.0, a review. *Journal of Economy and Technology*, *1*, 222–241. DOI: 10.1016/j.ject.2024.01.001

Souza, E. B., Carlos, R. L., de Mattos, C. A., & Scur, G. (2024). The role of blockchain platform in enabling circular economy practices. *Corporate Social Responsibility and Environmental Management*, *31*(6), 5730–5743. DOI: 10.1002/csr.2885

Stublić, H., Bilogrivić, M., & Zlodi, G. (2023). Blockchain and NFTs in the Cultural Heritage Domain: A Review of Current Research Topics. *Heritage*, *6*(4), 3801–3819. DOI: 10.3390/heritage6040202

Tahmasbi, N., Shan, G., & French, A. M. (2024). Identifying Washtrading Cases in NFT Sales Networks. *IEEE Transactions on Computational Social Systems*, *11*(2), 1696–1707. DOI: 10.1109/TCSS.2023.3319554

Tan, J. Y. (2024). *L.* NFT Security., DOI: 10.1007/978-3-031-58002-4_2

Tien, D. B., Phung, T. D., Nguyen, T. M., Vo, H. K., Dang, K. T., Trong, P. N., Khanh, B. L., & Kim, N. N. T. (2024). From Bricks to Bits: Revolutionizing Real Estate for the Digital World. *Lecture Notes in Computer Science (Including Subseries Lecture Notes in Artificial Intelligence and Lecture Notes in Bioinformatics), 14543 LNCS*, 106–117. DOI: 10.1007/978-3-031-60997-8_11

Tjiam, K., Wang, R., Chen, H., & Liang, K. (2021). Your Smart Contracts Are Not Secure: Investigating Arbitrageurs and Oracle Manipulators in Ethereum. *CYSARM 2021 - Proceedings of the 3rd Workshop on Cyber-Security Arms Race, Co-Located with CCS 2021*, 25–35. DOI: 10.1145/3474374.3486916

Tolmach, P., Li, Y., Lin, S. W., Liu, Y., & Li, Z. (2021). A Survey of Smart Contract Formal Specification and Verification. *ACM Computing Surveys, 54*(7), 1–38. Advance online publication. DOI: 10.1145/3464421

Tran, T. D., Phong, K. M., Le Bao, C. D., Cam, N. T., & Pham, V. H. (2024). Zk-Auction: A Cross-Blockchain System for Efficient Auctions combining Zero-Knowledge Proof and NFT. *ACM International Conference Proceeding Series*, 446–453. DOI: 10.1145/3654522.3654589

Trung, P. H. T., Khoa, T. D., Kha, H. N., Bao, Q. T., Trong, N. D. P., Loc, V. C. P., Hieu, D. M., & Bang, L. K. (2024). Decentralized Renewable Energy Trading: A Cross-Chain, NFT, and IPFS Framework. *Lecture Notes in Computer Science (Including Subseries Lecture Notes in Artificial Intelligence and Lecture Notes in Bioinformatics), 14792 LNCS*, 69–82. DOI: 10.1007/978-3-031-68005-2_6

Upadhyay, N., & Upadhyay, S. (2025). The dark side of non-fungible tokens: Understanding risks in the NFT marketplace from a fraud triangle perspective. *Financial Innovation, 11*(1), 1–29. DOI: 10.1186/s40854-024-00684-6

Uribe, D. (2020). Privacy Laws, Non-Fungible Tokens, and Genomics. *The Journal of The British Blockchain Association, 3*(2), 1–10. DOI: 10.31585/jbba-3-2-(5)2020

Vilkov, A., & Tian, G. (2023). Blockchain's Scope and Purpose in Carbon Markets: A Systematic Literature Review. *Sustainability 2023, Vol. 15, Page 8495, 15*(11), 8495. DOI: 10.3390/su15118495

Wang, J., Zheng, Q., & Shen, Y. (2024). Research on Multi-level Trustworthy Multimedia Data Broadcasting Network Based on Blockchain Oracles. *IEEE International Symposium on Broadband Multimedia Systems and Broadcasting, BMSB*. DOI: 10.1109/BMSB62888.2024.10608301

Wang, M., & Lau, N. (2023). NFT Digital Twins: A Digitalization Strategy to Preserve and Sustain Miao Silver Craftsmanship in the Metaverse Era. *Heritage*, *6*(2), 1921–1941. DOI: 10.3390/heritage6020103

Watanabe, H., Ichihara, K., & Aita, T. (2024). VELLET: Verifiable Embedded Wallet for Securing Authenticity and Integrity. *2024 IEEE International Conference on Blockchain and Cryptocurrency, ICBC 2024*, 254–258. DOI: 10.1109/ICBC59979.2024.10634467

Xie, M., Liu, J., Chen, S., & Lin, M. (2023). A survey on blockchain consensus mechanism: Research overview, current advances and future directions. *International Journal of Intelligent Computing and Cybernetics*, *16*(2), 314–340. DOI: 10.1108/IJICC-05-2022-0126

Yang, J., Liu, J., Lin, D., Wu, J., Huang, B., Li, Q., & Zheng, Z. (2024). Who Stole My NFT? Investigating Web3 NFT Phishing Scams on Ethereum. *IEEE Transactions on Information Forensics and Security*, *19*, 9301–9314. Advance online publication. DOI: 10.1109/TIFS.2024.3463541

Yang, S., Chen, J., Huang, M., Zheng, Z., & Huang, Y. (2024). Uncover the Premeditated Attacks: Detecting Exploitable Reentrancy Vulnerabilities by Identifying Attacker Contracts. *Proceedings - International Conference on Software Engineering*, 1573–1584. DOI: 10.1145/3597503.3639153

Yang, S., Chen, J., & Zheng, Z. (2023). Definition and Detection of Defects in NFT Smart Contracts. *ISSTA 2023 - Proceedings of the 32nd ACM SIGSOFT International Symposium on Software Testing and Analysis*, 373–384. DOI: 10.1145/3597926.3598063

Yang, X., & Li, W. (2020). A zero-knowledge-proof-based digital identity management scheme in blockchain. *Computers & Security*, *99*, 102050. DOI: 10.1016/j.cose.2020.102050

Zhang, W., Wei, L., Cheung, S. C., Liu, Y., Li, S., Liu, L., & Lyu, M. R. (2023). Combatting Front-Running in Smart Contracts: Attack Mining, Benchmark Construction and Vulnerability Detector Evaluation. *IEEE Transactions on Software Engineering*, *49*(6), 3630–3646. DOI: 10.1109/TSE.2023.3270117

Zheng, X. (2024). Research on blockchain smart contract technology based on resistance to quantum computing attacks. *PLoS One*, *19*(5), e0302325. DOI: 10.1371/journal.pone.0302325 PMID: 38781187

Zhu, H., Yang, L., Wang, L., & Sheng, V. S. (2024). A Survey on Security Analysis Methods of Smart Contracts. *IEEE Transactions on Services Computing*, *17*(6), 1–18. DOI: 10.1109/TSC.2024.3463394

ENDNOTES

1 https://www.theverge.com/2021/3/11/22325054/beeple-christies-nft-sale-cost-everydays-69-million

Conclusion

The journey through "Non-Fungible Tokens (NFTs) in Smart Cities: Advancements and Security Challenges" has illuminated the profound impact of blockchain and NFTs on the evolving urban landscape. As cities increasingly integrate sophisticated technologies like IoT and AI to foster sustainable and efficient environments, the imperative for robust security and governance frameworks becomes paramount. This volume has underscored how NFTs, with their inherent capacity for authenticating and tokenizing assets, offer innovative pathways to address these critical needs.

Throughout the book, we have explored the multifaceted role of NFTs in enhancing transparency, solidifying ownership, and fostering greater civic engagement within smart city ecosystems. We have delved into the intricate security risks associated with blockchain-integrated cyber-physical systems, offering analyses and potential countermeasures. Furthermore, the book has provided valuable comparative insights into emerging technologies, extending their relevance even to therapeutic contexts.

Since, the vision for smart cities is one of interconnected digital-physical environments. This book serves as a crucial guide, emphasizing the delicate yet vital balance between embracing technological innovation and upholding rigorous ethical and technical standards. By engaging with the comprehensive insights presented, readers are encouraged to envision a future where advanced web 3 technologies contribute not merely to urban efficiency, but fundamentally to the creation of more equitable, secure, and resilient cities for all.

Compilation of References

Abbaoui, W., Retal, S., Kharmoum, N., & Ziti, S. (2023). Artificial intelligence in the service of precision medicine. In J. Kacprzyk, M. Ezziyyani, & V. E. Balas (Eds.), International Conference on Advanced Intelligent Systems for Sustainable Development. AI2SD 2022 (Vol. 713, pp. 145-157). Springer, Cham. DOI: 10.1007/978-3-031-35248-5_9

Abbaoui, W., Retal, S., El Bhiri, B., Kharmoum, N., & Ziti, S. (2024). Towards revolutionizing precision healthcare: A systematic literature review of artificial intelligence methods in precision medicine. *Informatics in Medicine Unlocked*, *46*, 101475. DOI: 10.1016/j.imu.2024.101475

Abbas, K., Tawalbeh, L. A., Rafiq, A., Muthanna, A., Elgendy, I. A., & Abd El-Latif, A. A. (2021). Convergence of blockchain and IoT for secure transportation systems in smart cities. *Security and Communication Networks*, *2021*(1), 5597679. DOI: 10.1155/2021/5597679

Abideen, S. (2019). *Blockchain Expert* (Sainul Abideen CEO (ed.)). CYBROSYS Technologies. www.cybrosys.com, www.blockchainexpert.uk

Abideen, S. (2019). *Blockchain expert* (Abideen, S., Ed.). CYBROSYS Technologies.

Agarkhed, J., Patil, S. S., Raza, S. Y., & Patil, V. (2023). Secure Digital Identity using Non-Fungible Tokens. *Proceedings of the 5th International Conference on Inventive Research in Computing Applications, ICIRCA 2023*, 1196–1201. DOI: 10.1109/ICIRCA57980.2023.10220854

Agarwal, U., Singh, K., & Verma, R. (2022). An Overview of Non-Fungible Tokens (NFT). International Journal of Advanced Research in Science, Communication and Technology (IJARSCT, 2(1).

Agbo, C. C., & Mahmoud, Q. H. (2020). Blockchain in Healthcare: Opportunities, Challenges, and Possible Solutions. [IJHISI]. *International Journal of Healthcare Information Systems and Informatics*, *15*(3), 82–97. DOI: 10.4018/IJHISI.2020070105

Agrawal, A. V., Shashibhushan, G., Pradeep, S., Padhi, S., Sugumar, D., & Boopathi, S. (2023). Synergizing Artificial Intelligence, 5G, and Cloud Computing for Efficient Energy Conversion Using Agricultural Waste. In *Sustainable Science and Intelligent Technologies for Societal Development* (pp. 475–497). IGI Global.

Ahmed, F., Khan, S., & Kim, D. (2023). NFTs as a tool for digital rights management in healthcare. *Blockchain in Healthcare Today*, *6*, 1–12. DOI: 10.3099/bht.2023.0007

Al Shamsi, M., Smith, D., & Gleason, K. (2023). Space transition and the vulnerabilities of the NFT market to financial crime. *Journal of Financial Crime*, *30*(6), 1664–1673. DOI: 10.1108/JFC-09-2022-0218

Alasbali, N., Azzuhri, S. R. B., Salleh, R. B., Kiah, M. L. M., Shariffuddin, A. A. A. A., & Kamel, N. M. I. (2022). bin N. M., & Ismail, L. (2022). Rules of smart IoT networks within smart cities towards blockchain standardization. *Mobile Information Systems*, (1), 9109300.

Albuainain, A., Alansari, J., Alrashidi, S., Alqahtani, W., Alshaya, J., & Nagy, N. (2022). Experimental Implementation of Shor's Quantum Algorithm to Break RSA. *Proceedings - 2022 14th IEEE International Conference on Computational Intelligence and Communication Networks, CICN 2022*, 748–752. DOI: 10.1109/CICN56167.2022.10008287

Al-E'mari, S., & Sanjalawe, Y. (2025). A Review of Reentrancy Attack in Ethereum Smart Contracts. *Lecture Notes in Networks and Systems, 977 LNNS*, 53–70. DOI: 10.1007/978-981-97-2671-4_5

Ali, O., Momin, M., Shrestha, A., Das, R., Alhajj, F., & Dwivedi, Y. K. (2023). A review of the key challenges of non-fungible tokens. *Technological Forecasting and Social Change*, *187*, 122248. DOI: 10.1016/j.techfore.2022.122248

Almadhoun, R., Kadadha, M., Alhemeiri, M., Alshehhi, M., & Salah, K. (2019). A user authentication scheme of IoT devices using blockchain-enabled fog nodes. In *Proceedings of IEEE/ACS International Conference on Computer Systems and Applications (AICCSA)* (Vols. 2018–Novem).

Almadhoun, R., Kadadha, M., Alhemeiri, M., Alshehhi, M., & Salah, K. (2019). A User Authentication Scheme of IoT Devices using Blockchain-Enabled Fog Nodes. *Proceedings of IEEE/ACS International Conference on Computer Systems and Applications, AICCSA, 2018-Novem*. DOI: 10.1109/AICCSA.2018.8612856

Alnahari, M. S., & Ariaratnam, S. T. (2022). The application of blockchain technology to smart city infrastructure. *Smart Cities*, *5*(3), 979–993. DOI: 10.3390/smartcities5030049

Alrawi, O., Lever, C., Antonakakis, M., & Monrose, F. (2019). SoK: Security Evaluation of Home-Based IoT Deployments. *Proceedings - IEEE Symposium on Security and Privacy, 2019-May*, 1362–1380. DOI: 10.1109/SP.2019.00013

Alsaheel, A., Alhassoun, R., Alrashed, R., Almatrafi, N., Almallouhi, N., & Albahli, S. (2023). Deep fakes in healthcare: How deep learning can help to detect forgeries. *Computers, Materials & Continua, 76*(2), 2461–2482. DOI: 10.32604/cmc.2023.040257

Al-Sumaidaee, G., Alkhudary, R., & Zilic, Z. (2023). Non-fungible tokens (NFTs) as a means for blockchain networks integration in healthcare. 2023 5th Conference on Blockchain Research & Applications for Innovative Networks and Services (BRAINS), 1-2.

Aman, M. N., Chua, K. C., & Sikdar, B. (2017). Mutual Authentication in IoT Systems Using Physical Unclonable Functions. *IEEE Internet of Things Journal, 4*(5), 1327–1340. DOI: 10.1109/JIOT.2017.2703088

Ammi, M., Alarabi, S., & Benkhelifa, E. (2021). Customized blockchain-based architecture for secure smart home for lightweight IoT. *Information Processing & Management, 58*(3), 102482. DOI: 10.1016/j.ipm.2020.102482

Ante, L. (2023). Non-fungible token (NFT) markets on the Ethereum blockchain: Temporal development, cointegration and interrelations. *Economics of Innovation and New Technology, 32*(8), 1216–1234. DOI: 10.1080/10438599.2022.2119564

Arafat, S. (2023). *SoK: Can NFTs Solve the Economic Problems of Countries with Ancient Heritage? Egypt as a Case Study* (pp. 155–175). https://doi.org/DOI: 10.1007/978-3-031-31420-9_10

Arcenegui, J., Arjona, R., Román, R., & Baturone, I. (2021). Secure combination of IoT and blockchain by physically binding IoT devices to smart non-fungible tokens using PUFs. *Sensors (Basel), 21*(9), 3119. Advance online publication. DOI: 10.3390/s21093119 PMID: 33946227

Arif, S., Khan, M. A., Rehman, S. U., Kabir, M. A., & Imran, M. (2020). Investigating smart home security: Is blockchain the answer? *IEEE Access : Practical Innovations, Open Solutions, 8*, 117802–117816. DOI: 10.1109/ACCESS.2020.3004662

Armando, A., Carbone, R., Compagna, L., Cuellar, J., & Tobarra, L. (2008). Formal analysis of SAML 2.0 web browser single sign-on: Breaking the SAML-based single sign-on for google apps. *Proceedings of the ACM Conference on Computer and Communications Security*, 1–9. DOI: 10.1145/1456396.1456397

Arora, S., Li, Y., Feng, Y., & Xu, J. (2024). SecPLF: Secure Protocols for Loanable Funds against Oracle Manipulation Attacks. *ACM AsiaCCS 2024 - Proceedings of the 19th ACM Asia Conference on Computer and Communications Security*, 1394–1405. DOI: 10.1145/3634737.3637681

Atlam, H. F., Ekuri, N., Azad, M. A., & Lallie, H. S. (2024). Blockchain Forensics: A Systematic Literature Review of Techniques, Applications, Challenges, and Future Directions. *Electronics 2024, Vol. 13, Page 3568, 13*(17), 3568. DOI: 10.3390/electronics13173568

Ayres Principe, V., da Silva, G. C. P. S. M., de Souza Vale, R. G., & Moreira Nunes, R. de A. (. (2024). Blockchain and sports industry: A systematic literature review of Fan Tokens and their implications. *Retos, 60*, 823. DOI: 10.47197/retos.v60.107125

Azaria, A., Ekblaw, A., Vieira, T., & Lippman, A. (2016). MedRec: Using blockchain for medical data access and permission management. *2nd International Conference on Open and Big Data*, 25-30. DOI: 10.1109/OBD.2016.11

Babel, M., Gramlich, V., Körner, M. F., Sedlmeir, J., Strüker, J., & Zwede, T. (2022). Enabling end-to-end digital carbon emission tracing with shielded NFTs. *Energy Informatics, 5*(1), 1–21. DOI: 10.1186/s42162-022-00199-3 PMID: 35252758

Babu, B. S., Kamalakannan, J., Meenatchi, N., Karthik, S., & Boopathi, S. (2022). Economic impacts and reliability evaluation of battery by adopting Electric Vehicle. *IEEE Explore*, 1–6.

Bai, H., Li, Z., Chen, K., & Li, X. (2024). Blockchain-Based Responsibility Management Framework for Smart City Building Information Modeling Projects Using Non-Fungible Tokens. *Buildings (Basel, Switzerland), 14*(11), 3647. DOI: 10.3390/buildings14113647

Banaeian Far, S., & Hosseini Bamakan, S. M. (2023). NFT-based identity management in metaverses: Challenges and opportunities. *SN Applied Sciences, 5*(10), 1–12. DOI: 10.1007/s42452-023-05487-5

Bang, L. K., Khanh, H. V., Triet, M. N., Hung, N. N., Trinh, P. D., Bang, H. N., Anh, N. T., & Ngan, K. T. N. (2025). *Enhancing Election Security Through Blockchain: An In-Depth Study of Encrypted NFTs and Smart Contracts* (pp. 21–36). DOI: 10.1007/978-3-031-77153-8_3

Bansal, G., Rajgopal, K., Chamola, V., Xiong, Z., & Niyato, D. (2022). Healthcare in Metaverse: A Survey on Current Metaverse Applications in Healthcare. *IEEE Access : Practical Innovations, Open Solutions, 10*, 119914–119946. DOI: 10.1109/ACCESS.2022.3219845

Barczentewicz, M., Sarch, A., & Vasan, N. (2023). Blockchain Transaction Ordering as Market Manipulation. *Ohio State Technology Law Journal, 20*. https://heinonline.org/HOL/Page?handle=hein.journals/isjlpsoc20&id=7&div=&collection=

Batra, P., Singh, G. R., & Gandhi, R. (2023). NFT Marketplace. arXiv preprint arXiv:2304.10632.

Behl, A., Pereira, V., Nigam, A., Wamba, S., & Sindhwani, R. (2024). Knowledge development in non-fungible tokens (NFT): A scoping review. *Journal of Knowledge Management*, *28*(1), 232–267. DOI: 10.1108/JKM-12-2022-0937

BehrTech. (2020). *6 Leading Types of IoT Wireless Technologies | BehrTech Blog*. BEHRTECH Technologies Inc. https://behrtech.com/blog/6-leading-types-of-iot-wireless-tech-and-their-best-use-cases/

Bellagarda, J., & Abu-Mahfouz, A. M. (2022). Connect2NFT: A Web-Based, Blockchain Enabled NFT Application with the Aim of Reducing Fraud and Ensuring Authenticated Social, Non-Human Verified Digital Identity. *Mathematics, 10*(21), 3934. DOI: 10.3390/math10213934

Benkassioui, B., Retal, S., Kharmoum, N., Hadi, M. Y., & Rhalem, W. (2024). Information extraction for biomedical literature using artificial intelligence: A comparative study. In M. Ezziyyani, J. Kacprzyk, & V. E. Balas (Eds.), International Conference on Advanced Intelligent Systems for Sustainable Development (AI2SD'2023). AI2SD 2023. Lecture Notes in Networks and Systems (Vol. 904, pp. 211-225). Springer, Cham. DOI: 10.1007/978-3-031-52388-5_6

Bhujel, S., & Rahulamathavan, Y. (2022). A Survey: Security, Transparency, and Scalability Issues of NFT's and Its Marketplaces. *Sensors 2022, Vol. 22, Page 8833, 22*(22), 8833. DOI: 10.3390/s22228833

Bikash Chandra Saha, M. S., Deepa, R., Akila, A., & Sai Thrinath, B. V. (2022). *Sampath Boopathi *, J. Ramya*. IOT BASED SMART ENERGY METER FOR SMART GRID.

Binet, E., Sandford, R., Radomski, W., Cooke, A., Castonguay, P., & Therien, J. (2018). *EIP-1155: Multi-token standard*. Ethereum Improvement Proposals. https://eips.ethereum.org/EIPS/eip-1155

Bitcoin.it. (2018). Weaknesses - Bitcoin Wiki. *Bitcoin.it*. https://en.bitcoin.it/wiki/Weaknesses

Bitcoin.it. (2018). *Weaknesses - Bitcoin Wiki*. Bitcoin.It. https://en.bitcoin.it/wiki/Weaknesses#The_Finney_attack%0Ahttps://en.bitcoin.it/wiki/Weaknesses

Böhme, R., Christin, N., Edelman, B., & Moore, T. (2015). Bitcoin: Economics, technology, and governance. *The Journal of Economic Perspectives, 29*(2), 213–238. DOI: 10.1257/jep.29.2.213

Boitier, W., Del Pozzo, A., García-Pérez, Á., Gazut, S., Jobic, P., Lemaire, A., Mahe, E., Mayoue, A., Perion, M., Singh, D., Rezende, T. F., & Tucci-Piergiovanni, S. (2024). *Fantastyc: Blockchain-based federated learning made secure and practical.* ArXiv., DOI: 10.1109/SRDS64841.2024.00033

Bommu, S., Babburu, K. N. S., Thalluri, L. N., Gopalan, A., Mallapati, P. K., Guha, K., & Mohammad, H. R. (2023). Smart city IoT system network level routing analysis and blockchain security based implementation. *Journal of Electrical Engineering & Technology, 18*(2), 1351–1368. DOI: 10.1007/s42835-022-01239-4 PMID: 37521954

Bonadio, E., & Sganga, C. (2024b). *NFTs, Creativity and the Law.* Routledge., DOI: 10.4324/9781003395508

Boopathi, S. (2024). Balancing Innovation and Security in the Cloud: Navigating the Risks and Rewards of the Digital Age. In *Improving Security, Privacy, and Trust in Cloud Computing* (pp. 164–193). IGI Global.

Boopathi, S., Arigela, S. H., Raman, R., Indhumathi, C., Kavitha, V., & Bhatt, B. C. (2022). Prominent Rule Control-based Internet of Things: Poultry Farm Management System. *IEEE Explore*, 1–6.

Boopathi, S., Gavaskar, T., Dogga, A. D., Mahendran, R. K., Kumar, A., Kathiresan, G., N., V., Ganesan, M., Ishwarya, K. R., Ramana, G. V., & others. (2021, August 4). *Emergency medicine delivery transportation using unmanned aerial vehicle (Patent Grant).*

Boopathi, S., & Khang, A. (2023). AI-Integrated Technology for a Secure and Ethical Healthcare Ecosystem. In *AI and IoT-Based Technologies for Precision Medicine* (pp. 36–59). IGI Global. DOI: 10.4018/979-8-3693-0876-9.ch003

Borin, E., & Donato, F. (2022). *Cultural Ecosystem Approaches as Key for New Development Paths: A Reflection on Management and Governance Implications.*, DOI: 10.1007/978-3-031-14121-8_2

Bose, P., Das, D., Gritti, F., Ruaro, N., Kruegel, C., & Vigna, G. (2023). *Exploiting Unfair Advantages: Investigating Opportunistic Trading in the NFT Market.* https://arxiv.org/abs/2310.06844v1

Brown, K., Wilson, L., & Taylor, M. (2023). Ethical considerations of deepfake technology in healthcare. *Journal of Medical Ethics, 49*(5), 321–330. DOI: 10.1136/medethics-2022-108567

Bułkowska, K., Zielińska, M., & Bułkowski, M. (2023). Implementation of Blockchain Technology in Waste Management. *Energies 2023, Vol. 16, Page 7742, 16*(23), 7742. DOI: 10.3390/en16237742

Burhan, M., Rehman, R. A., Khan, B., & Kim, B. S. (2018). IoT elements, layered architectures and security issues: A comprehensive survey. *Sensors (Basel), 18*(9), 1–37. DOI: 10.3390/s18092796 PMID: 30149582

Burks, Z., Morgan, J., & Malone, B. J. S. (2020). *EIP-2981: NFT Royalty Standard.* Ethereum. https://eips.ethereum.org/EIPS/eip-2981

Burks, Z., Morgan, J., Malone, B., & Seibel, J. (2020). *EIP-2981: NFT royalty standard.* Ethereum. https://eips.ethereum.org/EIPS/eip-2981

Buterin, V. (2014). A next-generation smart contract and decentralized application platform. https://ethereum.org/en/whitepaper

Cao, B., Li, Y., Zhang, L., Zhang, L., Mumtaz, S., Zhou, Z., & Peng, M. (2019). When Internet of Things Meets Blockchain: Challenges in Distributed Consensus. *IEEE Network, 33*(6), 133–139. DOI: 10.1109/MNET.2019.1900002

Cao, Z., Zhen, Y., Fan, G., & Gao, S. (2022). *TokenPatronus: A Decentralized NFT Anti-theft Mechanism.* https://arxiv.org/abs/2208.05168v1

Caxton, S. V. M., Naveen, K., Karthik, R., & Bama, S. S. (2022, July). User-Centered Evaluation and Design Suggestions for NFT Marketplaces. In *2022 International Conference on Inventive Computation Technologies (ICICT)* (pp. 1214-1221). IEEE. DOI: 10.1109/ICICT54344.2022.9850815

Chaabouni, N., Mosbah, M., Zemmari, A., Sauvignac, C., & Faruki, P. (2019). Network Intrusion Detection for IoT Security Based on Learning Techniques. *IEEE Communications Surveys and Tutorials, 21*(3), 2671–2701. DOI: 10.1109/COMST.2019.2896380

Chan, C. C. K., Kumar, V., Delaney, S., & Gochoo, M. (2020). Combating deepfakes: Multi-LSTM and blockchain as proof of authenticity for digital media. 2020 IEEE / ITU International Conference on Artificial Intelligence for Good (AI4G), 55-62.

Chandrika, V., Sivakumar, A., Krishnan, T. S., Pradeep, J., Manikandan, S., & Boopathi, S. (2023). Theoretical Study on Power Distribution Systems for Electric Vehicles. In *Intelligent Engineering Applications and Applied Sciences for Sustainability* (pp. 1–19). IGI Global. DOI: 10.4018/979-8-3693-0044-2.ch001

Chaparala, H. K., Doddala, S. V., Showail, A., Singh, A., Gazzaz, S., & Nawab, F. (2022, August). Liftchain: A scalable multi-stage nft transaction protocol. In *2022 IEEE International Conference on Blockchain (Blockchain)* (pp. 362-369). IEEE. DOI: 10.1109/Blockchain55522.2022.00057

Chawda, K., Mehta, K., Borkar, T., & Ambadekar, S. (2024). NFTs and property tokenisation: Advancements and applications in blockchain technology. *International Journal of Blockchains and Cryptocurrencies*, *5*(1), 44–66. DOI: 10.1504/IJBC.2024.140167

Chen, R. J., Lu, M. Y., Chen, T. Y., Williamson, D. F. K., & Mahmood, F. (2021). Synthetic data in machine learning for medicine and healthcare. *Nature Biomedical Engineering*, *5*(6), 493–497. DOI: 10.1038/s41551-021-00751-8 PMID: 34131324

Chen, Y., Li, X., & Zhang, Q. (2023). Blockchain-based secure data sharing for healthcare applications: A comprehensive review. *IEEE Transactions on Biomedical Engineering*, *70*(4), 1234–1245. DOI: 10.1109/TBME.2023.3234567 PMID: 36288237

Cherian, A. K., Singh, A., & Singh, A. (2024). Sustainability-Mobility Solutions: A Pathway to Sustainable Urban Development. *2024 10th International Conference on Communication and Signal Processing (ICCSP)*, 1377–1382. https://doi.org/DOI: 10.1109/ICCSP60870.2024.10543902

Chesney, R., & Citron, D. (2019). Deepfakes and the New Disinformation War: The Coming Age of Post-Truth Geopolitics. *Foreign Affairs*, *98*(1), 147–155. https://www.jstor.org/stable/26798018

Chiacchio, F., D'urso, D., Oliveri, L. M., Spitaleri, A., Spampinato, C., & Giordano, D. (2022). A Non-Fungible Token Solution for the Track and Trace of Pharmaceutical Supply Chain. *Applied Sciences (Basel, Switzerland)*, *12*(8), 4019. DOI: 10.3390/app12084019

Chiang, M., & Zhang, T. (2016). Fog and IoT: An Overview of Research Opportunities. In *IEEE Internet of Things Journal* (Vol. 3, Issue 6, pp. 854–864). DOI: 10.1109/JIOT.2016.2584538

Cisco Academy. (2014). *Evolution of Software Defined Networking within Cisco ' s VMDC Challenges within the Data Center SDN Architectural Framework and Solution Characteristics.*

Cisco. (2020). Cisco: 2020 CISO Benchmark Report. In *Computer Fraud & Security* (Vol. 2020, Issue 3). DOI: 10.1016/S1361-3723(20)30026-9

Clifton, J., & Pal, L. A. (2022). The policy dilemmas of blockchain. *Policy and Society*, *41*(3), 321–327. DOI: 10.1093/polsoc/puac025

Crandall, J. (2023). Living on the block: How equitable is tokenized equity? *Big Data & Society*, *10*(2), 20539517231208455. Advance online publication. DOI: 10.1177/20539517231208455

Cruz, M., Oliveira, A., & Pinheiro, A. (2024). Metaverse Unveiled: From the Lens of Science to Common People Perspective. *Computers*, *13*(8), 193. DOI: 10.3390/computers13080193

Cryptopedia. (2021). What is tokenization? Blockchain token types. *Gemini*. https://www.gemini.com/cryptopedia/what-is-tokenization-definition-crypto-token

Cryptopedia. (2021). *What Is Tokenization? Blockchain Token Types*. https://www.gemini.com/cryptopedia/what-is-tokenization-definition-crypto-token

Dammak, M., Boudia, O. R. M., Messous, M. A., Senouci, S. M., & Gransart, C. (2019). Token-Based Lightweight Authentication to Secure IoT Networks. *2019 16th IEEE Annual Consumer Communications and Networking Conference, CCNC 2019*. DOI: 10.1109/CCNC.2019.8651825

Das, D., Bose, P., Ruaro, N., Kruegel, C., & Vigna, G. (2022, November). Understanding security issues in the NFT ecosystem. In *Proceedings of the 2022 ACM SIGSAC Conference on Computer and Communications Security* (pp. 667-681). DOI: 10.1145/3548606.3559342

Davis, S., Diemers, D., & Arsianian, H. G. D. (2019). 4 th ICO / STO Report - A Strategic Perspective. In *PWC Report*. https://www.pwc.ch/en/publications/2019/ch-20190308-strategyand-ico-sto-report-q1-2019.pdf

Davis, S., Diemers, D., Arsianian, H., & Dobrauz, G. (2019). *4th ICO/STO report: A strategic perspective.*

de Kruijff, J., & Weigand, H. (2017). Understanding the blockchain using enterprise ontology. In *Proceedings of the International Conference on Advanced Information Systems Engineering* (pp. 29–43). Springer. DOI: 10.1007/978-3-319-59536-8_3

Deng, W., Huang, T., & Wang, H. (2023). A Review of the Key Technology in a Blockchain Building Decentralized Trust Platform. *Mathematics*, *11*(1), 101. Advance online publication. DOI: 10.3390/math11010101

Department of the Army, H. (2006). *Supervisory Control and Data Acquisition (SCADA) Systems for command, control, communications, computer, intelligence, surveillance, and reconnaissance (C4ISR) facilities* (Issue January).

Deshpande, I., Sangitrao, R., & Panchal, L. (2023, January). Study of NFT Marketplace in the Metaverse. In International Conference on Data Management, Analytics & Innovation (pp. 855-862). Singapore: Springer Nature Singapore. DOI: 10.1007/978-981-99-1414-2_59

Dhanalakshmi, M., Tamilarasi, K., Saravanan, S., Sujatha, G., Boopathi, S., & Associates. (2024). Fog Computing-Based Framework and Solutions for Intelligent Systems: Enabling Autonomy in Vehicles. In *Computational Intelligence for Green Cloud Computing and Digital Waste Management* (pp. 330–356). IGI Global.

Divya, N., Dhawan, E., Sundar, H. S., Jain, H., & Dinakar, R. (2024). NFTGenesis - An NFT generation and authentication system with market intelligence using deep learning-based steganography. 2024 IEEE International Conference on Contemporary Computing and Communications (InC4), 1-6.

Domakonda, V. K., Farooq, S., Chinthamreddy, S., Puviarasi, R., Sudhakar, M., & Boopathi, S. (2022). Sustainable Developments of Hybrid Floating Solar Power Plants: Photovoltaic System. In *Human Agro-Energy Optimization for Business and Industry* (pp. 148–167). IGI Global.

Dorri, A., Kanhere, S. S., Jurdak, R., & Gauravaram, P. (2017). Blockchain for IoT security and privacy: The case study of a smart home. *2017 IEEE International Conference on Pervasive Computing and Communications Workshops, PerCom Workshops 2017*, 618–623. DOI: 10.1109/PERCOMW.2017.7917634

Doshi, R., Apthorpe, N., & Feamster, N. (2018). Machine learning DDoS detection for consumer internet of things devices. *Proceedings - 2018 IEEE Symposium on Security and Privacy Workshops, SPW 2018, Ml*, 29–35. DOI: 10.1109/SPW.2018.00013

Drosatos, G., & Kaldoudi, E. (2019). Blockchain applications in the biomedical domain: A scoping review. *Computational and Structural Biotechnology Journal, 17*, 229–240. DOI: 10.1016/j.csbj.2019.01.010 PMID: 30847041

Dwivedi, S. K., Amin, R., Vollala, S., & Khan, M. K. (2023). B-HAS: Blockchain-Assisted Efficient Handover Authentication and Secure Communication Protocol in VANETs. *IEEE Transactions on Network Science and Engineering*, •••, 1–14. DOI: 10.1109/TNSE.2023.3264829

Ekblaw, N.. (2016). A case study for blockchain in healthcare: "MedRec" prototype for electronic health records and medical research data. *Open Journal of Blockchains, 1*(1), 44–56.

Elangovan, D., Long, C. S., Bakrin, F. S., Tan, C. S., Goh, K. W., Hussain, Z., Al-Worafi, Y. M., Lee, K. S., Kassab, Y. W., & Ming, L. C. (2020). Application of Blockchain Technology in Hospital Information System. Dans CRC Press eBooks (p. 231-246). DOI: 10.1201/9781003038399-12

Elasri, C., Kharmoum, N., Saoiabi, F., Boukhlif, M., Ziti, S., & Rhalem, W. (2024). Applying graph theory to enhance software testing in medical applications: A comparative study. In M. Ezziyyani, J. Kacprzyk, & V. E. Balas (Eds.), International Conference on Advanced Intelligent Systems for Sustainable Development (AI2SD'2023). AI2SD 2023. Lecture Notes in Networks and Systems (Vol. 904, pp. 227-242). Springer, Cham. DOI: 10.1007/978-3-031-52388-5_7

Elsayed, M. A. S. (2021). Rearguard: A Novel Blockchain-based Automatic Worm Containment System. *2021 International Telecommunications Conference (ITC-Egypt)*, 1–8. DOI: 10.1109/ITC-Egypt52936.2021.9513932

Ennejjai, I., Ariss, A., Kharmoum, N., Rhalem, W., Ziti, S., & Ezziyyani, M. (2023). Artificial intelligence for fake news. In J. Kacprzyk, M. Ezziyyani, & V. E. Balas (Eds.), International Conference on Advanced Intelligent Systems for Sustainable Development. AI2SD 2022 (Vol. 637). Springer, Cham. DOI: 10.1007/978-3-031-26384-2_8

Entriken, W., Shirley, D., & Evans, J. N. S. (2018). *EIP-721: Non-Fungible Token Standard.* Ethereum Improvement Proposals. https://eips.ethereum.org/EIPS/eip-721

Entriken, W., Shirley, D., Evans, J., & Sachs, N. (2018). *EIP-721: Non-fungible token standard.* Ethereum Improvement Proposals. https://eips.ethereum.org/EIPS/eip-721

Eric Binet, R. S. W. R. A. C. P. C. J. T. (2018). "EIP-1155: Multi Token Standard. In *Ethereum Improvement Proposals*. https://eips.ethereum.org/EIPS/eip-1155

Esposito, C., Ficco, M., & Gupta, B. B. (2021). Blockchain-based authentication and authorization for smart city applications. *Information Processing & Management*, *58*(2), 102468. DOI: 10.1016/j.ipm.2020.102468

Ettaloui, N., Arezki, S., & Gadi, T. (2023). A blockchain-based electronic mental health records model. In Proceedings of the 2023 10th International Conference on Information Technology, Computer, and Electrical Engineering (ICITACEE) (pp. 320–325). IEEE. DOI: 10.1109/ICITACEE58587.2023.10277507

Fang, Y., Wu, D., Yi, X., Wang, S., Chen, Y., Chen, M., Liu, Y., & Jiang, L. (2023). Beyond "Protected" and "Private": An Empirical Security Analysis of Custom Function Modifiers in Smart Contracts. *ISSTA 2023 - Proceedings of the 32nd ACM SIGSOFT International Symposium on Software Testing and Analysis*, 1157–1168. DOI: 10.1145/3597926.3598125

Farooq, U., M., Waseem, M., Mazhar, S., Khairi, A., & Kamal, T. (. (2015). A Review on Internet of Things (IoT). *International Journal of Computer Applications*, *113*(1), 1–7. DOI: 10.5120/19787-1571

Ferrag, M. A., Maglaras, L., Derhab, A., & Bernabe, J. B. (2019). Authentication and Authorization for Mobile IoT Devices Using Biofeatures: Recent Advances and Future Trends. *Security and Communication Networks*, *2019*, 1–20. DOI: 10.1155/2019/5452870

Ferreira, C. M. S., Garrocho, C. T. B., Oliveira, R. A. R., Silva, J. S., & Cavalcanti, C. F. M. da C. (2021). IoT registration and authentication in smart city applications with blockchain. *Sensors (Basel)*, *21*(4), 1–23. DOI: 10.3390/s21041323 PMID: 33668415

Finkle, J., & Skariachan, D. (2013). Target cyber breach hits 40 million payment cards at holiday peak. In *Reuters US Edition: Vol. Cyber Crim* (p. https://www.reuters.com/news/technology/article/201). https://www.reuters.com/article/us-target-breach-idUSBRE9BH1GX20131219

Fisher, K. (2007). Jonah liberated by technology. In *Hart's E and P* (Issue AUG.). Uttarakhand Open University, 2017. http://uou.ac.in

Fisher, K. (2007). *Jonah liberated by technology*. Uttarakhand Open University.

Fotiou, N., Pittaras, I., Siris, V. A., Voulgaris, S., & Polyzos, G. C. (2021). *OAuth 2.0 Authorization using Blockchain-based Tokens*. DOI: 10.14722/diss.2020.23002

Fraga-Lamas, P., & Fernández-Caramés, T. (2019). Fake news, disinformation, and deepfakes: Leveraging distributed ledger technologies and blockchain to combat digital deception. *IT Professional*, *22*(2), 53–59. DOI: 10.1109/MITP.2020.2977589

Gallego Cuiñas, A., & Torres-Salinas, D. (2024). *Humanities and Big Data in Ibero-America: Theory, methodology and practical applications*. De Gruyter., DOI: 10.1515/9783110753523

Gebreab, S. A., Hasan, H. R., Salah, K., & Jayaraman, R. (2022). NFT-based traceability and ownership management of medical devices. *IEEE Access : Practical Innovations, Open Solutions*, *10*, 126394–126411. DOI: 10.1109/ACCESS.2022.3226128

German Steel Plant Suffers Significant Damage from Targeted Attack - Nouvelles de sécurité - Trend Micro FR. (2015). Nouvelles de Sécurité - Trend Micro. https://www.trendmicro.com/vinfo/fr/security/news/cyber-attacks/german-steel-plant-suffers-significant-damage-from-targeted-attack

Godwin Immanuel, D., Solaimalai, G., Chandrakala, B. M., Bharath, V. G., Singh, M. K., & Boopathi, S. (2024). Advancements in Electric Vehicle Management System: Integrating Machine Learning and Artificial Intelligence. In *Advances in Web Technologies and Engineering* (pp. 371–391). IGI Global. DOI: 10.4018/979-8-3693-1487-6.ch018

Gong, L., Alghazzawi, D. M., & Cheng, L. (2021). Bcot sentry: A blockchain-based identity authentication framework for iot devices. *Information (Basel)*, *12*(5), 1–20. DOI: 10.3390/info12050203

Goodfellow, I., Pouget-Abadie, J., Mirza, M., Xu, B., Warde-Farley, D., Ozair, S., Courville, A., & Bengio, Y. (2014). Generative adversarial nets. *Advances in Neural Information Processing Systems*, *27*, 2672–2680.

Gopal, M., Lurdhumary, J., Bathrinath, S., Priya, A. P., Sarojwal, A., & Boopathi, S. (2024). Energy Harvesting and Smart Highways for Sustainable Transportation Infrastructure: Revolutionizing Roads Using Nanotechnology. In *Principles and Applications in Speed Sensing and Energy Harvesting for Smart Roads* (pp. 136–165). IGI Global. DOI: 10.4018/978-1-6684-9214-7.ch005

Gope, P., & Sikdar, B. (2019). Lightweight and Privacy-Preserving Two-Factor Authentication Scheme for IoT Devices. *IEEE Internet of Things Journal*, *6*(1), 580–589. DOI: 10.1109/JIOT.2018.2846299

Gowda, C. (2025, June 4). Emerging trends in federated learning for data science AI. *Voval.Media*. https://vocal.media/education/emerging-trends-in-federated-learning-for-data-science-ai

Gubbi, J., Buyya, R., Marusic, S., & Palaniswami, M. (2013). Internet of Things (IoT): A vision, architectural elements, and future directions. *Future Generation Computer Systems*, *29*(7), 1645–1660. DOI: 10.1016/j.future.2013.01.010

Hai, T., Zhou, J., Srividhya, S. R., Jain, S. K., Young, P., & Agrawal, S. (2022). BV-FLEMR: An integrated federated learning and blockchain technology for cloud-based medical records recommendation system. *Journal of Cloud Computing (Heidelberg, Germany)*, *11*(1), 1–11. DOI: 10.1186/s13677-022-00294-6

Hammi, M. T., Bellot, P., & Serhrouchni, A. (2018). BCTrust: A decentralized authentication blockchain-based mechanism. In *IEEE Wireless Communications and Networking Conference (WCNC)* (Vol. 2018–April, pp. 1–6). DOI: 10.1109/WCNC.2018.8377413

Hammi, M. T., Bellot, P., & Serhrouchni, A. (2018). BCTrust: A decentralized authentication blockchain-based mechanism. *IEEE Wireless Communications and Networking Conference, WCNC, 2018-April*, 1–6. DOI: 10.1109/WCNC.2018.8376948

Han, Y., Wang, C., & Wang, H. (2024). Research on Blockchain Cross-Chain Model Based on "nFT + Cross-Chain Bridge.". *IEEE Access : Practical Innovations, Open Solutions, 12*, 77065–77078. DOI: 10.1109/ACCESS.2024.3401405

Hard, A., Rao, K., Mathews, R., Ramaswamy, S., Beaufays, F., Augenstein, S., Eichner, H., Kiddon, C., & Ramage, D. (2018). Federated learning for mobile keyboard prediction. *ArXiv*. https://arxiv.org/abs/1811.03604

Harris, C. G. (2024). Challenges and Opportunities of Integrating Non-Fungible Tokens (NFTs) and Self-Sovereign AI (SSAI) in Blockchain-Based Metaverse Projects. *2024 9th International Conference on Big Data Analytics (ICBDA)*, 288–296. https://doi.org/DOI: 10.1109/ICBDA61153.2024.10607366

Hasan, H. R., Salah, K., Battah, A., Madine, M., Yaqoob, I., Jayaraman, R., & Omar, M.HASAN. (2022). Incorporating Registration, Reputation, and Incentivization Into the NFT Ecosystem. *IEEE Access : Practical Innovations, Open Solutions, 10*, 76416–76433. DOI: 10.1109/ACCESS.2022.3192388

Hasan, H. R., Salah, K., Jayaraman, R., Yaqoob, I., & Omar, M. (2024). NFTs for combating deepfakes and fake metaverse digital contents. *Internet of Things : Engineering Cyber Physical Human Systems, 25*, 101133. DOI: 10.1016/j.iot.2024.101133

Hinrichs, T. (2019). Centralized vs. distributed authorization: The CAP theorem. *Styra Blog*. https://blog.styra.com/blog/centralized-vs.-distributed-authorization-the-cap-theorem

Hinrichs, T. (2019). *Centralized vs. Distributed Authorization: The CAP Theorem*. Styra. https://blog.styra.com/blog/centralized-vs.-distributed-authorization-the-cap-theorem

Hriez, S., Obeid, N., & Awajan, A. (2019). User authentication on smartphones using keystroke dynamics. *PervasiveHealth: Pervasive Computing Technologies for Healthcare, 2–5*, 1–4. Advance online publication. DOI: 10.1145/3368691.3368725

Hussain, F., Hussain, R., Hassan, S. A., & Hossain, E. (2020). Machine Learning in IoT Security: Current Solutions and Future Challenges. *IEEE Communications Surveys and Tutorials*, *22*(3), 1686–1721. DOI: 10.1109/COMST.2020.2986444

Ibrokhimov, S., Hui, K. L., Abdulhakim Al-Absi, A., Lee, H. J., & Sain, M. (2019). Multi-Factor Authentication in Cyber Physical System: A State of Art Survey. *International Conference on Advanced Communication Technology, ICACT, 2019-Febru*, 279–284. DOI: 10.23919/ICACT.2019.8701960

Jenkins, B. (2024). NFTs and the financialization of art. *Cultural Studies*. Advance online publication. DOI: 10.1080/09502386.2024.2329873

Jeong, D., & Kim, Y. (2024). The impact of Metaverse's social presence and NFT product characteristics on consumer satisfaction and continued engagement intention. *The Research Journal of the Costume Culture*, *32*(4), 453–467. DOI: 10.29049/rjcc.2024.32.4.453

Jeong, W., Park, H., & Park, C. (2023). KeyScrub: A Reliable Key Backup and Recovery Method for Blockchain. *IEEE Access : Practical Innovations, Open Solutions*, *11*, 91747–91755. DOI: 10.1109/ACCESS.2023.3308208

Jiang, Y. Y., & Zhou, J. T. (2022). Ticketing System Based On NFT. *2022 IEEE 24th International Workshop on Multimedia Signal Processing, MMSP 2022*. DOI: 10.1109/MMSP55362.2022.9948706

Johnson, E., & Martinez, R. (2023). Deepfake avatars in virtual reality therapy: Opportunities and risks. *Frontiers in Digital Health*, *5*, 78–92. DOI: 10.3389/fdgth.2023.00567

Johnson, E., & Martinez, R. (2023). Deepfake avatars in virtual reality therapy: Opportunities and risks. *Journal of Medicine and Virtual Reality : Computers, Imagery, Photonics and Robotic Applications*, *14*(4), 210–225. DOI: 10.1093/jmvr/2023.00456

Joost de Kruijff, H. W. (2017). Understanding the Blockchain Using Enterprise Ontology Joost. *Springer International Publishing AG 2017, 10253 LNCS*, 29–43. DOI: 10.1007/978-3-319-59536-8

Jose Diaz Rivera, J., Muhammad, A., & Song, W. C. (2024). Securing Digital Identity in the Zero Trust Architecture: A Blockchain Approach to Privacy-Focused Multi-Factor Authentication. *IEEE Open Journal of the Communications Society*, *5*, 2792–2814. DOI: 10.1109/OJCOMS.2024.3391728

Jung, Y. (2023). Current use cases, benefits and challenges of NFTs in the museum sector: Toward common pool model of NFT sharing for educational purposes. *Museum Management and Curatorship, 38*(4), 451–467. DOI: 10.1080/09647775.2022.2132995

Jung, Y., Vakharia, N., & Vecco, M. (Eds.). (2024). *The Oxford Handbook of Arts and Cultural Management*. Oxford University Press., DOI: 10.1093/oxfordhb/9780197621615.001.0001

Kaaniche, N., & Laurent, M. (2017). Data security and privacy preservation in cloud storage environments based on cryptographic mechanisms. *Computer Communications, 111*, 120–141. DOI: 10.1016/j.comcom.2017.07.006

Kafteranis, D., Unozkan, H., & Turksen, U. (2023). Know Your NFTs: Compliance and Enforcement Challenges in Trading of Non-Fungible Tokens. *International Journal of Law in Changing World, 2*. https://heinonline.org/HOL/Page?handle=hein.journals/inljlolwic2&id=145&div=&collection=

Kaisto, J., Juutilainen, T., & Kauranen, J. (2024). Non-fungible tokens, tokenization, and ownership. *Computer Law & Security Review, 54*, 105996. DOI: 10.1016/j.clsr.2024.105996

Kalinaki, K. (2024). IoT and Blockchain Integration for Enhanced AI-Driven Business Intelligence. In *Intersection of AI and Business Intelligence in Data-Driven Decision-Making* (pp. 21–52). IGI Global., DOI: 10.4018/979-8-3693-5288-5.ch002

Kalinaki, K., Alli, A. A., Asuman, B., & Zakari, R. Y. (2024). Secure federated learning in the Internet of Health Things for improved patient privacy and data security. In *Federated Learning for Digital Healthcare Systems* (pp. 387–408). Elsevier., DOI: 10.1016/B978-0-443-13897-3.00003-5

Kalinaki, K., Thilakarathne, N. N., Mubarak, H. R., Malik, O. A., & Abdullatif, M. (2023). Cybersafe Capabilities and Utilities for Smart Cities. In *Cybersecurity for Smart Cities* (pp. 71–86). Springer., DOI: 10.1007/978-3-031-24946-4_6

Kalinaki, K., Yahya, U., Malik, O. A., & Lai, D. T. C. (2024). A Review of Big Data Analytics and Artificial Intelligence in Industry 5.0 for Smart Decision-Making. In *Human-Centered Approaches in Industry 5.0* (pp. 24–47). Human-Machine Interaction, Virtual Reality Training, and Customer Sentiment Analysis., DOI: 10.4018/979-8-3693-2647-3.ch002

Kamble, M., Chaudhari, T., Korewar, M., & Umale, A. NFT MARKETPLACE WEB APPLICATION.

Kanimozhi, P., Jayasri, A. R., Ananth Kumar, T., & Arunmozhiselvi, S. (2023). *Smart Contracts for Enhanced Water Resource Management.*, DOI: 10.4018/979-8-3693-0497-6.ch011

Kaushik, S., & El Madhoun, N. (2023). Analysis of Blockchain Security: Classic Attacks, Cybercrime and Penetration Testing. *Proceedings of the 2023 8th International Conference on Mobile and Secure Services, MobiSecServ 2023*. DOI: 10.1109/MobiSecServ58080.2023.10329210

Kavitha, C., Varalatchoumy, M., Mithuna, H., Bharathi, K., Geethalakshmi, N., & Boopathi, S. (2023). Energy Monitoring and Control in the Smart Grid: Integrated Intelligent IoT and ANFIS. In *Applications of Synthetic Biology in Health, Energy, and Environment* (pp. 290–316). IGI Global.

Kazi, S., Kazi, A., D'souza, L., & Loke, A. (2023, April). NiftyPlace: An NFT Marketplace Using Blockchain. In International Conference on Soft Computing for Security Applications (pp. 299-314). Singapore: Springer Nature Singapore.

Kelley, M. B. (2013). The Stuxnet Attack On Iran's Nuclear Plant Was "Far More Dangerous" Than Previously Thought. *Business Insider*, 1. https://www.businessinsider.com/stuxnet-was-far-more-dangerous-than-previous-thought-2013-11

Keshk, M., Turnbull, B., Moustafa, N., Vatsalan, D., & Choo, K. K. R. (2020). A privacy-preserving-framework-based blockchain and deep learning for protecting smart power networks. *IEEE Transactions on Industrial Informatics*, *16*(8), 5110–5118. DOI: 10.1109/TII.2019.2957140

Khalid, U., Asim, M., Baker, T., Hung, P. C. K., Tariq, M. A., & Rafferty, L. (2020). A decentralized lightweight blockchain-based authentication mechanism for IoT systems. *Cluster Computing*, *23*(3), 2067–2087. DOI: 10.1007/s10586-020-03058-6

Khalil, U., Malik, O. A., Hong, O. W., & Uddin, M. (2022). DSCOT: An NFT-based blockchain architecture for the authentication of IoT-enabled smart devices in smart cities. SSRN Electronic Journal. DOI: 10.2139/ssrn.4355848

Khalil, U., Malik, O. A., Hong, O. W., & Uddin, M. (2023). Leveraging a novel NFT-enabled blockchain architecture for the authentication of IoT assets in smart cities. *Scientific Reports 2023 13:1, 13*(1), 1–26. DOI: 10.1038/s41598-023-45212-1

Khalil, U., Malik, O. A., Hong, O. W., & Uddin, M. (2022). Decentralized Smart City of Things: A Blockchain Tokenization-enabled Architecture for Digitization and Authentication of Assets in Smart Cities. *ACM International Conference Proceeding Series*. https://doi.org/DOI: 10.1145/3569507.3569513

Khalil, U., Malik, O. A., Lai, D. T. C., & King, O. S. (2023). Profiling obese subgroups in national health and nutritional status survey data using machine learning techniques: A case study from Brunei Darussalam. *Biomedical Journal of Scientific & Technical Research, 48*(3), 39629–39643. DOI: 10.26717/BJSTR.2023.48.007641

Khalil, U., Malik, O. A., Uddin, M., & Chen, C.-L. (2022). A Comparative Analysis on Blockchain and Centralized Authentication Architectures for IoT-Enabled Smart Devices in Smart Cities : A Comprehensive Review, Recent Advances, and Future Research Directions. *Sensors (Basel), 22*(12), 1–52. DOI: 10.3390/s22145168 PMID: 35890848

Khalil, U., Mueen, U., Malik, O. A., & Hussain, S. (2022). A Blockchain Footprint for Authentication of IoT-Enabled Smart Devices in Smart Cities: State-of-the-Art Advancements, Challenges and Future Research Directions. *IEEE Access : Practical Innovations, Open Solutions, 10*, 76805–76823. DOI: 10.1109/ACCESS.2022.3189998

Khalil, U., Uddin, M., Malik, O. A., & Hong, O. W. (2024). A Novel NFT Solution for Assets Digitization and Authentication in Cyber-Physical Systems: Blueprint and Evaluation. *IEEE Open Journal of the Computer Society, 5*, 131–143. Advance online publication. DOI: 10.1109/OJCS.2024.3378424

Khan, A., & Anjum, A. (2023). Optimizing Data Distribution to Balance Scalability-Redundancy Trade-off for Collaborative Blockchain Storage. *2023 IEEE International Conference on Pervasive Computing and Communications Workshops and Other Affiliated Events, PerCom Workshops 2023*, 249–255. DOI: 10.1109/PerComWorkshops56833.2023.10150226

Khanal, K. (2024). *Blockchain-Driven NFTs.*, DOI: 10.4018/979-8-3693-1878-2.ch004

Khanh, B. L. Phung, Trinh. D., Nguyen, T. M., Vo, H. K., Dang, K. T., Trong, P. N., Kim, N. N. T., & Kha, N. H. (2024). *Property and Pixels: Redefining Real Estate in the Digital Era* (pp. 162–177). DOI: 10.1007/978-3-031-65154-0_10

Khan, M. A., Abbas, S., Rehman, A., Saeed, Y., Zeb, A., Uddin, M. I., Nasser, N., & Ali, A. (2021). A machine learning approach for blockchain-based smart home networks security. *IEEE Network, 35*(3), 223–229. DOI: 10.1109/MNET.011.2000514

Khan, M. A., & Salah, K. (2018). IoT security: Review, blockchain solutions, and open challenges. *Future Generation Computer Systems, 82*, 395–411. DOI: 10.1016/j.future.2017.11.022

Khoa, T. V., Son, D. H., Hoang, D. T., Trung, N. L., Thuy Quynh, T. T., Nguyen, D. N., Ha, N. V., & Dutkiewicz, E. (2024). Real-time Cyberattack Detection with Collaborative Learning for Blockchain Networks. *IEEE Wireless Communications and Networking Conference, WCNC*. DOI: 10.1109/WCNC57260.2024.10571103

Kim, H., Cui, J., Jang, E., Lee, C., Lee, Y., Chung, J.-W., & Shin, S. (2023). *DRAIN-CLoG: Detecting Rogue Accounts with Illegally-obtained NFTs using Classifiers Learned on Graphs*. DOI: 10.14722/ndss.2024.24888

King, N., & Raja, V. (2018). Protecting privacy in medical data: A blockchain-based approach. *Journal of Medical Systems*, *42*(8), 1–9.

Kireyev, P. (2022). NFT marketplace design and market intelligence.

Konagari, A., Kusuma, H. P., Chetharasi, S., Kuchipudi, R., Babu, P. R., & Murthy, T. S. (2023, June). NFT Marketplace for Blockchain based Digital Assets using ERC-721 Token Standard. In *2023 International Conference on Sustainable Computing and Smart Systems (ICSCSS)* (pp. 1394-1398). IEEE. DOI: 10.1109/ICSCSS57650.2023.10169350

Kostick-Quenet, K. (2022, April 19). What if our medical records became NFTs? LADN.

Kraken. (2021). *Kraken report: Non-fungible tokens (NFTs): Redefining digital scarcity*.

Kraken. (2021). Kraken Report: Non-Fungible Tokens (NFTs): Redefining Digital Scarcity. In *NCFA (National Crowdfunding and Fintech Association) Canada* (Issue September). kraken.com/subscribe/intelligence

Kräussl, R., & Tugnetti, A. (2024). Non-Fungible Tokens (NFTs): A Review of Pricing Determinants, Applications and Opportunities. *Journal of Economic Surveys*, *38*(2), 555–574. DOI: 10.1111/joes.12597

Kumar, P. R., Meenakshi, S., Shalini, S., Devi, S. R., & Boopathi, S. (2023). Soil Quality Prediction in Context Learning Approaches Using Deep Learning and Blockchain for Smart Agriculture. In *Effective AI, Blockchain, and E-Governance Applications for Knowledge Discovery and Management* (pp. 1–26). IGI Global. DOI: 10.4018/978-1-6684-9151-5.ch001

Kumar, S., Patel, R., & Lee, T. (2022). Blockchain-based secure data sharing for therapeutic applications: A review. *Health Informatics Journal*, *28*(4), 1–15. DOI: 10.1177/14604582221123456

Kumar, S., Patel, R., & Lee, T. (2023). A blockchain-based framework for secure and private health data sharing. *Health Informatics Journal, 29*(2), 146–160. DOI: 10.1177/14604582231123456

Kushwaha, S. S., Joshi, S., Singh, D., Kaur, M., & Lee, H. N. (2022). Systematic Review of Security Vulnerabilities in Ethereum Blockchain Smart Contract. *IEEE Access : Practical Innovations, Open Solutions, 10*, 6605–6621. DOI: 10.1109/ACCESS.2021.3140091

Kute, S., Desai, C., & Jadhav, M. (2024). Analysis of RSA and Shor's algorithm for cryptography: A quantum perspective. *AIP Conference Proceedings, 3156*(1), 040004. Advance online publication. DOI: 10.1063/5.0227773

Kuznetsov, O., Frontoni, E., Kuznetsova, K., Shevchuk, R., & Karpinski, M. (2024). NFT Technology for Enhanced Global Digital Registers: A Novel Approach to Tokenization. *Future Internet 2024, Vol. 16, Page 252, 16*(7), 252. DOI: 10.3390/fi16070252

La Morgia, M., Mei, A., Mongardini, A. M., & Nemmi, E. N. (2022). Nft wash trading in the ethereum blockchain. arXiv preprint arXiv:2212.01225.

Ladd, V. (2024, June 4). Blockchain for AI federated learning and decentralized authentication and privacy. Medium. https://medium.com/@oracle_43885/blockchain-powered-ai-federated-learning-secured-with-decentralized-authentication-and-privacy-ad5812719b1a

Lakhan, A., Mohammed, M. A., Abdulkareem, K. H., Deveci, M., Marhoon, H. A., Memon, S., Nedoma, J., & Martinek, R. (2024). BEDS: Blockchain energy efficient IoE sensors data scheduling for smart home and vehicle applications. *Applied Energy, 369*, 123535. DOI: 10.1016/j.apenergy.2024.123535

Lampson, B., Abadi, M., Burrows, M., & Wobber, E. (1992). Authentication in distributed systems. In *ACM Transactions on Computer Systems* (Vol. 10, Issue 4, pp. 265–310). DOI: 10.1145/138873.138874

Lampson, B., Abadi, M., Burrows, M., & Wobber, E. (1991). Authentication in distributed systems: Theory and practice. *Proceedings of the 13th ACM Symposium on Operating Systems Principles, SOSP 1991*, 165–182. DOI: 10.1145/121132.121160

Lax, G., Canino, A., & Musarella, L. (2024). A Blockchain-Based Approach for Certifying Information at Different Levels of Granularity According to the Data Minimization Principle of the GDPR. *Proceedings - 2024 8th International Conference on Computer, Software and Modeling, ICCSM 2024*, 31–35. DOI: 10.1109/ICCSM63823.2024.00014

Lee, I., & Lee, K. (2015). The Internet of Things (IoT): Applications, investments, and challenges for enterprises. *Business Horizons*, *58*(4), 431–440. DOI: 10.1016/j.bushor.2015.03.008

Leible, S., Schlager, S., Schubotz, M., & Gipp, B. (2019). A review on blockchain technology and blockchain projects fostering open science. *Frontiers in Blockchain*, *2*, 16. DOI: 10.3389/fbloc.2019.00016

Leong, W. Y., Leong, Y. Z., & Leong, W. S. (2024). Enhancing Blockchain Security. *2024 IEEE Symposium on Wireless Technology & Applications (ISWTA)*, 108–112. DOI: 10.1109/ISWTA62130.2024.10651753

Letichevsky, A. A., Letychevskyi, O. O., Skobelev, V. G., & Volkov, V. A. (2017). Cyber-physical systems. *Cybernetics and Systems Analysis*, *53*(6), 821–834. DOI: 10.1007/s10559-017-9984-9

Lewis, A. (2015). Blockchain Technology Explained. In *Blockchain Technologies*. https://www.blockchaintechnologies.com/blockchain-definition

Lewis, A. (2015). *Blockchain technology explained.*

Liao, X., Li, Q., Chan, S., Chu, J., & Zhang, Y. (2024). Interconnections and contagion among cryptocurrencies, DeFi, NFT and traditional financial assets: Some new evidence from tail risk driven network. *Physica A*, *647*, 129892. DOI: 10.1016/j.physa.2024.129892

Liddell, F. (2024). THE DISTRIBUTED MUSEUM: Using Smart Contracts and NFTs to Find Financial Equity in Co-produced Exhibitions. *Financial Management in Museums: Theory, Practice, and Context*, 314–329. DOI: 10.4324/9781003308003-26

Lin, Y., Gao, Z., Tu, Y., Du, H., Niyato, D., Kang, J., & Yang, H. (2023). A Blockchain-Based Semantic Exchange Framework for Web 3.0 Toward Participatory Economy. *IEEE Communications Magazine*, *61*(8), 94–100. DOI: 10.1109/MCOM.003.2200817

Li, S. (2018). Application of blockchain technology in smart city infrastructure. *2018 IEEE International Conference on Smart Internet of Things (SmartIoT)*, 276–2766. DOI: 10.1109/SmartIoT.2018.00056

Li, T., Yang, C., Yang, Q., Lan, S., Zhou, S., Luo, X., Huang, H., & Zheng, Z. (2023). Metaopera: A Cross-Metaverse Interoperability Protocol. *IEEE Wireless Communications*, *30*(5), 136–143. DOI: 10.1109/MWC.011.2300042

Liu, H. X., & Holopainen, J. P. (2024). Calling for Play-oriented Research on Blockchain Video Games: An Overview Study. *Distributed Ledger Technologies: Research and Practice*. https://doi.org/DOI: 10.1145/3674154

Liu, Z., Zhang, X., Li, G., Cui, H., Wang, J., & Xiao, B. (2024). A Secure and Reliable Blockchain-based Audit Log System. *ICC 2024 - IEEE International Conference on Communications*, 2010–2015. DOI: 10.1109/ICC51166.2024.10623012

Li, X., Wang, Y., & Zhang, Q. (2022). A blockchain-based framework for authenticating digital therapeutic assets. *IEEE Transactions on Biomedical Engineering*, *69*(5), 1789–1801. DOI: 10.1109/TBME.2022.3145678

Li, X., Wang, Y., & Zhang, Q. (2023). Integrating blockchain and AI for secure and efficient healthcare data management. *IEEE Journal of Biomedical and Health Informatics*, *27*(6), 2890–2901. DOI: 10.1109/JBHI.2023.1234567

Lohachab, A., & Urovi, V. (2024). A Blockchain-Based Approach for Model Card Accountability and Regulatory Compliance. *Lecture Notes in Business Information Processing*, *521*, 37–48. DOI: 10.1007/978-3-031-61003-5_4

López-Pimentel, J. C., Morales-Rosales, L. A., Algredo-Badillo, I., & Del-Valle-Soto, C. (2023). NFT-Vehicle: A Blockchain-Based Tokenization Architecture to Register Transactions over a Vehicle's Life Cycle. *Mathematics*, *11*(13), 2801. DOI: 10.3390/math11132801

Madine, M., Salah, K., Jayaraman, R., Battah, A., Hasan, H. R., & Yaqoob, I. (2022). Blockchain and NFTs for time-bound access and monetization of private data. *IEEE Access : Practical Innovations, Open Solutions*, *10*, 94186–94202. DOI: 10.1109/ACCESS.2022.3204274

Maguluri, L. P., Ananth, J., Hariram, S., Geetha, C., Bhaskar, A., & Boopathi, S. (2023). Smart Vehicle-Emissions Monitoring System Using Internet of Things (IoT). In *Handbook of Research on Safe Disposal Methods of Municipal Solid Wastes for a Sustainable Environment* (pp. 191–211). IGI Global.

Maguluri, L. P., Arularasan, A., & Boopathi, S. (2023). Assessing Security Concerns for AI-Based Drones in Smart Cities. In *Effective AI, Blockchain, and E-Governance Applications for Knowledge Discovery and Management* (pp. 27–47). IGI Global. DOI: 10.4018/978-1-6684-9151-5.ch002

Malathi, J., Kusha, K., Isaac, S., Ramesh, A., Rajendiran, M., & Boopathi, S. (2024). IoT-Enabled Remote Patient Monitoring for Chronic Disease Management and Cost Savings: Transforming Healthcare. In *Advances in Explainable AI Applications for Smart Cities* (pp. 371–388). IGI Global.

Marin, O., Cioara, T., Toderean, L., Mitrea, D., & Anghel, I. (2023). Review of Blockchain Tokens Creation and Valuation. *Future Internet 2023, Vol. 15, Page 382, 15*(12), 382. DOI: 10.3390/fi15120382

Mateen, A. Q., & Hong, O. W. (2018). Implementation and evaluation of IoT system using cloud storage platform. *ACM International Conference Proceeding Series*, 157–161. DOI: 10.1145/3289430.3289465

Matta, P., & Pant, B. (2019). Internet-of-things: Genesis, challenges and applications. *Journal of Engineering Science and Technology*, *14*(3), 1717–1750.

Meneguzzo, S., Selabi, E. G. K., Favenza, A., Gatteschi, V., & Schifanella, C. (2024). Enabling Citizen Sustainable Behaviors in Urban Mobility through Blockchain and Tokenization. In *Blockchain Technology in the Automotive Industry* (pp. 245–279). CRC Press., DOI: 10.1201/9781003450306-17

Mir, O., Roland, M., & Mayrhofer, R. (2020). DAMFA: Decentralized anonymous multi-factor authentication. *BSCI 2020 - Proceedings of the 2nd ACM International Symposium on Blockchain and Secure Critical Infrastructure, Co-Located with AsiaCCS 2020*, 10–19. DOI: 10.1145/3384943.3409417

Miyachi, K., & Mackey, T. K. (2021). hOCBS: A privacy-preserving blockchain framework for healthcare data leveraging an on-chain and off-chain system design. *Information Processing & Management*, *58*(3), 102535. DOI: 10.1016/j.ipm.2021.102535

Mohammed Abdul, S. S., Shrestha, A., & Yong, J. (2024). CrossDeFi: A Novel Cross-Chain Communication Protocol. *Future Internet*, *16*(9), 314. DOI: 10.3390/fi16090314

Mohanty, A., Venkateswaran, N., Ranjit, P., Tripathi, M. A., & Boopathi, S. (2023). Innovative Strategy for Profitable Automobile Industries: Working Capital Management. In *Handbook of Research on Designing Sustainable Supply Chains to Achieve a Circular Economy* (pp. 412–428). IGI Global.

Mohanty, A., Jothi, B., Jeyasudha, J., Ranjit, P., Isaac, J. S., & Boopathi, S. (2023). Additive Manufacturing Using Robotic Programming. In *AI-Enabled Social Robotics in Human Care Services* (pp. 259–282). IGI Global. DOI: 10.4018/978-1-6684-8171-4.ch010

Mollajafari, S., & Bechkoum, K. (2023). Blockchain Technology and Related Security Risks: Towards a Seven-Layer Perspective and Taxonomy. *Sustainability 2023, Vol. 15, Page 13401, 15*(18), 13401. DOI: 10.3390/su151813401

Moniruzzaman, M., Khezr, S., Yassine, A., & Benlamri, R. (2020). Blockchain for smart homes: Review of current trends and research challenges. *Computers & Electrical Engineering*, *83*, 106585. DOI: 10.1016/j.compeleceng.2020.106585

Monti, M., & Rasmussen, S. (2017). RAIN: A Bio-Inspired Communication and Data Storage Infrastructure. *Artificial Life*, *23*(4), 552–557. DOI: 10.1162/ARTL_a_00247 PMID: 28985116

Morris, A., & Ford, B. (2019). *Blockchain for beginners* (Vol. 107).

MORRIS. A., & Ford, B. (2019). Blockchain for Beginners. In *Quill* (Vol. 107, Issue 1). http://search.ebscohost.com/login.aspx?direct=true&db=ufh&AN=135307185&site=eds-live

Muda, I., Santosh, K., Aarif, M., Natrayan, L., Kaliappan, S., & Muthuperumal, S. (2024). Innovative Blockchain Protocol for Enhancing Transaction Security and Integrity in Decentralized Financial Ecosystems. *2nd IEEE International Conference on Data Science and Network Security, ICDSNS 2024*. DOI: 10.1109/ICDSNS62112.2024.10691288

Mumtaz, M., Akram, J., & Ping, L. (2019). An RSA based authentication system for smart IoT environment. *Proceedings - 21st IEEE International Conference on High Performance Computing and Communications, 17th IEEE International Conference on Smart City and 5th IEEE International Conference on Data Science and Systems, HPCC/SmartCity/DSS 2019*, 758–765. DOI: 10.1109/HPCC/SmartCity/DSS.2019.00112

Musamih, A., Dirir, A., Yaqoob, I., Salah, K., Jayaraman, R., & Puthal, D. (2024). NFTs in Smart Cities: Vision, Applications, and Challenges. *IEEE Consumer Electronics Magazine*, *13*(2), 9–23. Advance online publication. DOI: 10.1109/MCE.2022.3217660

Musamih, A., Yaqoob, I., Salah, K., Jayaraman, R., Omar, M., & Ellahham, S. (2022a). NFTs in healthcare: Vision, opportunities, and challenges. *IEEE Consumer Electronics Magazine*, •••, 21–32. https://ieeexplore.ieee.org/document/9850370

Musamih, A., Yaqoob, I., Salah, K., Jayaraman, R., Omar, M., & Ellahham, S. (2022a). NFTs in Healthcare: Vision, Opportunities, and Challenges. *IEEE Consumer Electronics Magazine*. Advance online publication. DOI: 10.1109/MCE.2022.3196480

Musamih, A., Yaqoob, I., Salah, K., Jayaraman, R., Omar, M., & Ellahham, S. (2022b). Using NFTs for Product Management, Digital Certification, Trading, and Delivery in the Healthcare Supply Chain. *IEEE Transactions on Engineering Management*, •••, 1–22. DOI: 10.1109/TEM.2022.3215793

Naik, M., Singh, A. P., Pradhan, N. R., Kumar, N., Nayak, A., & Guizani, M. (2024). TokenGreen: A Versatile NFT Framework for Peer-to-Peer Energy Trading and Asset Ownership of Electric Vehicles. *IEEE Internet of Things Journal*, *11*(8), 13636–13646. DOI: 10.1109/JIOT.2023.3340155

Nakamoto, S. (2008). Bitcoin: A peer-to-peer electronic cash system. https://bitcoin.org/bitcoin.pdf

Nanda, A. K., Sharma, A., Augustine, P. J., Cyril, B. R., Kiran, V., & Sampath, B. (2024). Securing Cloud Infrastructure in IaaS and PaaS Environments. In *Improving Security, Privacy, and Trust in Cloud Computing* (pp. 1–33). IGI Global. DOI: 10.4018/979-8-3693-1431-9.ch001

Napoli, E. A., & Gatteschi, V. (2023). A Platform for the Aggregation of Blockchain-based Services for Municipalities and Smart-cities, Enabling Automatic Conversion based on Saved CO2 Units. *ACM International Conference Proceeding Series*. https://doi.org/DOI: 10.1145/3582515.3609545

Naqvi, N. (2023). Metaverse for Public Good: Embracing the Societal Impact of Metaverse Economies. *The Journal of The British Blockchain Association*, *6*(1), 1–17. DOI: 10.31585/jbba-6-1-(6)2023

Narayanan, G., Cvitić, I., Peraković, D., & Raja, S. P. (2024). Role of Blockchain Technology in Supplychain Management. *IEEE Access : Practical Innovations, Open Solutions*, *12*, 19021–19034. DOI: 10.1109/ACCESS.2024.3361310

NerdWallet. (2023). *11 Best Crypto Wallets of January 2023 - NerdWallet*. https://www.nerdwallet.com/article/investing/best-bitcoin-cryptocurrency-wallet

NerdWallet. (2023). 11 best crypto wallets of January 2023. *NerdWallet*. https://www.nerdwallet.com/article/investing/best-bitcoin-cryptocurrency-wallet

NFTs and the Art World: Understanding the Role of Social Media in the Emergence of Digital Collections. (2023). *British Journal of Arts and Humanities*, 277–290. https://doi.org/DOI: 10.34104/bjah.02302770290

Nicolazzi, L., & Tai, M. G. (2024). *NFT and Blockchain Technology for a Sustainable Future of Cultural Heritage*., DOI: 10.1007/978-3-031-47347-0_9

Ning, W., Zhu, Y., Song, C., Li, H., Zhu, L., Xie, J., Chen, T., Xu, T., Xu, X., & Gao, J. (2024). Blockchain-based federated learning: A survey and new perspectives. *Applied Sciences (Basel, Switzerland)*, *14*(20), 9459. DOI: 10.3390/app14209459

Niu, Y., Li, X., Peng, H., & Li, W. (2024). Unveiling Wash Trading in Popular NFT Markets. *WWW 2024 Companion - Companion Proceedings of the ACM Web Conference*, 730–733. DOI: 10.1145/3589335.3651580

Norta, A., Udokwu, C., & Craß, S. (2024). Real-World Asset Identity Authentication in Blockchain Enabled Inter-Organizational Process-Aware Systems Involving Adjustable Challenge-Response Evaluation Sets. *SN Computer Science*, *5*(7), 1–16. DOI: 10.1007/s42979-024-03265-7

Odom, W. (2016). *Cisco cert guide* (B. Bartow, S. Schroeder, C. Cleveland, T. Simpson, K. Cline, C. Hutchinson, & A. Adams, Eds.). Cisco Press.

Odom, W. (2016). *Cisco Cert Guide* (E. B. Bartow, Brett, Sandra Schroeder Senior, Christopher Cleveland, Tonya Simpson, Keith Cline, Chuck Hutchinson, Aubrey Adams (Ed.)). ciscopress.com. https://doi.org/DOI: 1-58720-580-7

Oladoyinbo, T. O., Olabanji, S. O., Olaniyi, O. O., Adebiyi, O. O., Okunleye, O. J., & Alao, A. I. (2024). Exploring the Challenges of Artificial Intelligence in Data Integrity and its Influence on Social Dynamics. *Asian Journal Of Advanced Research And Reports*, *18*(2), 1–23. DOI: 10.9734/ajarr/2024/v18i2601

Onder, I. (2023). ENHANCING SUSTAINABLE TOURISM THROUGH BLOCKCHAIN-BASED TOKENIZATION. *Blockchain for Tourism and Hospitality Industries*, 105–121. DOI: 10.4324/9781003351917-8

Orabi, M. M., Emam, O., & Fahmy, H. (2025). Adapting security and decentralized knowledge enhancement in federated learning using blockchain technology: Literature review. *Journal of Big Data*, *12*(1), 1–24. DOI: 10.1186/s40537-025-01099-5

Otoni, R., Marescotti, M., Alt, L., Eugster, P., Hyvärinen, A., & Sharygina, N. (2023). A Solicitous Approach to Smart Contract Verification. *ACM Transactions on Privacy and Security*, *26*(2), 1–28. Advance online publication. DOI: 10.1145/3564699

Oza, V. J., Nikte, A., Bhanushali, V., & Rote, U. (2024). Smart Contracts and Tokenization: Revolutionizing Real Estate Transactions with Blockchain Technology. *2024 International Conference on Inventive Computation Technologies (ICICT)*, 1598–1604. DOI: 10.1109/ICICT60155.2024.10544886

Pajooh, H. H., Rashid, M., Alam, F., & Demidenko, S. (2021). Multi-Layer Blockchain-Based Security Architecture for Internet of Things. *Sensors 2021, Vol. 21, Page 772, 21*(3), 772. DOI: 10.3390/s21030772

Palattella, M. R., Ladid, L., Ziegler, S., Kastner, W., Jung, M., Kofler, M., Drajic, D. D., Krco, S., Nam, G., & Marin Perez, R. (2019). *IoT-IPv6 integration for SMEs*. IoT6 European Project (STREP) of the 7th Framework Program.

Palattella, M. R., Ladid, L., Ziegler, S., Kastner, W., Jung, M., Kofler, M., Drajic, D. D., Krco, S., Nam, G., & Perez, R. M. (2019). *IoT-IPv6 Integration for SMEs*. IoT6 European Project (STREP) of the 7th Framework Program. www.iot6.eu

Pasumarthy, R., Mohammed, S., Laxman, V., Krishnamoorthy, V., Durga, S., & Boopathi, S. (2024). Digital Transformation in Developing Economies: Forecasting Trends, Impact, and Challenges in Industry 5.0. In *Convergence of Human Resources Technologies and Industry 5.0* (pp. 47–68). IGI Global. DOI: 10.4018/979-8-3693-1343-5.ch003

Pawelzik, L., & Thies, F. (2022). Selling digital art for millions-a qualitative analysis of NFT art marketplaces. In *Proceedings of the Thirtieth European Conference on Information Systems (ECIS 2022)*, Timisoara, Romania.

Pelechrinis, K., Liu, X., Krishnamurthy, P., & Babay, A. (2023). Spotting anomalous trades in NFT markets: The case of NBA TopShot. *PLoS One*, *18*(6), e0287262. DOI: 10.1371/journal.pone.0287262 PMID: 37319178

Peng, G., Shi, X., Zhang, J., Gao, L., Tan, Y., Xiang, N., & Wang, W. (2024). BGFL: A blockchain-enabled group federated learning at wireless industrial edges. *Journal of Cloud Computing (Heidelberg, Germany)*, *13*(1), 1–16. DOI: 10.1186/s13677-024-00700-1

Perera, C., Zaslavsky, A., Christen, P., & Georgakopoulos, D. (2014). Sensing as a service model for smart cities supported by Internet of Things. *Transactions on Emerging Telecommunications Technologies*, *25*(1), 81–93. DOI: 10.1002/ett.2704

Permenev, A., Dimitrov, D., Tsankov, P., Drachsler-Cohen, D., & Vechev, M. (2020). VerX: Safety verification of smart contracts. *Proceedings - IEEE Symposium on Security and Privacy, 2020-May*, 1661–1677. DOI: 10.1109/SP40000.2020.00024

Piccardo, G., Conti, L., & Martino, A. (2024). Blockchain Technology and Its Potential to Benefit Public Services Provision: A Short Survey. *Future Internet*, *16*(8), 290. DOI: 10.3390/fi16080290

PKtronics: Structure of a wireless sensor node : (2017). http://pktronics.blogspot.com/2017/10/structure-of-wireless-sensor-node.html

Prihatno, A. T., Suryanto, N., Oh, S., Le, T.-T.-H., & Kim, H. (2023). NFT image plagiarism check using EfficientNet-based deep neural network with triplet semi-hard loss. *Applied Sciences (Basel, Switzerland)*, *13*(5), 3072. DOI: 10.3390/app13053072

Punia, A., Gupta, D., & Jaiswal, S. (2017). A perspective on available security techniques in IoT. *RTEICT 2017 - 2nd IEEE International Conference on Recent Trends in Electronics, Information and Communication Technology, Proceedings, 2018-Janua*, 1553–1559. DOI: 10.1109/RTEICT.2017.8256859

Putz, B., & Pernul, G. (2020). Detecting Blockchain Security Threats. *Proceedings - 2020 IEEE International Conference on Blockchain, Blockchain 2020*, 313–320. DOI: 10.1109/Blockchain50366.2020.00046

Quy, T. L., K. V., Huong, H. L., Khiem, H. G., P. N., N. K., T. N., B. K., Trong, D. P. N., Hieu, M. D., Bao, Q. T., & Khoa, D. T. (2023). Decentralized management of medical test results utilizing blockchain, smart contracts, and NFTs. *International Journal of Advanced Computer Science and Applications.*

Radanovic, I., & Likić, R. (2018). Opportunities for the use of blockchain technology in medicine. *Applied Health Economics and Health Policy*, *16*(5), 583–590. DOI: 10.1007/s40258-018-0412-8 PMID: 30022440

Rahamathunnisa, U., Subhashini, P., Aancy, H. M., Meenakshi, S., & Boopathi, S. (2023). Solutions for Software Requirement Risks Using Artificial Intelligence Techniques. In *Handbook of Research on Data Science and Cybersecurity Innovations in Industry 4.0 Technologies* (pp. 45–64). IGI Global.

Rai, S., Chaurasia, B., Gupta, R., & Verma, S. (2023). Blockchain-based NFT for Healthcare System. 2023 IEEE 12th International Conference on Communication Systems and Network Technologies (CSNT), 12, 700-704.

Rai, S., Chaurasia, B., Gupta, R., & Verma, S. (2023). Blockchain-based NFT for healthcare system. 2023 IEEE 12th International Conference on Communication Systems and Network Technologies (CSNT), 700-704.

Raible, M. (2017). *What the Heck is OAuth? | Okta Developer*. Okta. https://developer.okta.com/blog/2017/06/21/what-the-heck-is-oauth

Rajeswari, M., & Magesh, R. (2024). Hierarchical Escalations of Incidents in Block Chain Technology. *Organization, Purpose and Values: Integrating Diversity, Equity and Inclusion*, 327–344. DOI: 10.4324/9781003501374-24

Rameder, H., di Angelo, M., & Salzer, G. (2022). Review of Automated Vulnerability Analysis of Smart Contracts on Ethereum. *Frontiers in Blockchain*, *5*, 814977. DOI: 10.3389/fbloc.2022.814977

Ramudu, K., Mohan, V. M., Jyothirmai, D., Prasad, D., Agrawal, R., & Boopathi, S. (2023). Machine Learning and Artificial Intelligence in Disease Prediction: Applications, Challenges, Limitations, Case Studies, and Future Directions. In *Contemporary Applications of Data Fusion for Advanced Healthcare Informatics* (pp. 297–318). IGI Global.

Ranjbar Alvar, S., Akbari, M., Yue, D., & Zhang, Y. (2023, August). NFT-Based Data Marketplace with Digital Watermarking. In *Proceedings of the 29th ACM SIGKDD Conference on Knowledge Discovery and Data Mining* (pp. 4756-4767).

Rapal, H. (2024, June 4). Smart contracts and regulatory compliance: Navigating the legal landscape. Legitt AI. https://legittai.com/blog/smart-contracts-and-regulatory-compliance

Rashid, M. M., Suk, H. L., & Kwon, K. R. (2021). Blockchain technology for combating deepfake and protecting video/image integrity.

Ratkovic, N. (2022). Improving home security using blockchain. International Journal of Computations [IJCIM]. *Information and Manufacturing*, *2*(1), 2022. DOI: 10.54489/ijcim.v2i1.72

Ravisankar, A., Shanthi, A., Lavanya, S., Ramaratnam, M., Krishnamoorthy, V., & Boopathi, S. (2024). Harnessing 6G for Consumer-Centric Business Strategies Across Electronic Industries. In *AI Impacts in Digital Consumer Behavior* (pp. 241–270). IGI Global.

Ray, P. P. (2023). Web3: A comprehensive review on background, technologies, applications, zero-trust architectures, challenges and future directions. In *Internet of Things and Cyber-Physical Systems* (Vol. 3). https://doi.org/DOI: 10.1016/j.iotcps.2023.05.003

Razi, Q., Devrani, A., Abhyankar, H., Chalapathi, G. S. S., Hassija, V., & Guizani, M. (2024). Non-Fungible Tokens (NFTs) - Survey of Current Applications, Evolution, and Future Directions. *IEEE Open Journal of the Communications Society*, *5*, 2765–2791. Advance online publication. DOI: 10.1109/OJCOMS.2023.3343926

Reddy, P. Y., Madan, B. S., Anandaram, H., Rathod, P., Vasanthaseelan, S., & Boopathi, S. (2024). Analyzing Fuel Cell Vehicles Through Intelligent Battery Management Systems (BMS): AI and ML Technologies for E-Mobility. In *Advances in Web Technologies and Engineering* (pp. 335–355). IGI Global. DOI: 10.4018/979-8-3693-1487-6.ch016

Rehman, Z. U., Altaf, S., & Iqbal, S. (2019). Survey of Authentication Schemes for Health Monitoring: A Subset of Cyber Physical System. *Proceedings of 2019 16th International Bhurban Conference on Applied Sciences and Technology, IBCAST 2019*, 653–660. DOI: 10.1109/IBCAST.2019.8667166

Ren, S., Kim, E., & Lee, C. (2024). A scalable blockchain-enabled federated learning architecture for edge computing. *PLoS One*, *19*(8), e0308991. DOI: 10.1371/journal.pone.0308991 PMID: 39150937

Ren, Y., Xie, R., Yu, F. R., Huang, T., & Liu, Y. (2022). Green Intelligence Networking for Connected and Autonomous Vehicles in Smart Cities. *IEEE Transactions on Green Communications and Networking*, *6*(3), 1591–1603. Advance online publication. DOI: 10.1109/TGCN.2022.3148293

Revathi, S., Babu, M., Rajkumar, N., Meti, V. K. V., Kandavalli, S. R., & Boopathi, S. (2024). Unleashing the Future Potential of 4D Printing: Exploring Applications in Wearable Technology, Robotics, Energy, Transportation, and Fashion. In *Human-Centered Approaches in Industry 5.0: Human-Machine Interaction, Virtual Reality Training, and Customer Sentiment Analysis* (pp. 131–153). IGI Global.

Riggs, W., Vyas, V., & Sethi, M. (2022). Blockchain and Distributed Autonomous Community Ecosystems: Opportunities to Democratize Finance and Delivery of Transport, Housing, Urban Greening and Community Infrastructure. SSRN *Electronic Journal*. https://doi.org/DOI: 10.2139/ssrn.4045363

Rotună, C., GHEORGHI Ă, A., Zamfiroiu, A., & SMADA ANAGRAMA, D. (2019). Smart City Ecosystem Using Blockchain Technology. *Informatica Economica, 23*(4).

Rubino, F., Agostino, D., & Spallazzo, D. (2024). Strategizing blockchain adoption in public cultural services: a comprehensive scoping review. *International Journal of Public Sector Management, ahead-of-print*(ahead-of-print). DOI: 10.1108/IJPSM-12-2023-0383

Russell, J. (2018). *The crypto world's latest hack sees Bancor lose $23.5M*. https://techcrunch.com/2018/07/10/bancor-loses-23-5m/

Saeed, H., Malik, H., Bashir, U., Ahmad, A., Riaz, S., Ilyas, M., Bukhari, W. A., & Khan, M. I. A. (2022). Blockchain technology in healthcare: A systematic review. *PLoS One*, *17*(4), e0266974. DOI: 10.1371/journal.pone.0266462 PMID: 35404955

Sai, S., Hassija, V., Chamola, V., & Guizani, M. (2024). Federated learning and NFT-based privacy-preserving medical-data-sharing scheme for intelligent diagnosis in smart healthcare. *IEEE Internet of Things Journal*, *11*(4), 5568–5577. DOI: 10.1109/JIOT.2023.3308991

Samuel, R. M., M R, J., M R, G., N B, S. S., & Rao, S. N. (2023). Web 3.0 and NFTs enabled eWaste Management System for Smart City. *2023 International Conference on Wireless Communications Signal Processing and Networking (WiSPNET)*, 01–07. https://doi.org/DOI: 10.1109/WiSPNET57748.2023.10134167

Sandoval, K. (2017). *OAuth 2.0 – Why It's Vital to IoT Security*. https://nordicapis.com/why-oauth-2-0-is-vital-to-iot-security/

Sandoval, K. (2017). OAuth 2.0 – Why it's vital to IoT security. *Nordic APIs*. https://nordicapis.com/why-oauth-2-0-is-vital-to-iot-security/

Saoiabi, F., Kharmoum, N., Elasri, C., Boukhari, M. E., Ziti, S., & Rhalem, W. (2024). Agile software engineering in medical environments: Challenges and opportunities. In M. Ezziyyani, J. Kacprzyk, & V. E. Balas (Eds.), International Conference on Advanced Intelligent Systems for Sustainable Development (AI2SD'2023) (Vol. 904). Springer, Cham. DOI: 10.1007/978-3-031-52388-5_8

Satav, S. D., Hasan, D. S., Pitchai, R., Mohanaprakash, T., Sultanuddin, S., & Boopathi, S. (2023). Next generation of internet of things (ngiot) in healthcare systems. In *Sustainable Science and Intelligent Technologies for Societal Development* (pp. 307–330). IGI Global.

Saxena, U., Sodhi, J. S., & Tanwar, R. (2020). Augmenting smart home network security using blockchain technology. *International Journal of Electronic Security and Digital Forensics*, *12*(1), 99–117. DOI: 10.1504/IJESDF.2020.103881

Sebastian-Cardenas, D. J., Gourisetti, S. N. G., Wang, P., Smith, J. J., Borkum, M. I., & Mukherjee, M. (2022). *Smart Contract Architectures and Templates for Blockchain-based Energy Markets (V.1.0)*. DOI: 10.2172/1987264

Sechting, C., & Raschke, P. (2024). A Taxonomy of Anti-Fraud Measures within Token Economy: Insights from Rug Pull Schemes. *2024 6th Conference on Blockchain Research & Applications for Innovative Networks and Services (BRAINS)*, 1–9. DOI: 10.1109/BRAINS63024.2024.10732222

Serada, A. (2022). Fairness by Design: The Fair Game and the Fair Price on a Blockchain-Based Marketplace. *Lecture Notes in Networks and Systems*, *382*, 63–75. DOI: 10.1007/978-3-030-93780-5_6

Sestino, A., Guido, G., & Peluso, A. M. (2022). Non-Fungible Tokens (NFTs). In *Non-Fungible Tokens (NFTs)*. Springer International Publishing., DOI: 10.1007/978-3-031-07203-1

Shafik, W. (2023). Artificial intelligence and Blockchain technology enabling cybersecurity in telehealth systems. In *Artificial Intelligence and Blockchain Technology in Modern Telehealth Systems* (pp. 285–326). Institution of Engineering and Technology. https://doi.org/DOI: 10.1049/PBHE061E_ch11

Shafik, W., Kalinaki, K., & Zakari, R. Y. (2024). Blockchain's Motivation for IoT-Enabled Smart City. *Secure and Intelligent IoT-Enabled Smart Cities*, 195–221. DOI: 10.4018/979-8-3693-2373-1.ch010

Shafik, W. (2024). *Data Privacy and Security Safeguarding Customer Information in ChatGPT Systems.*, DOI: 10.4018/979-8-3693-1239-1.ch003

Shalabi, K., Al-Haija, Q. A., & Al-Fayoumi, M. (2024). A Blockchain-based Intrusion Detection/Prevention Systems in IoT Network: A Systematic Review. *Procedia Computer Science*, *236*, 410–419. DOI: 10.1016/j.procs.2024.05.048

Sharma, A. K., Dubey, R. K., Goswami, P., & Sarang, R. P. (2024). Securing smart homes with blockchain-enabled systems. In 2024 IEEE 4th International Conference on ICT in Business Industry and Government (ICTBIG 2024). IEEE. DOI: 10.1109/ICTBIG64922.2024.10911074

Sharma, A., Sharma, A., Tripathi, A., & Chaudhary, A. (2024). Real Estate Registry Platform Through NFT Tokenization Using Blockchain. *2024 2nd International Conference on Disruptive Technologies (ICDT)*, 335–340. DOI: 10.1109/ICDT61202.2024.10488945

Sharma, M., Sharma, M., Sharma, N., & Boopathi, S. (2024). Building Sustainable Smart Cities Through Cloud and Intelligent Parking System. In *Handbook of Research on AI and ML for Intelligent Machines and Systems* (pp. 195–222). IGI Global.

Shepherd, J. (2019). *The Ultimate Authentication Playbook.* Okta. https://www.okta.com/blog/2019/02/the-ultimate-authentication-playbook/

Shi, J. (2011). A survey of cyber-physical systems.

Shiba, K. (2020). *EIP-2615: Non-fungible token with mortgage and rental functions.* Ethereum Improvement Proposals. https://eips.ethereum.org/EIPS/eip-2615

Shiba, K. (2020). *EIP-2615: Non-Fungible Token with mortgage and rental functions.* https://eips.ethereum.org/EIPS/eip-2615

Sibanda, K., Ndayizigamiye, P., & Twinomurinzi, H. (2024). Non-fungible tokens (NFTs) in healthcare: A thematic analysis and research agenda. *Frontiers in Digital Health*, *6*, 6. DOI: 10.3389/fdgth.2024.1377531 PMID: 38919876

Siddiqui, A. S., Gui, Y., Lawrence, D., Laval, S., Plusquellic, J., Manjrekar, M., Chowdhury, B., & Saqib, F. (2018). Hardware assisted security architecture for smart grid. *Proceedings: IECON 2018 - 44th Annual Conference of the IEEE Industrial Electronics Society, 1*(1566530), 2890–2895. DOI: 10.1109/IECON.2018.8591401

Sifat, I., Tariq, S. A., & van Donselaar, D. (2024). Suspicious trading in nonfungible tokens (NFTs). *Information & Management, 61*(1), 103898. DOI: 10.1016/j.im.2023.103898

Singh, S., Sharma, P. K., Yoon, B., Shojafar, M., Cho, G. H., & Ra, I.-H. (2020). Convergence of blockchain and artificial intelligence in IoT network for the sustainable smart city. *Sustainable Cities and Society, 63*, 102364. DOI: 10.1016/j.scs.2020.102364

Smith, J., Brown, A., & Garcia, M. (2023). Ethical implications of deepfake technology in virtual reality therapy. *Journal of Medical Ethics and Technology, 15*(3), 112–125. DOI: 10.1093/jmet/2023.00345

Sonia, R., Gupta, N., Manikandan, K., Hemalatha, R., Kumar, M. J., & Boopathi, S. (2024). Strengthening Security, Privacy, and Trust in Artificial Intelligence Drones for Smart Cities. In *Analyzing and Mitigating Security Risks in Cloud Computing* (pp. 214–242). IGI Global. DOI: 10.4018/979-8-3693-3249-8.ch011

Soori, M., Dastres, R., & Arezoo, B. (2023). AI-powered blockchain technology in industry 4.0, a review. *Journal of Economy and Technology, 1*, 222–241. DOI: 10.1016/j.ject.2024.01.001

Souza, E. B., Carlos, R. L., de Mattos, C. A., & Scur, G. (2024). The role of blockchain platform in enabling circular economy practices. *Corporate Social Responsibility and Environmental Management, 31*(6), 5730–5743. DOI: 10.1002/csr.2885

Sree Kumar, C., Lenka, A. K., Dora, S. A., Sharma, A., Fiore, U., & Roy, D. S. (2023, June). TokenFuse: A Versatile NFT Marketplace. In International Conference on Computational Science and Its Applications (pp. 179-192). Cham: Springer Nature Switzerland.

Stublić, H., Bilogrivić, M., & Zlodi, G. (2023). Blockchain and NFTs in the cultural heritage domain: A review of current research topics. *Heritage, 6*(1), 256–274. DOI: 10.3390/heritage6040202

Subha, S., Inbamalar, T., Komala, C., Suresh, L. R., Boopathi, S., & Alaskar, K. (2023). A Remote Health Care Monitoring system using internet of medical things (IoMT). *IEEE Explore*, 1–6.

Swan, M. (2015). *Blockchain: Blueprint for a new economy*. O'Reilly Media.

Syahla, H. D., & Ogi, D. (2021). Implementation of secure parking based on cyber-physical system using one-time password scheme to overcome replay attack. In 8th International Conference on ICT for Smart Society (ICISS 2021), 1–6. DOI: 10.1109/ICISS53185.2021.9533246

Syamala, M., Komala, C., Pramila, P., Dash, S., Meenakshi, S., & Boopathi, S. (2023). Machine Learning-Integrated IoT-Based Smart Home Energy Management System. In *Handbook of Research on Deep Learning Techniques for Cloud-Based Industrial IoT* (pp. 219–235). IGI Global. DOI: 10.4018/978-1-6684-8098-4.ch013

Tahir, M., Sardaraz, M., Muhammad, S., & Khan, M. S. (2020). A lightweight authentication and authorization framework for blockchain-enabled IoT network in health-informatics. *Sustainability (Basel)*, *12*(17), 6960. Advance online publication. DOI: 10.3390/su12176960

Tahmasbi, N., Shan, G., & French, A. M. (2024). Identifying Washtrading Cases in NFT Sales Networks. *IEEE Transactions on Computational Social Systems*, *11*(2), 1696–1707. DOI: 10.1109/TCSS.2023.3319554

Tan, J. Y. (2024). *L.* NFT Security., DOI: 10.1007/978-3-031-58002-4_2

Teicher, J. (2018). *The little-known story of the first IoT device - IBM Industries.* Ibm. https://www.ibm.com/blogs/industries/little-known-story-first-iot-device/

Theodorou, S., & Sklavos, N. (2019). Blockchain-based security and privacy in smart cities. In *Smart cities cybersecurity and privacy* (pp. 21–37). Elsevier. DOI: 10.1016/B978-0-12-815032-0.00003-2

Thomas, Y. C., & Woo, S. S. L. (2014). Distributed Systems. *Distributed Systems*, *25*(1), 39–52. DOI: 10.1201/b17224

Thottungal Valapu, S., Sarkar, T., Coleman, J., Avyukt, A., Embrechts, H., Torfs, D., . . . Krishnamachari, B. (2023, September). DARSAN: A Decentralized Review System Suitable for NFT Marketplaces. In International Conference on Blockchain (pp. 3-20). Cham: Springer Nature Switzerland. DOI: 10.1007/978-3-031-44920-8_1

Tien, D. B., Phung, T. D., Nguyen, T. M., Vo, H. K., Dang, K. T., Trong, P. N., Khanh, B. L., & Kim, N. N. T. (2024). From Bricks to Bits: Revolutionizing Real Estate for the Digital World. *Lecture Notes in Computer Science (Including Subseries Lecture Notes in Artificial Intelligence and Lecture Notes in Bioinformatics), 14543 LNCS*, 106–117. DOI: 10.1007/978-3-031-60997-8_11

Tjiam, K., Wang, R., Chen, H., & Liang, K. (2021). Your Smart Contracts Are Not Secure: Investigating Arbitrageurs and Oracle Manipulators in Ethereum. *CYSARM 2021 - Proceedings of the 3rd Workshop on Cyber-Security Arms Race, Co-Located with CCS 2021*, 25–35. DOI: 10.1145/3474374.3486916

Tolmach, P., Li, Y., Lin, S. W., Liu, Y., & Li, Z. (2021). A Survey of Smart Contract Formal Specification and Verification. *ACM Computing Surveys*, *54*(7), 1–38. Advance online publication. DOI: 10.1145/3464421

Tran, T. D., Phong, K. M., Le Bao, C. D., Cam, N. T., & Pham, V. H. (2024). Zk-Auction: A Cross-Blockchain System for Efficient Auctions combining Zero-Knowledge Proof and NFT. *ACM International Conference Proceeding Series*, 446–453. DOI: 10.1145/3654522.3654589

Trung, P. H. T., Khoa, T. D., Kha, H. N., Bao, Q. T., Trong, N. D. P., Loc, V. C. P., Hieu, D. M., & Bang, L. K. (2024). Decentralized Renewable Energy Trading: A Cross-Chain, NFT, and IPFS Framework. *Lecture Notes in Computer Science (Including Subseries Lecture Notes in Artificial Intelligence and Lecture Notes in Bioinformatics), 14792 LNCS*, 69–82. DOI: 10.1007/978-3-031-68005-2_6

Tschorsch, F., & Scheuermann, B. (2016). Bitcoin and beyond: A technical survey on decentralized digital currencies. *IEEE Communications Surveys and Tutorials*, *18*(3), 2084–2123. DOI: 10.1109/COMST.2016.2535718

Underwood, S. (2016). Blockchain beyond bitcoin. *Communications of the ACM*, *59*(11), 15–17. DOI: 10.1145/2994581

Upadhyay, N., & Upadhyay, S. (2025). The dark side of non-fungible tokens: Understanding risks in the NFT marketplace from a fraud triangle perspective. *Financial Innovation*, *11*(1), 1–29. DOI: 10.1186/s40854-024-00684-6

Uribe, D. (2020). Privacy Laws, Non-Fungible Tokens, and Genomics. *The Journal of The British Blockchain Association*, *3*(2), 1–10. DOI: 10.31585/jbba-3-2-(5)2020

Vasan, K., Janosov, M., & Barabási, A. L. (2022). Quantifying NFT-driven networks in crypto art. *Scientific Reports*, *12*(1), 2769. DOI: 10.1038/s41598-022-05146-6 PMID: 35177628

Vegh, L. (2018). Cyber-physical systems security through multi-factor authentication and data analytics. *Proceedings of the IEEE International Conference on Industrial Technology, 2018-Febru*, 1369–1374. DOI: 10.1109/ICIT.2018.8352379

Venkateswaran, N., Vidhya, K., Ayyannan, M., Chavan, S. M., Sekar, K., & Boopathi, S. (2023). A Study on Smart Energy Management Framework Using Cloud Computing. In *5G, Artificial Intelligence, and Next Generation Internet of Things: Digital Innovation for Green and Sustainable Economies* (pp. 189–212). IGI Global. DOI: 10.4018/978-1-6684-8634-4.ch009

Venkateswaran, N., Vidhya, R., Naik, D. A., Raj, T. M., Munjal, N., & Boopathi, S. (2023). Study on Sentence and Question Formation Using Deep Learning Techniques. In *Digital Natives as a Disruptive Force in Asian Businesses and Societies* (pp. 252–273). IGI Global. DOI: 10.4018/978-1-6684-6782-4.ch015

Venugopalan, S., & Aydt, H. (2023). Incentivising Building Data Availability and Accessibility Using Tokenized Data Assets. *2023 5th International Conference on Blockchain Computing and Applications, BCCA 2023*. https://doi.org/DOI: 10.1109/BCCA58897.2023.10338916

Vergani, F., & Jiang, J. (2022). *Digital Solutions Supporting Citizen Participation in Urban Environment.*

Verma, S. (2013). Network Topologies in Wireless Sensor Networks: A Review 1. *International Journal of Electronics & Communication Technology, 4*(3), 93–97. https://doi.org/ISSN : 2230-7109 (Online)

Verma, R., Christiana, M. B. V., Maheswari, M., Srinivasan, V., Patro, P., Dari, S. S., & Boopathi, S. (2024). Intelligent Physarum Solver for Profit Maximization in Oligopolistic Supply Chain Networks. In *AI and Machine Learning Impacts in Intelligent Supply Chain* (pp. 156–179). IGI Global. DOI: 10.4018/979-8-3693-1347-3.ch011

Viano, C. (2024). Context-based civic blockchain: Localising blockchain for local civic participation. *Digital Geography and Society, 6*, 100090. DOI: 10.1016/j.diggeo.2024.100090

Vilkov, A., & Tian, G. (2023). Blockchain's Scope and Purpose in Carbon Markets: A Systematic Literature Review. *Sustainability 2023, Vol. 15, Page 8495, 15*(11), 8495. DOI: 10.3390/su15118495

Vinet, L., & Zhedanov, A. (2011). A "missing" family of classical orthogonal polynomials. *Journal of Physics. A, Mathematical and Theoretical, 44*(8), 1–11. DOI: 10.1088/1751-8113/44/8/085201

Wang, H., Liu, J., & Zhang, L. (2023). NFTs for medical data ownership: A new paradigm in healthcare. *Journal of Medical Internet Research, 25*(3), e45678. DOI: 10.2196/45678

Wang, J., Zheng, Q., & Shen, Y. (2024). Research on Multi-level Trustworthy Multimedia Data Broadcasting Network Based on Blockchain Oracles. *IEEE International Symposium on Broadband Multimedia Systems and Broadcasting, BMSB*. DOI: 10.1109/BMSB62888.2024.10608301

Wang, M., & Lau, N. (2023). NFT Digital Twins: A Digitalization Strategy to Preserve and Sustain Miao Silver Craftsmanship in the Metaverse Era. *Heritage*, *6*(2), 1921–1941. DOI: 10.3390/heritage6020103

Wang, Z., Dong, X., Li, Y., Fang, L., & Chen, P. (2018). IoT Security Model and Performance Evaluation: A Blockchain Approach. *Proceedings of 2018 6th IEEE International Conference on Network Infrastructure and Digital Content, IC-NIDC 2018*, 260–264. DOI: 10.1109/ICNIDC.2018.8525716

Watanabe, H., Ichihara, K., & Aita, T. (2024). VELLET: Verifiable Embedded Wallet for Securing Authenticity and Integrity. *2024 IEEE International Conference on Blockchain and Cryptocurrency, ICBC 2024*, 254–258. DOI: 10.1109/ICBC59979.2024.10634467

Wei, X., Zhang, W., Bai, G., & Li, B. (2023). Research on technology against deepfake. 2023 3rd International Conference on Mobile Networks and Wireless Communications (ICMNWC), 1-5.

Weiser, M. (1991). The Computer for the 21st Century - Specialized elements of hardware and software, connected by wires, radio waves and infrared, will be so ubiquitous that no one will notice their presence. *Readings in Human–Computer Interaction*, 933–940. https://www.lri.fr/~mbl/Stanford/CS477/papers/Weiser-SciAm.pdf

Westerlund, M. (2019). The emergence of deepfake technology: A review. *Technology Innovation Management Review*, *9*(11), 39–52. DOI: 10.22215/timreview/1282

What Is Token-Based Authentication? (2021). Okta Inc. https://www.okta.com/identity-101/what-is-token-based-authentication/

White, B., Mahanti, A., & Passi, K. (2022, April). Characterizing the OpenSea NFT marketplace. In Companion Proceedings of the Web Conference 2022 (pp. 488-496). DOI: 10.1145/3487553.3524629

Wikström, E., & Emilsson, U. M. (2014). Autonomy and Control in Everyday Life in Care of Older People in Nursing Homes. In *Journal of Housing for the Elderly* (Vol. 28, Issue 1). DOI: 10.1080/02763893.2013.858092

Work, O. S. (2020). *A Developer's History of Authentication*. Workos.Com. https://workos.com/blog/a-developers-history-of-authentication

Wright, K. L., Martinez, M., Chadha, U., & Krishnamachari, B. (2018). SmartEdge: A Smart Contract for Edge Computing. *Proceedings - IEEE 2018 International Congress on Cybermatics: 2018 IEEE Conferences on Internet of Things, Green Computing and Communications, Cyber, Physical and Social Computing, Smart Data, Blockchain, Computer and Information Technology, IThings/Gree*, 1685–1690. DOI: 10.1109/Cybermatics_2018.2018.00281

X-Force. I. (2017). *Mirai Botnet Loader Campaign*. IBM X-Force Threat Research. https://exchange.xforce.ibmcloud.com/collection/Mirai-Botnet-Loader-Campaign-7e8131a283d50a0f13d43ae5f1d0058b

Xie, M., Liu, J., Chen, S., & Lin, M. (2023). A survey on blockchain consensus mechanism: Research overview, current advances and future directions. *International Journal of Intelligent Computing and Cybernetics*, *16*(2), 314–340. DOI: 10.1108/IJICC-05-2022-0126

Xihua, Z., & Goyal, S. (2022). Security and privacy challenges using IoT-blockchain technology in a smart city: Critical analysis. *Int. J. Electr. Electron. Res*, *10*(2), 190–195. DOI: 10.37391/ijeer.100224

Yaghy, A., Alberto, N. R., & Ristovska, L. (2023). The potential use of non-fungible tokens (NFTs) in healthcare and medical research. *PLOS Digital Health*, *2*(7), 2. DOI: 10.1371/journal.pdig.0000312 PMID: 37498836

Yang, L., Liu, X. Y., & Gong, W. (2020). Secure smart home systems: A blockchain perspective. *IEEE INFOCOM 2020 - IEEE Conference on Computer Communications Workshops, INFOCOM WKSHPS 2020*, 1003–1008. DOI: 10.1109/INFOCOMWKSHPS50562.2020.9162648

Yang, S., Chen, J., & Zheng, Z. (2023). Definition and Detection of Defects in NFT Smart Contracts. *ISSTA 2023 - Proceedings of the 32nd ACM SIGSOFT International Symposium on Software Testing and Analysis*, 373–384. DOI: 10.1145/3597926.3598063

Yang, S., Chen, J., Huang, M., Zheng, Z., & Huang, Y. (2024). Uncover the Premeditated Attacks: Detecting Exploitable Reentrancy Vulnerabilities by Identifying Attacker Contracts. *Proceedings - International Conference on Software Engineering*, 1573–1584. DOI: 10.1145/3597503.3639153

Yang, J., Liu, J., Lin, D., Wu, J., Huang, B., Li, Q., & Zheng, Z. (2024). Who Stole My NFT? Investigating Web3 NFT Phishing Scams on Ethereum. *IEEE Transactions on Information Forensics and Security*, *19*, 9301–9314. Advance online publication. DOI: 10.1109/TIFS.2024.3463541

Yang, Q., & Wang, H. (2021). Privacy-preserving transactive energy management for IoT-aided smart homes via blockchain. *IEEE Internet of Things Journal*, *8*(14), 11463–11475. DOI: 10.1109/JIOT.2021.3051323

Yang, X., & Li, W. (2020). A zero-knowledge-proof-based digital identity management scheme in blockchain. *Computers & Security*, *99*, 102050. DOI: 10.1016/j.cose.2020.102050

Yazdinejad, A., Parizi, R., Srivastava, G., & Dehghantanha, A. (2020). Making sense of blockchain for AI deepfakes technology. 2020 IEEE Globecom Workshops (GC Wkshps), 1-6.

Yetis, R., & Sahingoz, O. K. (2019). Blockchain Based Secure Communication for IoT Devices in Smart Cities. *7th International Istanbul Smart Grids and Cities Congress and Fair, ICSG 2019 - Proceedings*, 134–138. DOI: 10.1109/SGCF.2019.8782285

Yli-Huumo, J., Ko, D., Choi, S., Park, S., & Smolander, K. (2016). Where is current research on blockchain technology? — A systematic review. *PLoS One*, *11*(10), 11. DOI: 10.1371/journal.pone.0163477 PMID: 27695049

Zhang, L., Chen, Y., & Wang, H. (2023). The role of NFTs in digital art therapy: A new frontier for mental health interventions. *Journal of Digital Psychology*, *8*(2), 45–60. DOI: 10.1016/j.jdp.2023.100123

Zhang, W., Wei, L., Cheung, S. C., Liu, Y., Li, S., Liu, L., & Lyu, M. R. (2023). Combatting Front-Running in Smart Contracts: Attack Mining, Benchmark Construction and Vulnerability Detector Evaluation. *IEEE Transactions on Software Engineering*, *49*(6), 3630–3646. DOI: 10.1109/TSE.2023.3270117

Zhaofeng, M., Jialin, M., Jihui, W., & Zhiguang, S. (2021). Blockchain-Based Decentralized Authentication Modeling Scheme in Edge and IoT Environment. *IEEE Internet of Things Journal*, *8*(4), 2116–2123. DOI: 10.1109/JIOT.2020.3037733

Zheng, X. (2024). Research on blockchain smart contract technology based on resistance to quantum computing attacks. *PLoS One*, *19*(5), e0302325. DOI: 10.1371/journal.pone.0302325 PMID: 38781187

Zhu, H., Yang, L., Wang, L., & Sheng, V. S. (2024). A Survey on Security Analysis Methods of Smart Contracts. *IEEE Transactions on Services Computing*, *17*(6), 1–18. DOI: 10.1109/TSC.2024.3463394

Zyskind, G., Nathan, O., & Pentland, A. (2015). Decentralizing privacy: Using blockchain to protect personal data. IEEE Security and Privacy Workshops, 180-184.

About the Contributors

Usman Khalil, Dr., is associated with School of Digital Sciences as Eminent Visiting Professor (EVP) at Universiti Brunei Darussalam (UBD) in Brunei Darussalam. He is associated as a Researcher in Robotics Lab (RoboLab), School of Digital Science, UBD. He also worked with Faculty of Integrated Science as Eminent Visiting Professor (EVP) at Universiti Brunei Darussalam (UBD) which is an Engineering School in Brunei Darussalam and the Virginia Tech Lab at UBD which is an international collaboration laboratory between UBD and Virginia Polytechnic Institute and State University (Virginia Tech-VT) United States. He obtained his Ph.D. and MS in Computer Science majoring in Cybersecurity and Data Science from Universiti Brunei Darussalam (UBD) in 2024 and 2019 respectively. With over fourteen years of professional experience in the telecom industry in Pakistan and Malaysia, Usman Khalil previously worked as a Telecom professional. His research interests focus on exploratory pattern recognition algorithms for the analysis, data mining, clustering, integration of the Internet of Things with cloud computing, and the integration of the Internet of Things with Blockchain. He is serving as an invited Editor in the Innovative Informatics and Artificial Intelligence Research (IIAIR). He is also serving as an invited reviewer in reputed journals, including IEEE Access, Scientific Reports, Blockchain: Research and Applications, Journal of Electrical Engineering & Technology, SN Applied Sciences, Bulletin of Electrical Engineering, and Informatics, PLOS ONE, Measurement Sensors, Cluster Computing, The Journal of Super Computing, Peer to Peer Networking and Applications etc. Position (s) and affiliation (s): Eminent Visiting Professor (EVP) – School of Digital Science, Universiti Brunei Darussalam, Jalan Tungku Link, Gadong BE1410, Brunei Darussalam. Researcher – RoboLab, School of Digital Science, Universiti Brunei Darussalam, Jalan Tungku Link, Gadong BE1410, Brunei Darussalam.

Mueen Uddin, Dr. (Sr. Member IEEE) has been included in the Top 2% of Research Scientists (Stanford and Elsevier report 2022 and 2023). He received his PhD from Universiti Teknologi Malaysia UTM in 2013. He has around 15 years of Research and Teaching experience in the domain of Data and Cybersecurity, Blockchain, and Security of Cyber-Physical Systems. Currently, he works as an Associate Professor of Data and Cybersecurity at the University of Doha for Science and Technology Qatar. Dr. Mueen was a Postdoctoral Research Fellow with Khalifa University UAE from 2019-2020. Dr. Mueen has developed an excellent track record of research and academic leadership including the development, management, and implementation of various funded projects supported by agencies in Malaysia, Saudi Arabia, UAE, and Brunei Darussalam. Dr. Mueen has co-authored over 170 peer-reviewed research papers in highly cited journals and conferences. He is currently serving as Editor/ Associate Editor/GE in various prestigious journals. He is a Senior Member IEEE, ACM, AIS and was awarded a Higher Education Academy (HEA) Fellowship from the UK. He has also served as a technical committee member and session chair for various international and local conferences in Computer Sciences and Information Systems. Position (s) and affiliation (s): Associate Professor of Data and Cybersecurity, College of Computing and IT, University of Doha for Science and Technology, Doha, 24449, Qatar

Owais A. Malik, Dr. (Sr. Member IEEE) received the M.S. degree in computer science from KFUPM, Dhahran, Saudi Arabia, in 2002, and the Ph.D. degree in computer science from Universiti Brunei Darussalam, Bandar Seri Begawan, Brunei, in 2015. He is currently a Senior Assistant Professor of Mathematical and Computing Sciences with the Department of Digital Sciences, University Brunei Darussalam. He graduated as a Computer System Engineer from NED, Pakistan in 1998 and has more than ten years of progressive experience in academia and research in computer science and engineering. He has been teaching various undergraduate courses, including machine learning, data mining, machine perception, programming fundamentals, design and analysis of algorithms, software engineering, and operating systems in different national/international universities. He has authored or coauthored several articles in internationally reputable journals and conferences. His research interests include designing and exploring different intelligent/pattern recognition algorithms to analyze and classify biodiversity and cyber-security data, applied biomechanics, bio-signal processing, and Big Data analytics. Position (s) and affiliation (s): Sr. Assistant Professor, School of Digital Science, Universiti Brunei Darussalam, Jalan Tungku Link, Gadong BE1410, Brunei Darussalam. Director, Institute of Applied Data Analytics, Universiti Brunei Darussalam, Jalan Tungku Link, Gadong BE1410, Brunei Darussalam.

Abdulhalim Dandoush, Dr., is the Head of the IT department and an Associate Professor in IT and Computer Science at UDST, Qatar since June 2023. Additionally, he holds the position of associated researcher at the Esme Research Lab in France and at L2TI lab of Sorbonne University Paris Nord, France. Previously, Abdulhalim was the Director of Expertise Areas in "Computing, Modeling, and Digital Technologies" at ESME in France from September 2015 to July 2022. He holds a Master's degree in Networking and a Ph.D. in Information Technology from INRIA and the University of Nice-Sophia Antipolis in 2006 and 2010, respectively. Before his tenure at ESME, he worked as an Expert Engineer at INRIA-Sophia Antipolis within the INRIA-Alstom Transport joint Lab. His research interests encompass the performance evaluation and optimization of network protocols, as well as the intelligent management of new-generation networks. Abdulhalim co-led the ONF/ONOS teaching brigade in 2017/2018 and served as an assistant and associate for research and teaching at the University of Nice-Sophia Antipolis in France from 2006 to 2010. He also held positions as an Assistant Professor at the University of Tishreen in Syria and the Arab Academy for Sciences and Technology in Egypt from 2011 to 2014. He served as a TPC member and co-chair in many international conferences and workshops. Position (s) and affiliation (s): Associate Professor of Information Technology, Head of IT department, College of Computing and IT, University of Doha for Science and Technology, Doha, 24449, Qatar. Home Page I ORCID I Google Scholar I ResearchGate I LinkedIn

***

Btissam Acim currently pursuing her Doctorate in Computer Science at the Faculty of Sciences, University of Rabat, specializing in Deepfake Technology and Artificial Intelligence. She earned her state engineering degree in Data and Knowledge Engineering in 2016. Her current research focuses on designing innovative techniques to improve the quality and accuracy of deepfakes in potential application areas. Prof. Acim has extensive professional experience, with over 8 years of experience as a data scientist in major organizations such as the Deposit and Management Fund (CDG), Bank Al-Maghrib (BKAM), and the Royal Society of Horse Encouragement (SOREC), which enhances her current research on deepfakes and generative models with a strong expertise in data analysis.

Gusti Ahmad Fanshuri Alfarisy is an Assistant Professor at Institut Teknologi Kalimantan at the Department of Informatics. He has compleetd his Ph.D. degree in Artificial Intelligence at the School of Digital Science, Universiti Brunei Darussalam under supervision of Dr. Owais Ahmed Malik and Dr. Ong Wee Hong.He has been teaching several topics including algorithms and programming languages, data structures, numerical methods, machine learning, and software engineering. I have reviewed several articles in Springer and Elsevier Journals. His research interest includes Open-World Lifelong Machine Learning, Computer Vision, Web Intelligence, Natural Language Processing, LLM, Ecological and Environmental Informatics, and Healthcare Informatics.

Kassim Kalinaki (MIEEE) is a computer science researcher, technologist, and educator with more than ten years of experience in the industry and academia. He received his Diploma in Computer engineering from Kyambogo University, a BSc in computer science and engineering, and an MSc. Computer Science and Engineering from Bangladesh's Islamic University of Technology (IUT). Since 2014, He has lectured at the Islamic University in Uganda (IUIU), where he most recently served as the Head of Department Computer Science department (2019-2022). In 2025, he graduated with a PhD in Computer Science at the School of Digital Science, Universiti Brunei Darussalam (UBD). He's the founder and principal investigator of Borderline Research Laboratory (BRLab) and his areas of research include Ecological Informatics, Data Analytics, Computer Vision, ML/DL, Digital Image Processing, Cybersecurity, IoT/AIoMT, Remote Sensing, and Educational Technologies. He has authored and co-authored several published peer-reviewed articles in renowned journals and publishers, including Springer, Elsevier, Taylor & Francis, IGI Global, Emerald, and IEEE.

Nassim Kharmoum, Ph.D. and Assistant Professor. He received his diploma of doctor Degree in Computer Science from the Mohammed V University in Rabat. Currently, he is an Assis-tant Professor in Software Engineering at the National Center for Scientific and Technical Research in Morocco. He proposed different validated methods in scientific articles published in international journals, books, and conferences. His research interest focuses on artificial intelligence, data science, analysis and conceptual modeling, software requirements, multi-agent systems modeling, and modernization of legacy systems.

Nassanga Jalia is both a lecturer for computer science and systems developer with over seven years of experience in the Industry.Currently, she serves as a lecturer at Islamic University in Uganda where she lectures computer science students and also supervises research for undergraduate students.She holds a Masters degree in Computing from Uganda Technology and Management University and a bachelors degree in Computer Science from Islamic University in Uganda.

Abdelaziz Ouajdouni is an Associate Professor at Ibn Zohr University, Agadir, and a PhD in Management Sciences from the National School of Business and Management of Tangier, Abdelmalek Essaadi University, Morocco. He holds a variety of academic distinctions, including a master of science (M.Sc) in accounting, control, and audit from UQAM's School of Management (ESG) in Canada and a master's degree in management from Orléans Graduate School of Management (IAE, Orléans University) in France.

Hamid Ouhnni currently pursuing his Doctorate in Computer Science at the Faculty of Sciences, University of Rabat, specializing in Big Data and Artificial Intelligence in Virtual Reality (VR). He earned his Master's degree in Data Engineering and Software Development in 2021 and holds a Professional Bachelor's degree in Multimedia and Web Technologies, among other qualifications. His research interests focus on advanced computer science topics, including machine learning,and software development. Hehas a rich professional background, currently teaching web development. He has also served as an instructor at the Faculty of Sciences in Rabat. His experience includes developing a machine learning and working as a secondary school computer science teacher since 2019. His technical expertise spans multiple programming languages, web frameworks, virtual reality, and machine learning techniques. Hecombines his extensive knowledge with practical teaching and development experience.

Wasswa Shafik (Member, IEEE) received a Bachelor of Science degree in information technology from Ndejje University, Uganda, a Master of Engineering degree in Information Technology (Computer and Communication Networks) from Yazd University, Iran, and a PhD in Computer Science with the School of Digital Science, Universiti Brunei Darussalam, Brunei Darussalam. He is also the Founder and Research Director of the Dig Connectivity Research Laboratory (DCRLab) after serving as a Research Associate at the Network Interconnectivity Research Laboratory at Yazd University. Prior to this, he worked as a Community Data Analyst at Population Services International (PSI-Uganda), a Community Data Officer at the Programme for Accessible Health Communication (PACE-Uganda), a Research Assistant at the Socio-Economic Data Centre (SEDC-Uganda), Uganda, an Assistant Data Officer at TechnoServe, Kampala, Uganda, and Asmaah Charity Organization as Cheif Executive Officer. He has hundreds of publications with renowned publishers. His research interests include Artificial Intelligence, Smart Agriculture, Digital Health, Green Computing, Security and Privacy.

Ali Tufail is currently working as a Senior Assistant Professor of Distributed and Cyber Physical Systems at the School of Digital Science (SDS), Universiti Brunei Darussalam. He completed his PhD in Information and Communication Engineering at Ajou University South Korea in 2011, Masters of Science in Advanced Computing at the University of Bristol UK in 2006 and Bachelor's degree in Information Technology at the National University of Sciences and Technology Pakistan in 2005. Dr. Ali's teaching and research specializations are in the areas of Wireless Sensor Networks, Internet of Things and Vehicular Adhoc Networks. Dr. Ali has more than 10 years of teaching experience in countries such as Pakistan, South Korea, Turkey and Saudi Arabia. He has 25+ publications in renowned journals and conferences. Dr. Ali is also serving as SDS Seminar Coordinator and Learning Technology Advisor.

Soumia Ziti completed her Doctorate in Computer Science at the Faculty of Sciences, University of Orléans from 2003-2006. She is currently a professor at the Faculty of Sciences of Rabat, Mohammed V University, where she has been teaching and conducting research since March 2021. Her previous roles include Professor Accredited to Supervise Research from January 2015 to March 2021 and assistant professor from March 2007 to May 2015 at the same institution. She also served as a part-time instructor in computer science at the University of Orléans from September 2003 to February 2007. She earned a Diploma of Advanced Studies in Fundamental Computer Science from the University of Orléans, a Master's degree in Computer Science with a focus on Software Engineering, and a DEUG in Mathematics and Physics from Hassan II University. She began her academic journey with a Baccalaureate in Mathematical Sciences from El Alia Hight School, Mohammedia. Her research interests are primarily in computer science and software engineering, where she has made significant contributions through numerous publications and projects. She is renowned for her expertise and has served as a consultant on various high-profile projects. She has represented her institution in numerous academic conferences and workshops, contributing to the advancement of knowledge in her field. Her dedication to education and research has made her a prominent figure in the academic community.

Index

N

P

R

S

T

U

W

www.ingramcontent.com/pod-product-compliance
Lightning Source LLC
LaVergne TN
LVHW061539290926
849162LV00004B/851

9798369388761